⑩

LOVE and LIES by MUSAWO

# CONTENTS

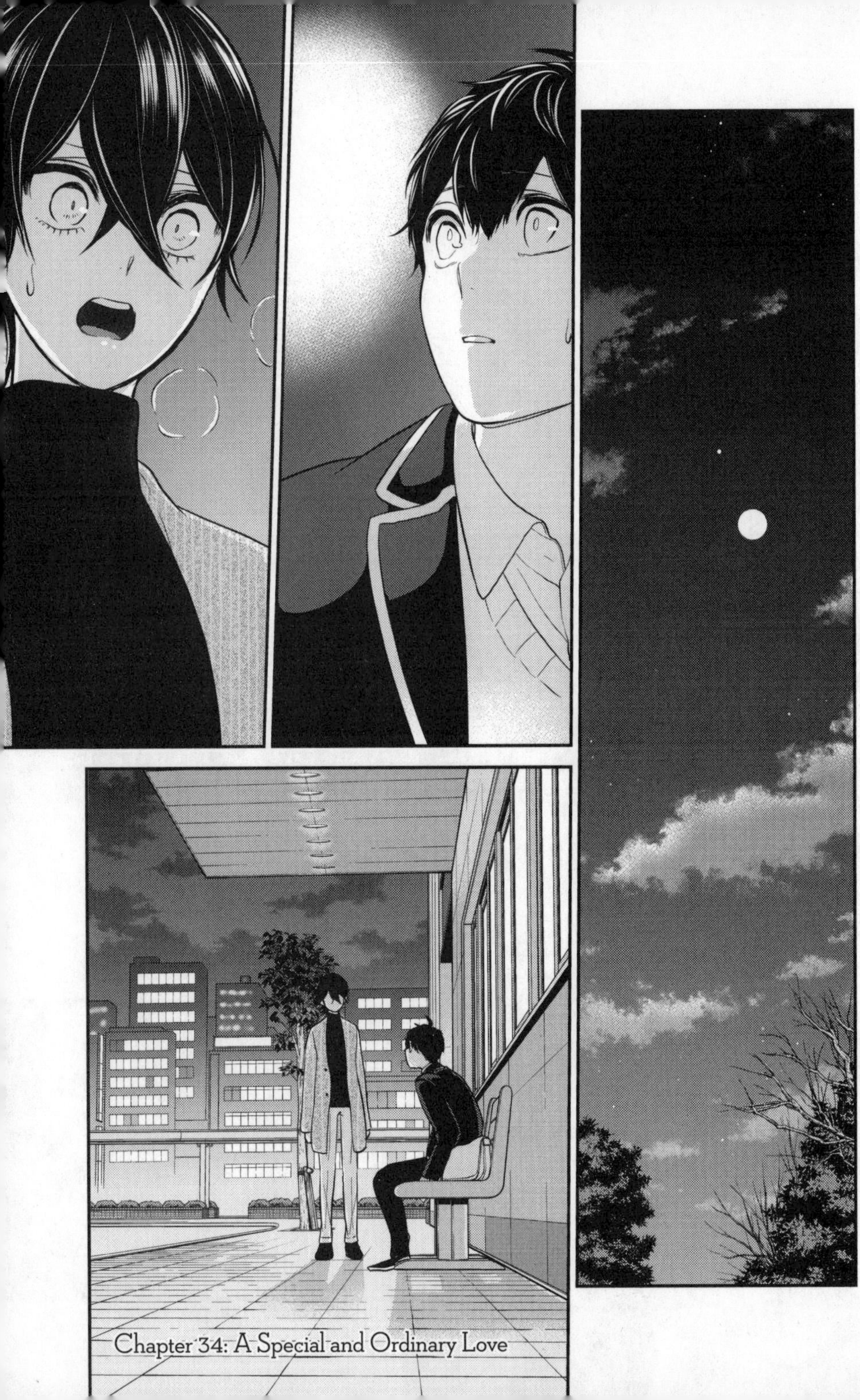
Chapter 34: A Special and Ordinary Love

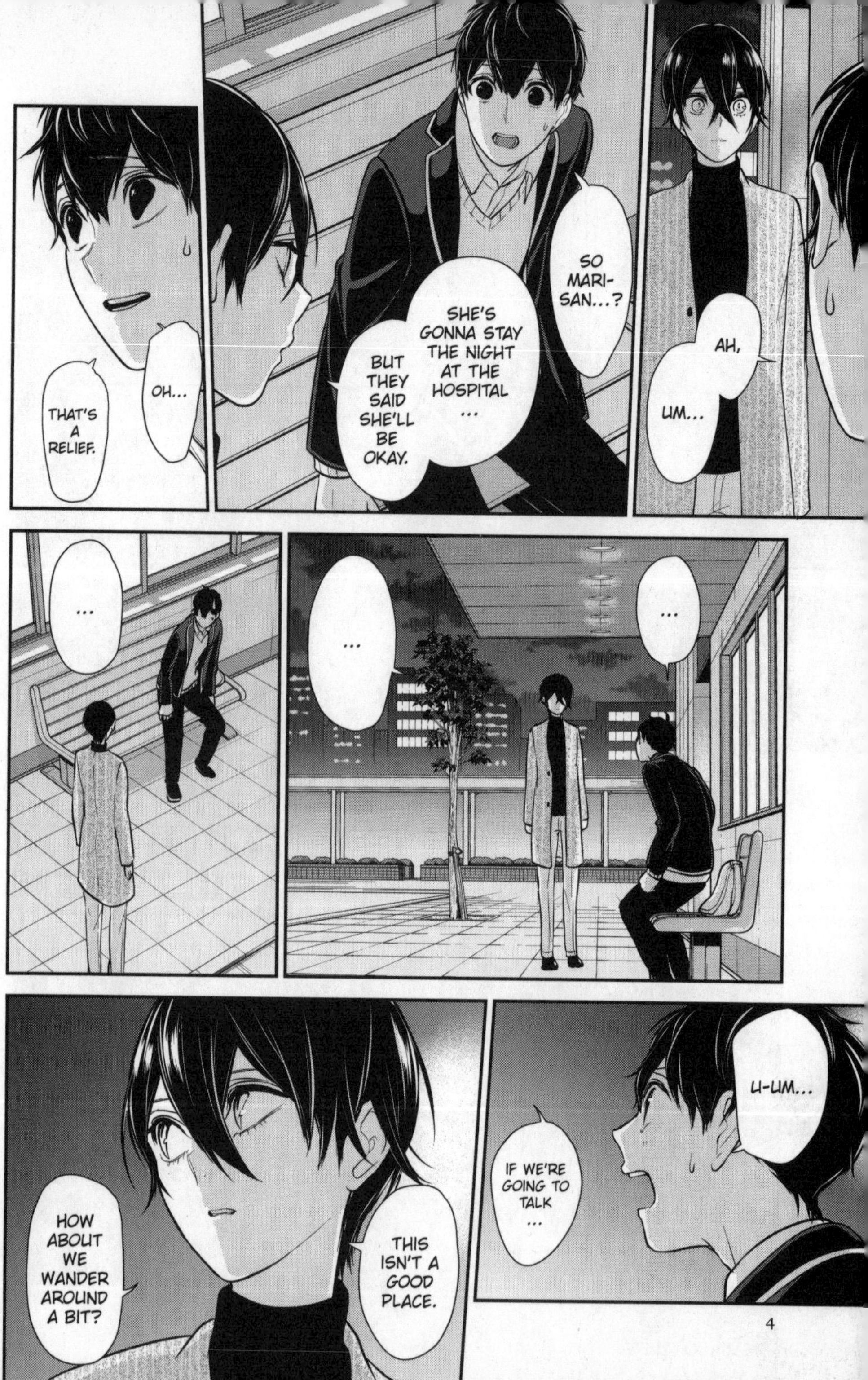
AH,
UM...
SO MARI-SAN...?
SHE'S GONNA STAY THE NIGHT AT THE HOSPITAL ...
BUT THEY SAID SHE'LL BE OKAY.
OH...
THAT'S A RELIEF.
...
...
...
U-UM...
IF WE'RE GOING TO TALK ...
THIS ISN'T A GOOD PLACE.
HOW ABOUT WE WANDER AROUND A BIT?

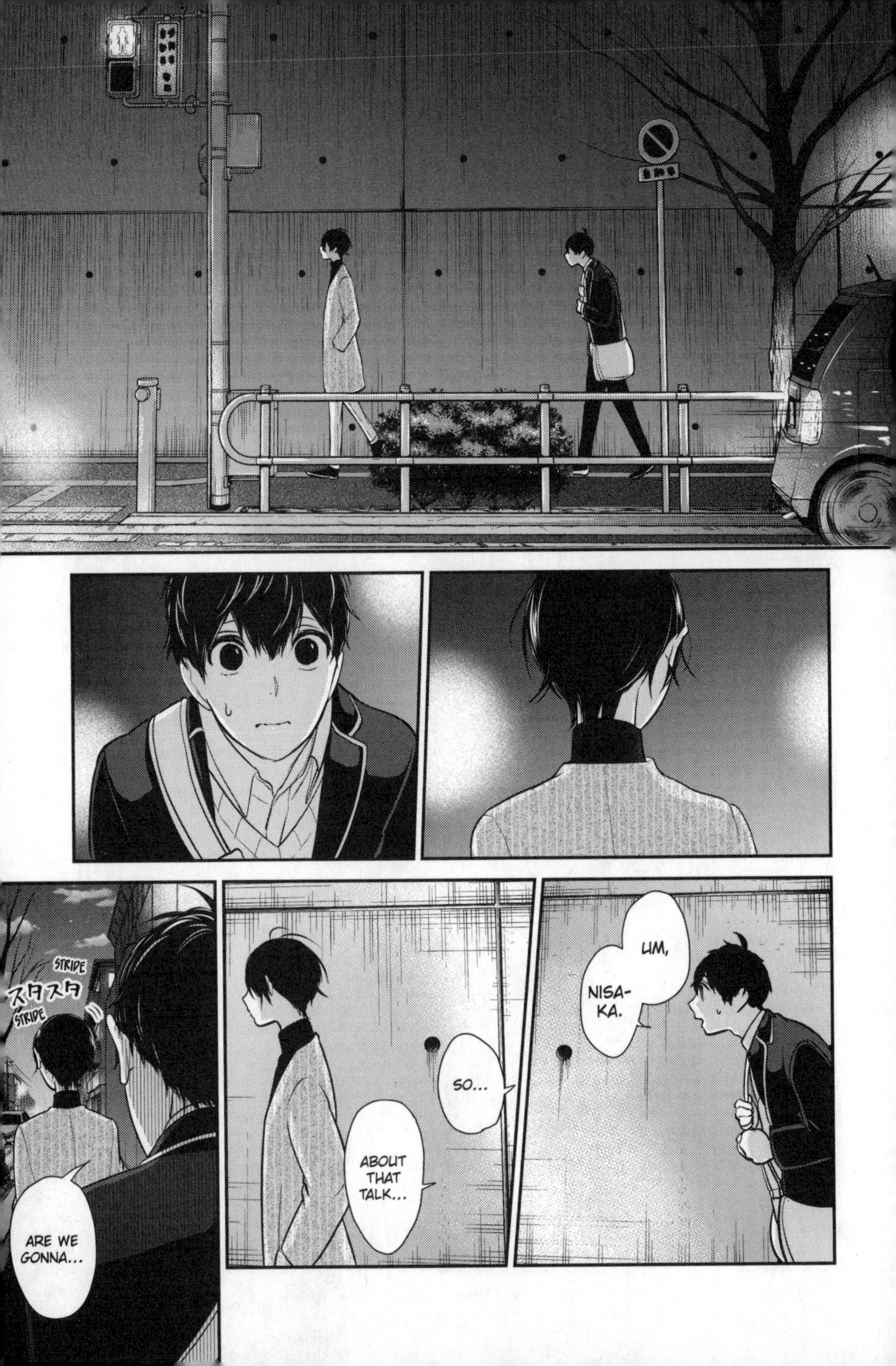
UM,
NISA-KA.
SO...
ABOUT THAT TALK...
STRIDE
スタスタ
STRIDE
ARE WE GONNA...

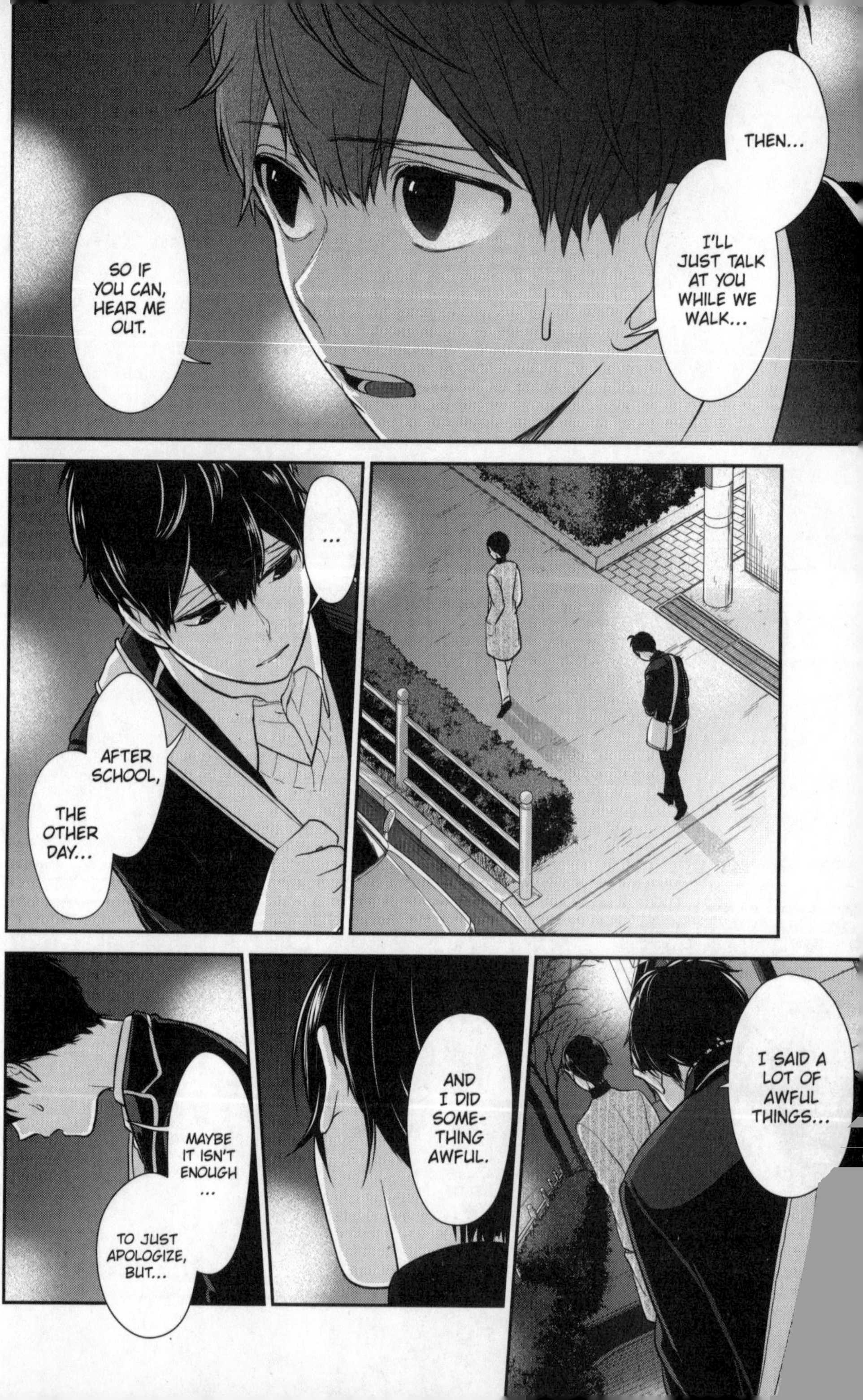
THEN...
I'LL JUST TALK AT YOU WHILE WE WALK...
SO IF YOU CAN, HEAR ME OUT.
...
AFTER SCHOOL,
THE OTHER DAY...
I SAID A LOT OF AWFUL THINGS...
AND I DID SOME-THING AWFUL.
MAYBE IT ISN'T ENOUGH ...
TO JUST APOLOGIZE, BUT...

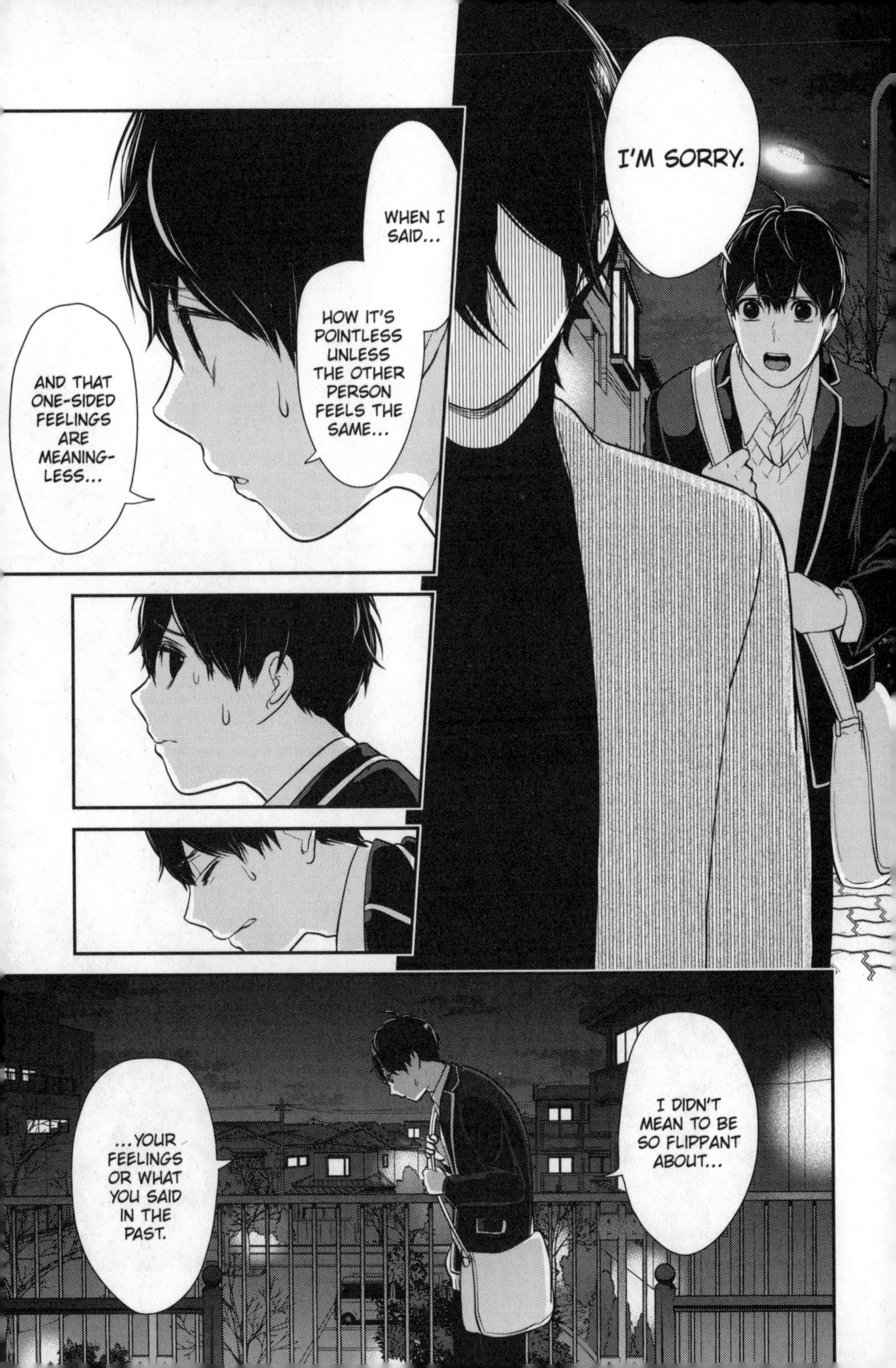
I'M SORRY.
WHEN I SAID...
HOW IT'S POINTLESS UNLESS THE OTHER PERSON FEELS THE SAME...
AND THAT ONE-SIDED FEELINGS ARE MEANING-LESS...
I DIDN'T MEAN TO BE SO FLIPPANT ABOUT...
...YOUR FEELINGS OR WHAT YOU SAID IN THE PAST.

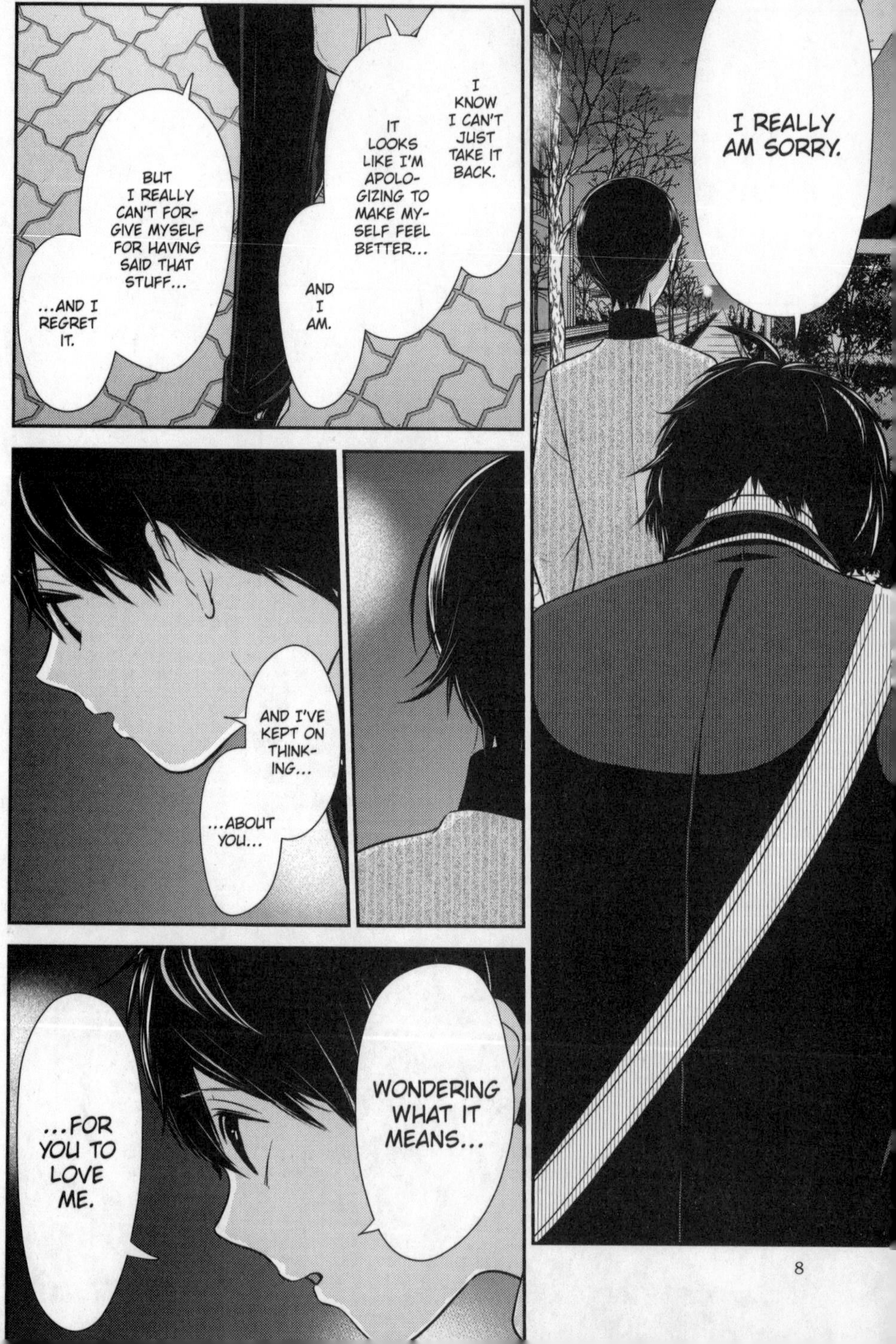
I REALLY AM SORRY.
I KNOW I CAN'T JUST TAKE IT BACK.
IT LOOKS LIKE I'M APOLOGIZING TO MAKE MYSELF FEEL BETTER...
AND I AM.
BUT I REALLY CAN'T FORGIVE MYSELF FOR HAVING SAID THAT STUFF...
...AND I REGRET IT.
AND I'VE KEPT ON THINKING...
...ABOUT YOU...
WONDERING WHAT IT MEANS...
...FOR YOU TO LOVE ME.

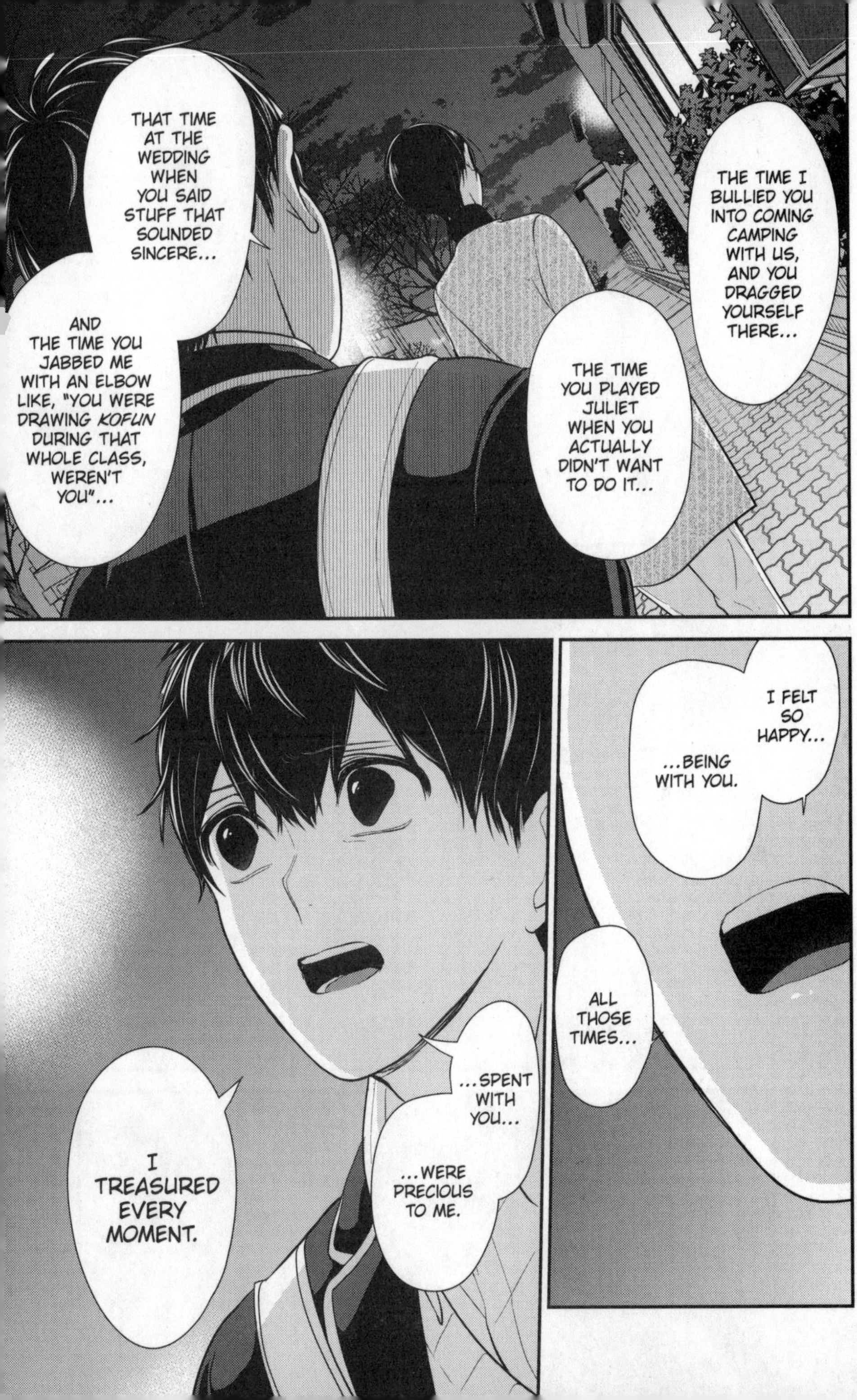
THE TIME I BULLIED YOU INTO COMING CAMPING WITH US, AND YOU DRAGGED YOURSELF THERE...
THE TIME YOU PLAYED JULIET WHEN YOU ACTUALLY DIDN'T WANT TO DO IT...
THAT TIME AT THE WEDDING WHEN YOU SAID STUFF THAT SOUNDED SINCERE...
AND THE TIME YOU JABBED ME WITH AN ELBOW LIKE, "YOU WERE DRAWING *KOFUN* DURING THAT WHOLE CLASS, WEREN'T YOU"...
I FELT SO HAPPY...
...BEING WITH YOU.
ALL THOSE TIMES...
...SPENT WITH YOU...
...WERE PRECIOUS TO ME.
I TREASURED EVERY MOMENT.

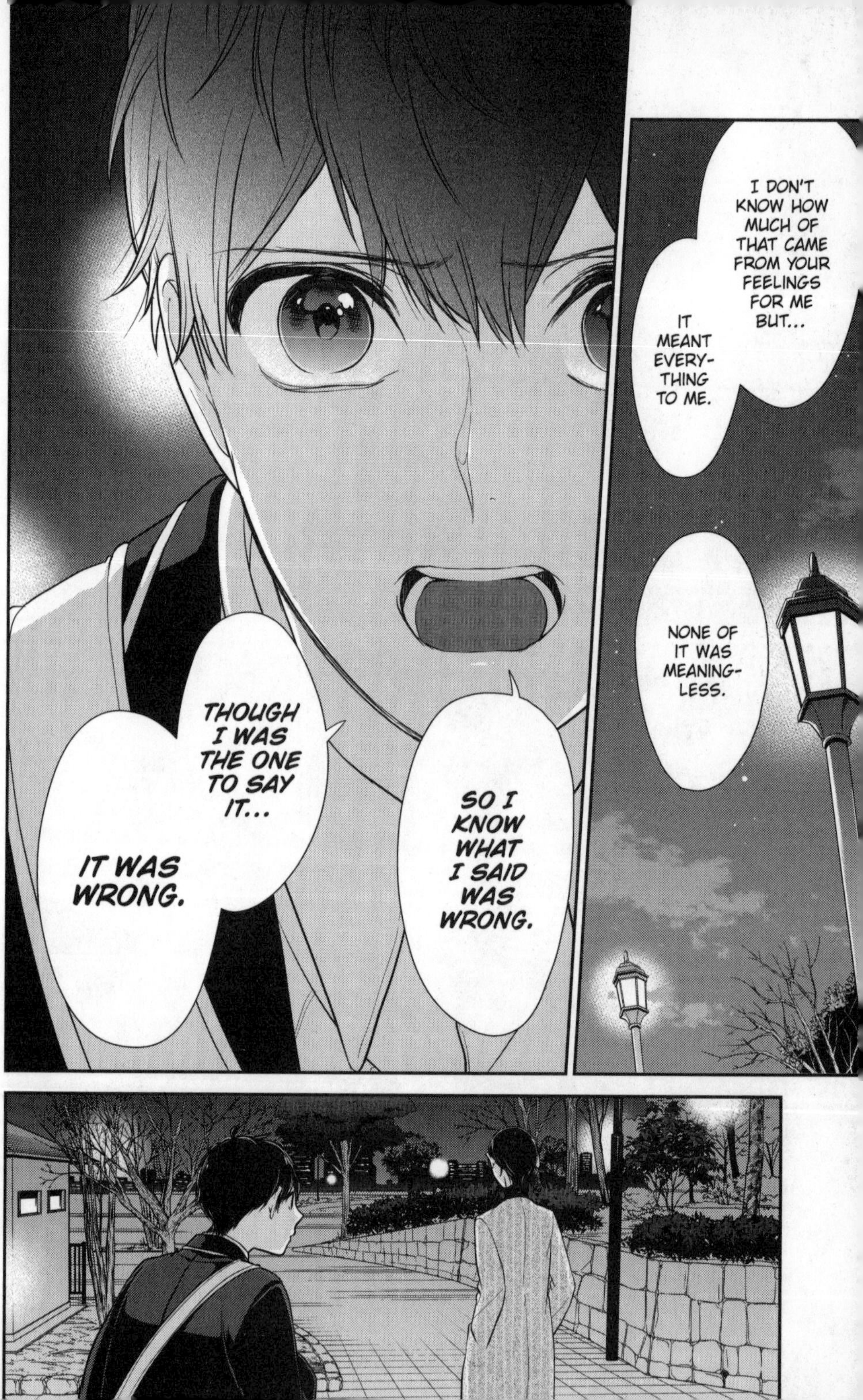
I DON'T KNOW HOW MUCH OF THAT CAME FROM YOUR FEELINGS FOR ME BUT...
IT MEANT EVERY-THING TO ME.
NONE OF IT WAS MEANING-LESS.
SO I KNOW WHAT I SAID WAS WRONG.
THOUGH I WAS THE ONE TO SAY IT... IT WAS WRONG.

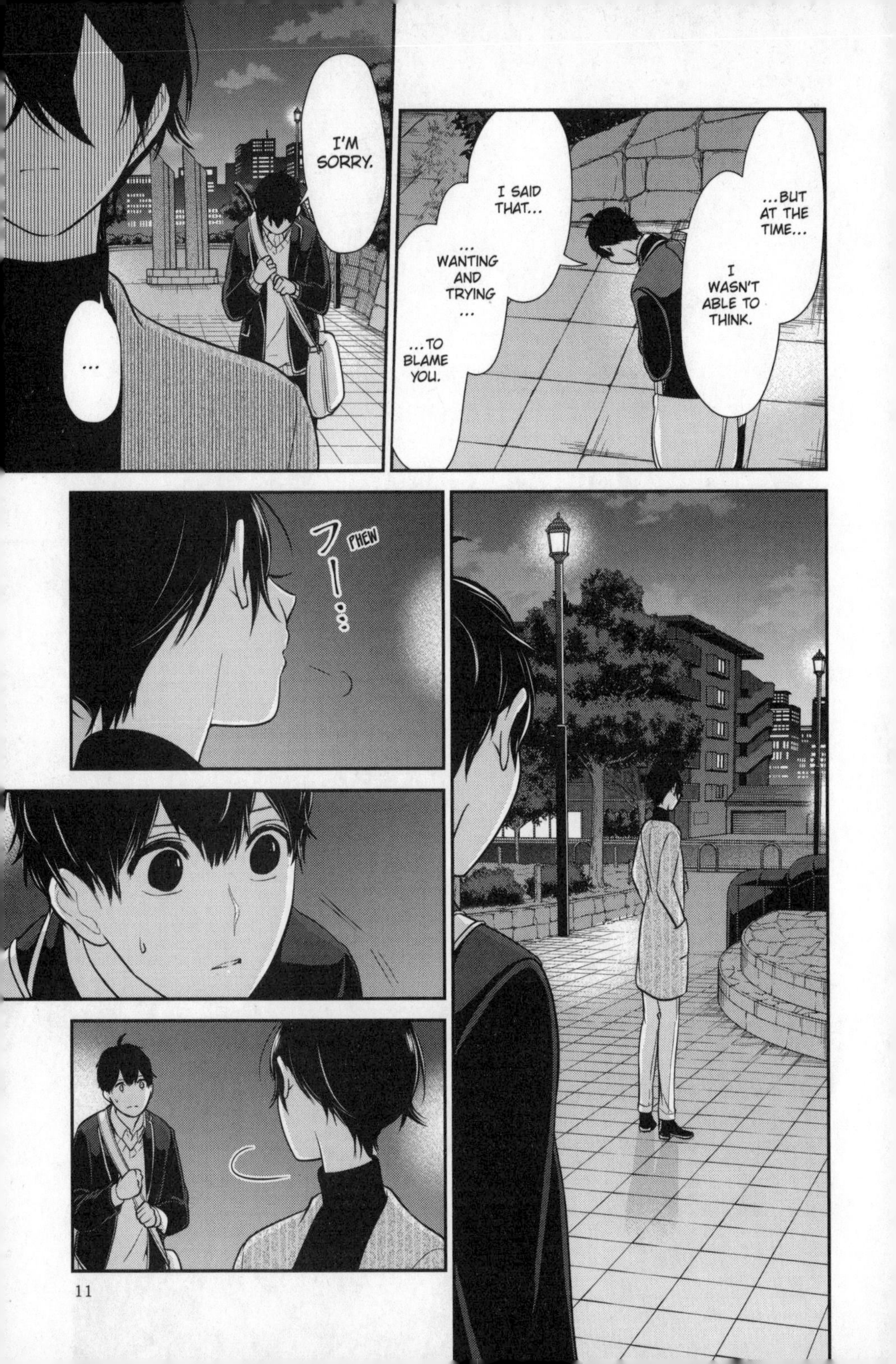
...BUT AT THE TIME...
I WASN'T ABLE TO THINK.
I SAID THAT...
...WANTING AND TRYING...
...TO BLAME YOU.
I'M SORRY.
...
フー...
PHEW

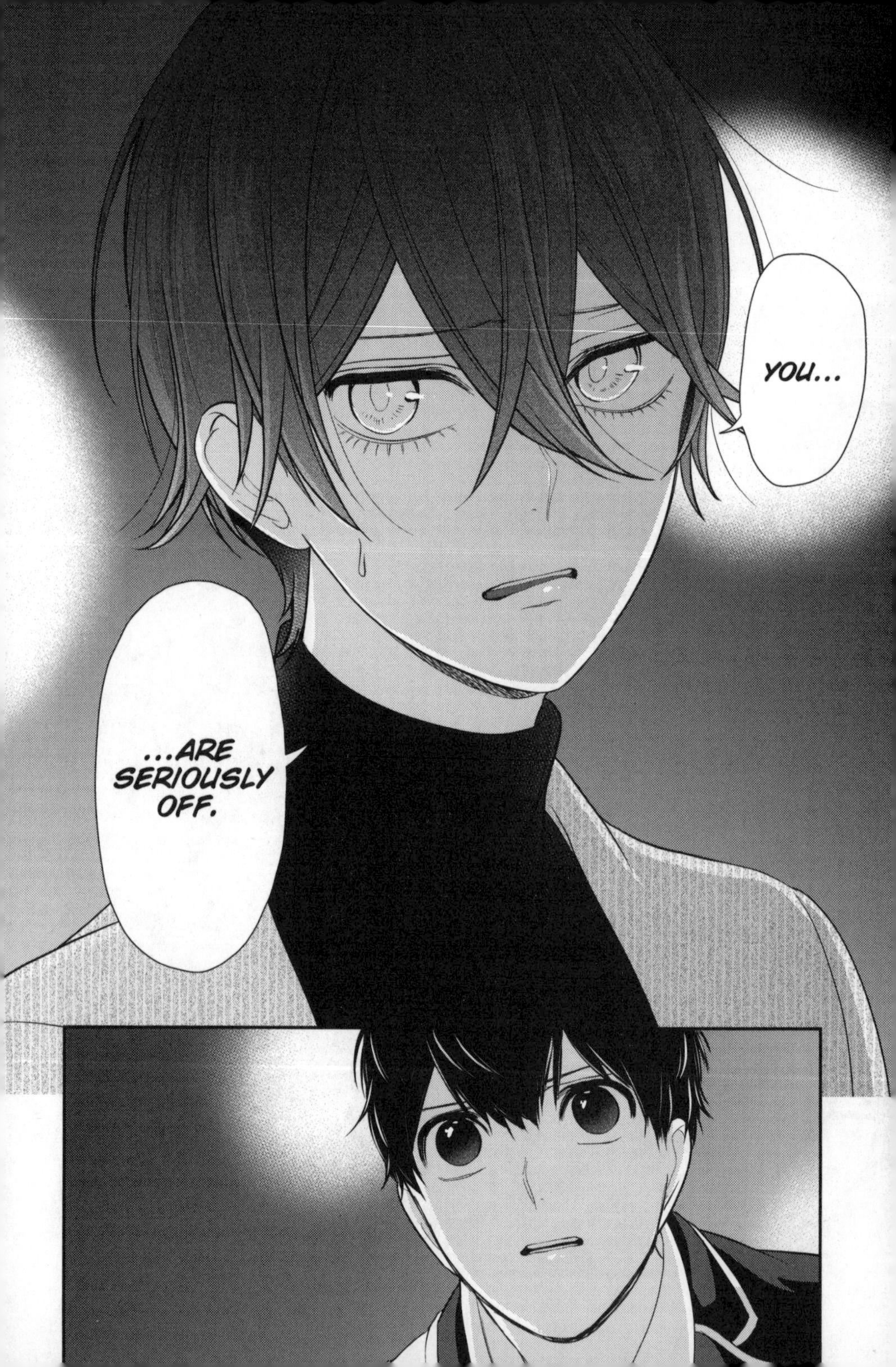
YOU...
...ARE SERIOUSLY OFF.

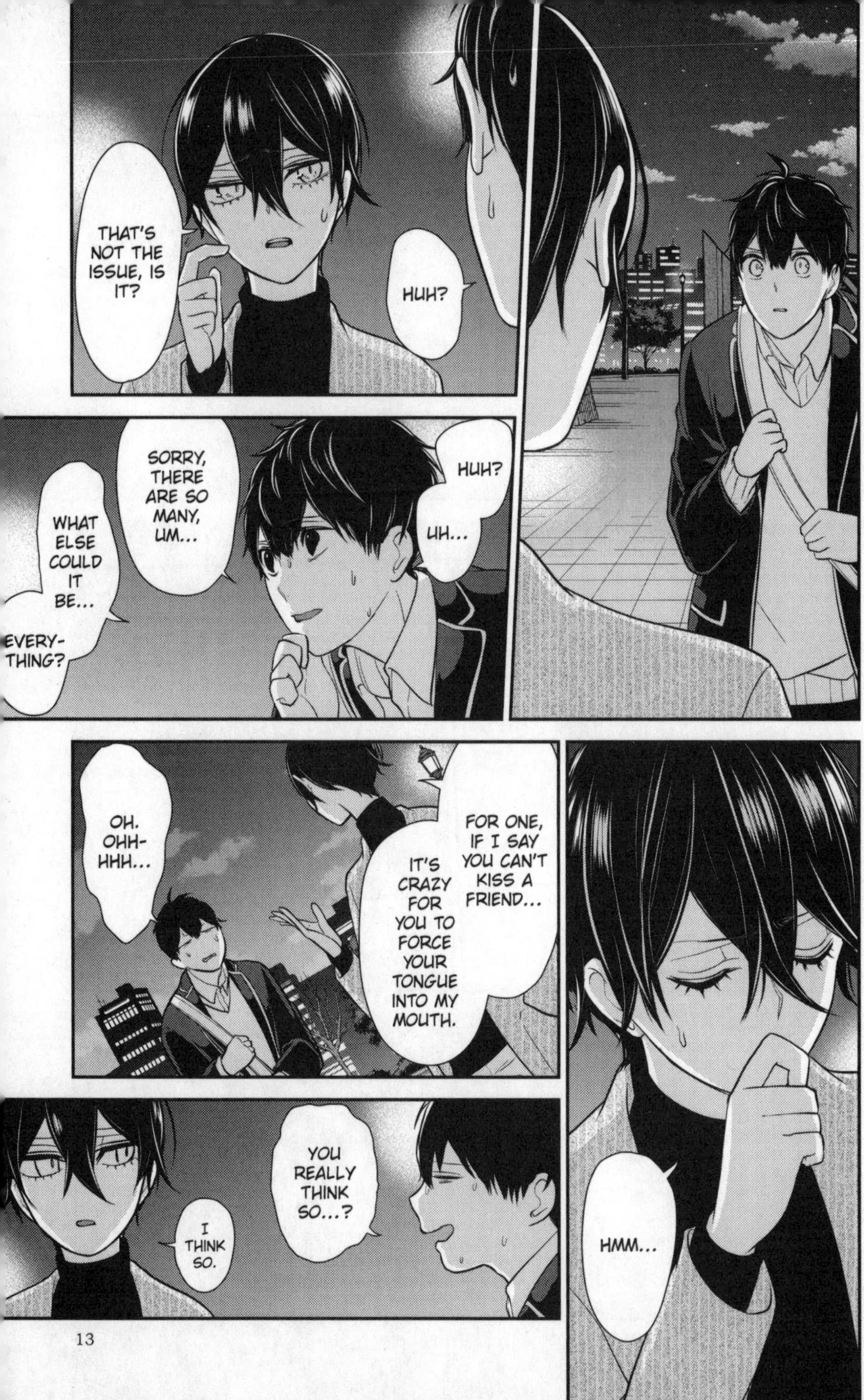
THAT'S NOT THE ISSUE, IS IT?
HUH?
HUH?
UH...
SORRY, THERE ARE SO MANY, UM...
WHAT ELSE COULD IT BE...
EVERY-THING?
HMM...
FOR ONE, IF I SAY YOU CAN'T KISS A FRIEND...
IT'S CRAZY FOR YOU TO FORCE YOUR TONGUE INTO MY MOUTH.
OH. OHH-HHH...
YOU REALLY THINK SO...?
I THINK SO.

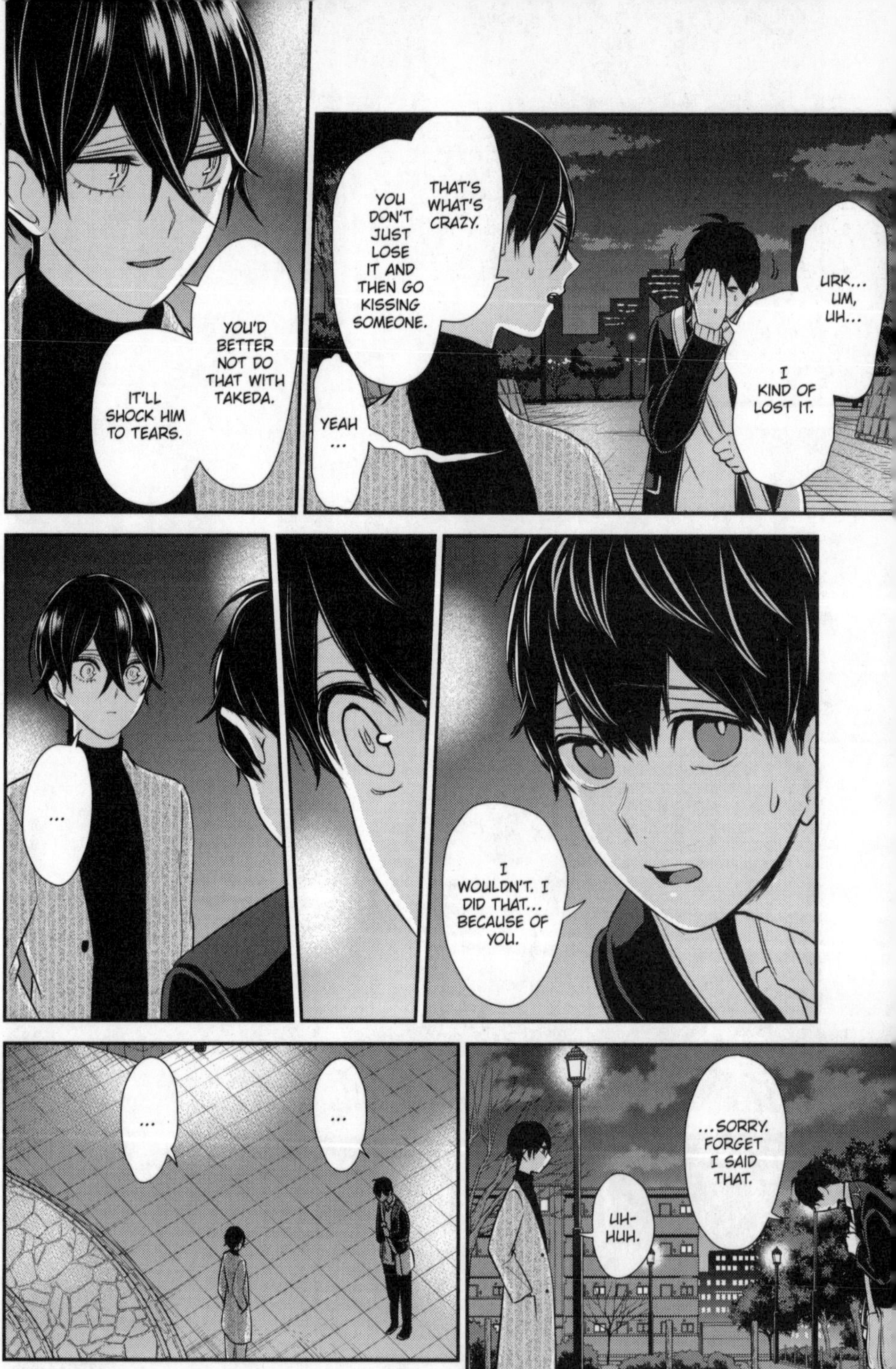
URK... UM, UH...
I KIND OF LOST IT.
THAT'S WHAT'S CRAZY.
YOU DON'T JUST LOSE IT AND THEN GO KISSING SOMEONE.
YEAH...
YOU'D BETTER NOT DO THAT WITH TAKEDA.
IT'LL SHOCK HIM TO TEARS.
I WOULDN'T. I DID THAT... BECAUSE OF YOU.
...
...SORRY. FORGET I SAID THAT.
UH-HUH.
...
...

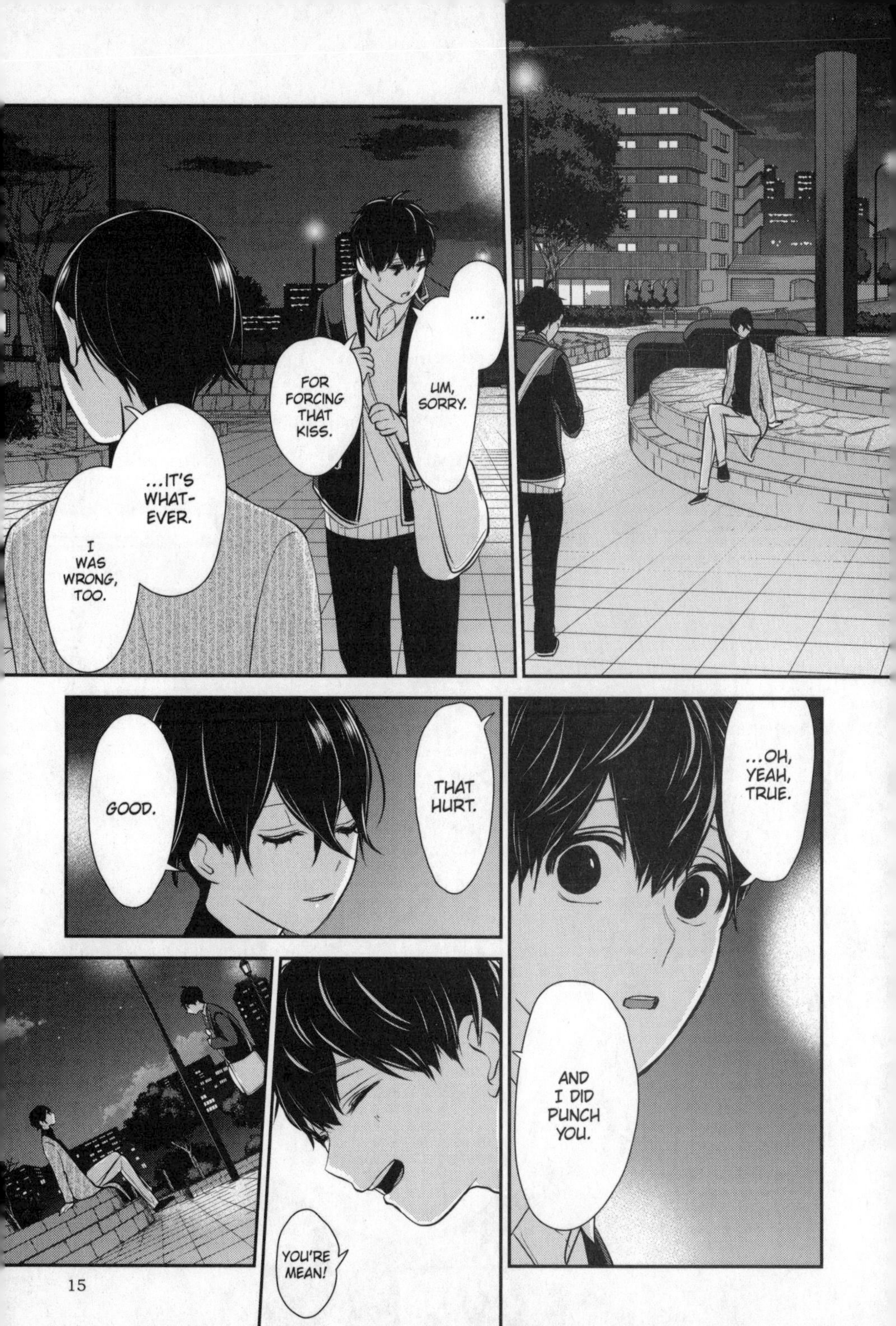
...
UM, SORRY.
FOR FORCING THAT KISS.
...IT'S WHAT-EVER.
I WAS WRONG, TOO.
...OH, YEAH, TRUE.
AND I DID PUNCH YOU.
THAT HURT.
GOOD.
YOU'RE MEAN!

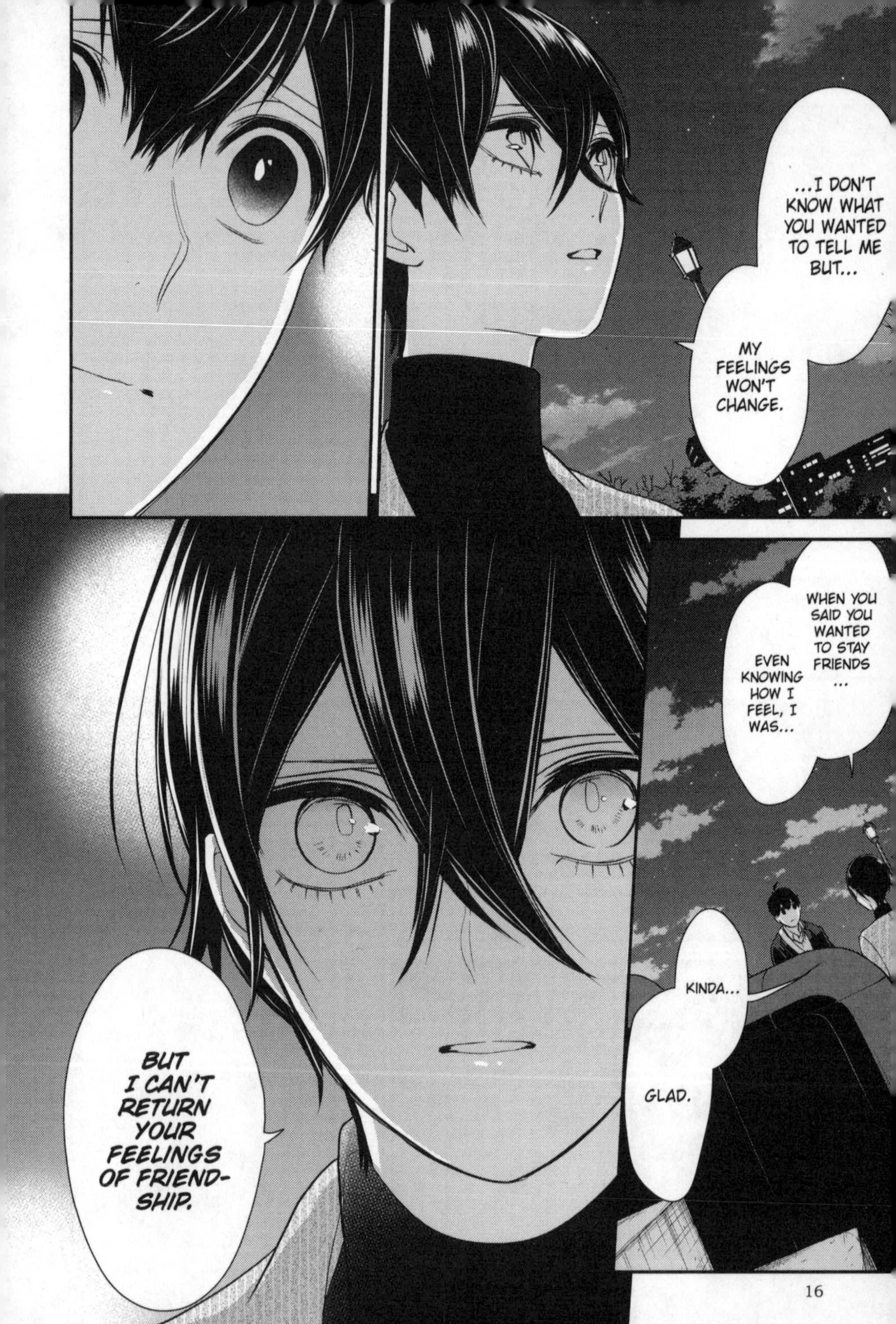
...I DON'T KNOW WHAT YOU WANTED TO TELL ME BUT...
MY FEELINGS WON'T CHANGE.
WHEN YOU SAID YOU WANTED TO STAY FRIENDS...
EVEN KNOWING HOW I FEEL, I WAS...
KINDA...
GLAD.
BUT I CAN'T RETURN YOUR FEELINGS OF FRIEND-SHIP.

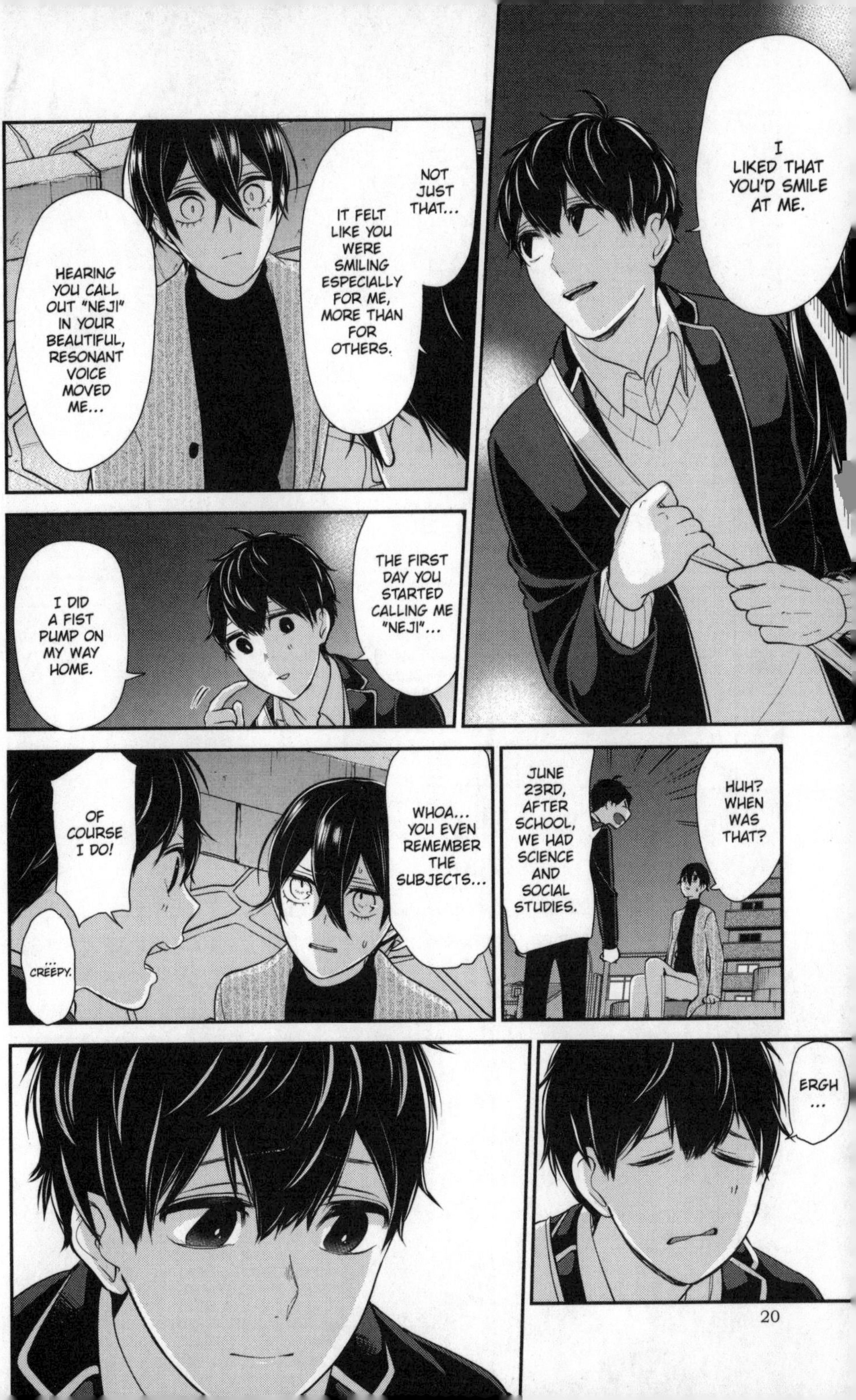
I LIKED THAT YOU'D SMILE AT ME.
NOT JUST THAT...
IT FELT LIKE YOU WERE SMILING ESPECIALLY FOR ME, MORE THAN FOR OTHERS.
HEARING YOU CALL OUT "NEJI" IN YOUR BEAUTIFUL, RESONANT VOICE MOVED ME...
THE FIRST DAY YOU STARTED CALLING ME "NEJI"...
I DID A FIST PUMP ON MY WAY HOME.
HUH? WHEN WAS THAT?
JUNE 23RD, AFTER SCHOOL, WE HAD SCIENCE AND SOCIAL STUDIES.
WHOA... YOU EVEN REMEMBER THE SUBJECTS...
OF COURSE I DO!
... CREEPY.
ERGH ...

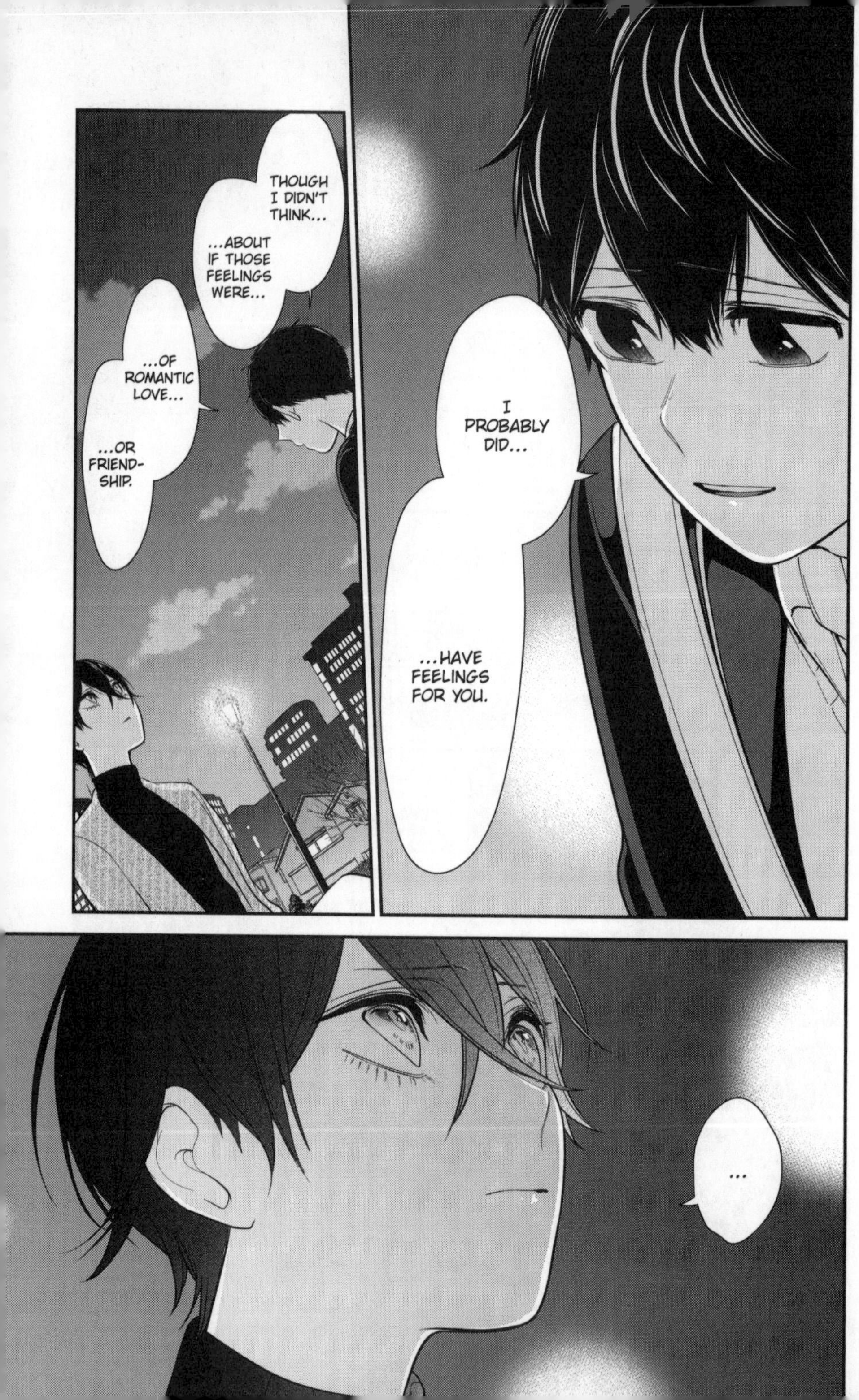
I PROBABLY DID...
...HAVE FEELINGS FOR YOU.
THOUGH I DIDN'T THINK...
...ABOUT IF THOSE FEELINGS WERE...
...OF ROMANTIC LOVE...
...OR FRIEND-SHIP.
...

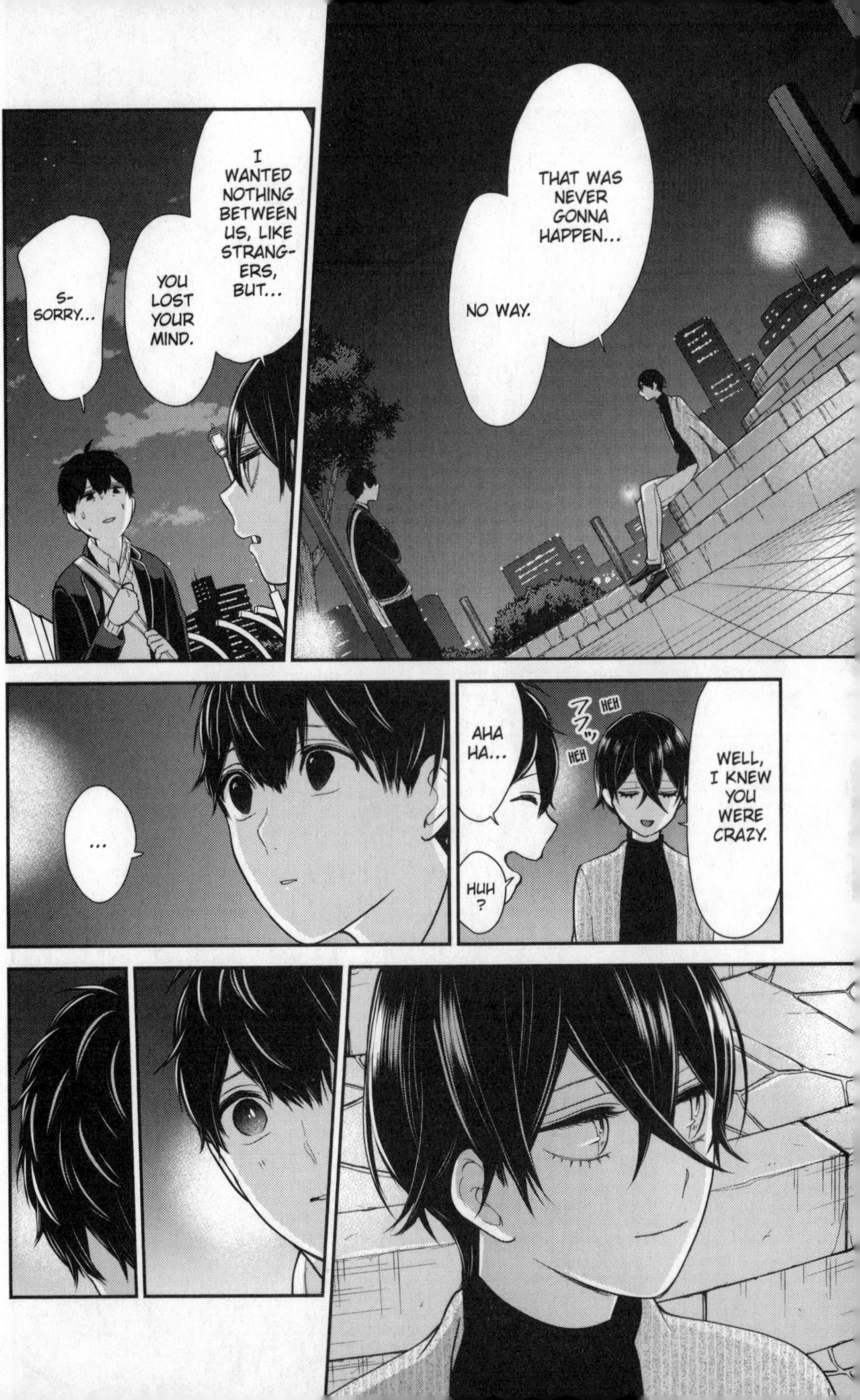
THAT WAS NEVER GONNA HAPPEN...
NO WAY.
I WANTED NOTHING BETWEEN US, LIKE STRANG-ERS, BUT...
YOU LOST YOUR MIND.
S-SORRY...
WELL, I KNEW YOU WERE CRAZY.
HEH HEH
AHA HA...
HUH?
...

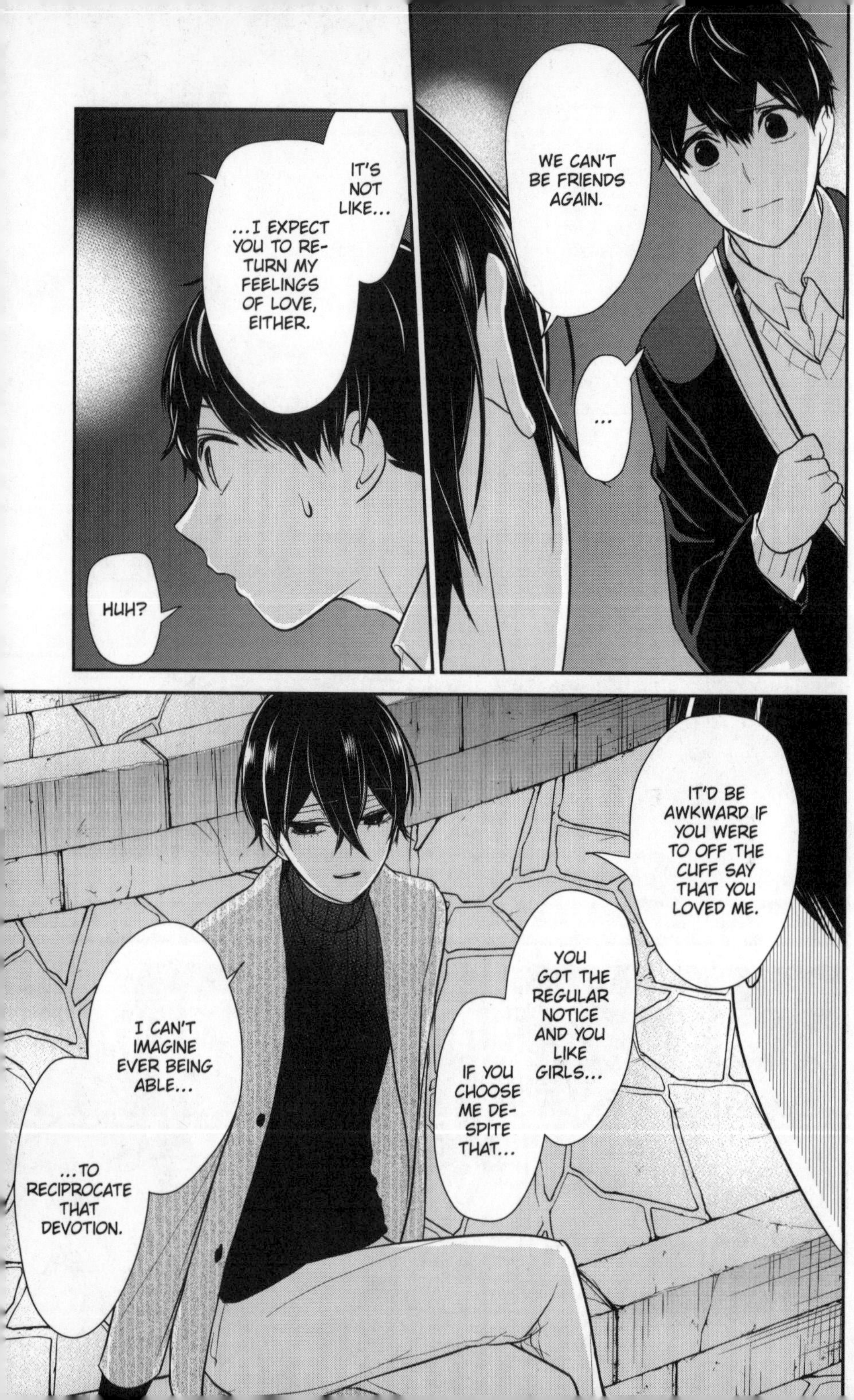
WE CAN'T BE FRIENDS AGAIN.
...
IT'S NOT LIKE...
...I EXPECT YOU TO RETURN MY FEELINGS OF LOVE, EITHER.
HUH?
IT'D BE AWKWARD IF YOU WERE TO OFF THE CUFF SAY THAT YOU LOVED ME.
YOU GOT THE REGULAR NOTICE AND YOU LIKE GIRLS...
IF YOU CHOOSE ME DESPITE THAT...
I CAN'T IMAGINE EVER BEING ABLE...
...TO RECIPROCATE THAT DEVOTION.

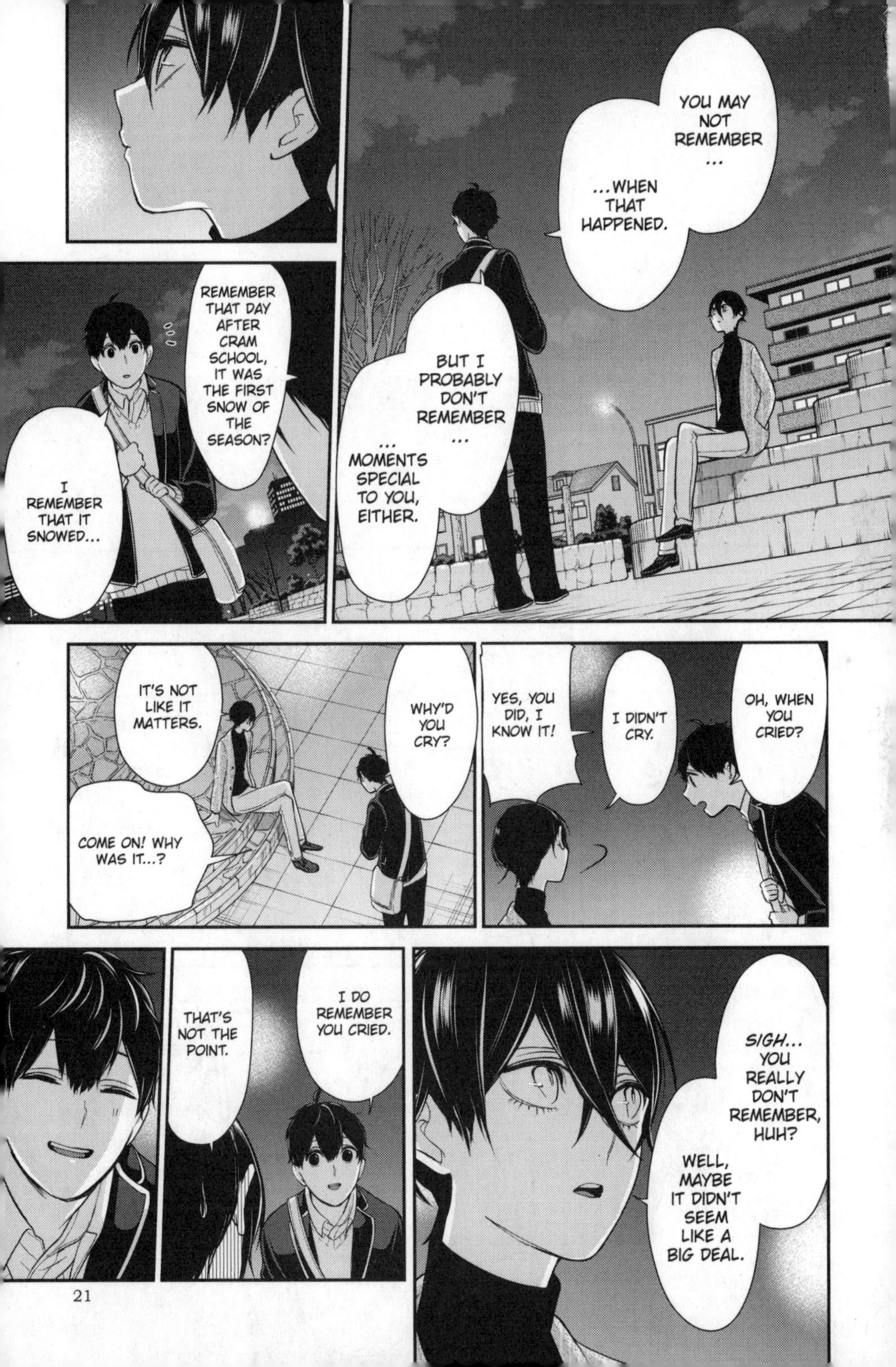
YOU MAY NOT REMEMBER ...
...WHEN THAT HAPPENED.
BUT I PROBABLY DON'T REMEMBER ...
... MOMENTS SPECIAL TO YOU, EITHER.
REMEMBER THAT DAY AFTER CRAM SCHOOL, IT WAS THE FIRST SNOW OF THE SEASON?
I REMEMBER THAT IT SNOWED...
OH, WHEN YOU CRIED?
I DIDN'T CRY.
YES, YOU DID, I KNOW IT!
WHY'D YOU CRY?
IT'S NOT LIKE IT MATTERS.
COME ON! WHY WAS IT...?
SIGH... YOU REALLY DON'T REMEMBER, HUH?
WELL, MAYBE IT DIDN'T SEEM LIKE A BIG DEAL.
I DO REMEMBER YOU CRIED.
THAT'S NOT THE POINT.

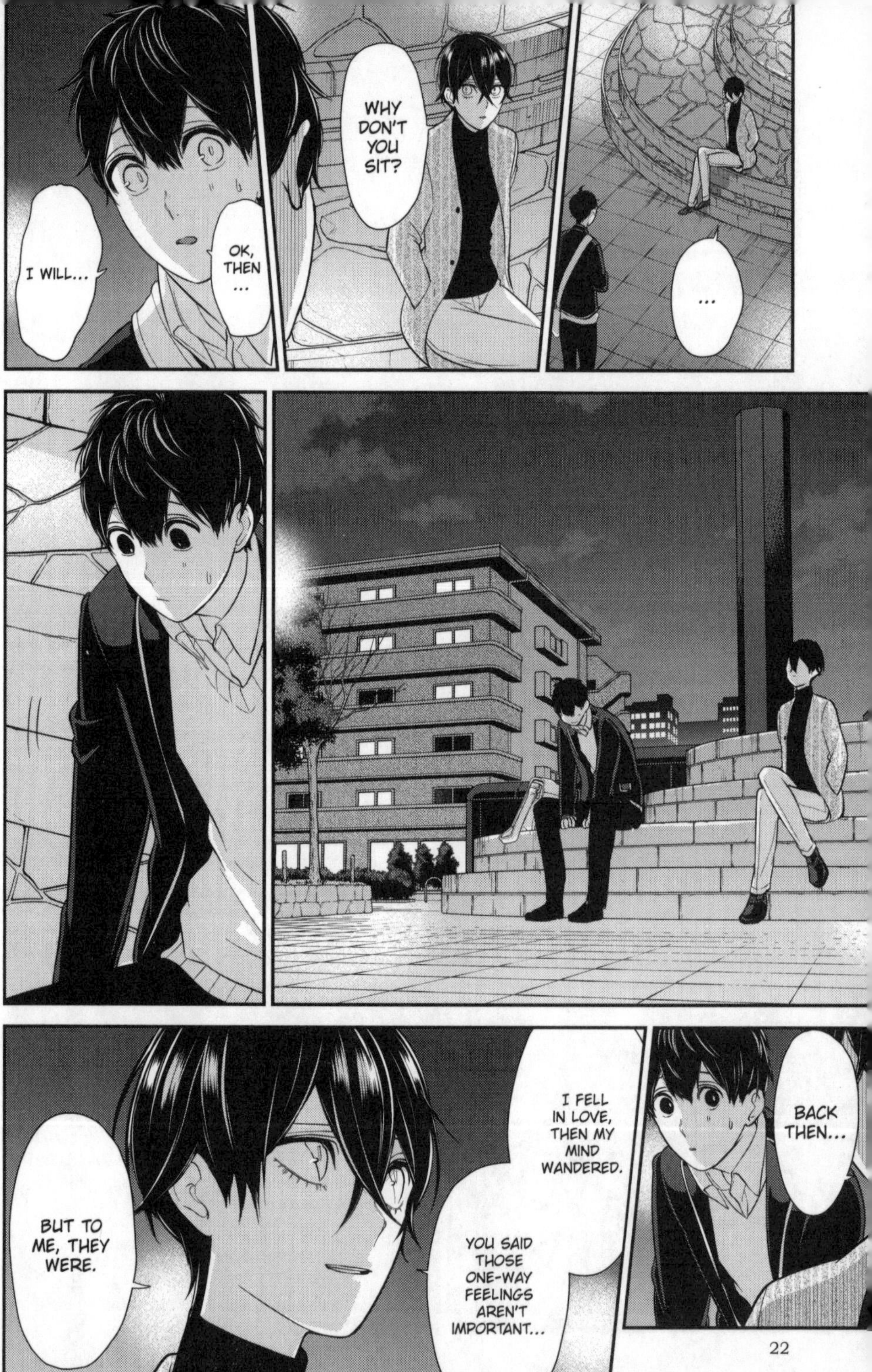
...
WHY DON'T YOU SIT?
OK, THEN...
I WILL...
BACK THEN...
I FELL IN LOVE, THEN MY MIND WANDERED.
YOU SAID THOSE ONE-WAY FEELINGS AREN'T IMPORTANT...
BUT TO ME, THEY WERE.

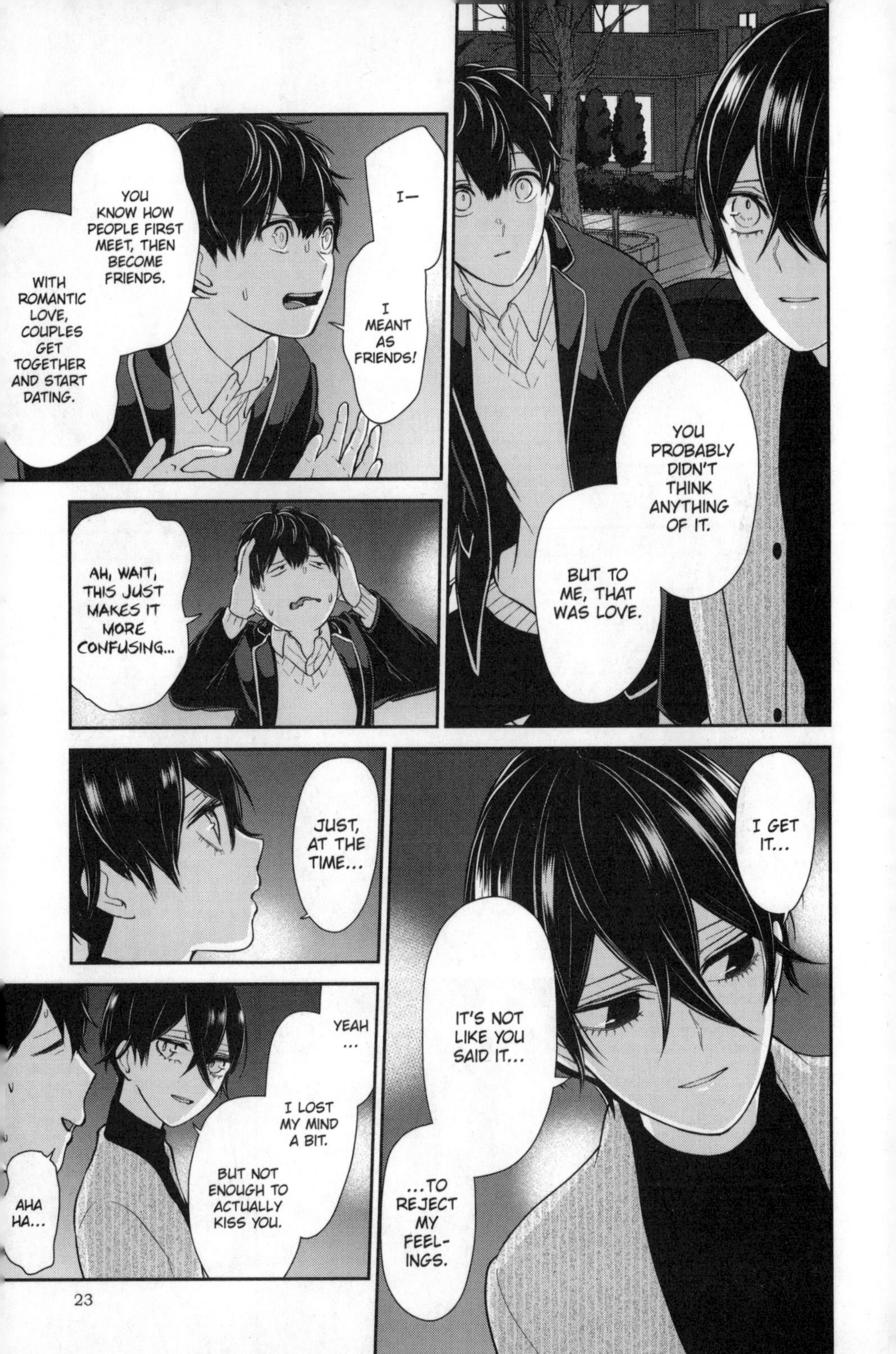
YOU PROBABLY DIDN'T THINK ANYTHING OF IT.
BUT TO ME, THAT WAS LOVE.
I—
I MEANT AS FRIENDS!
YOU KNOW HOW PEOPLE FIRST MEET, THEN BECOME FRIENDS.
WITH ROMANTIC LOVE, COUPLES GET TOGETHER AND START DATING.
AH, WAIT, THIS JUST MAKES IT MORE CONFUSING...
I GET IT...
IT'S NOT LIKE YOU SAID IT...
...TO REJECT MY FEEL-INGS.
JUST, AT THE TIME...
YEAH ...
I LOST MY MIND A BIT.
BUT NOT ENOUGH TO ACTUALLY KISS YOU.
AHA HA...

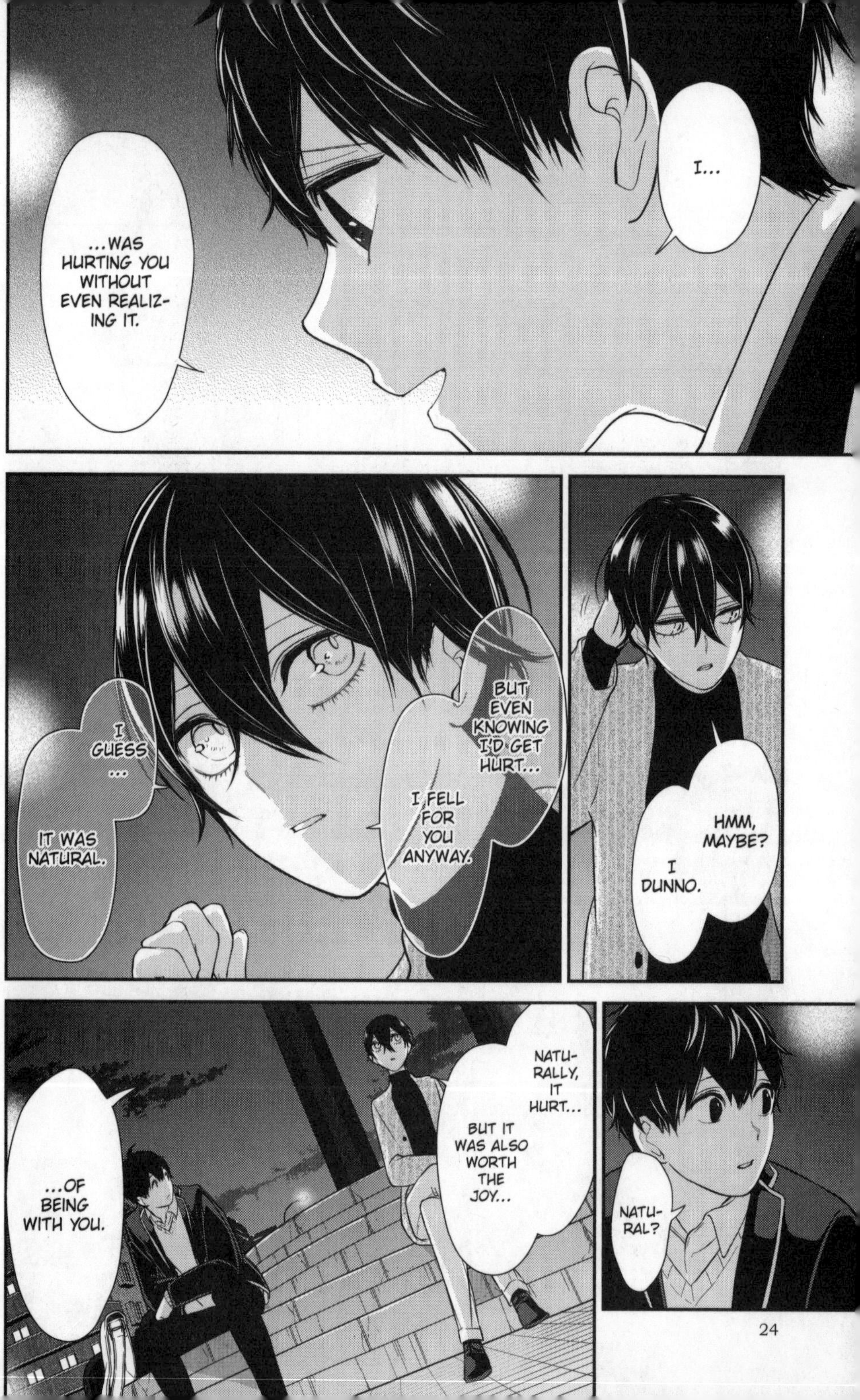
I...
...WAS HURTING YOU WITHOUT EVEN REALIZ-ING IT.
HMM, MAYBE? I DUNNO.
BUT EVEN KNOWING I'D GET HURT... I FELL FOR YOU ANYWAY.
I GUESS... IT WAS NATURAL.
NATU-RAL?
NATU-RALLY, IT HURT... BUT IT WAS ALSO WORTH THE JOY...
...OF BEING WITH YOU.

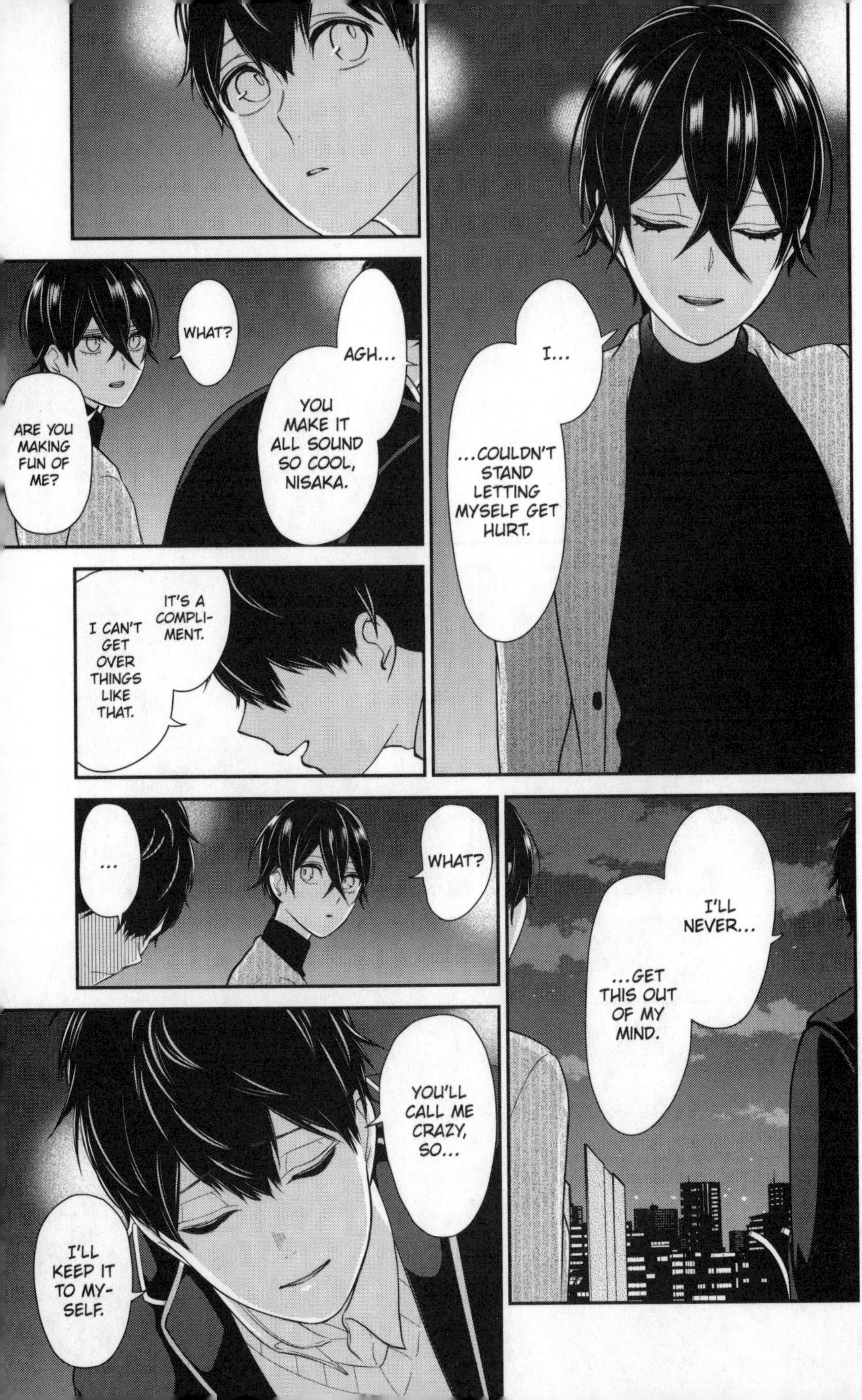
I...
...COULDN'T STAND LETTING MYSELF GET HURT.
AGH...
YOU MAKE IT ALL SOUND SO COOL, NISAKA.
WHAT?
ARE YOU MAKING FUN OF ME?
IT'S A COMPLI-MENT.
I CAN'T GET OVER THINGS LIKE THAT.
I'LL NEVER...
...GET THIS OUT OF MY MIND.
WHAT?
...
YOU'LL CALL ME CRAZY, SO...
I'LL KEEP IT TO MY-SELF.

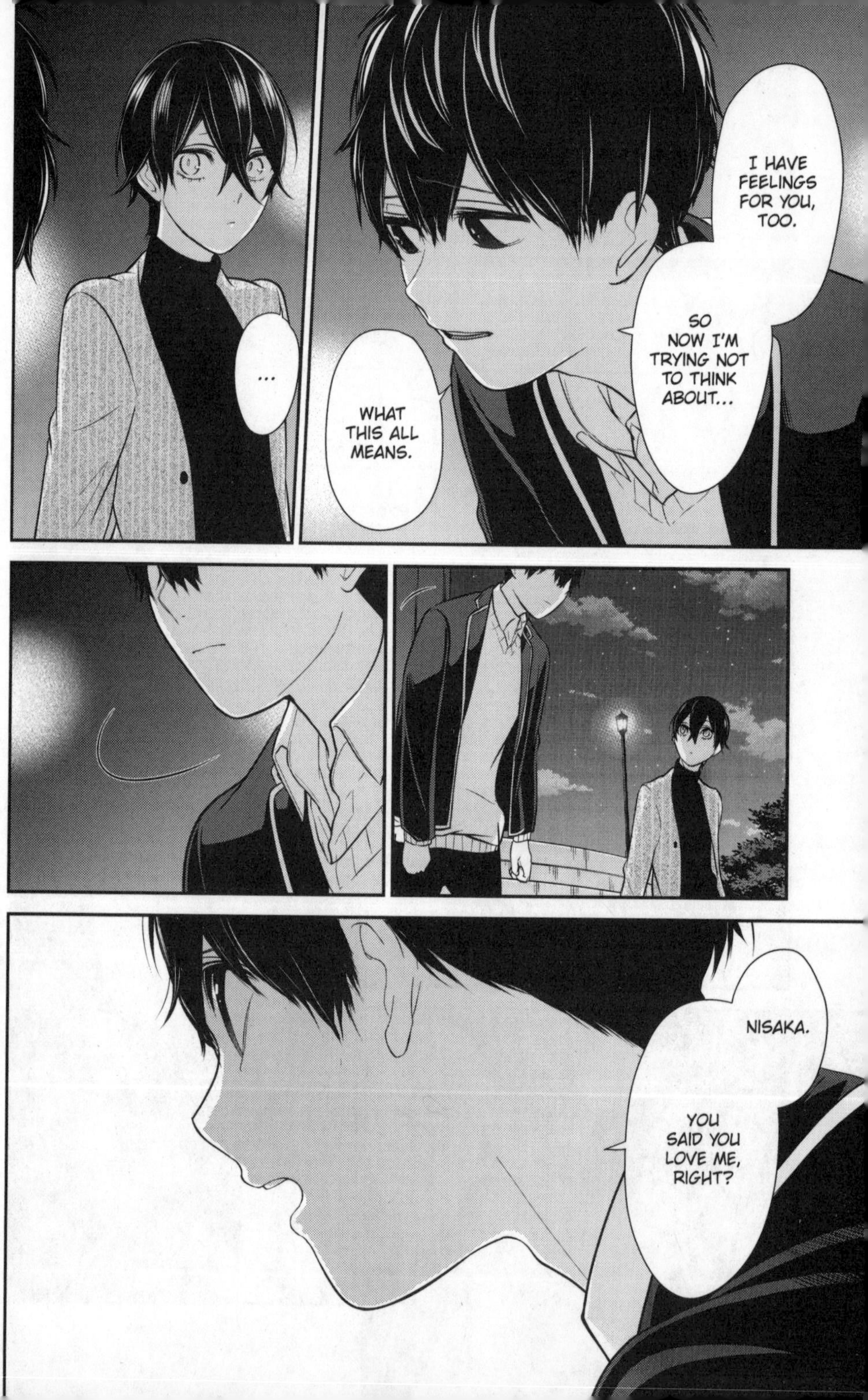
I HAVE FEELINGS FOR YOU, TOO.
SO NOW I'M TRYING NOT TO THINK ABOUT...
WHAT THIS ALL MEANS.
...
NISAKA.
YOU SAID YOU LOVE ME, RIGHT?

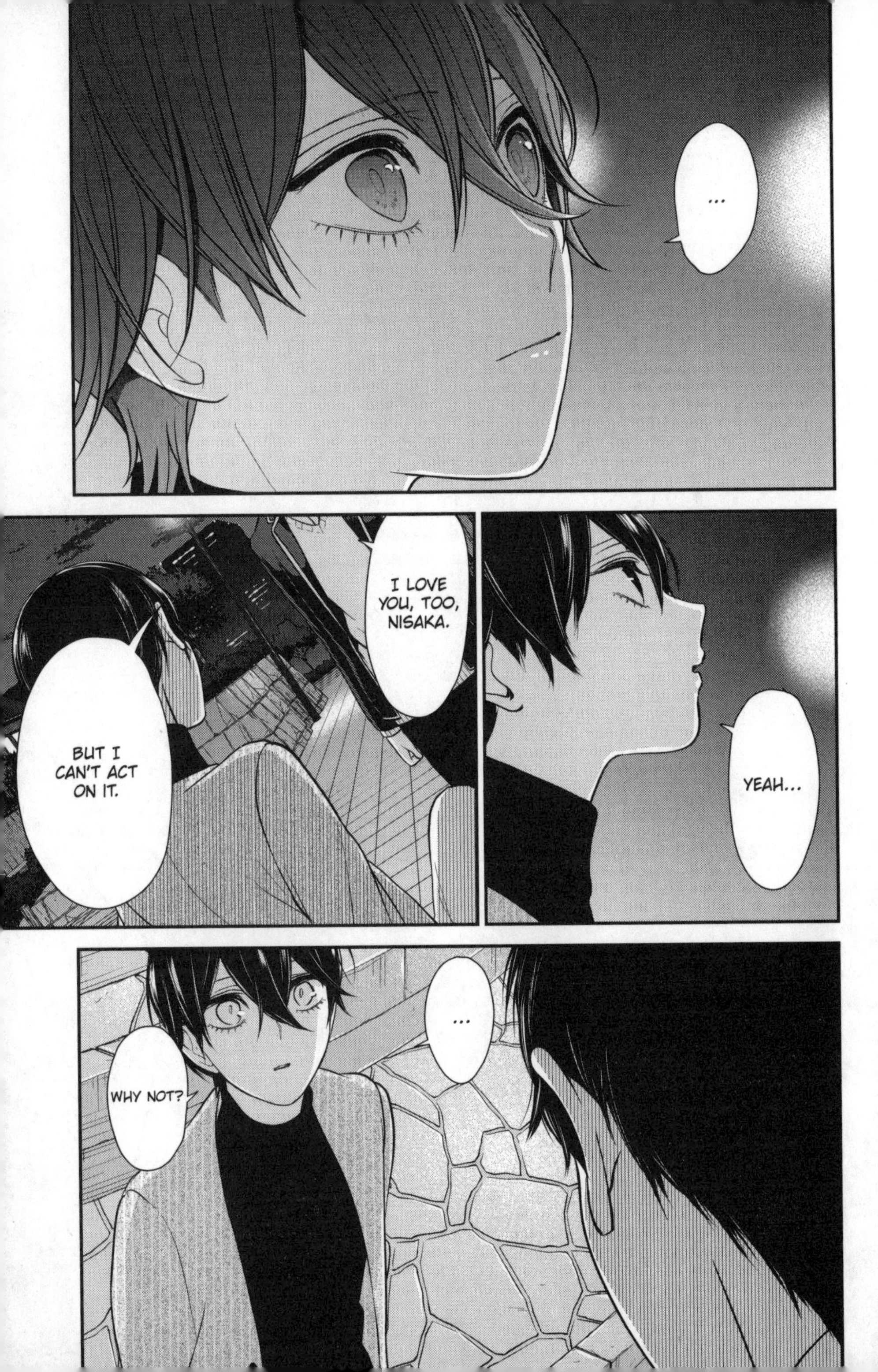
...
YEAH...
I LOVE YOU, TOO, NISAKA.
BUT I CAN'T ACT ON IT.
...
WHY NOT?

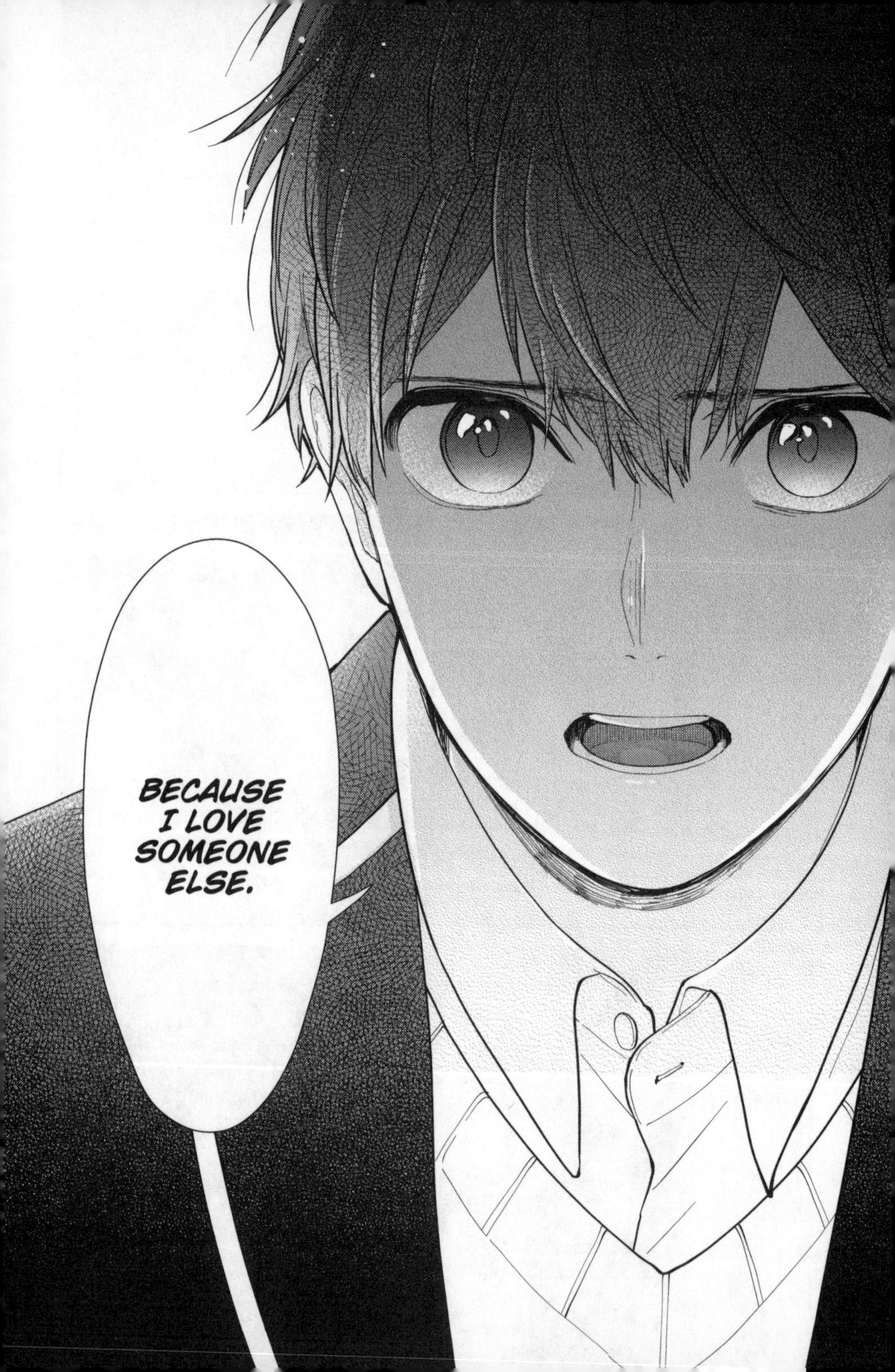
BECAUSE I LOVE SOMEONE ELSE.

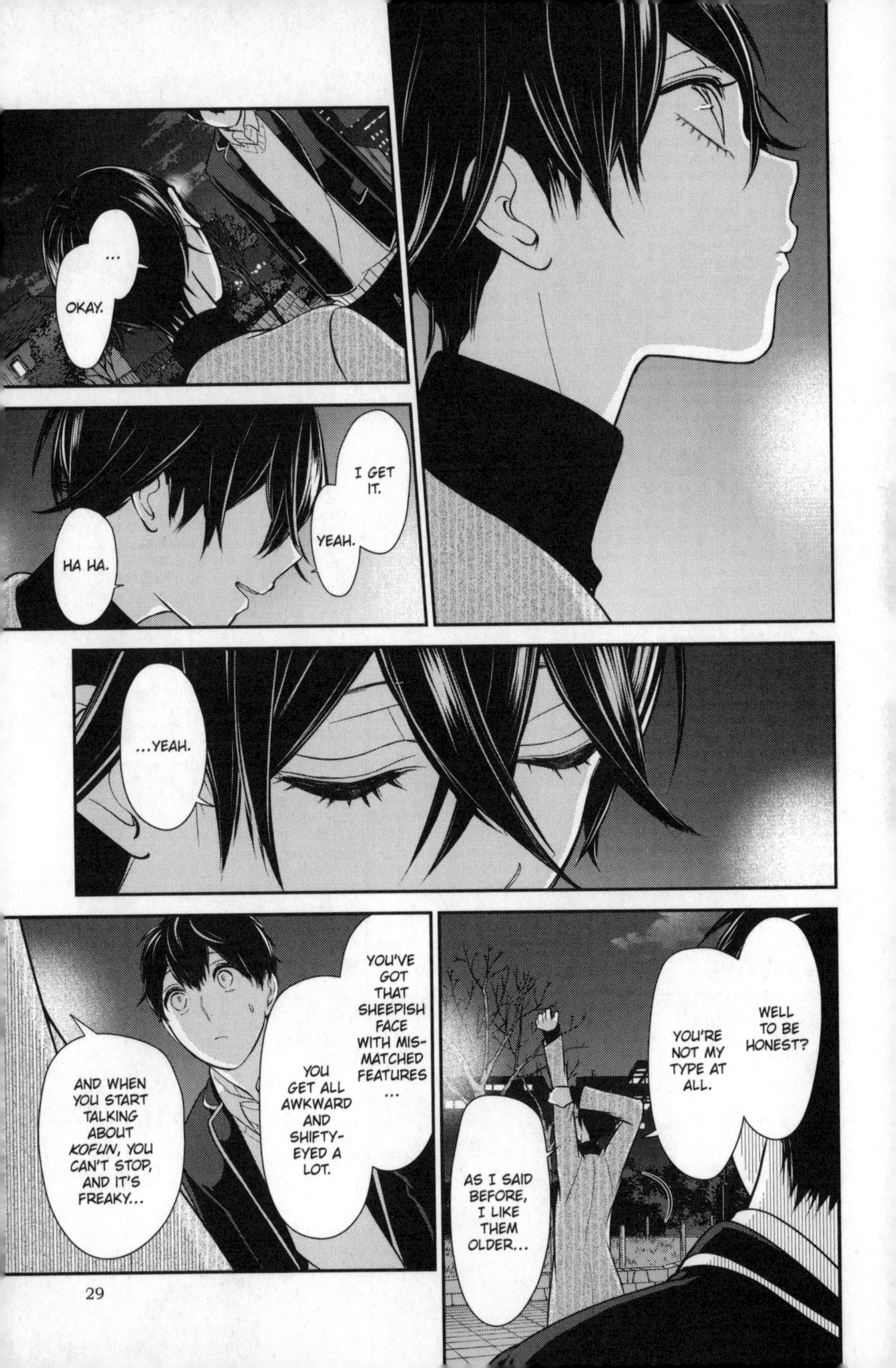
...
OKAY.
I GET IT.
YEAH.
HA HA.
...YEAH.
WELL TO BE HONEST?
YOU'RE NOT MY TYPE AT ALL.
AS I SAID BEFORE, I LIKE THEM OLDER...
YOU'VE GOT THAT SHEEPISH FACE WITH MIS-MATCHED FEATURES...
YOU GET ALL AWKWARD AND SHIFTY-EYED A LOT.
AND WHEN YOU START TALKING ABOUT *KOFUN*, YOU CAN'T STOP, AND IT'S FREAKY...

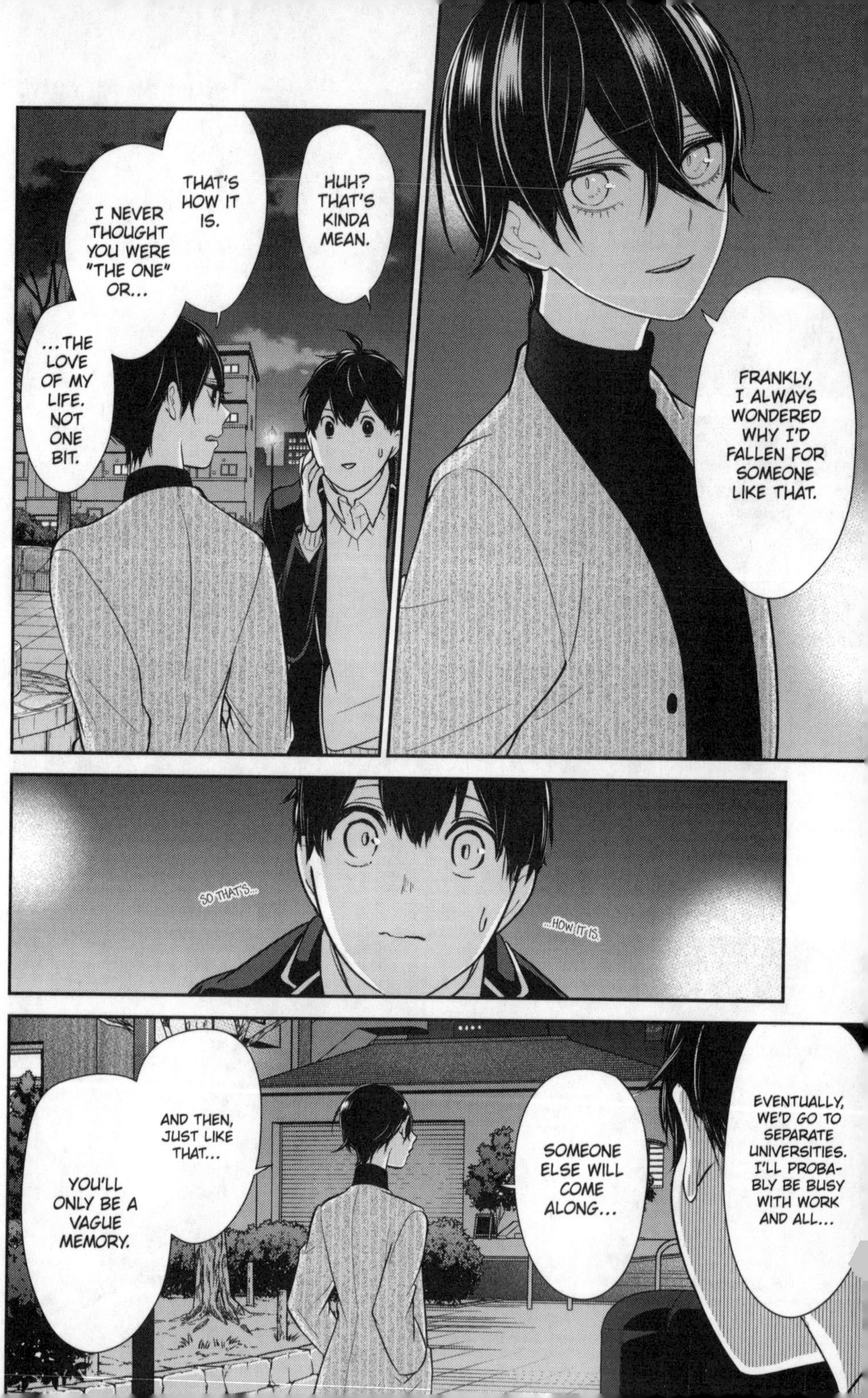
FRANKLY, I ALWAYS WONDERED WHY I'D FALLEN FOR SOMEONE LIKE THAT.
HUH? THAT'S KINDA MEAN.
THAT'S HOW IT IS.
I NEVER THOUGHT YOU WERE "THE ONE" OR...
...THE LOVE OF MY LIFE. NOT ONE BIT.
SO THAT'S...
...HOW IT IS.
EVENTUALLY, WE'D GO TO SEPARATE UNIVERSITIES. I'LL PROBABLY BE BUSY WITH WORK AND ALL...
SOMEONE ELSE WILL COME ALONG...
AND THEN, JUST LIKE THAT...
YOU'LL ONLY BE A VAGUE MEMORY.

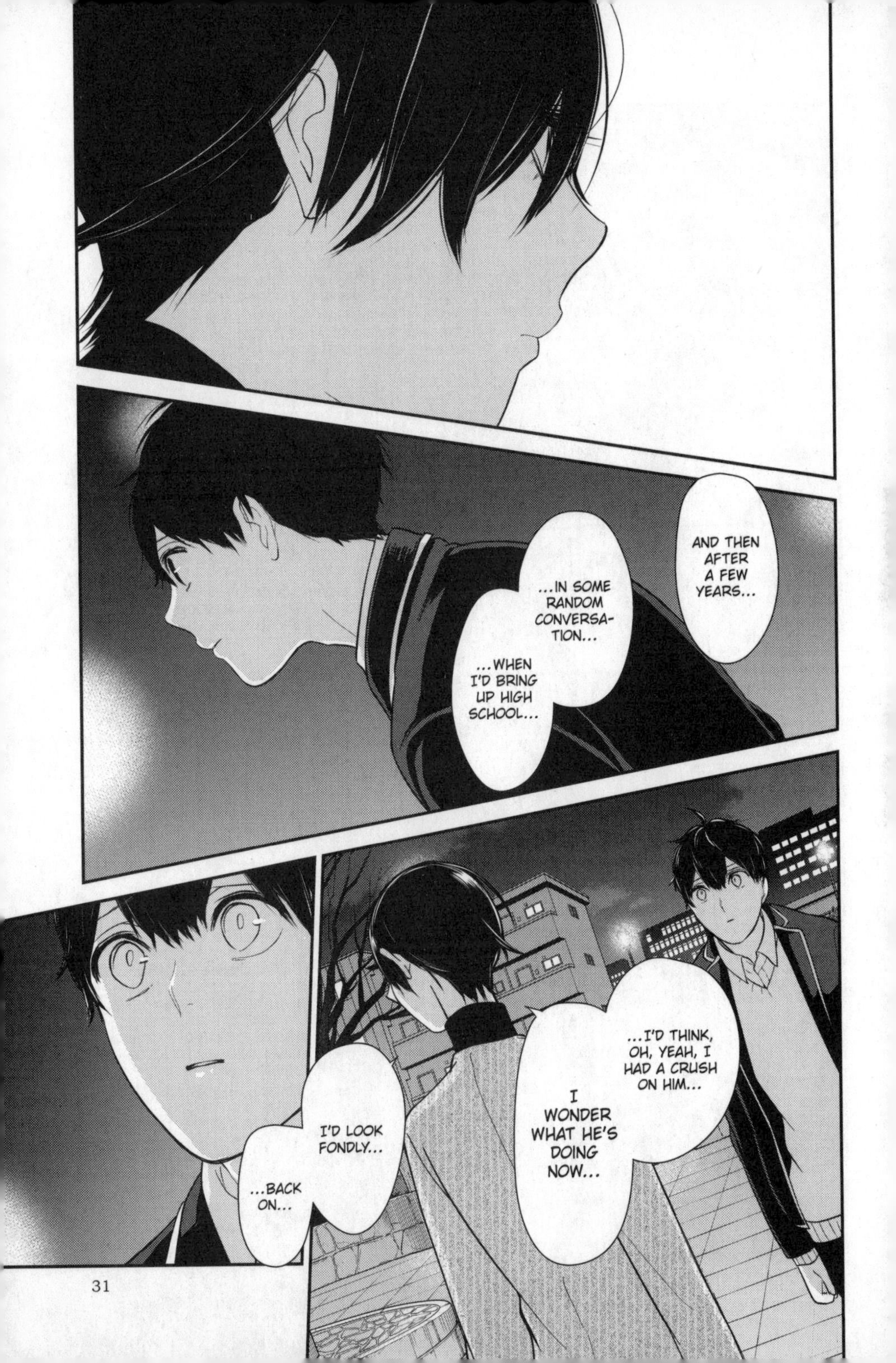
AND THEN AFTER A FEW YEARS...
...IN SOME RANDOM CONVERSATION...
...WHEN I'D BRING UP HIGH SCHOOL...
...I'D THINK, OH, YEAH, I HAD A CRUSH ON HIM...
I WONDER WHAT HE'S DOING NOW...
I'D LOOK FONDLY...
...BACK ON...

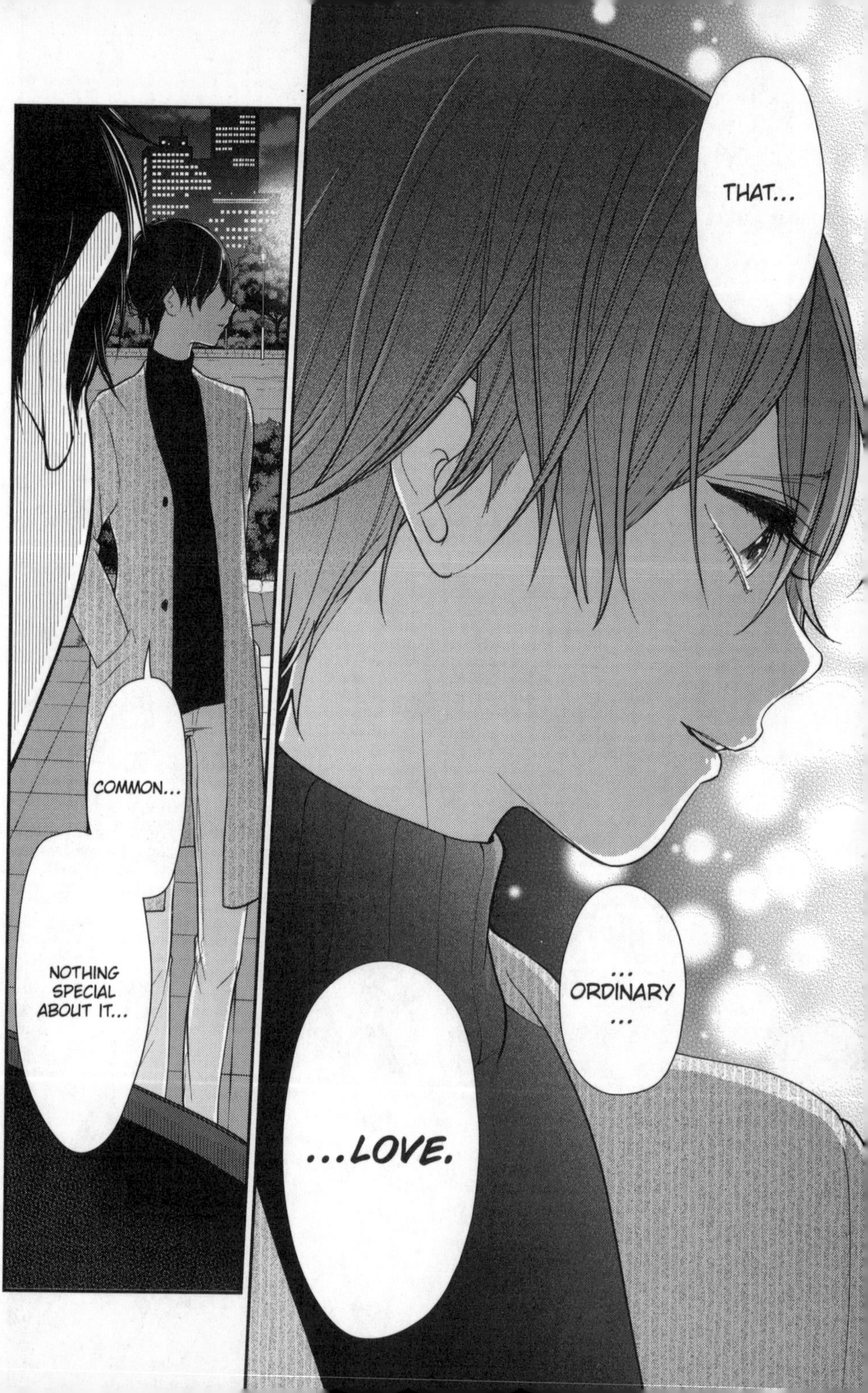
THAT...
... ORDINARY ...
...LOVE.
COMMON...
NOTHING SPECIAL ABOUT IT...

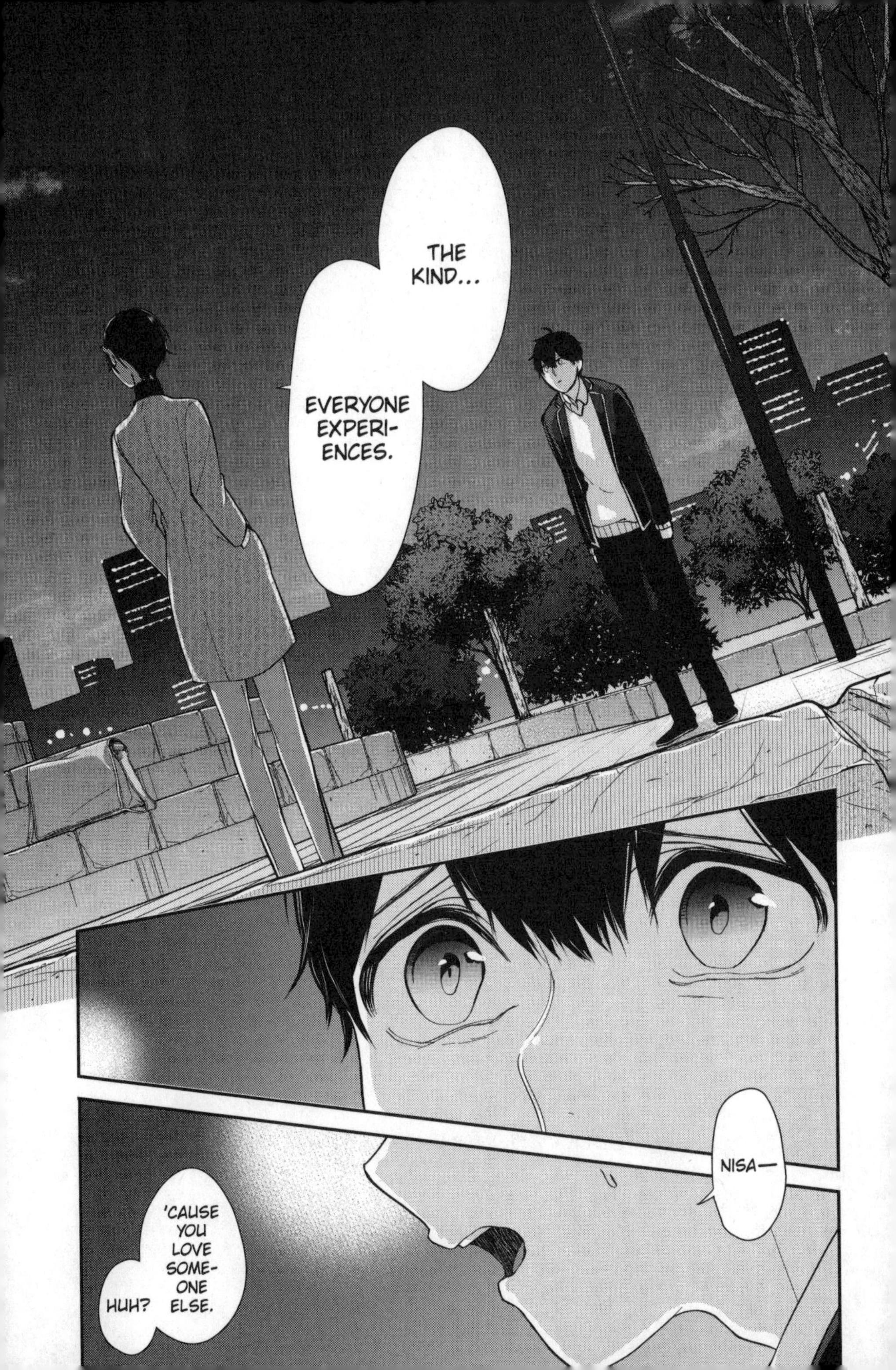
THE KIND...
EVERYONE EXPERI-ENCES.
NISA—
'CAUSE YOU LOVE SOME-ONE ELSE.
HUH?

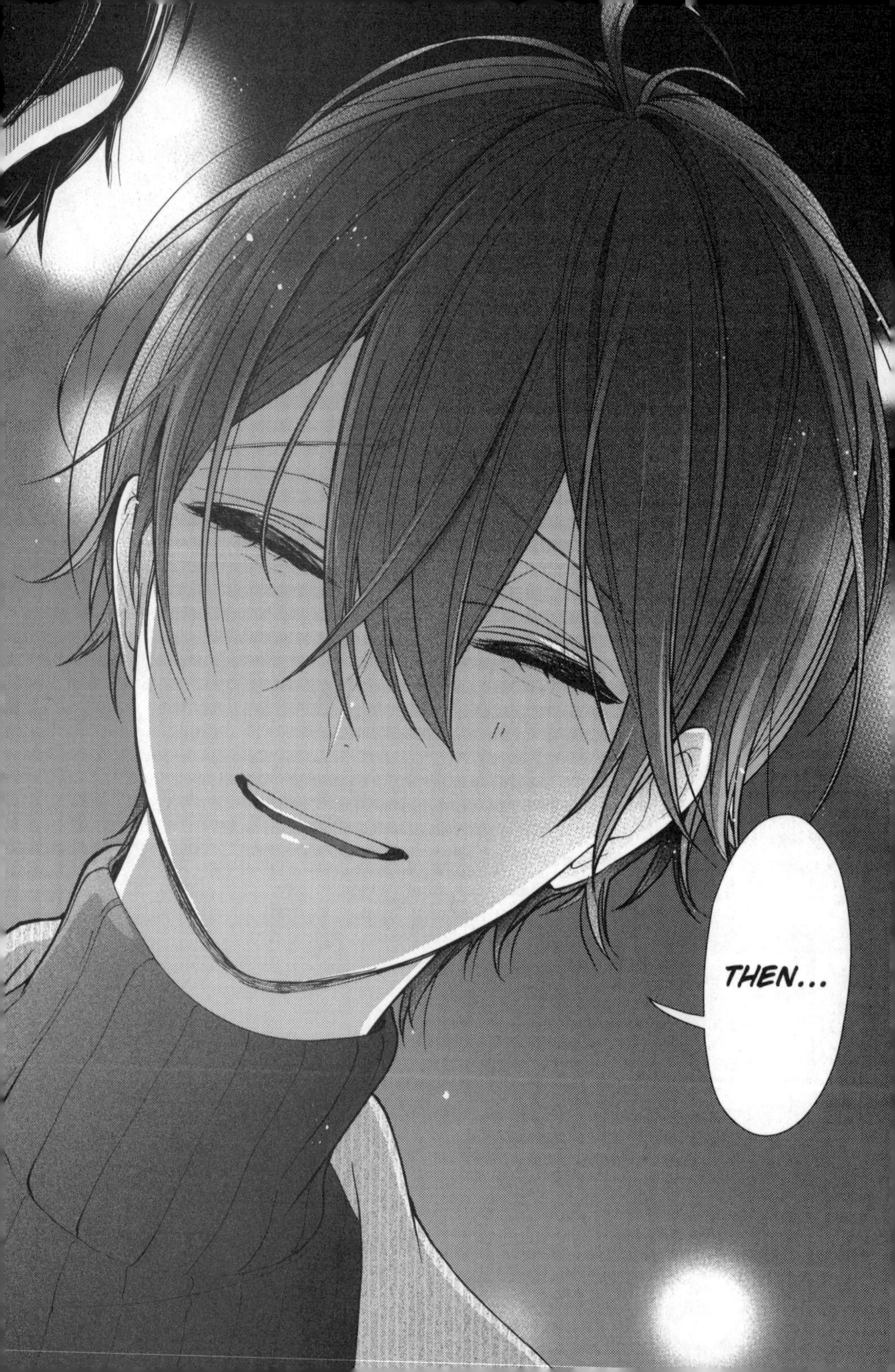
THEN...

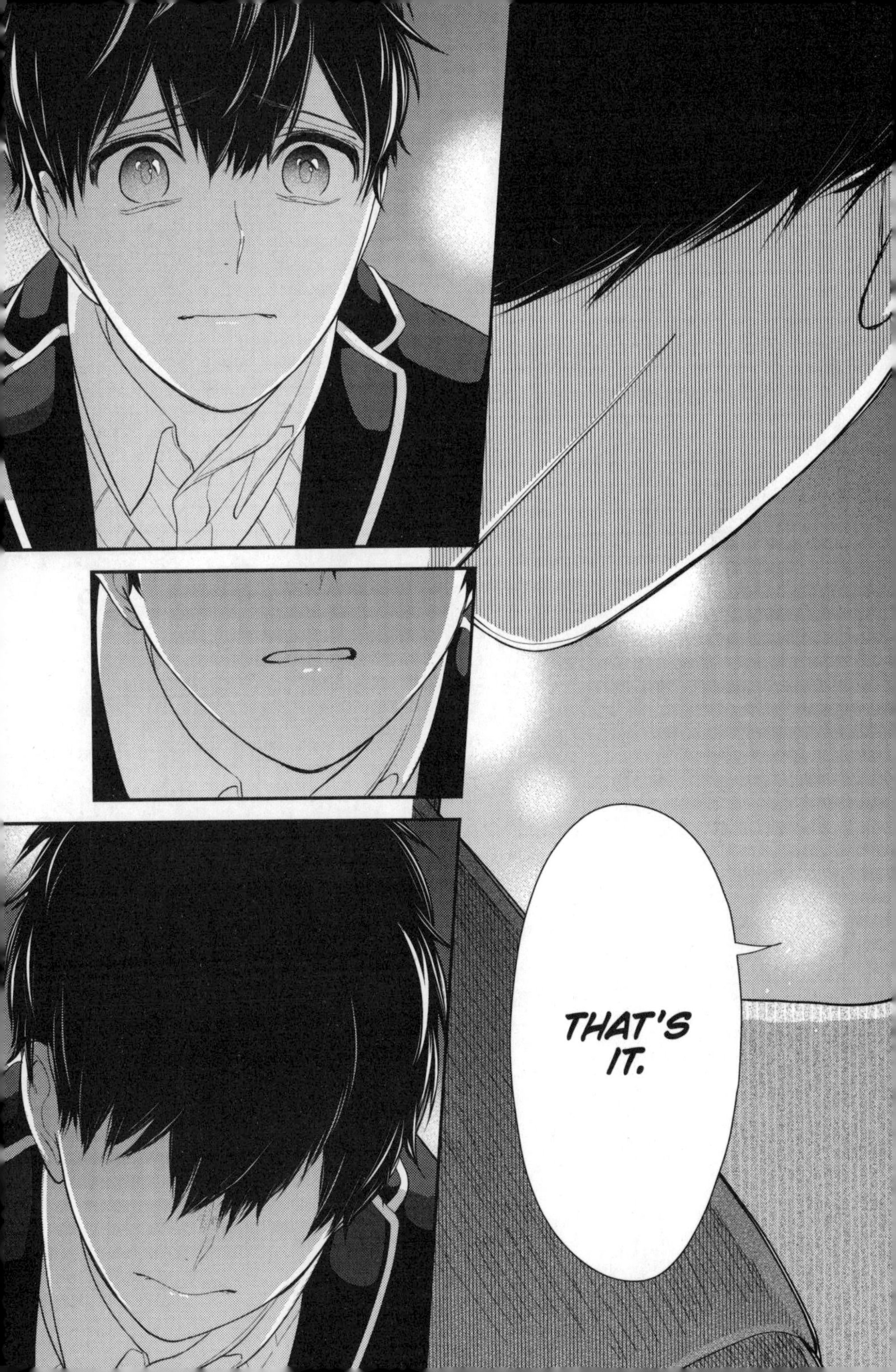
THAT'S IT.

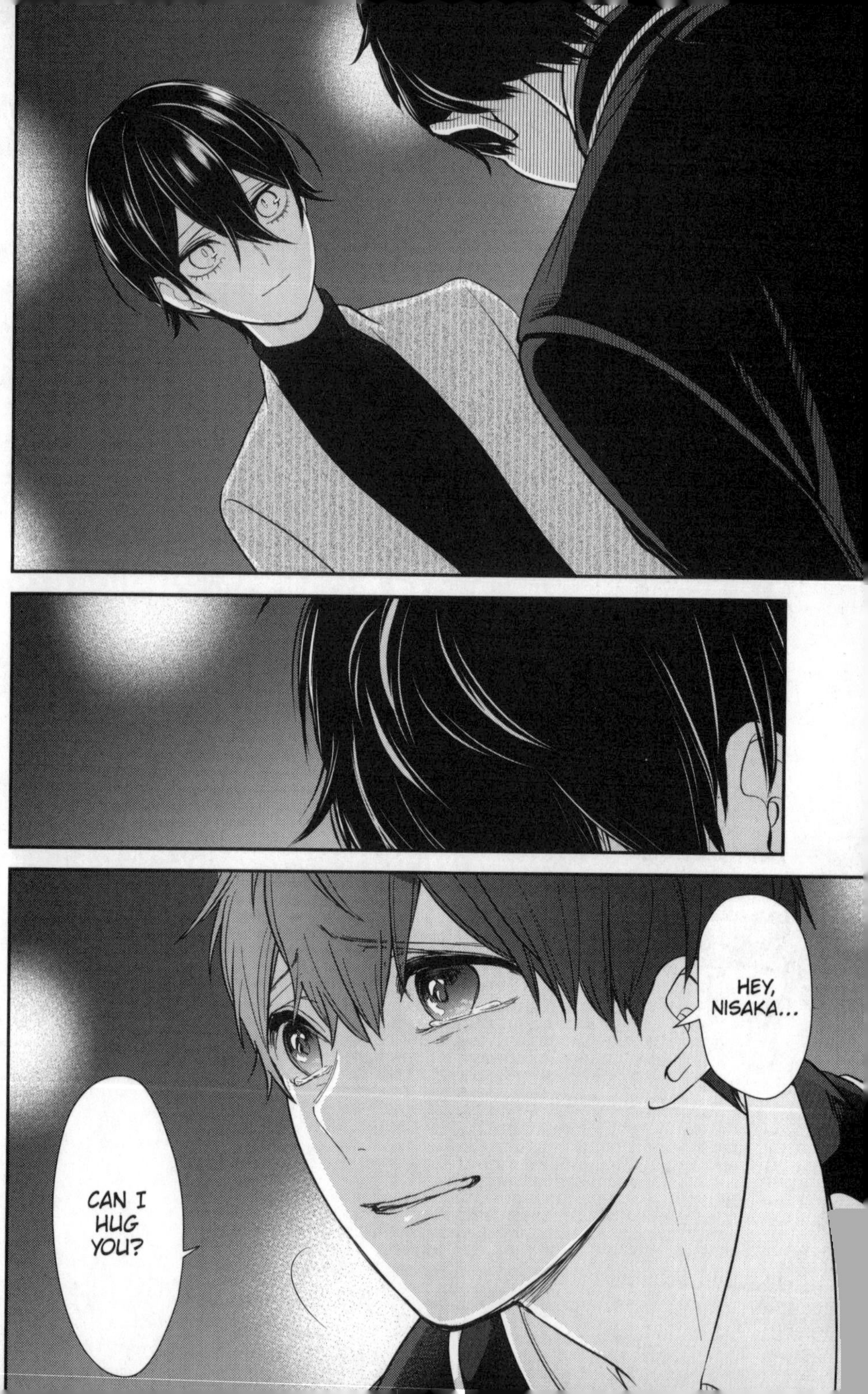
HEY, NISAKA...
CAN I HUG YOU?

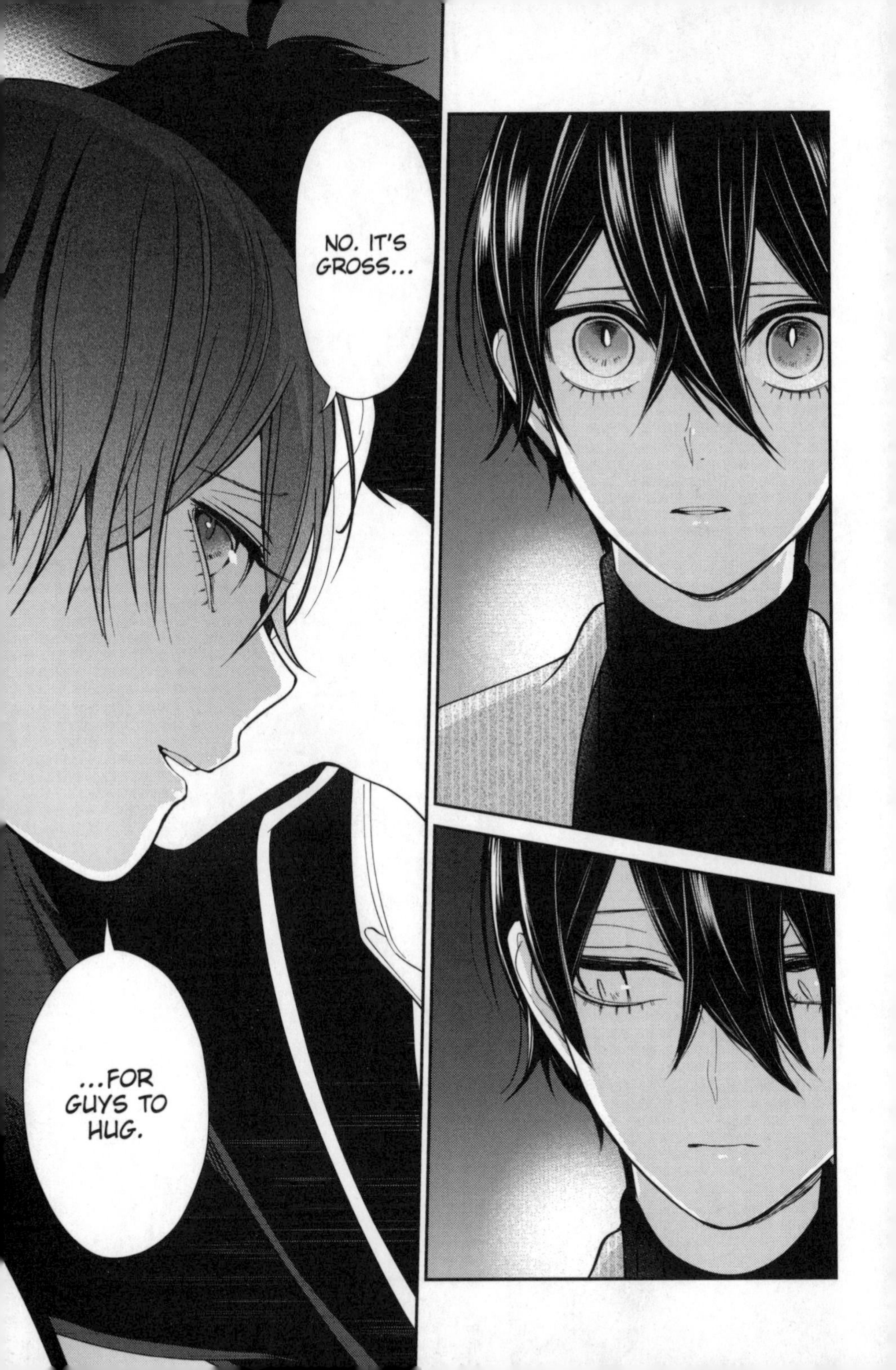
NO. IT'S GROSS...
...FOR GUYS TO HUG.

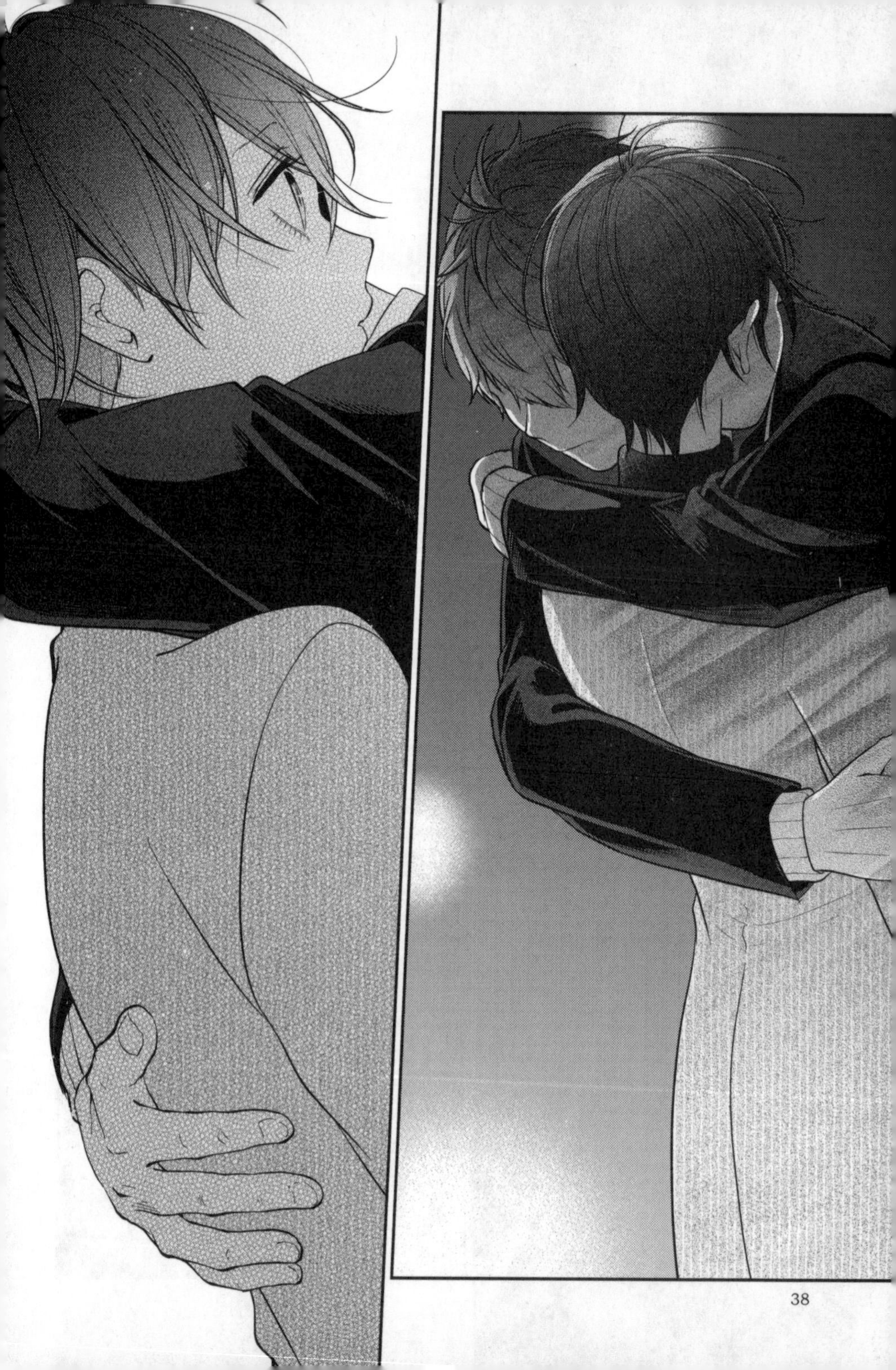

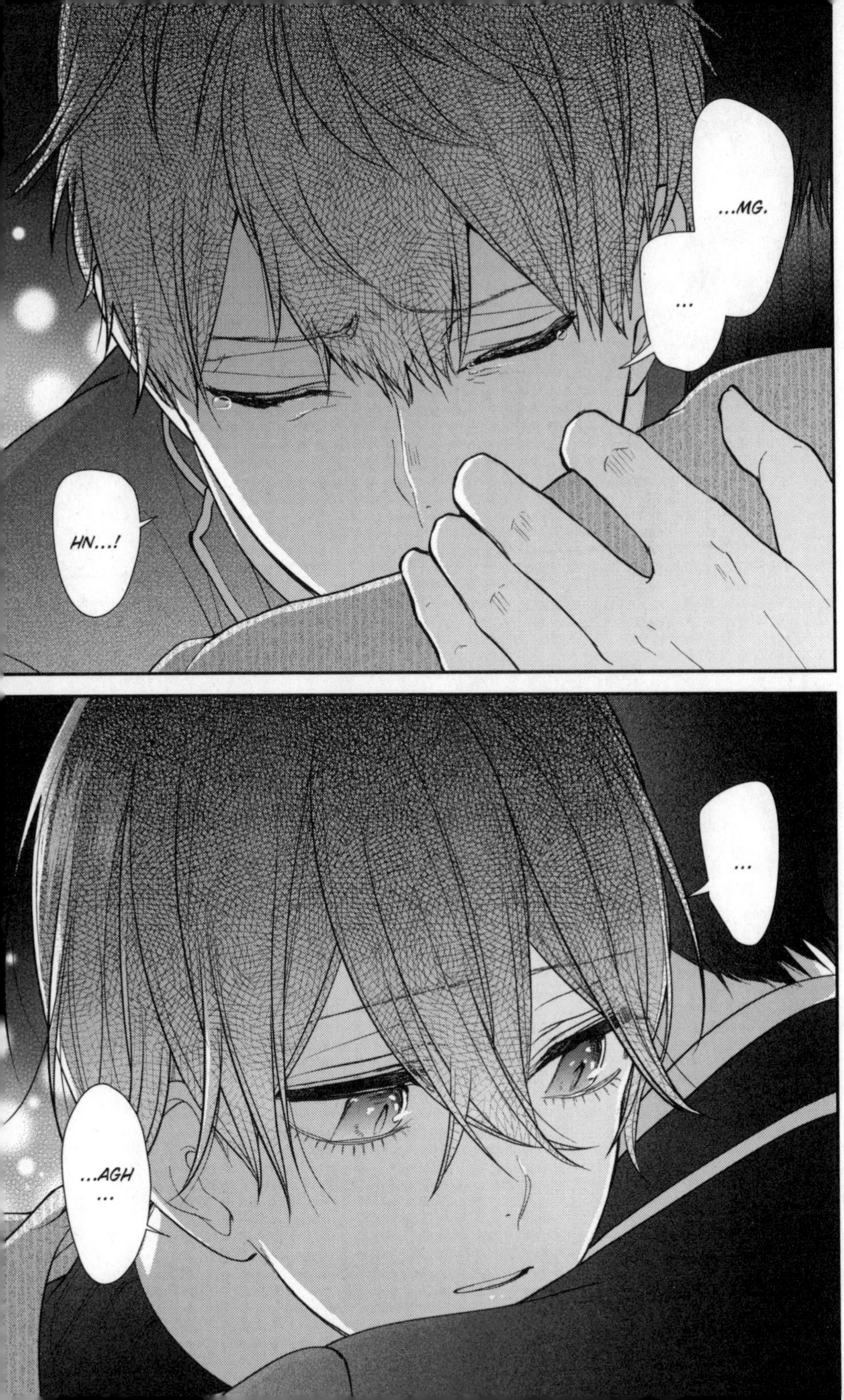
...MG.
...
HN...!
...
...AGH
...

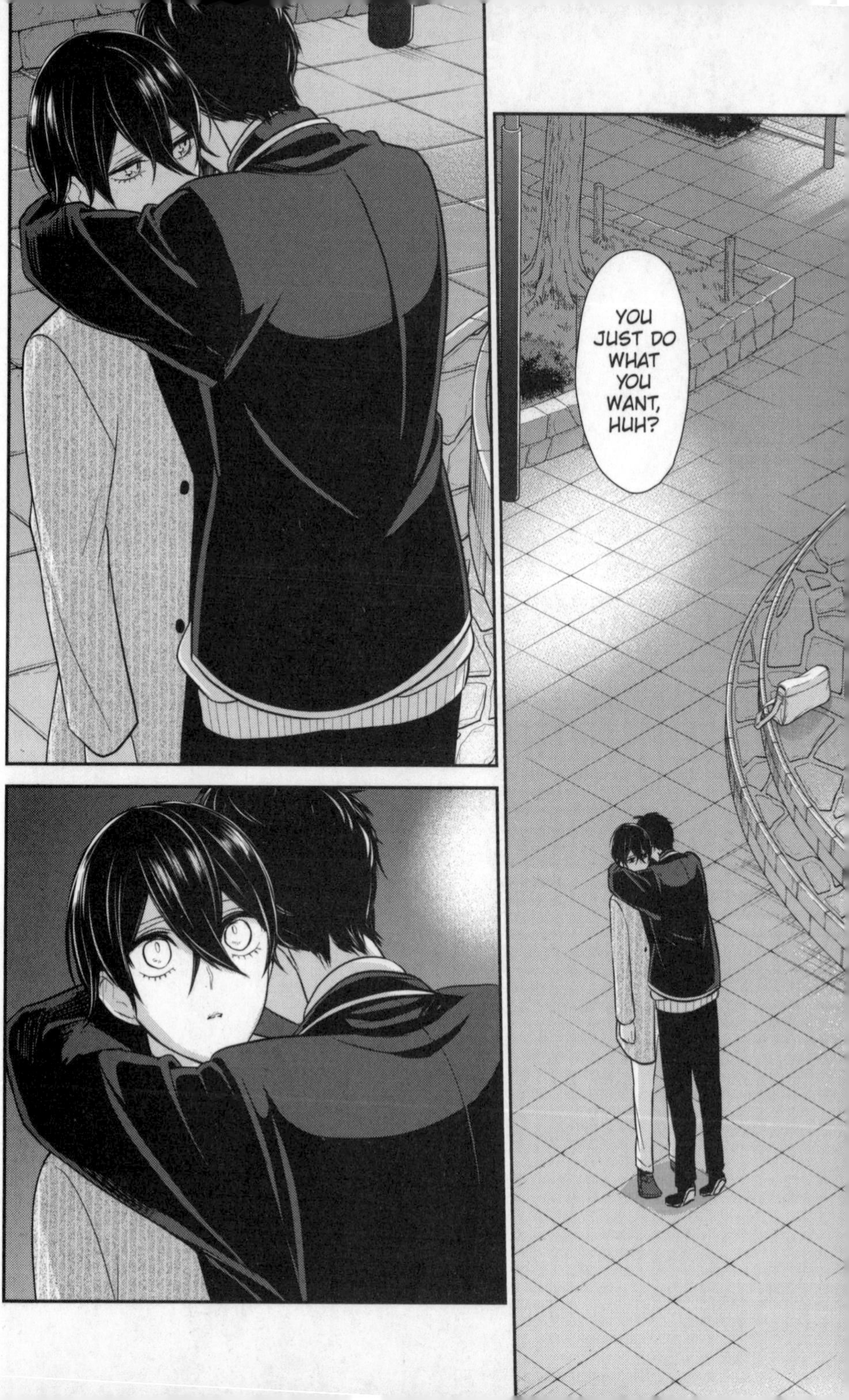
YOU JUST DO WHAT YOU WANT, HUH?

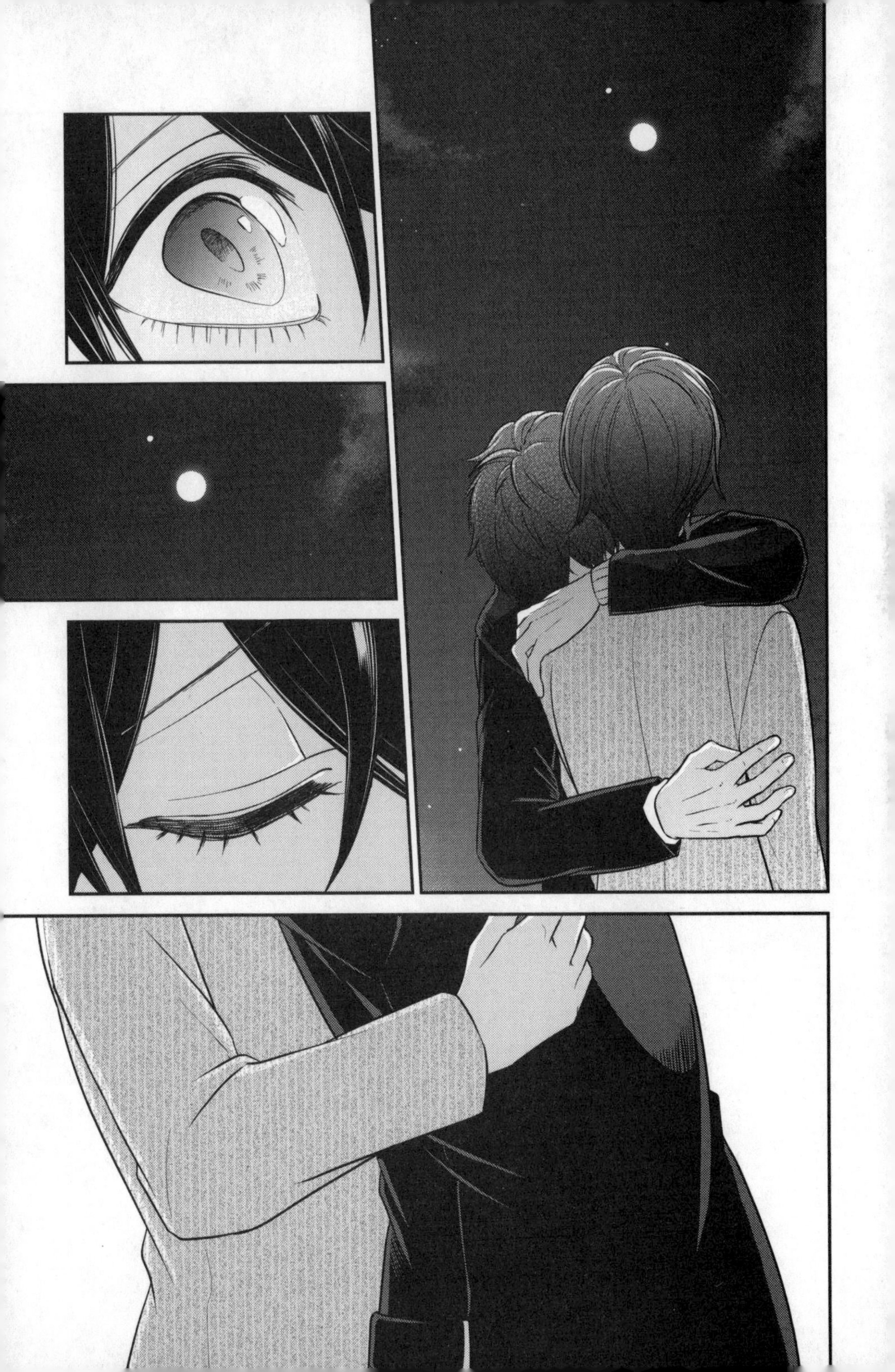

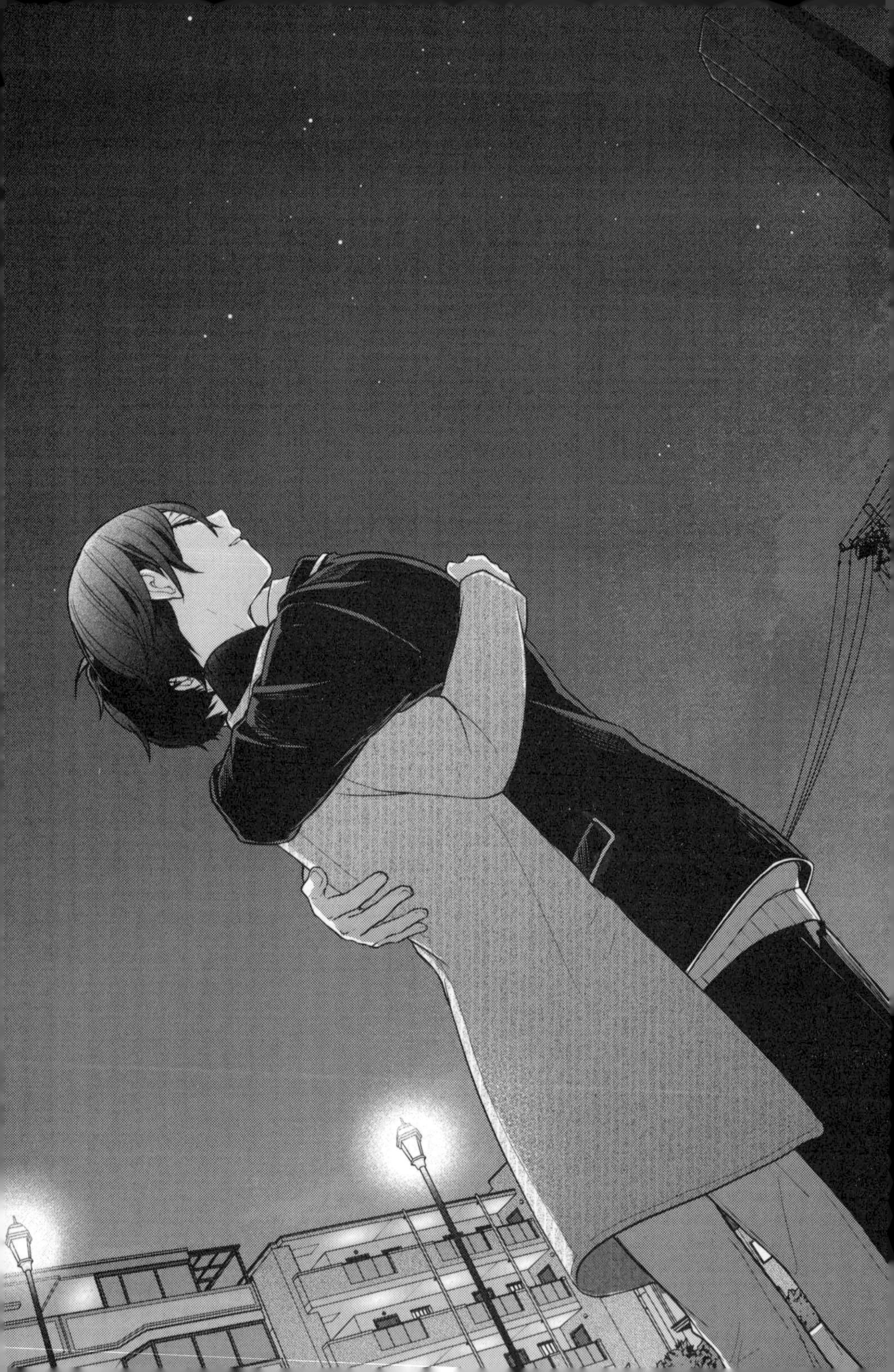

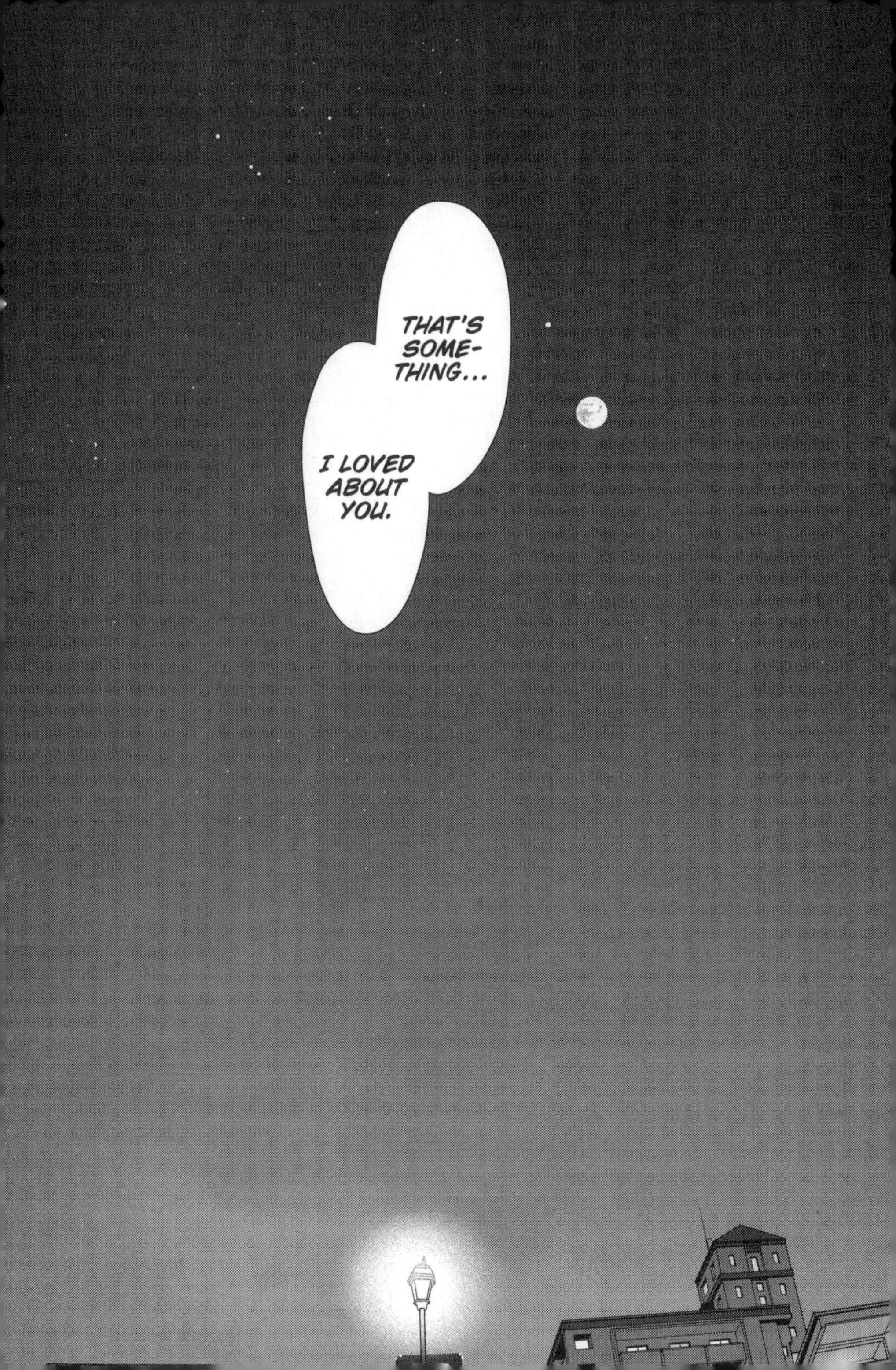
THAT'S SOME-THING...
I LOVED ABOUT YOU.

Love & Lies

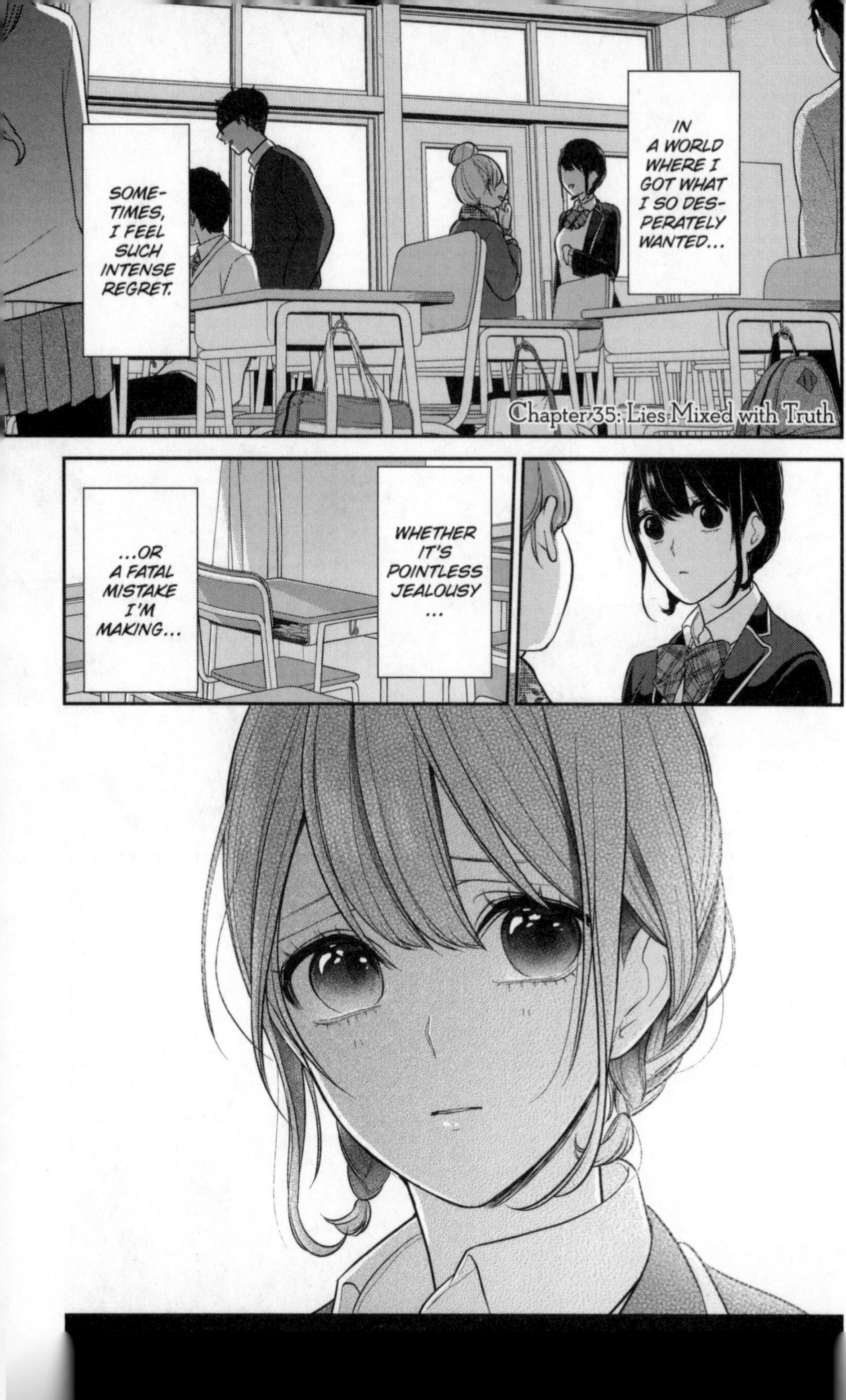
IN A WORLD WHERE I GOT WHAT I SO DES-PERATELY WANTED...
SOME-TIMES, I FEEL SUCH INTENSE REGRET.
Chapter 35: Lies Mixed with Truth
WHETHER IT'S POINTLESS JEALOUSY...
...OR A FATAL MISTAKE I'M MAKING...

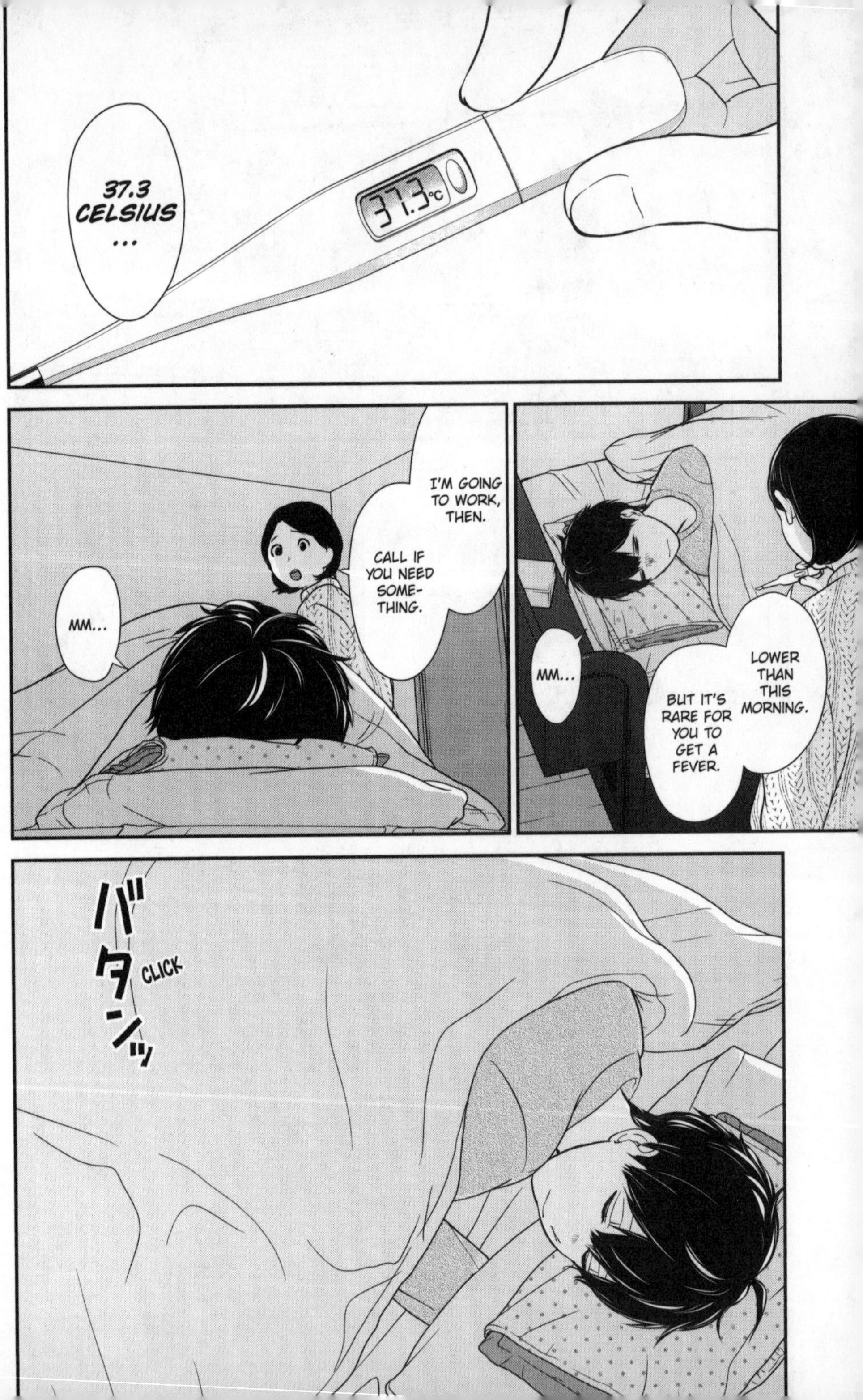
37.3 CELSIUS ...
37.3°C
LOWER THAN THIS MORNING.
BUT IT'S RARE FOR YOU TO GET A FEVER.
MM...
I'M GOING TO WORK, THEN.
CALL IF YOU NEED SOME-THING.
MM...
バタンッ
CLICK

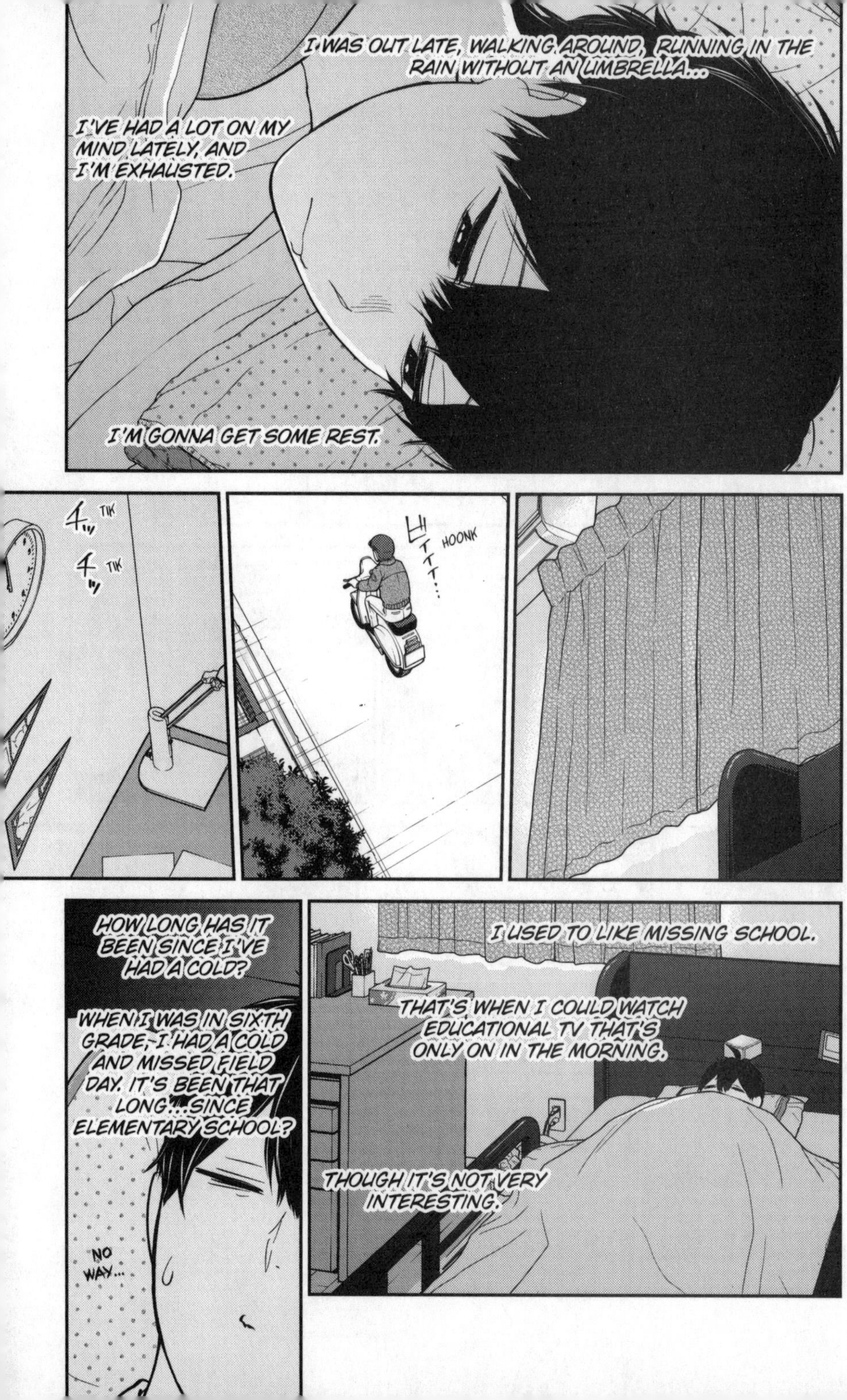
I WAS OUT LATE, WALKING AROUND, RUNNING IN THE RAIN WITHOUT AN UMBRELLA...
I'VE HAD A LOT ON MY MIND LATELY, AND I'M EXHAUSTED.
I'M GONNA GET SOME REST.
HOONK
TIK
TIK
I USED TO LIKE MISSING SCHOOL.
THAT'S WHEN I COULD WATCH EDUCATIONAL TV THAT'S ONLY ON IN THE MORNING.
THOUGH IT'S NOT VERY INTERESTING.
HOW LONG HAS IT BEEN SINCE I'VE HAD A COLD?
WHEN I WAS IN SIXTH GRADE, I HAD A COLD AND MISSED FIELD DAY. IT'S BEEN THAT LONG...SINCE ELEMENTARY SCHOOL?
NO WAY...

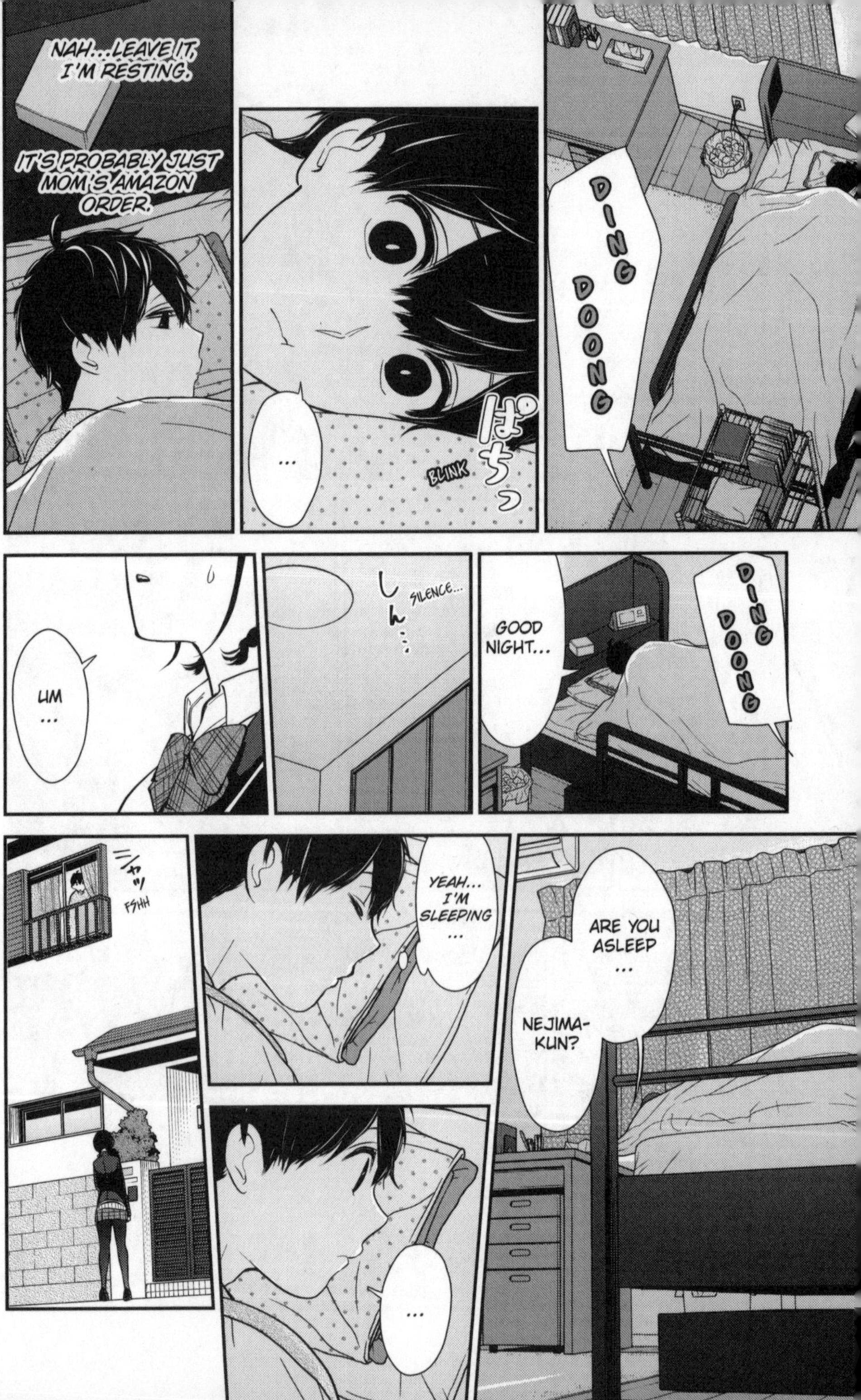
DING DOONG
...
ぱちっ
BLINK
NAH...LEAVE IT, I'M RESTING.
IT'S PROBABLY JUST MOM'S AMAZON ORDER.
DING DOONG
GOOD NIGHT...
しん…
SILENCE...
UM ...
ARE YOU ASLEEP ...
NEJIMA-KUN?
YEAH... I'M SLEEPING ...
...
シャッ
FSHH

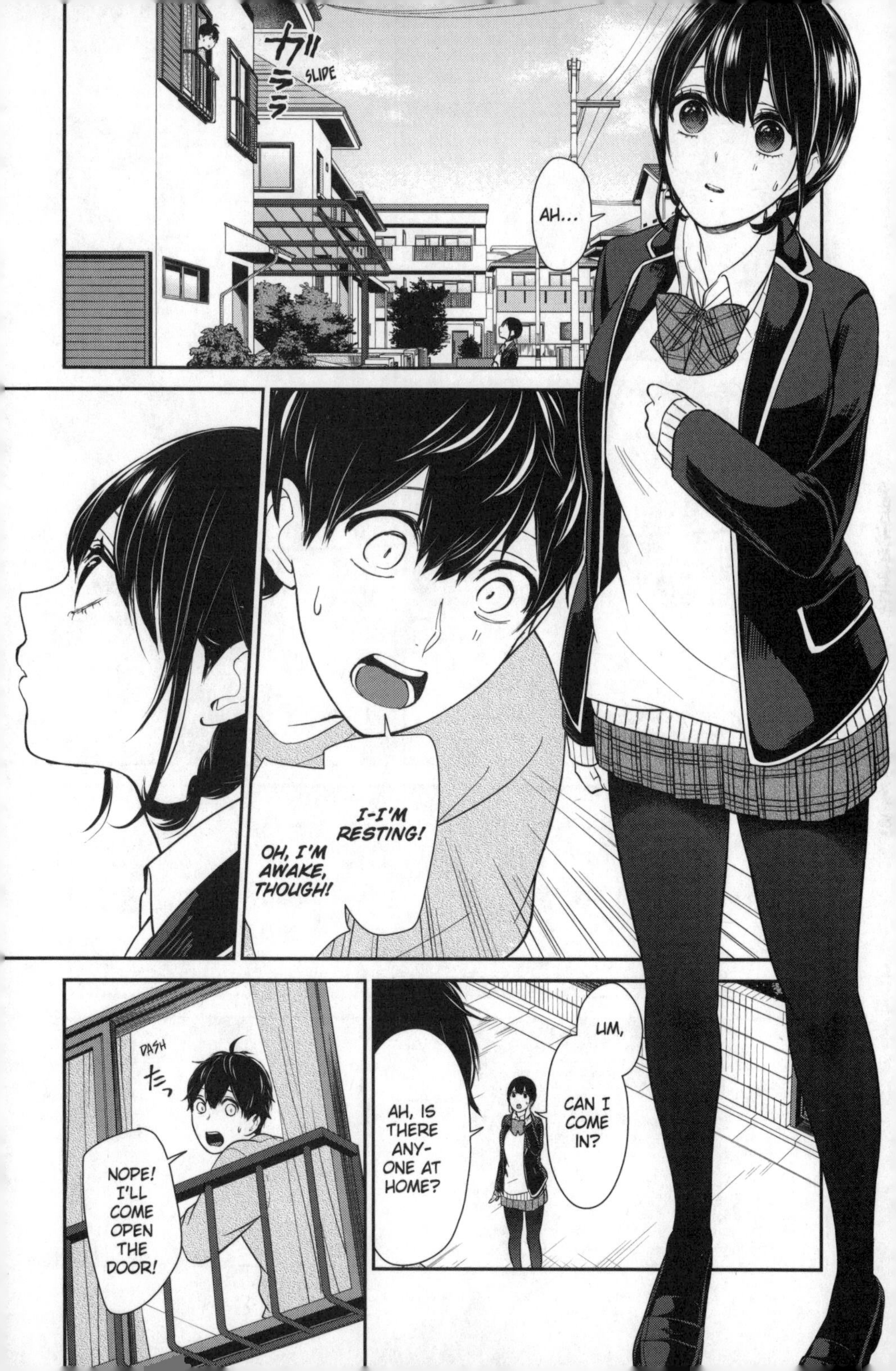
SLIDE
AH...
I-I'M RESTING!
OH, I'M AWAKE, THOUGH!
UM,
CAN I COME IN?
AH, IS THERE ANY-ONE AT HOME?
DASH
NOPE! I'LL COME OPEN THE DOOR!

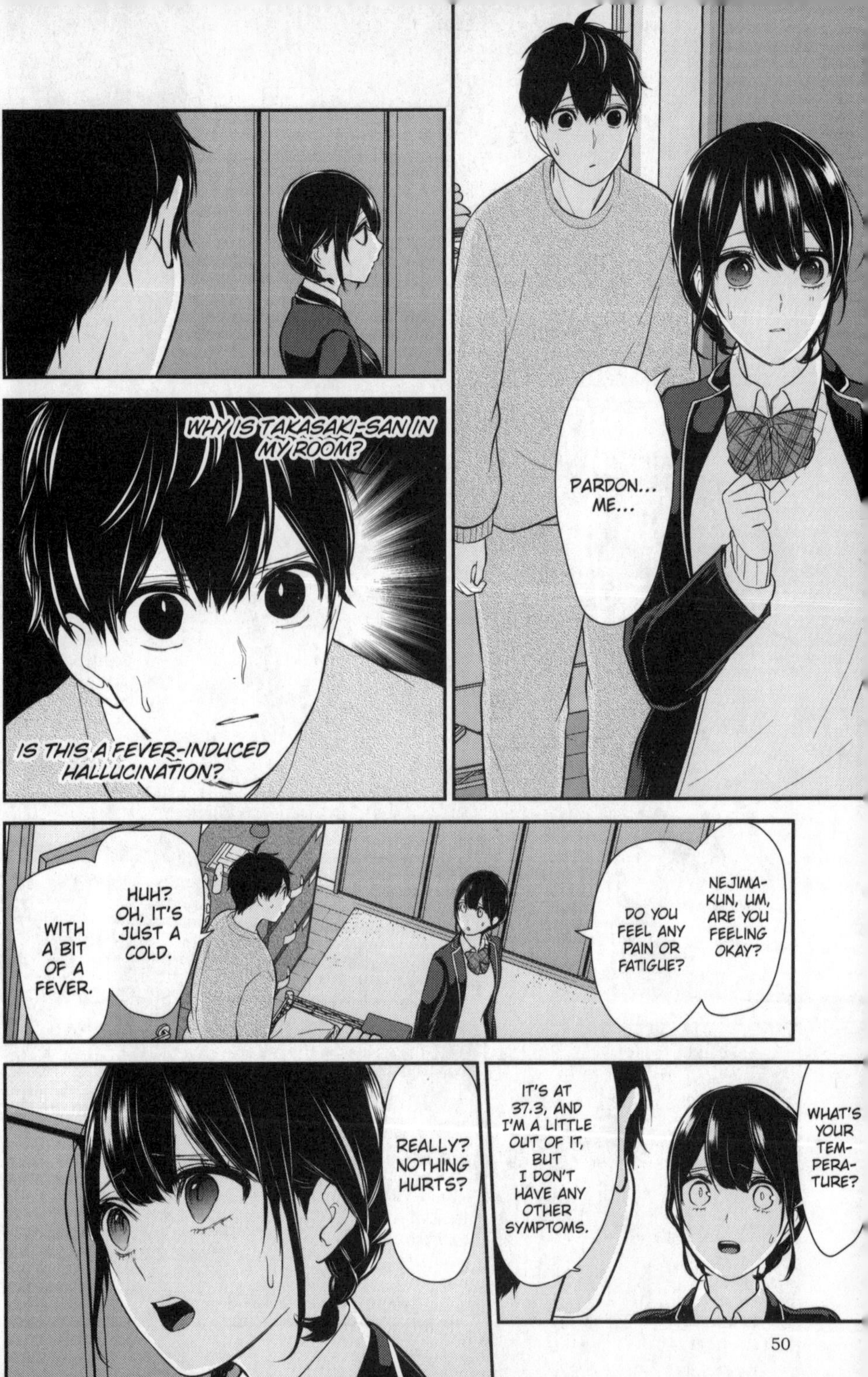
PARDON... ME...
WHY IS TAKASAKI-SAN IN MY ROOM?
IS THIS A FEVER-INDUCED HALLUCINATION?
NEJIMA-KUN, UM, ARE YOU FEELING OKAY?
DO YOU FEEL ANY PAIN OR FATIGUE?
HUH? OH, IT'S JUST A COLD.
WITH A BIT OF A FEVER.
WHAT'S YOUR TEMPERATURE?
IT'S AT 37.3, AND I'M A LITTLE OUT OF IT, BUT I DON'T HAVE ANY OTHER SYMPTOMS.
REALLY? NOTHING HURTS?

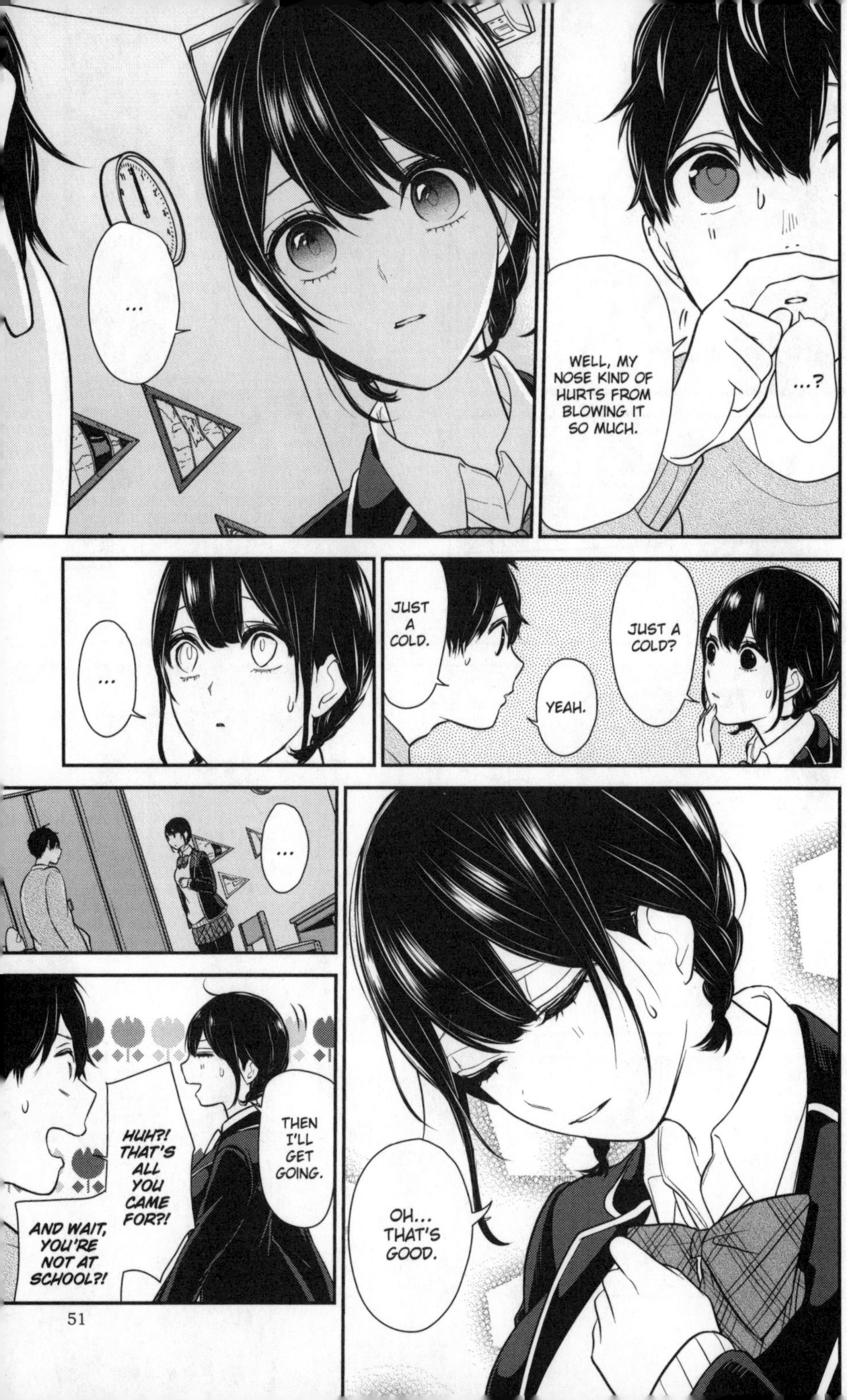
...?
WELL, MY NOSE KIND OF HURTS FROM BLOWING IT SO MUCH.
...
JUST A COLD?
YEAH.
JUST A COLD.
...
OH... THAT'S GOOD.
...
THEN I'LL GET GOING.
HUH?! THAT'S ALL YOU CAME FOR?!
AND WAIT, YOU'RE NOT AT SCHOOL?!

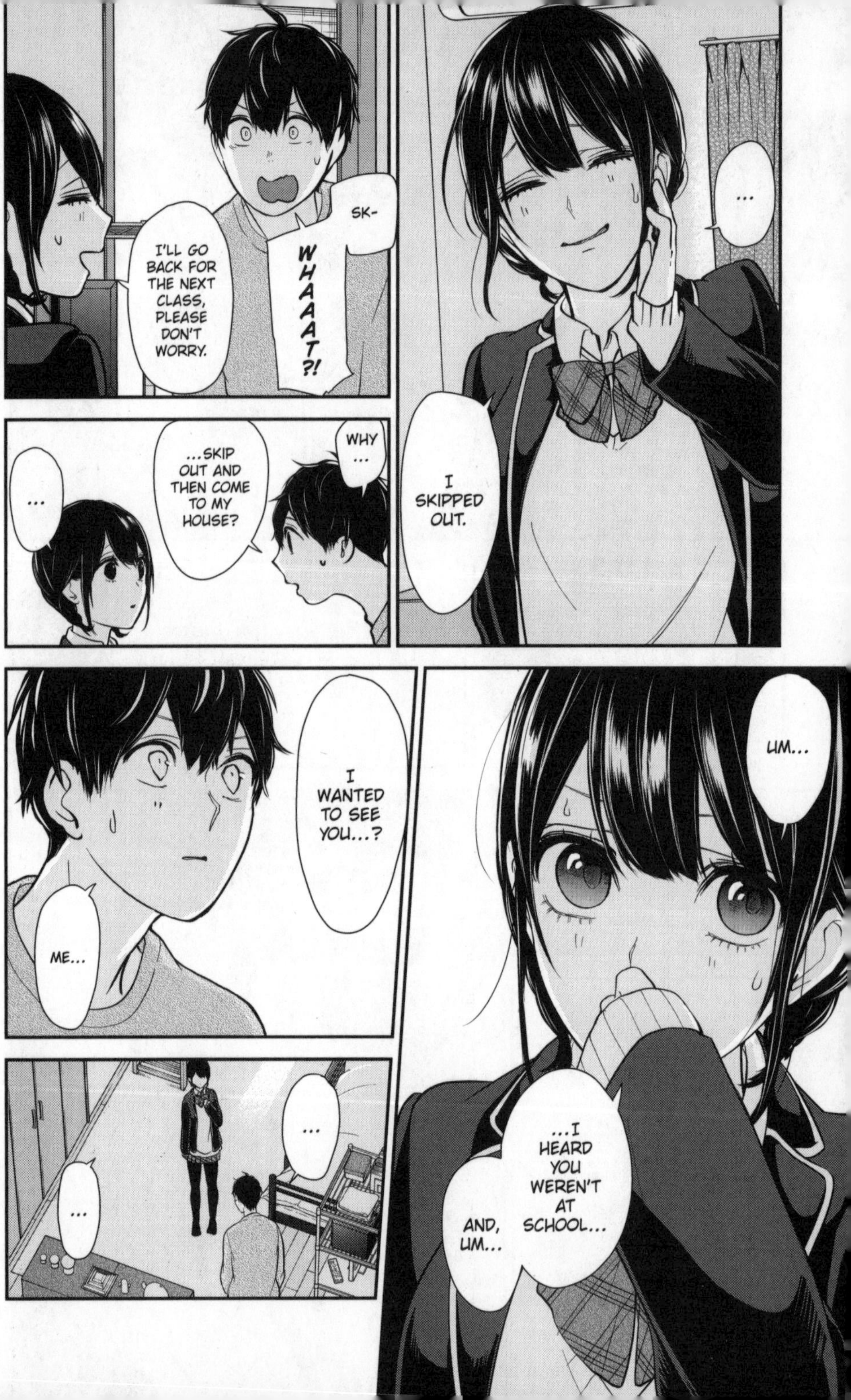
...
I SKIPPED OUT.
SK-
WHAAAT?!
I'LL GO BACK FOR THE NEXT CLASS, PLEASE DON'T WORRY.
WHY...
...SKIP OUT AND THEN COME TO MY HOUSE?
...
UM...
...I HEARD YOU WEREN'T AT SCHOOL...
AND, UM...
I WANTED TO SEE YOU...?
ME...
...
...

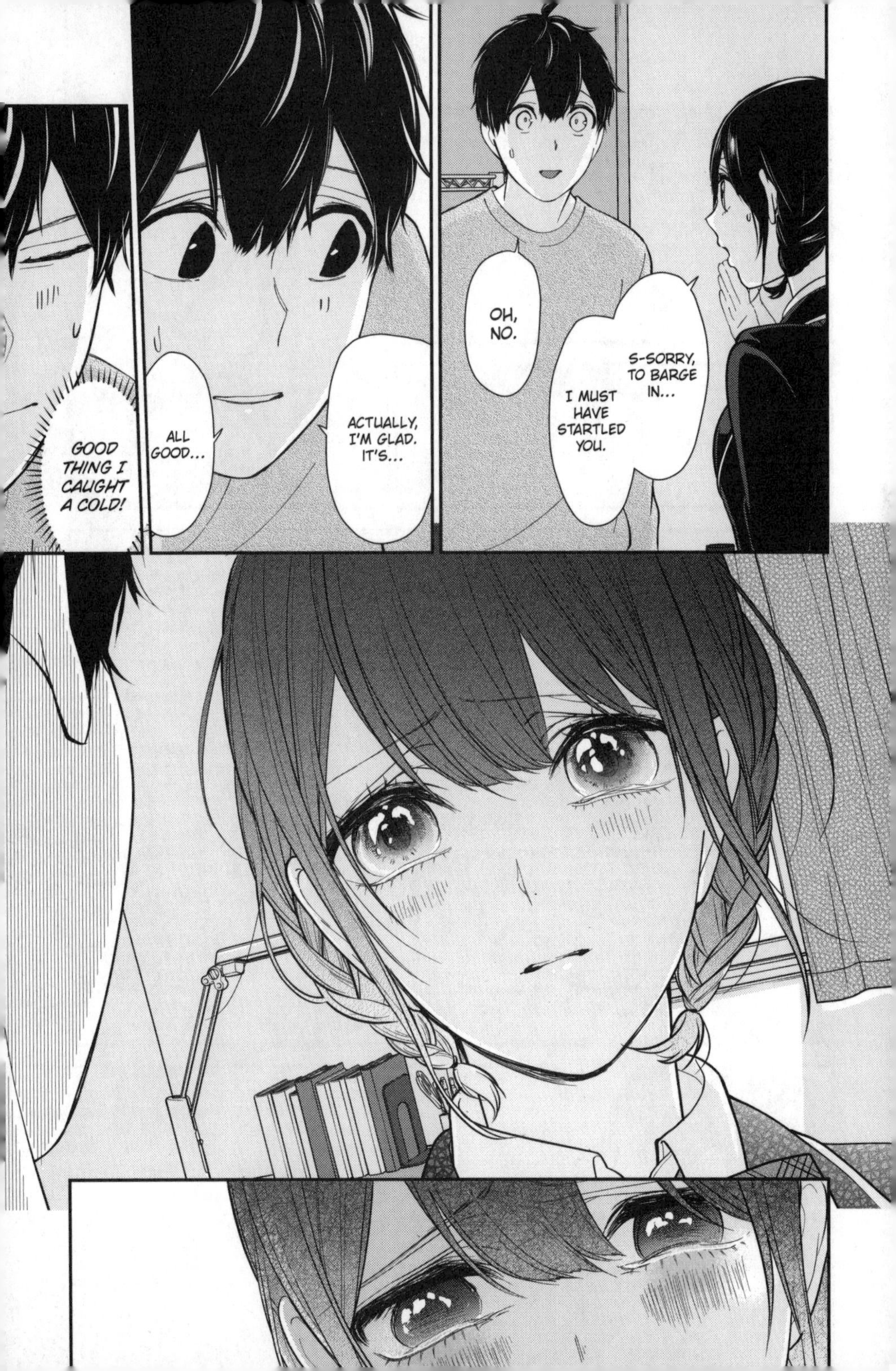
S-SORRY, TO BARGE IN...
I MUST HAVE STARTLED YOU.
OH, NO.
ACTUALLY, I'M GLAD. IT'S...
ALL GOOD...
GOOD THING I CAUGHT A COLD!

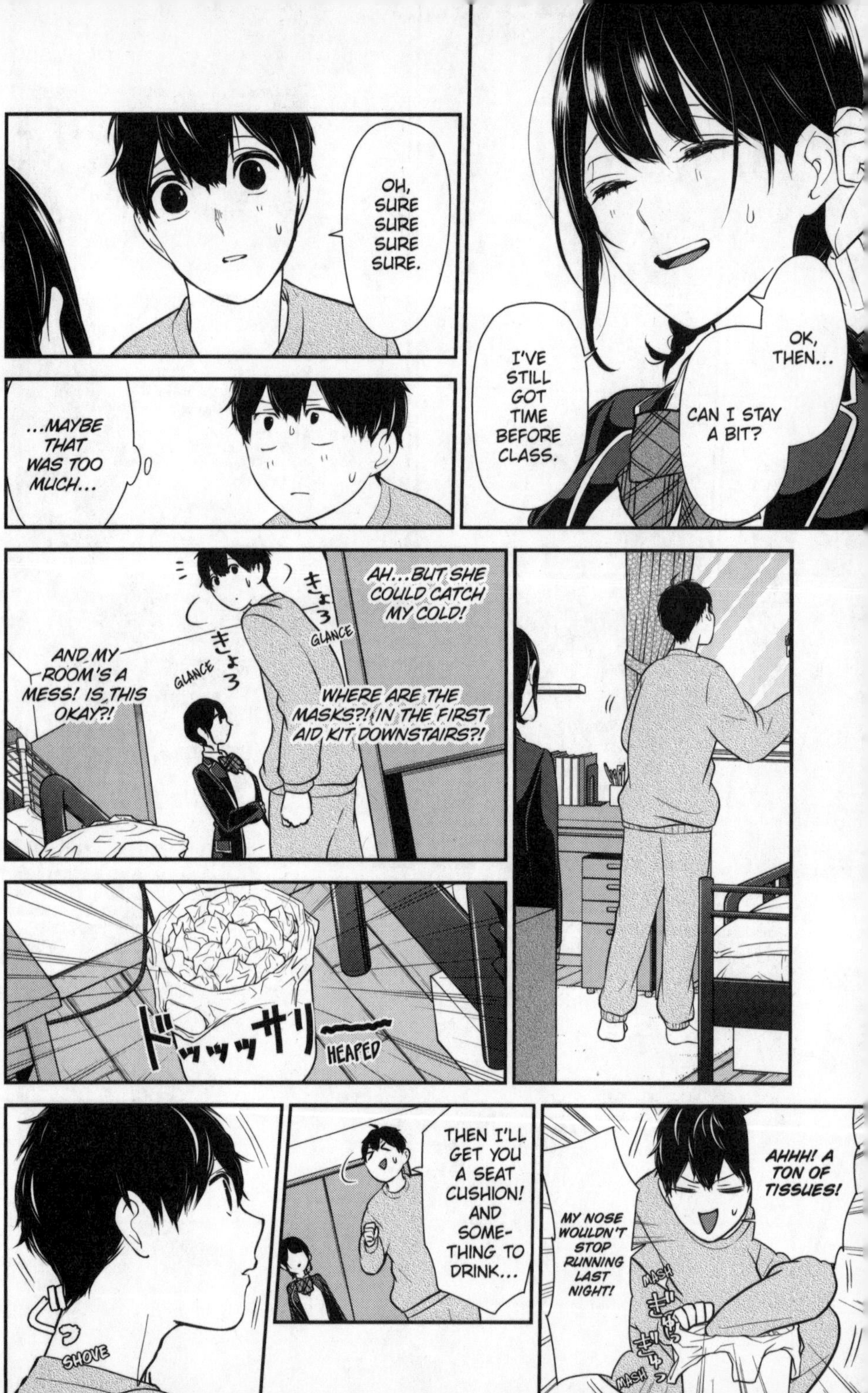
OK, THEN...
CAN I STAY A BIT?
I'VE STILL GOT TIME BEFORE CLASS.
OH, SURE SURE SURE SURE.
...MAYBE THAT WAS TOO MUCH...
AH...BUT SHE COULD CATCH MY COLD!
きょろ
GLANCE
WHERE ARE THE MASKS?! IN THE FIRST AID KIT DOWNSTAIRS?!
きょろ
GLANCE
AND MY ROOM'S A MESS! IS THIS OKAY?!
ドッッッサリ
HEAPED
AHHH! A TON OF TISSUES!
MY NOSE WOULDN'T STOP RUNNING LAST NIGHT!
MASH
MASH
THEN I'LL GET YOU A SEAT CUSHION! AND SOME-THING TO DRINK...
SHOVE

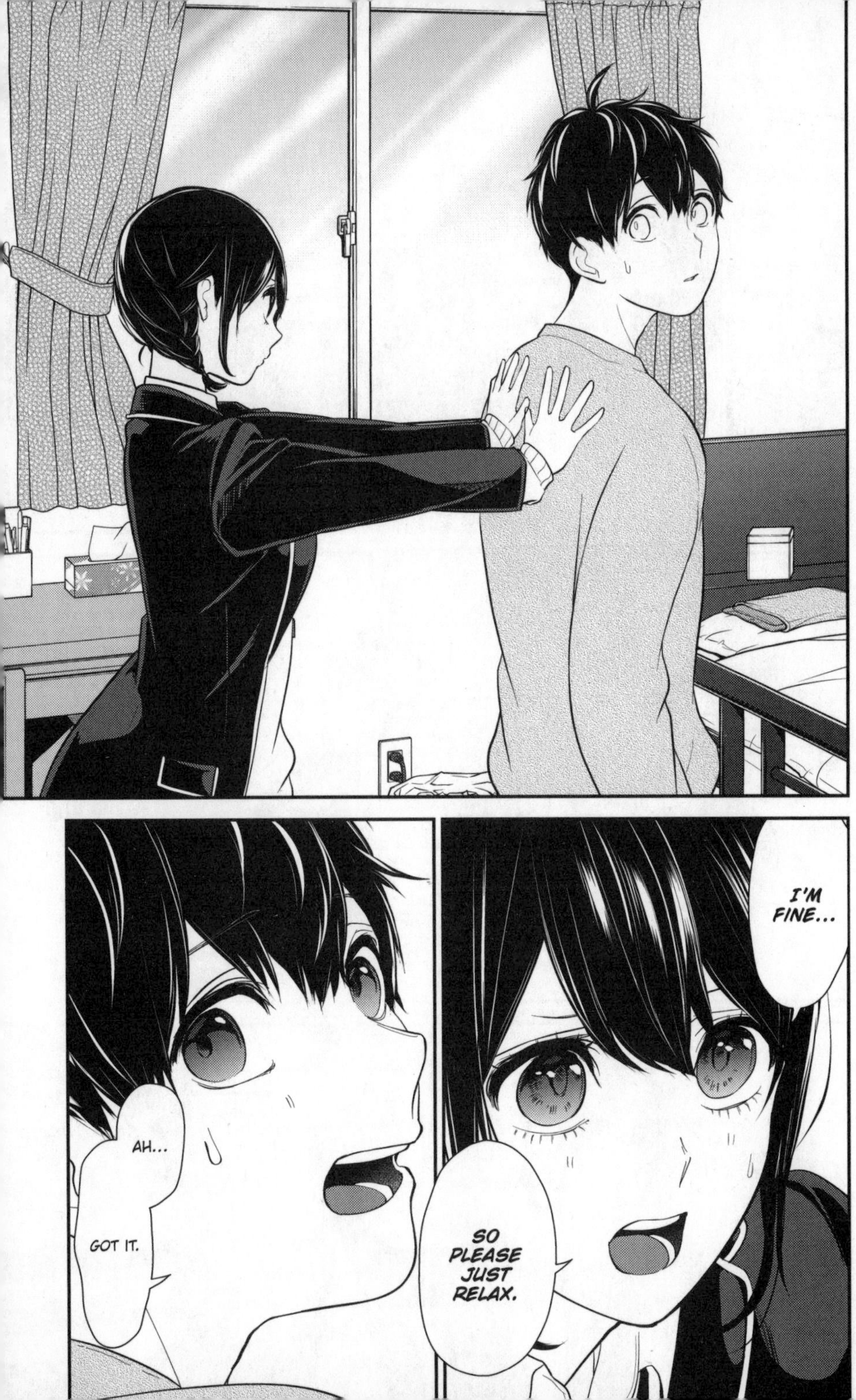
I'M FINE...
SO PLEASE JUST RELAX.
AH...
GOT IT.

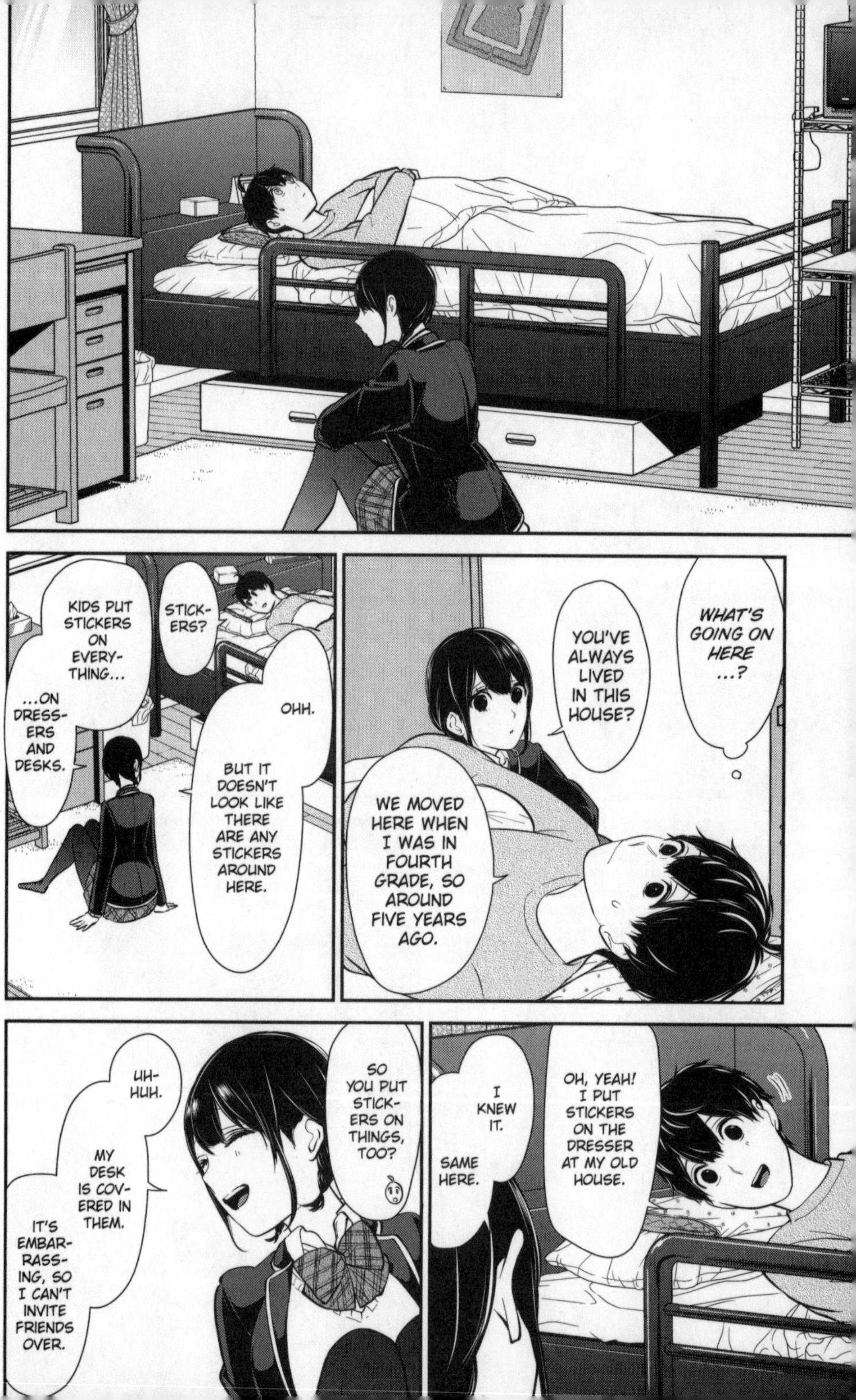

WHAT'S GOING ON HERE ...?
YOU'VE ALWAYS LIVED IN THIS HOUSE?
WE MOVED HERE WHEN I WAS IN FOURTH GRADE, SO AROUND FIVE YEARS AGO.
STICKERS?
KIDS PUT STICKERS ON EVERYTHING...
...ON DRESSERS AND DESKS.
OHH.
BUT IT DOESN'T LOOK LIKE THERE ARE ANY STICKERS AROUND HERE.
OH, YEAH! I PUT STICKERS ON THE DRESSER AT MY OLD HOUSE.
I KNEW IT.
SAME HERE.
SO YOU PUT STICKERS ON THINGS, TOO?
UH-HUH.
MY DESK IS COVERED IN THEM.
IT'S EMBARRASSING, SO I CAN'T INVITE FRIENDS OVER.

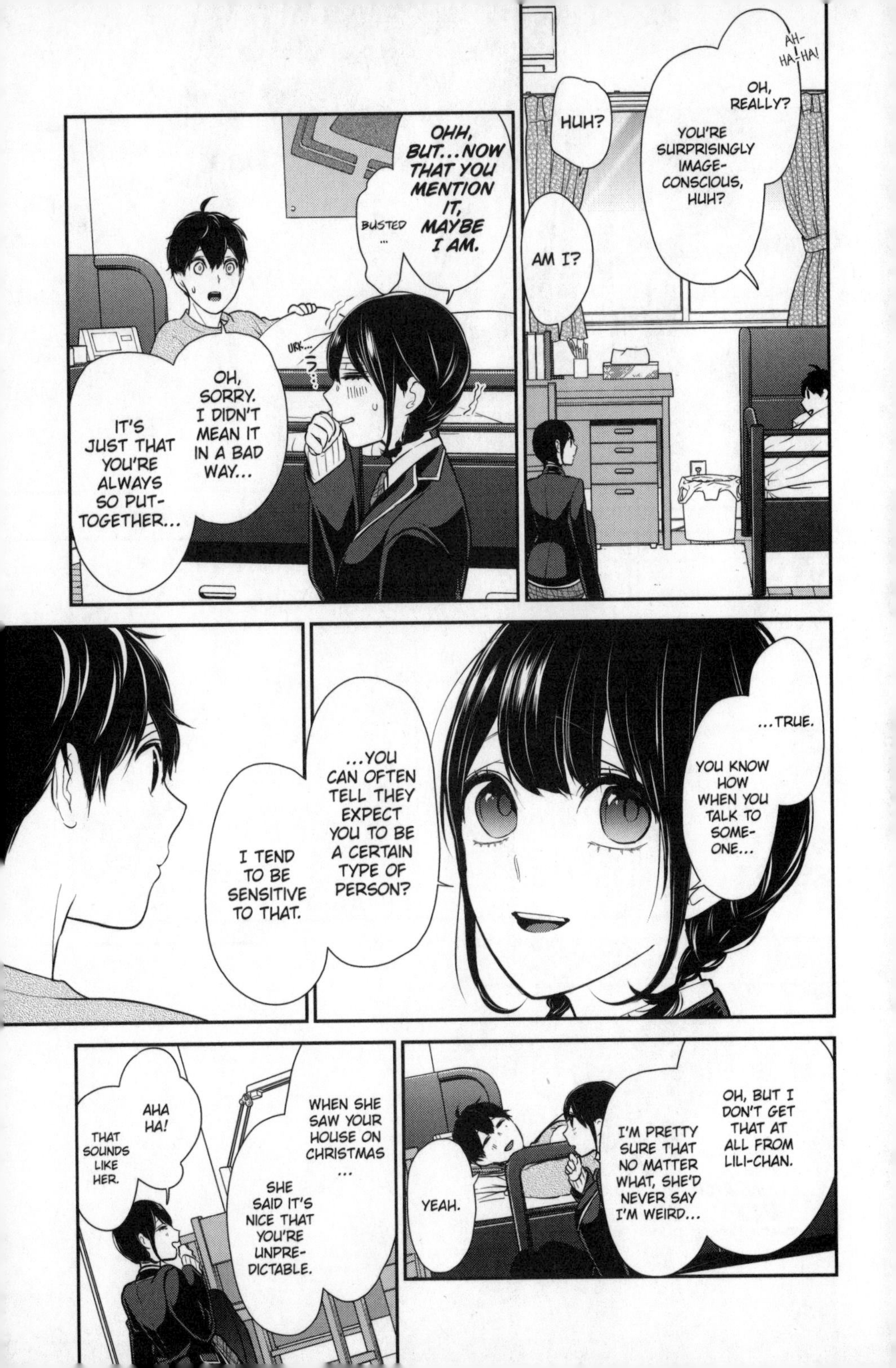
AH-HA-HA!
OH, REALLY? YOU'RE SURPRISINGLY IMAGE-CONSCIOUS, HUH?
HUH?
AM I?
OHH, BUT...NOW THAT YOU MENTION IT, MAYBE I AM.
BUSTED...
URK...
OH, SORRY. I DIDN'T MEAN IT IN A BAD WAY...
IT'S JUST THAT YOU'RE ALWAYS SO PUT-TOGETHER...
...TRUE.
YOU KNOW HOW WHEN YOU TALK TO SOMEONE...
...YOU CAN OFTEN TELL THEY EXPECT YOU TO BE A CERTAIN TYPE OF PERSON?
I TEND TO BE SENSITIVE TO THAT.
OH, BUT I DON'T GET THAT AT ALL FROM LILI-CHAN.
I'M PRETTY SURE THAT NO MATTER WHAT, SHE'D NEVER SAY I'M WEIRD...
YEAH.
WHEN SHE SAW YOUR HOUSE ON CHRISTMAS...
SHE SAID IT'S NICE THAT YOU'RE UNPREDICTABLE.
AHA HA!
THAT SOUNDS LIKE HER.

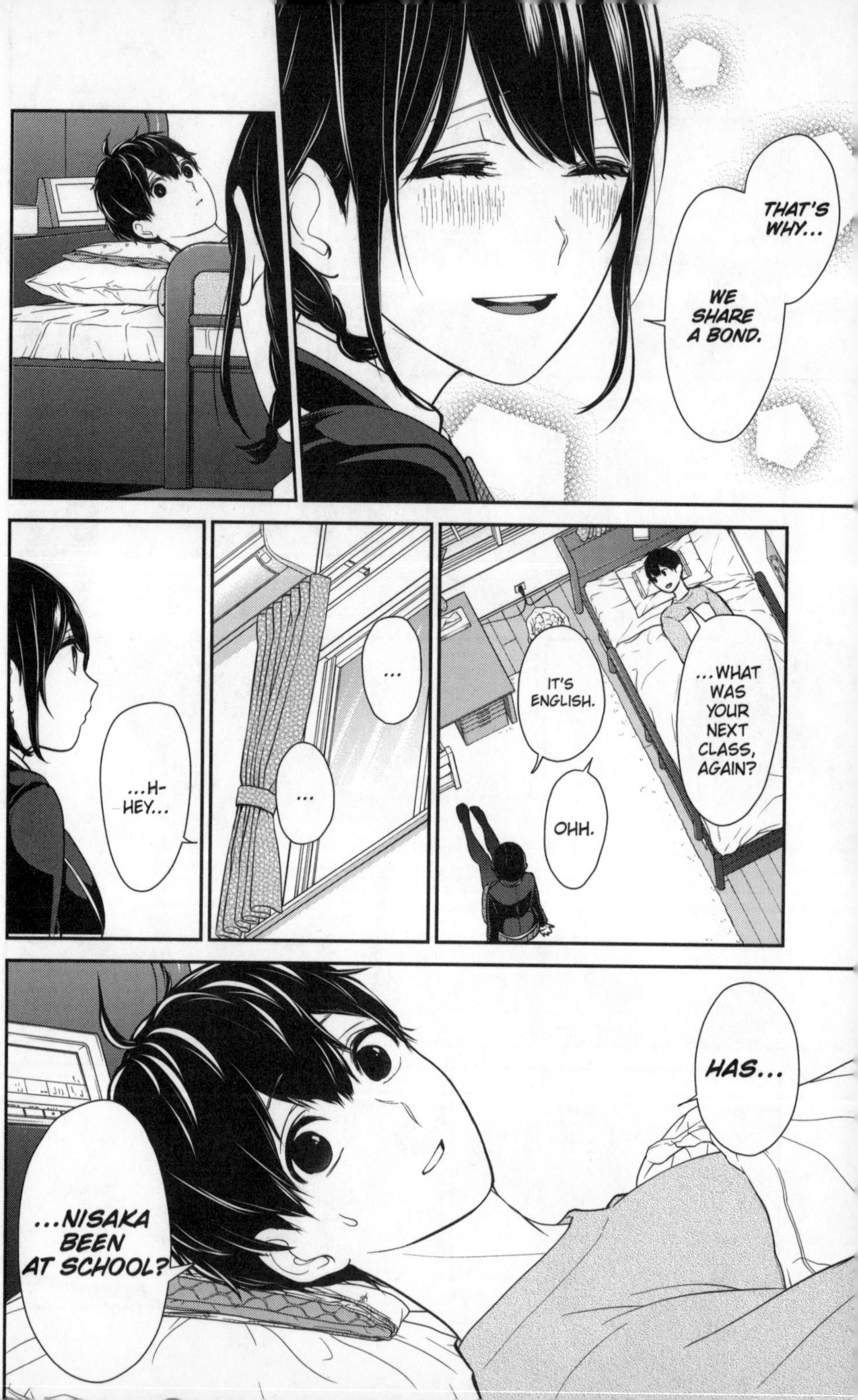
THAT'S WHY...
WE SHARE A BOND.
...WHAT WAS YOUR NEXT CLASS, AGAIN?
IT'S ENGLISH.
OHH.
...
...
...H-HEY...
HAS...
...NISAKA BEEN AT SCHOOL?

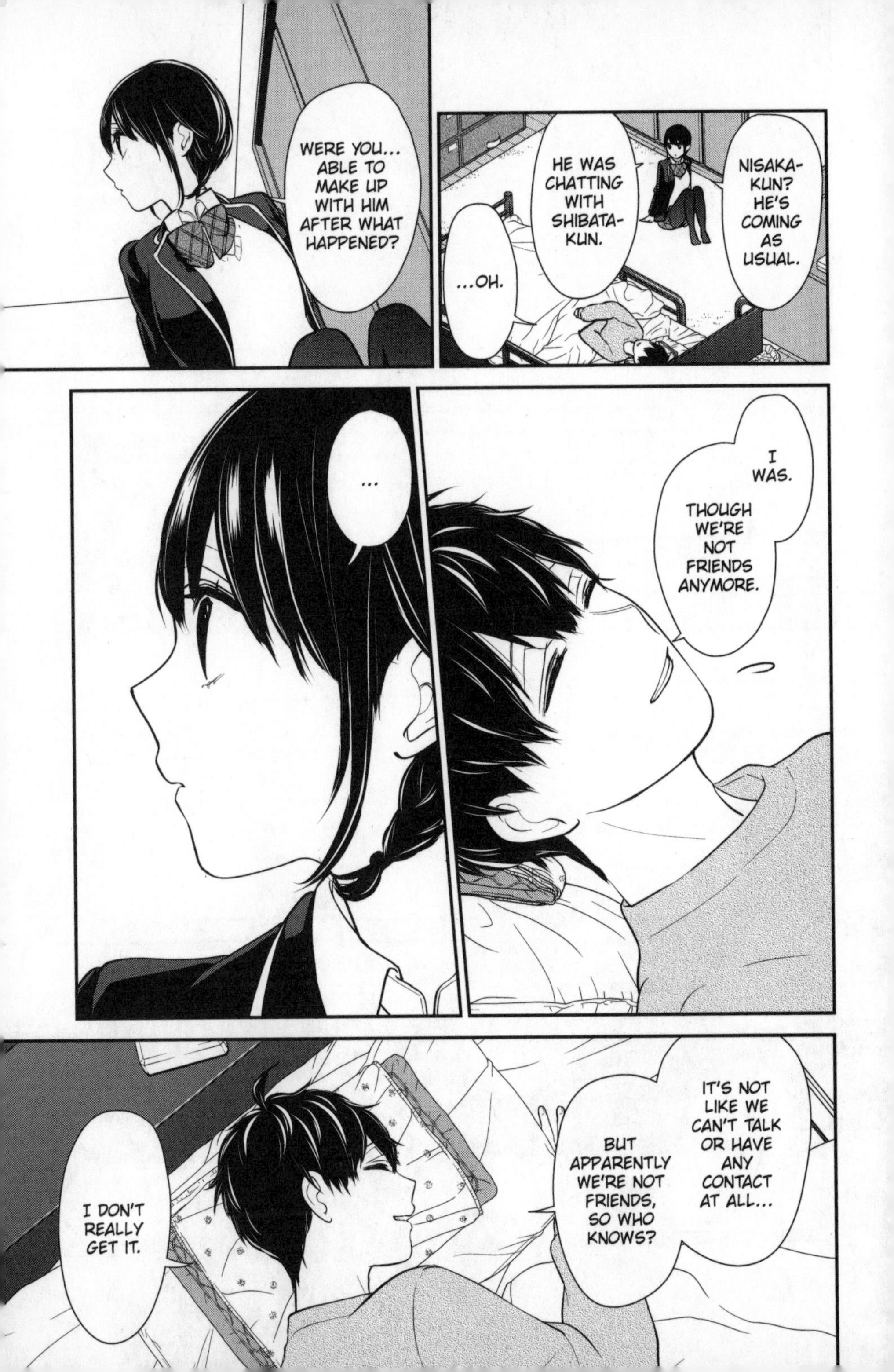
NISAKA-KUN? HE'S COMING AS USUAL.
HE WAS CHATTING WITH SHIBATA-KUN.
...OH.
WERE YOU... ABLE TO MAKE UP WITH HIM AFTER WHAT HAPPENED?
I WAS.
THOUGH WE'RE NOT FRIENDS ANYMORE.
...
IT'S NOT LIKE WE CAN'T TALK OR HAVE ANY CONTACT AT ALL...
BUT APPARENTLY WE'RE NOT FRIENDS, SO WHO KNOWS?
I DON'T REALLY GET IT.

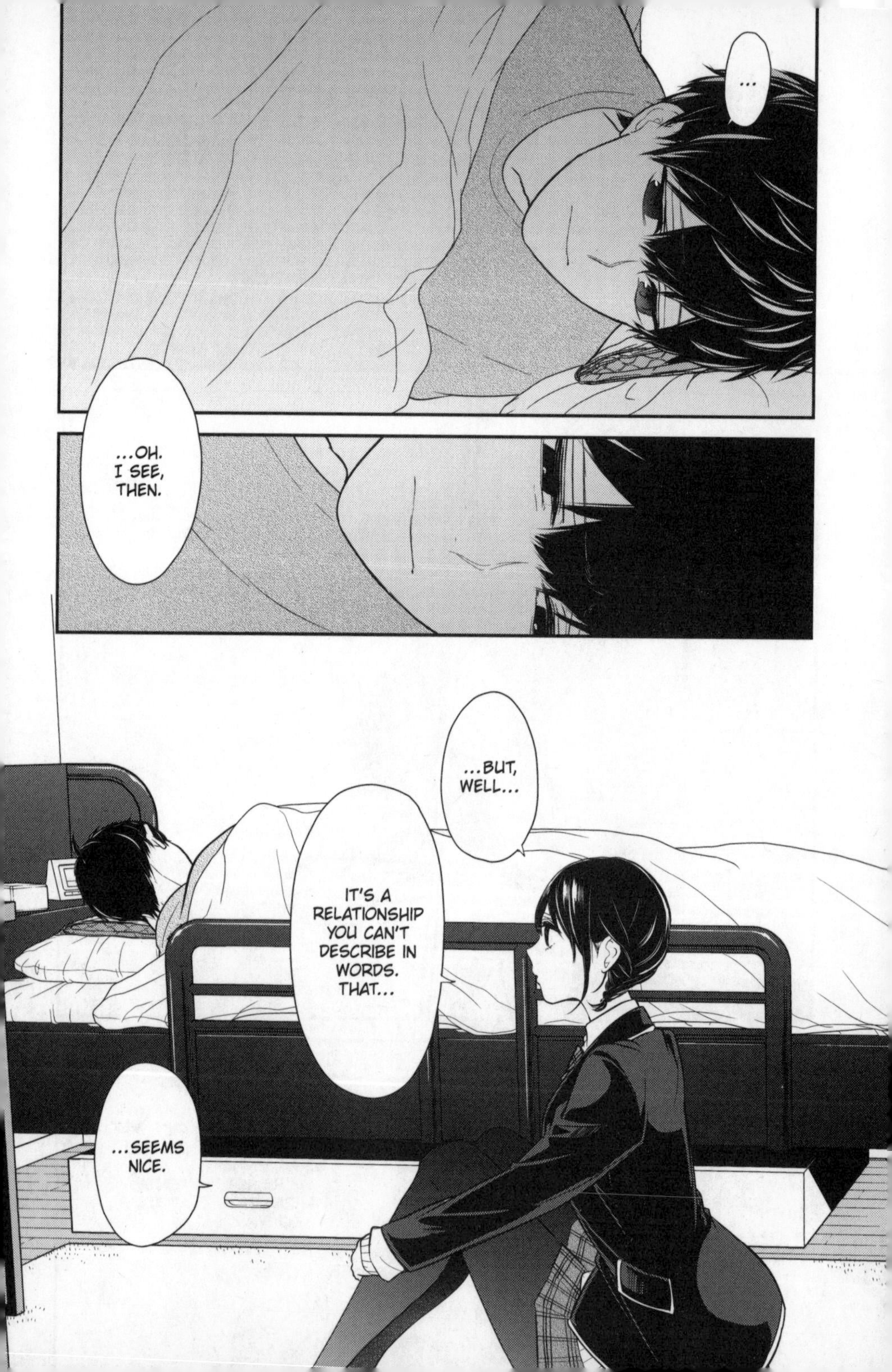
...
...OH. I SEE, THEN.
...BUT, WELL...
IT'S A RELATIONSHIP YOU CAN'T DESCRIBE IN WORDS. THAT...
...SEEMS NICE.

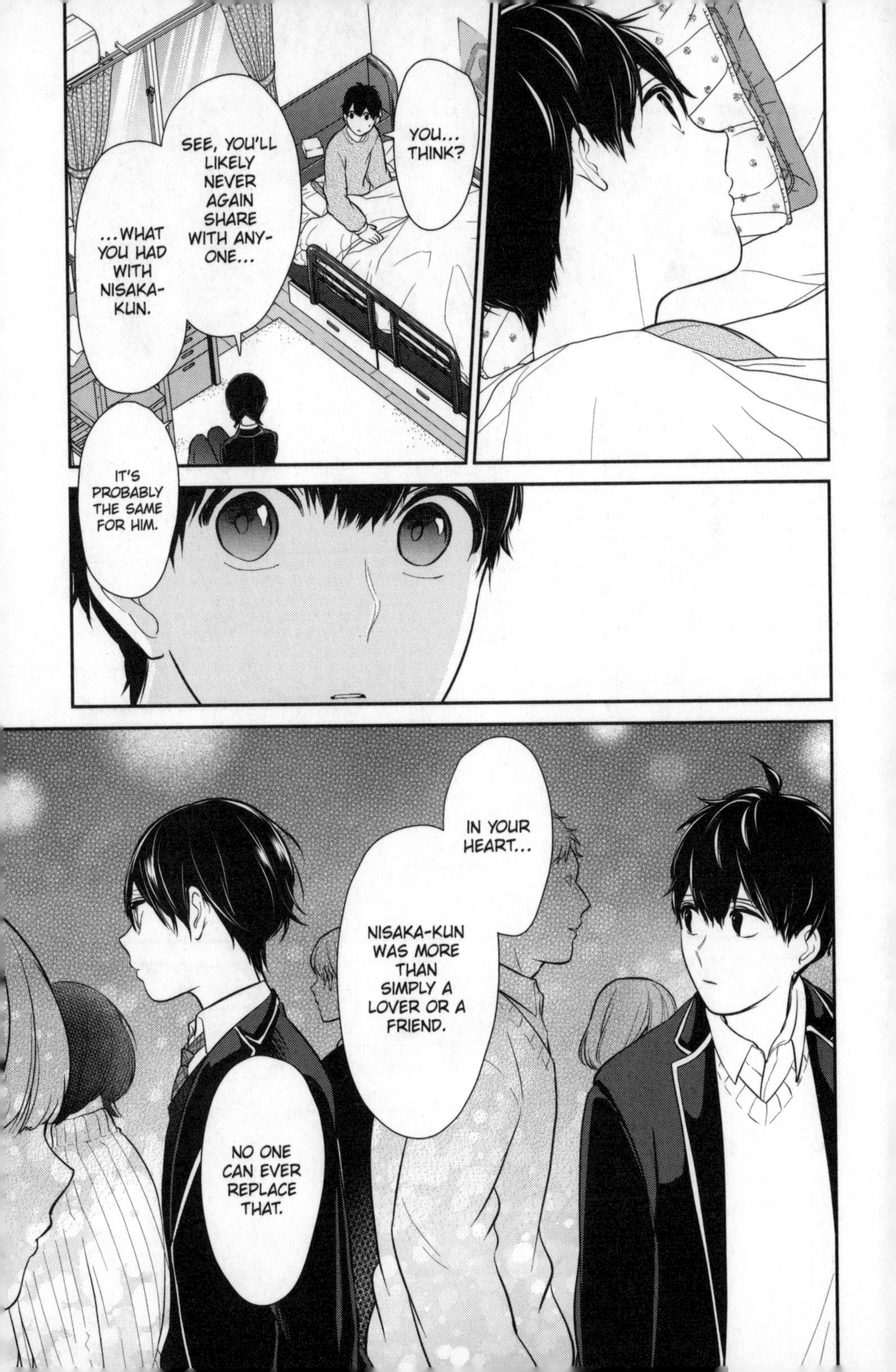
YOU... THINK?
SEE, YOU'LL LIKELY NEVER AGAIN SHARE WITH ANY-ONE...
...WHAT YOU HAD WITH NISAKA-KUN.
IT'S PROBABLY THE SAME FOR HIM.
IN YOUR HEART...
NISAKA-KUN WAS MORE THAN SIMPLY A LOVER OR A FRIEND.
NO ONE CAN EVER REPLACE THAT.

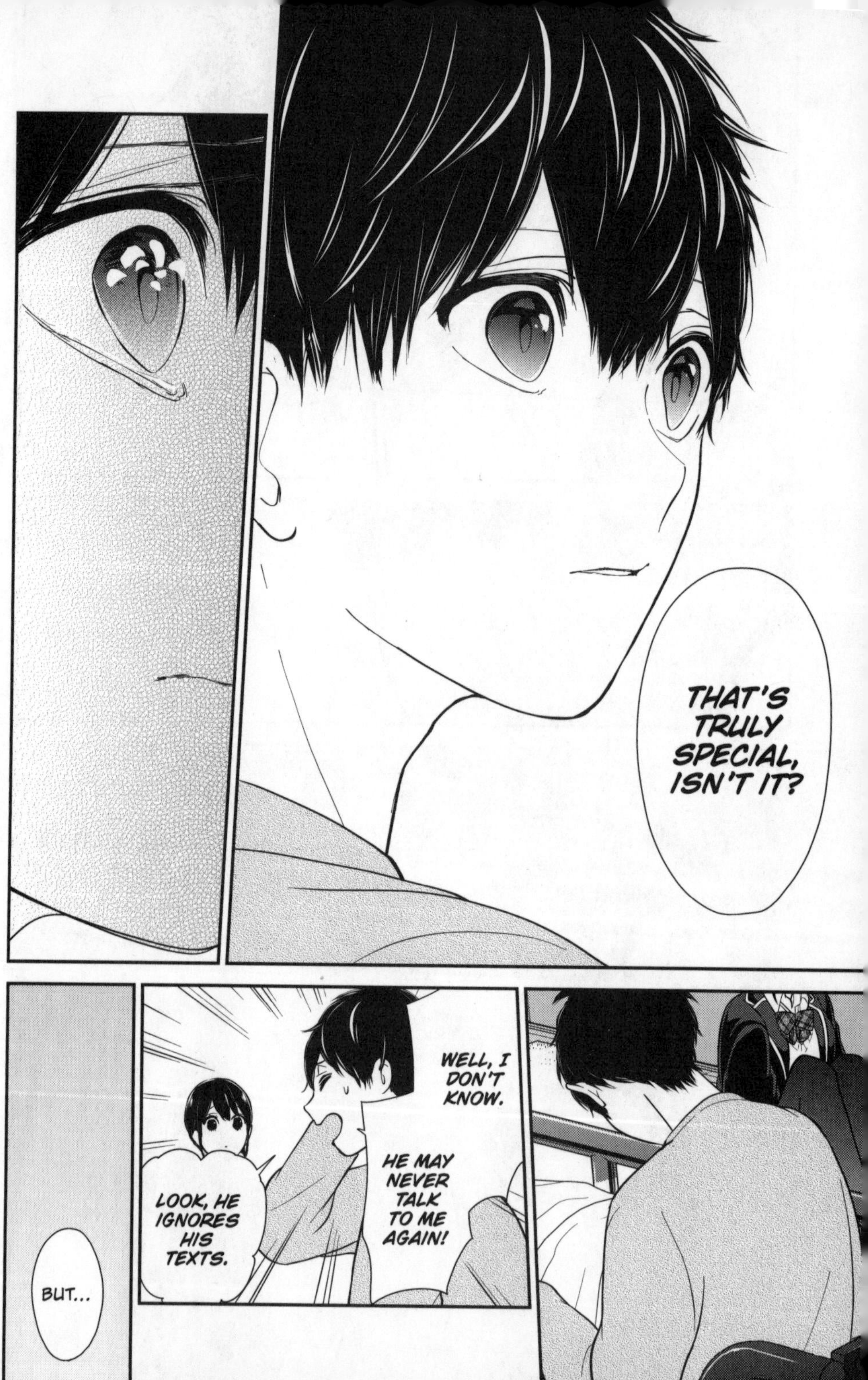
THAT'S TRULY SPECIAL, ISN'T IT?
WELL, I DON'T KNOW.
HE MAY NEVER TALK TO ME AGAIN!
LOOK, HE IGNORES HIS TEXTS.
BUT...

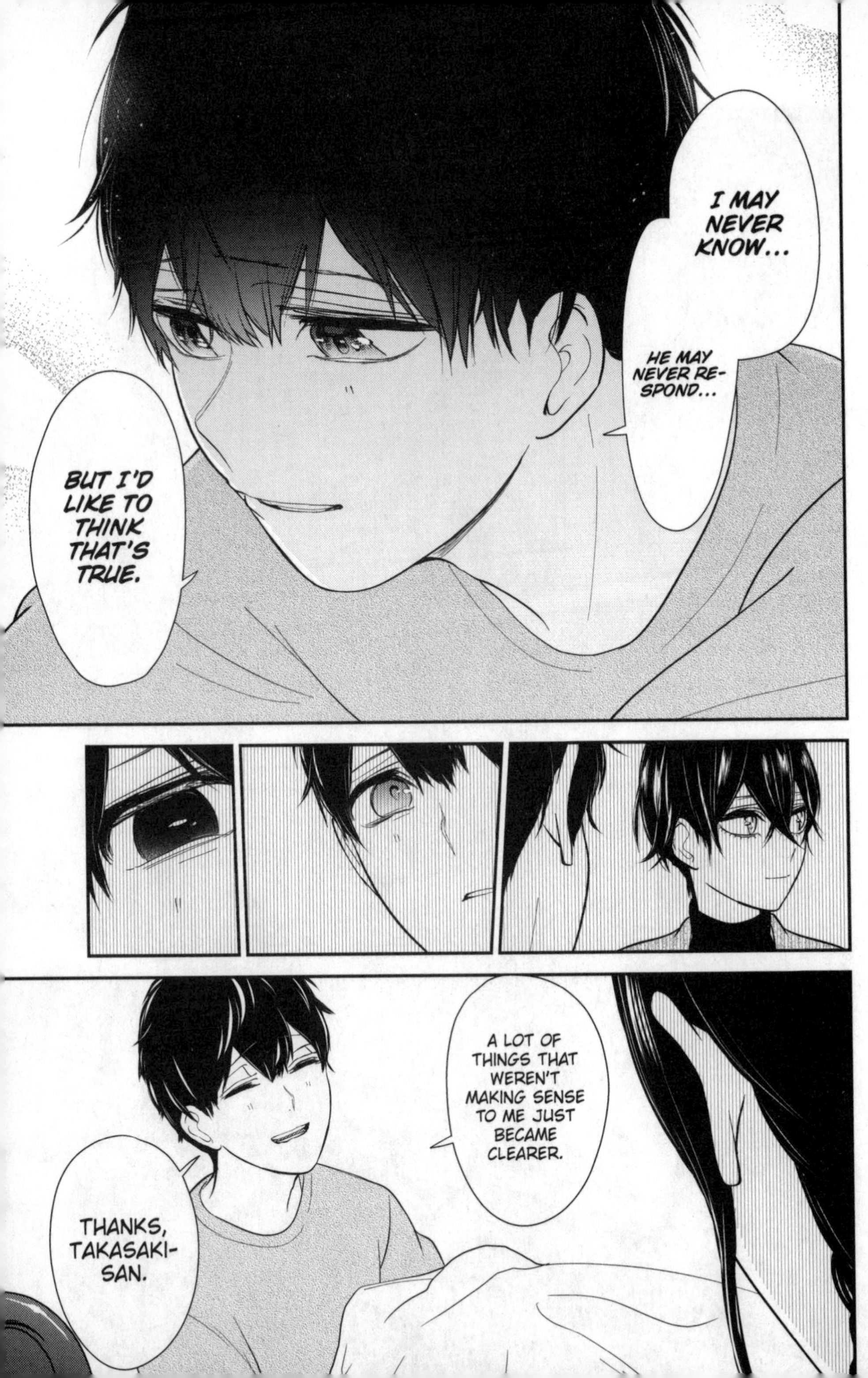
I MAY NEVER KNOW...
HE MAY NEVER RE-SPOND...
BUT I'D LIKE TO THINK THAT'S TRUE.
A LOT OF THINGS THAT WEREN'T MAKING SENSE TO ME JUST BECAME CLEARER.
THANKS, TAKASAKI-SAN.

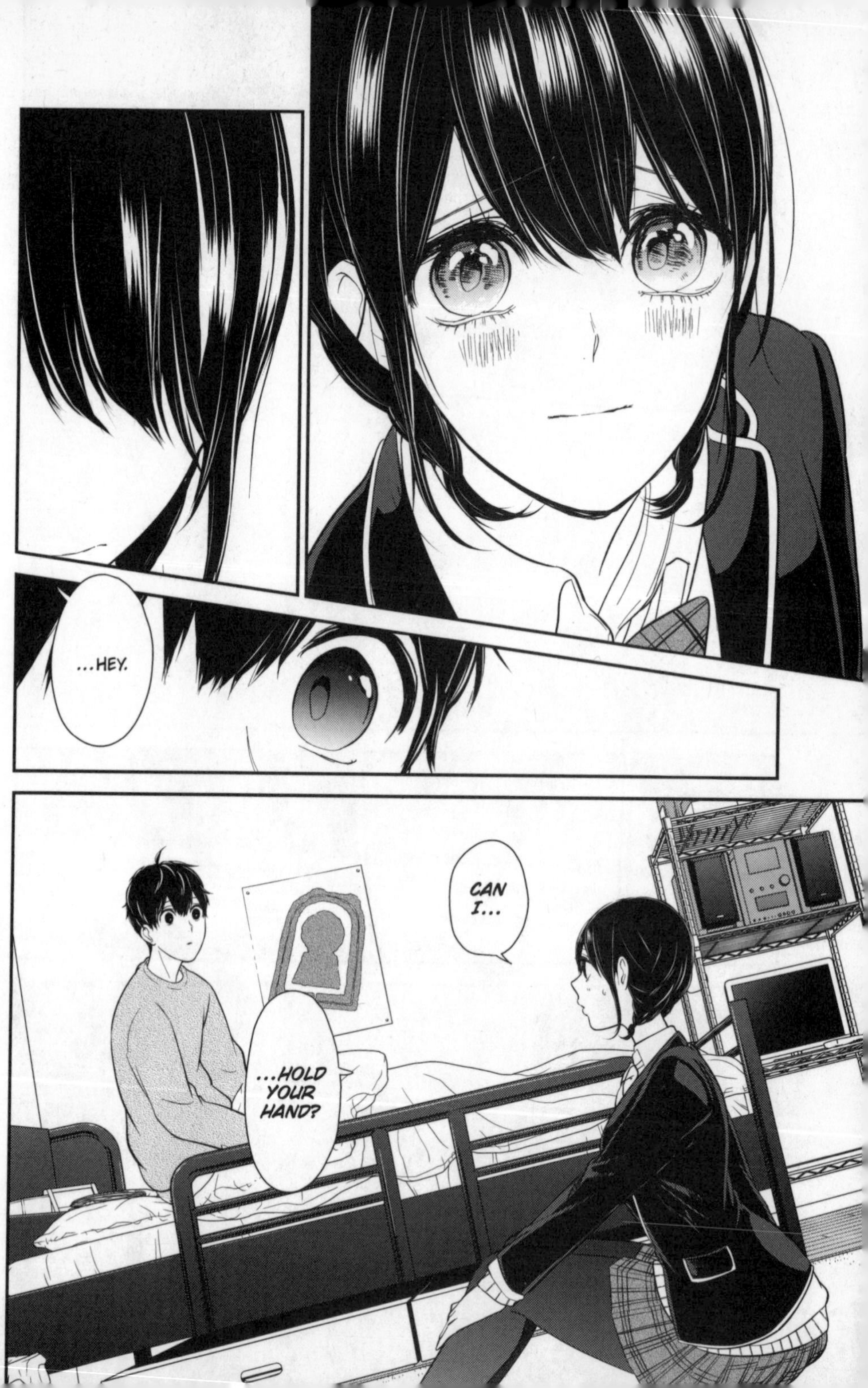
...HEY.
CAN I...
...HOLD YOUR HAND?

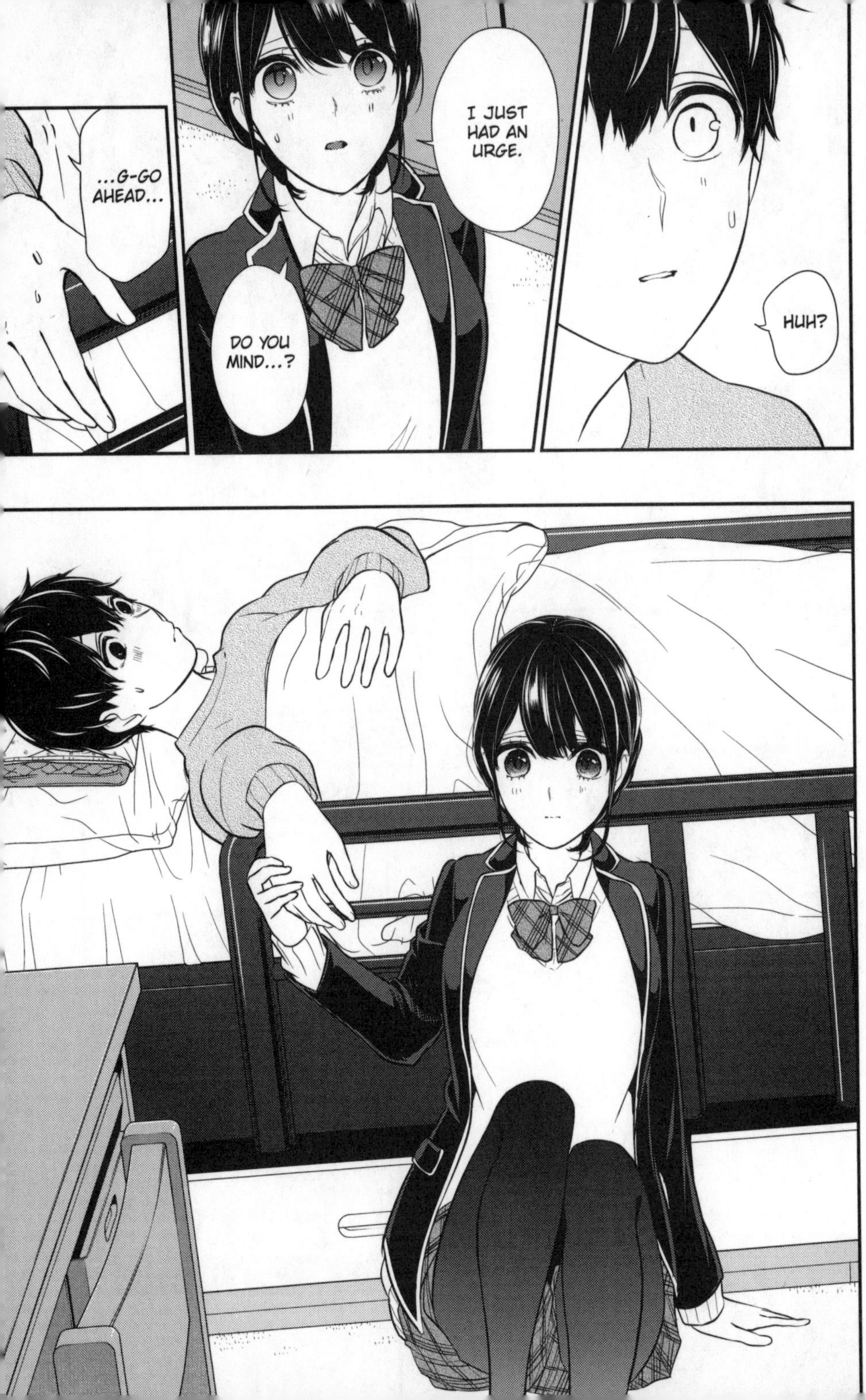
HUH?
I JUST HAD AN URGE.
DO YOU MIND...?
...G-GO AHEAD...

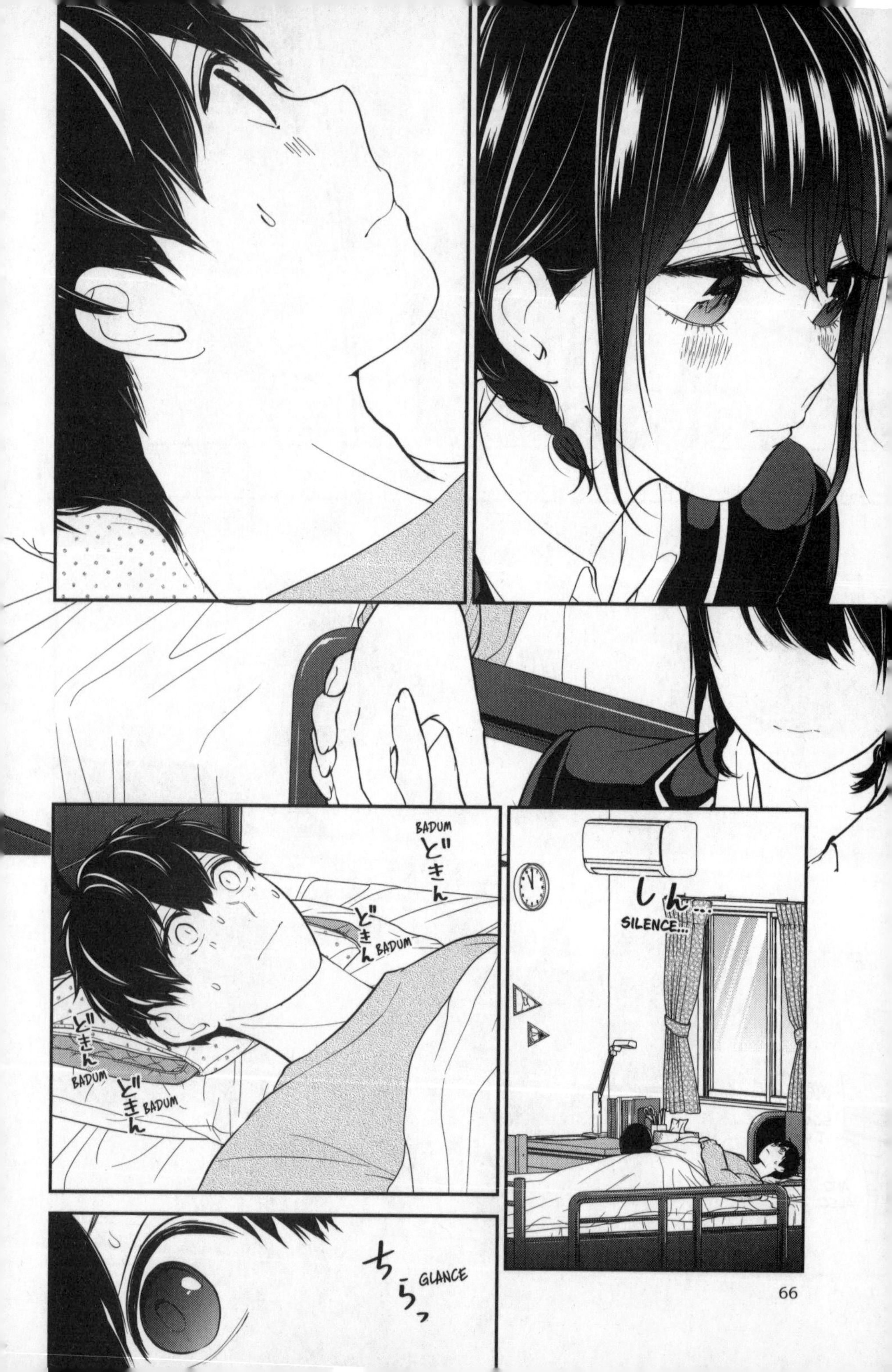
しん…
SILENCE…
どきん
BADUM
どきん
BADUM
どきん
BADUM
どきん
BADUM
ちらっ
GLANCE

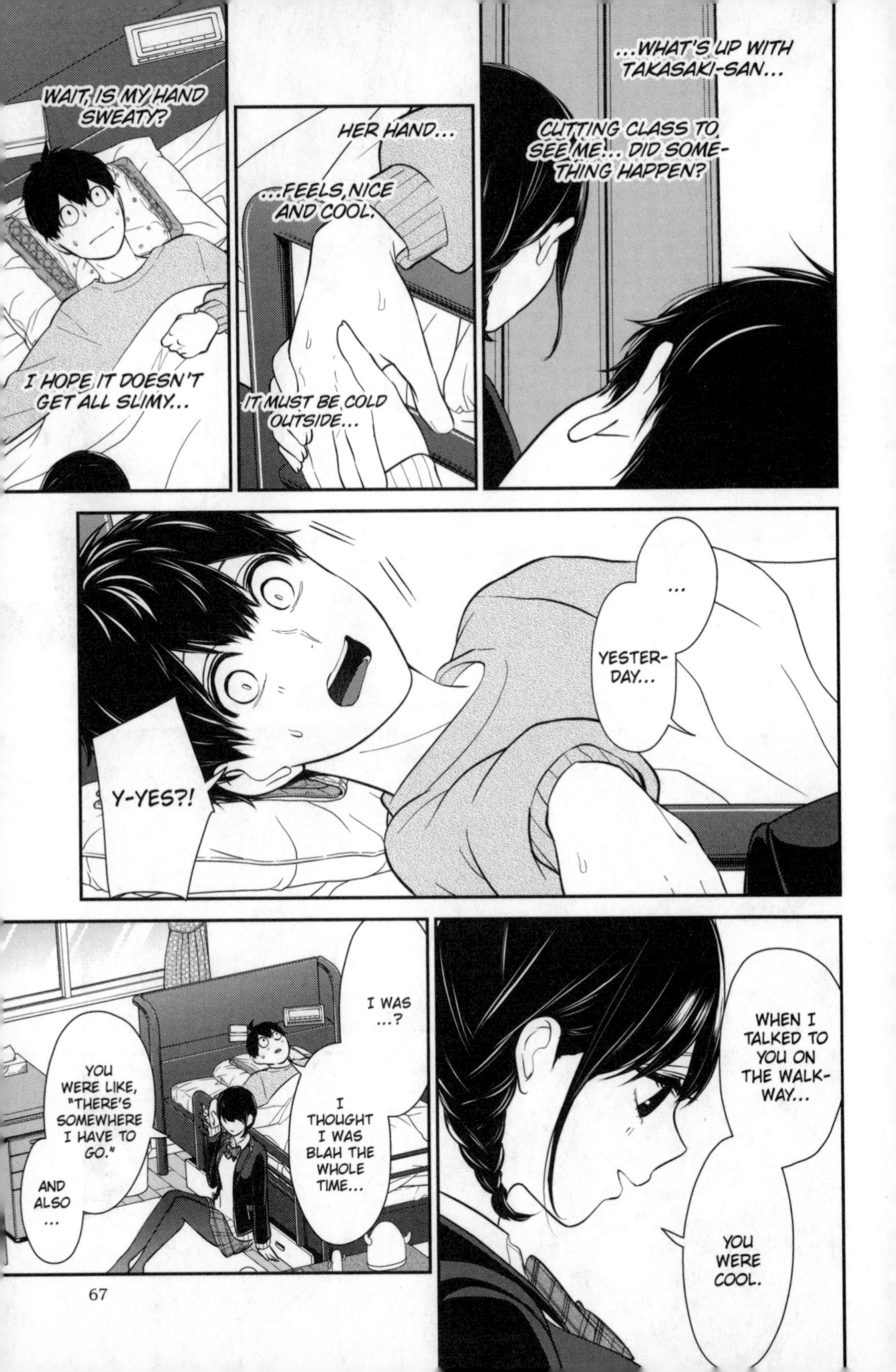
...WHAT'S UP WITH TAKASAKI-SAN...
CUTTING CLASS TO SEE ME... DID SOMETHING HAPPEN?
HER HAND...
...FEELS NICE AND COOL.
IT MUST BE COLD OUTSIDE...
WAIT, IS MY HAND SWEATY?
I HOPE IT DOESN'T GET ALL SLIMY...
...
YESTERDAY...
Y-YES?!
WHEN I TALKED TO YOU ON THE WALKWAY...
YOU WERE COOL.
I WAS ...?
I THOUGHT I WAS BLAH THE WHOLE TIME...
YOU WERE LIKE, "THERE'S SOMEWHERE I HAVE TO GO."
AND ALSO ...

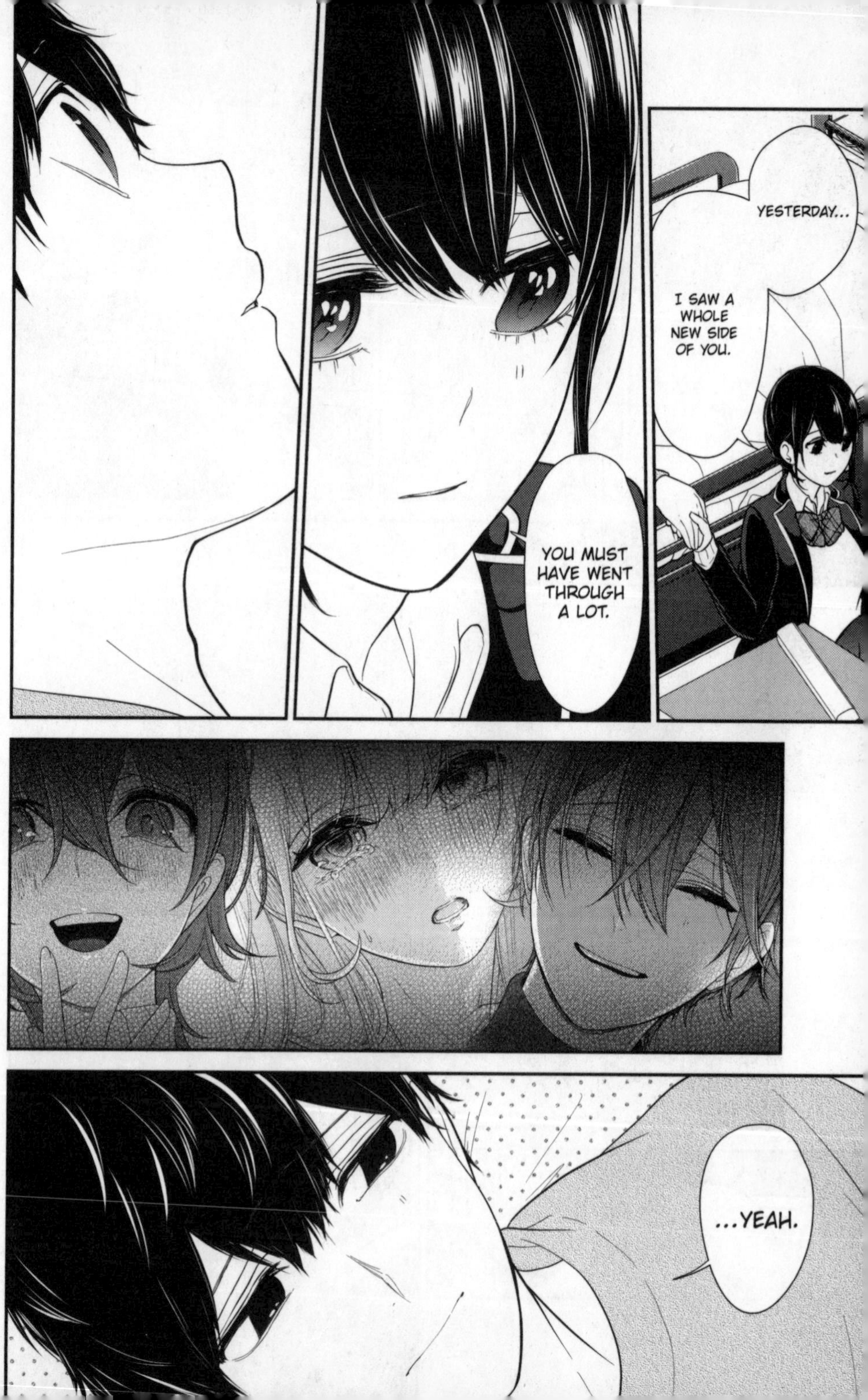

YESTERDAY...
I SAW A WHOLE NEW SIDE OF YOU.
YOU MUST HAVE WENT THROUGH A LOT.
...YEAH.

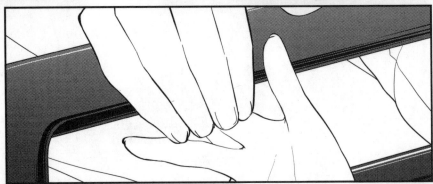

NO MATTER HOW TOUGH OR EXHAUSTING IT GOT...

EVEN WHEN YOU HAD THE URGE TO RUN AWAY...

YOU STILL FACED IT HEAD-ON.

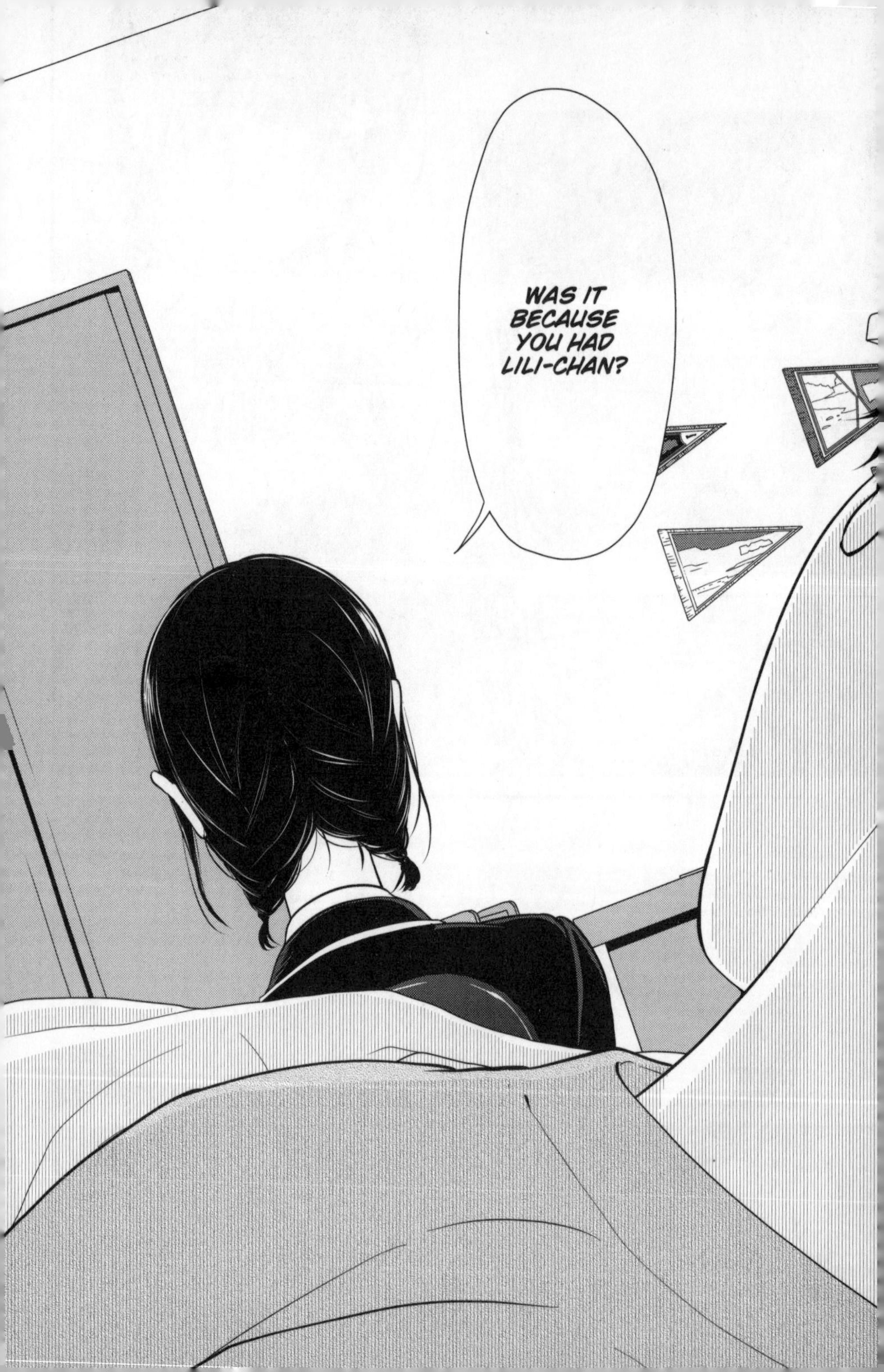
WAS IT BECAUSE YOU HAD LILI-CHAN?

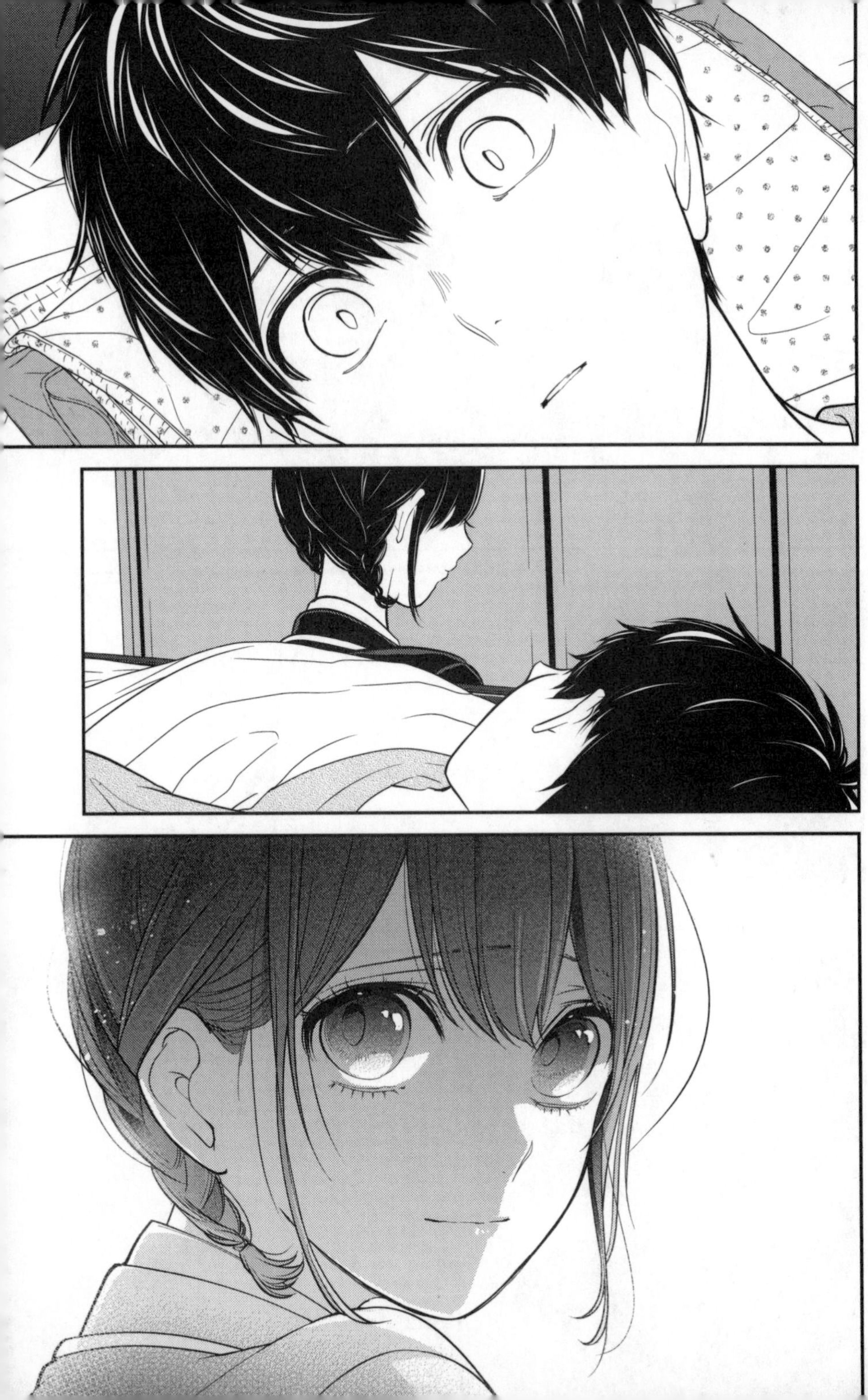

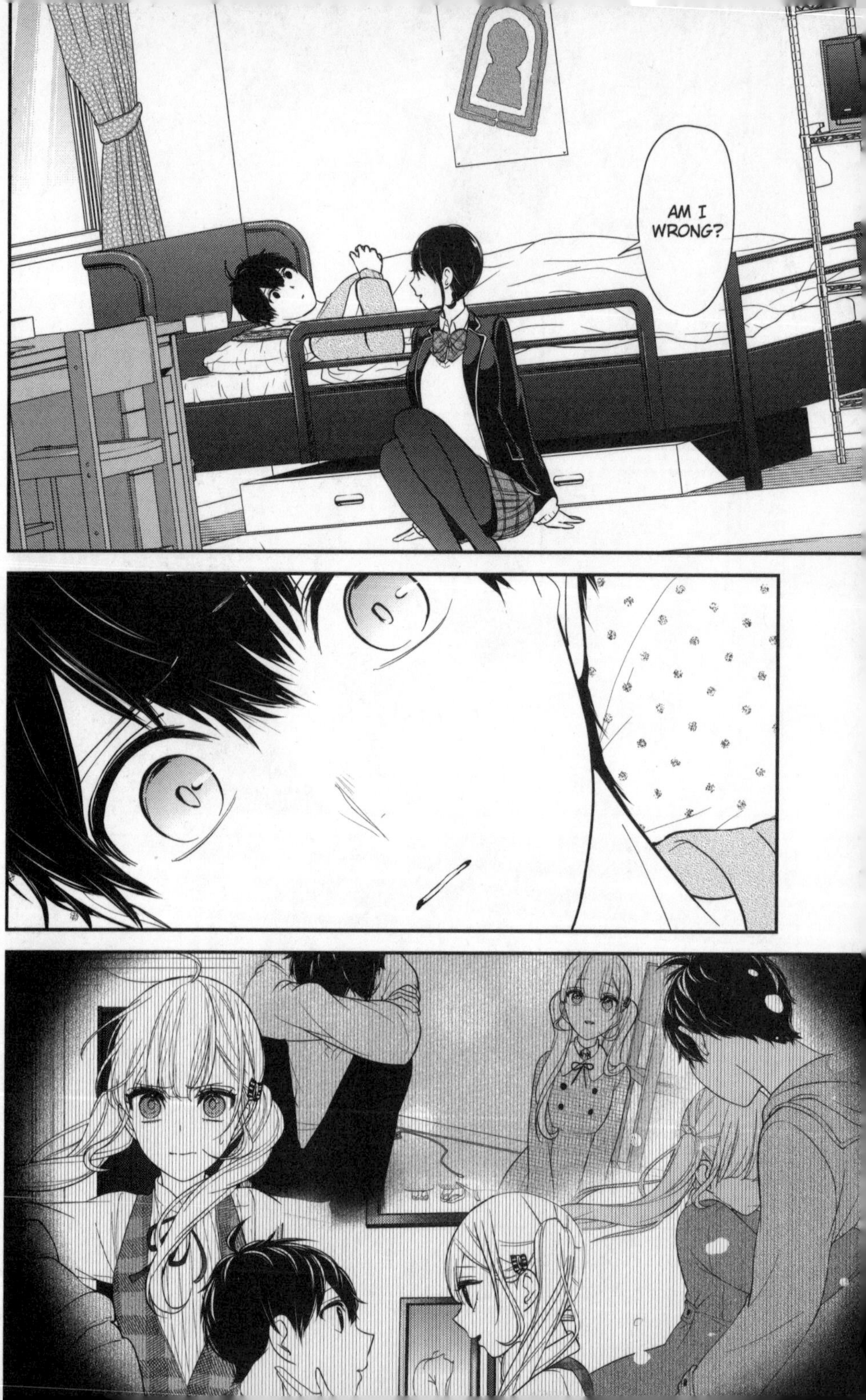
AM I WRONG?

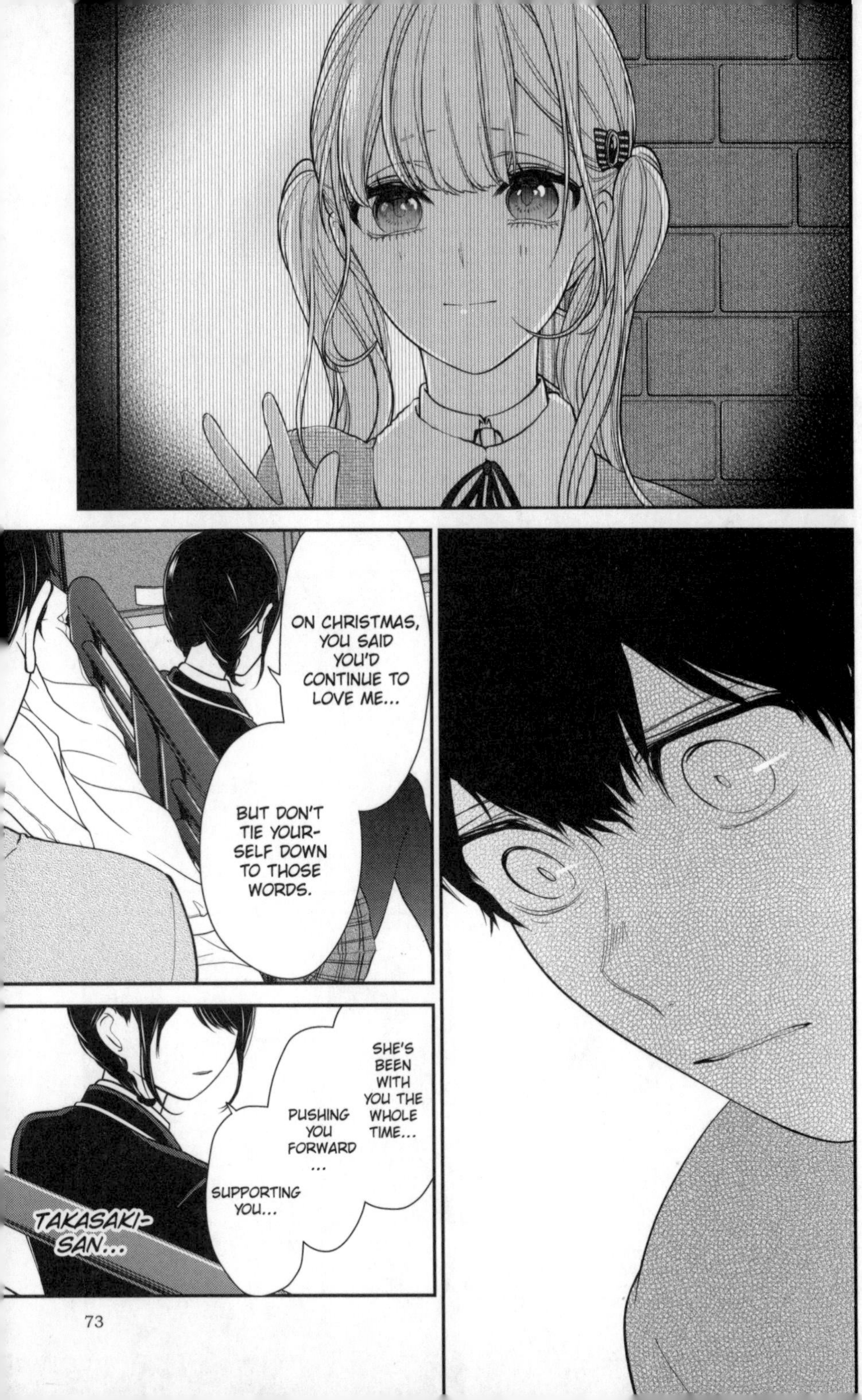
ON CHRISTMAS, YOU SAID YOU'D CONTINUE TO LOVE ME...
BUT DON'T TIE YOUR-SELF DOWN TO THOSE WORDS.
SHE'S BEEN WITH YOU THE WHOLE TIME...
PUSHING YOU FORWARD ...
SUPPORTING YOU...
TAKASAKI-SAN...

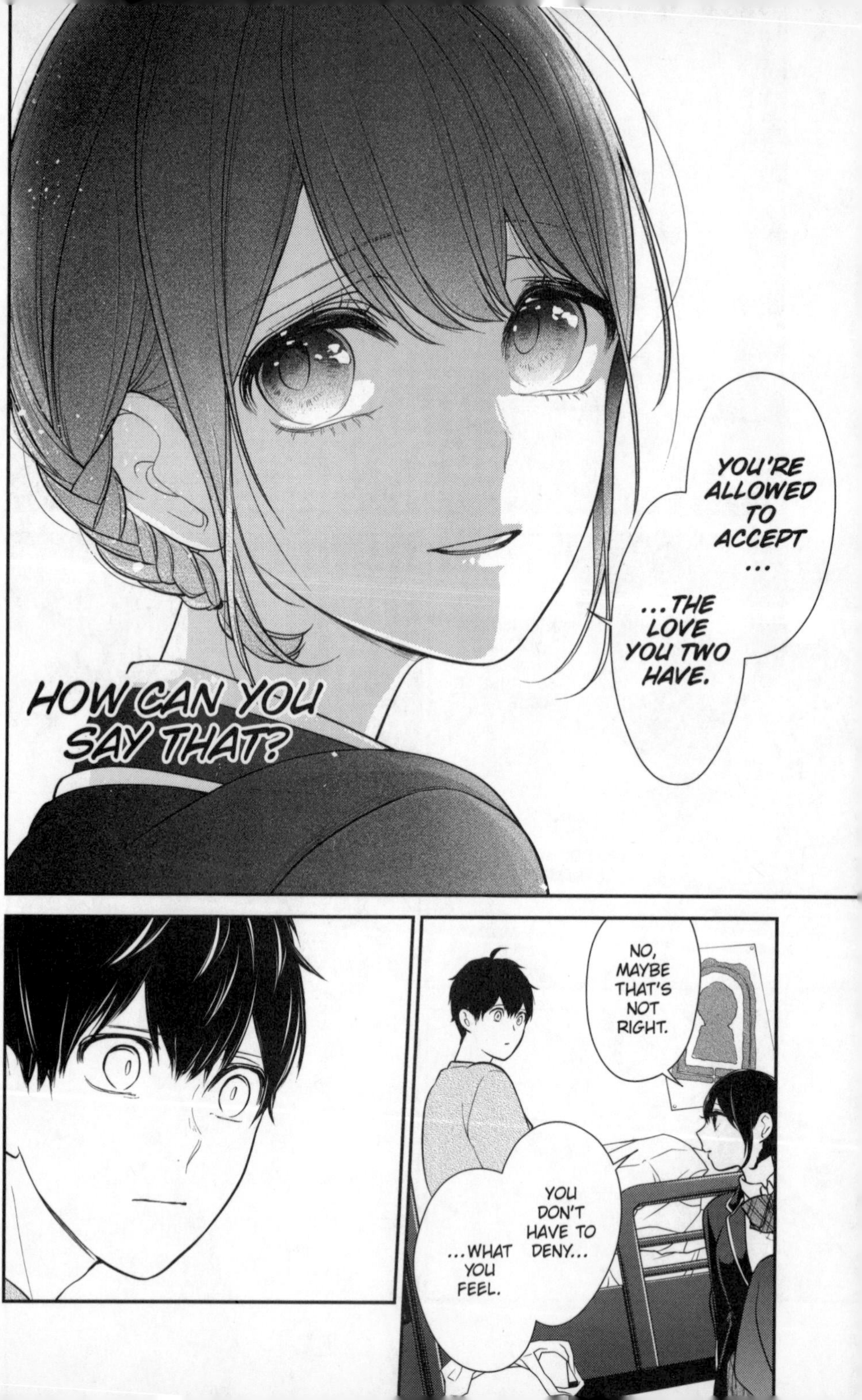
YOU'RE ALLOWED TO ACCEPT...
...THE LOVE YOU TWO HAVE.
HOW CAN YOU SAY THAT?
NO, MAYBE THAT'S NOT RIGHT.
YOU DON'T HAVE TO DENY...
...WHAT YOU FEEL.

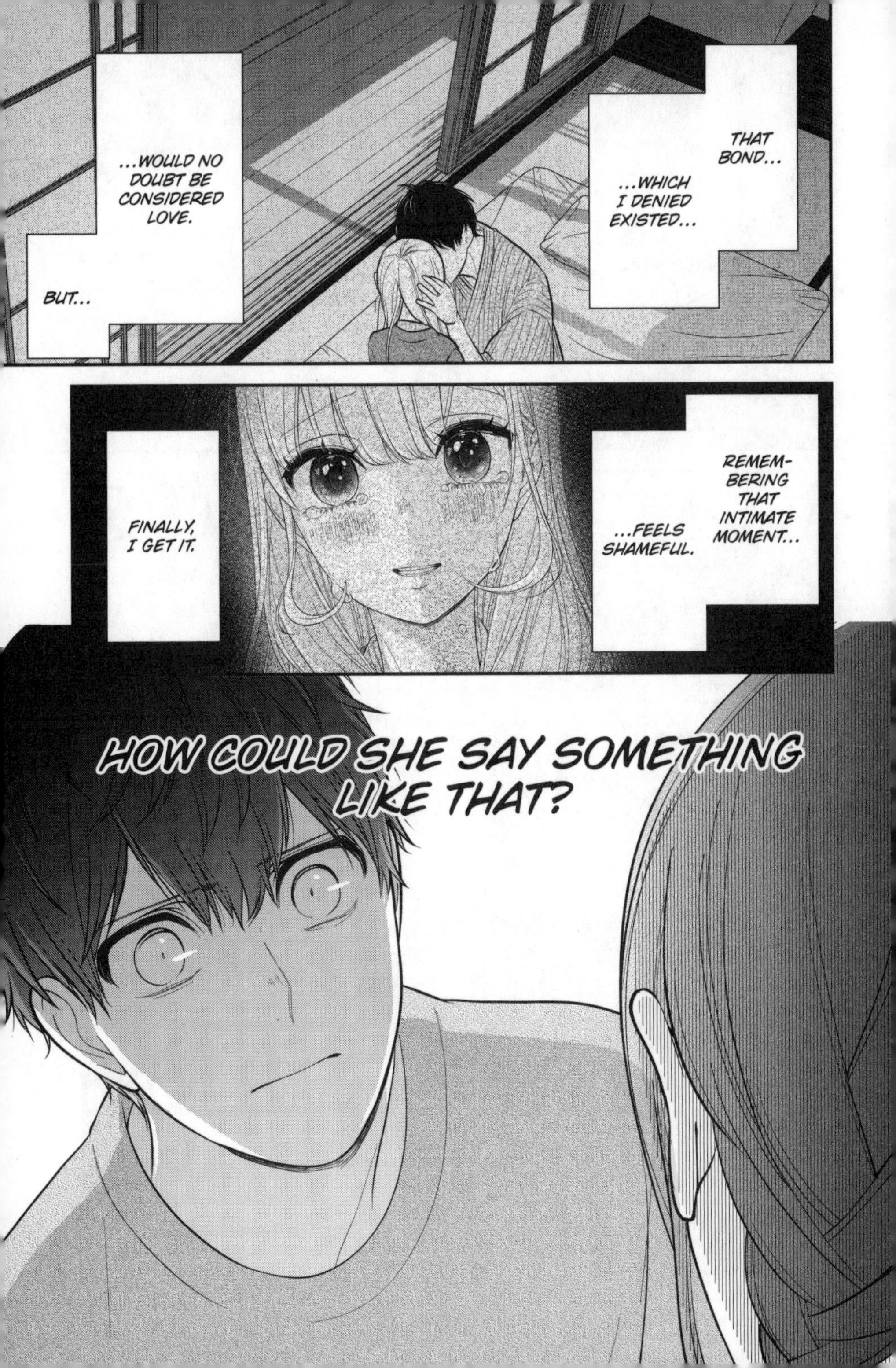
THAT BOND...
...WHICH I DENIED EXISTED...
...WOULD NO DOUBT BE CONSIDERED LOVE.
BUT...
REMEMBERING THAT INTIMATE MOMENT...
...FEELS SHAMEFUL.
FINALLY, I GET IT.
HOW COULD SHE SAY SOMETHING LIKE THAT?

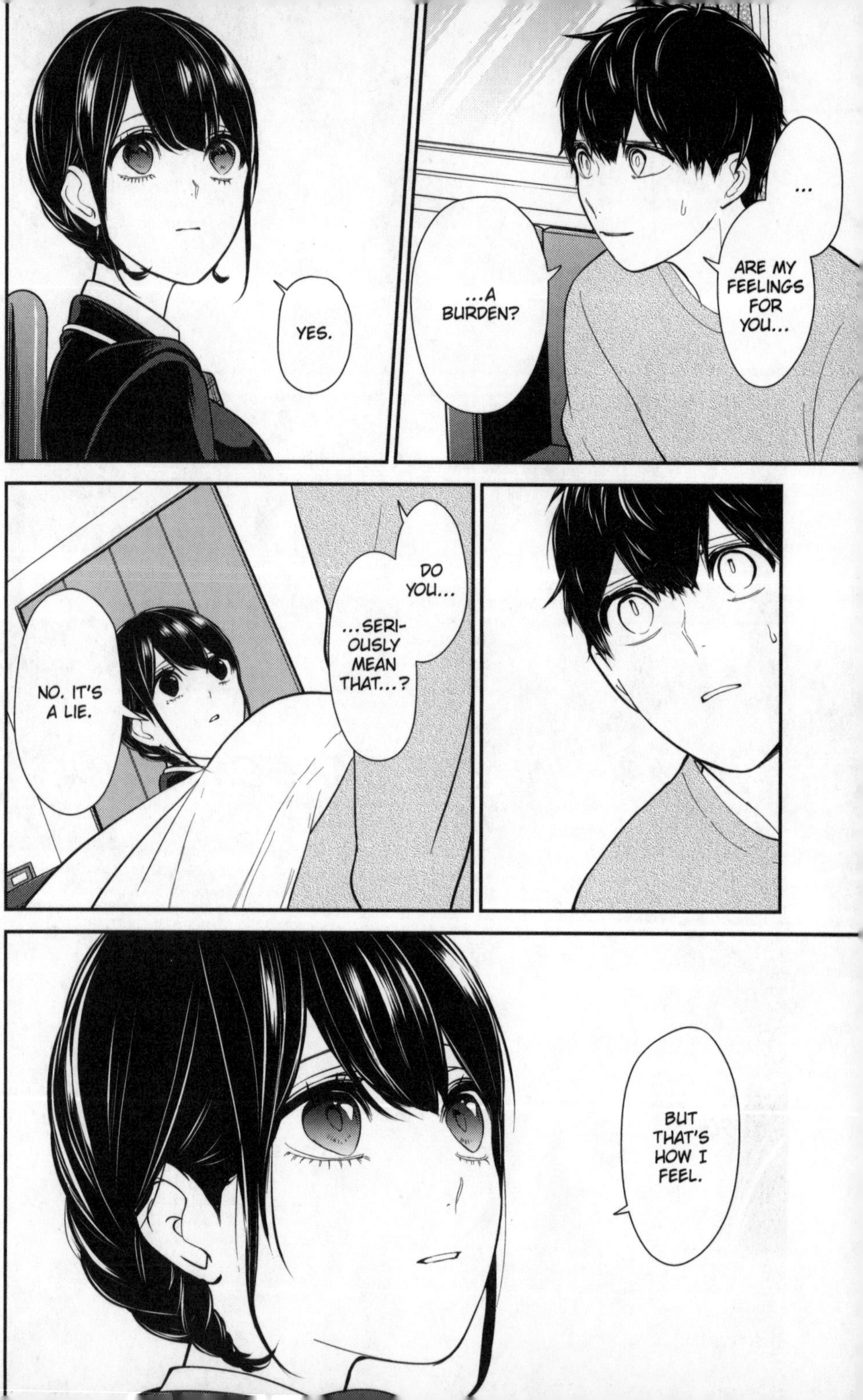
...
ARE MY FEELINGS FOR YOU...
...A BURDEN?
YES.
DO YOU...
...SERIOUSLY MEAN THAT...?
NO. IT'S A LIE.
BUT THAT'S HOW I FEEL.

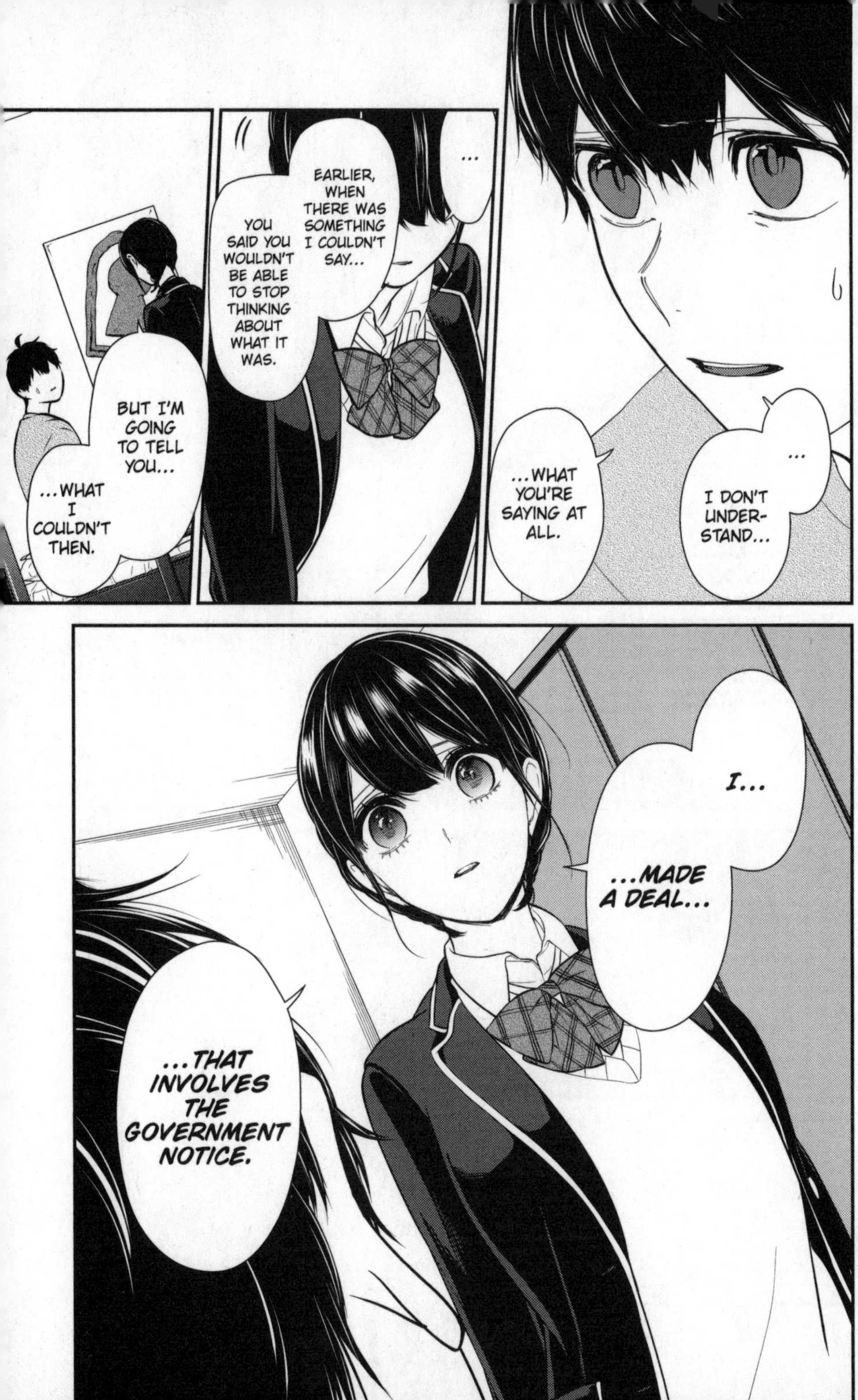
...
I DON'T UNDER-STAND...
...WHAT YOU'RE SAYING AT ALL.
...
EARLIER, WHEN THERE WAS SOMETHING I COULDN'T SAY...
YOU SAID YOU WOULDN'T BE ABLE TO STOP THINKING ABOUT WHAT IT WAS.
BUT I'M GOING TO TELL YOU...
...WHAT I COULDN'T THEN.
I...
...MADE A DEAL...
...THAT INVOLVES THE GOVERNMENT NOTICE.

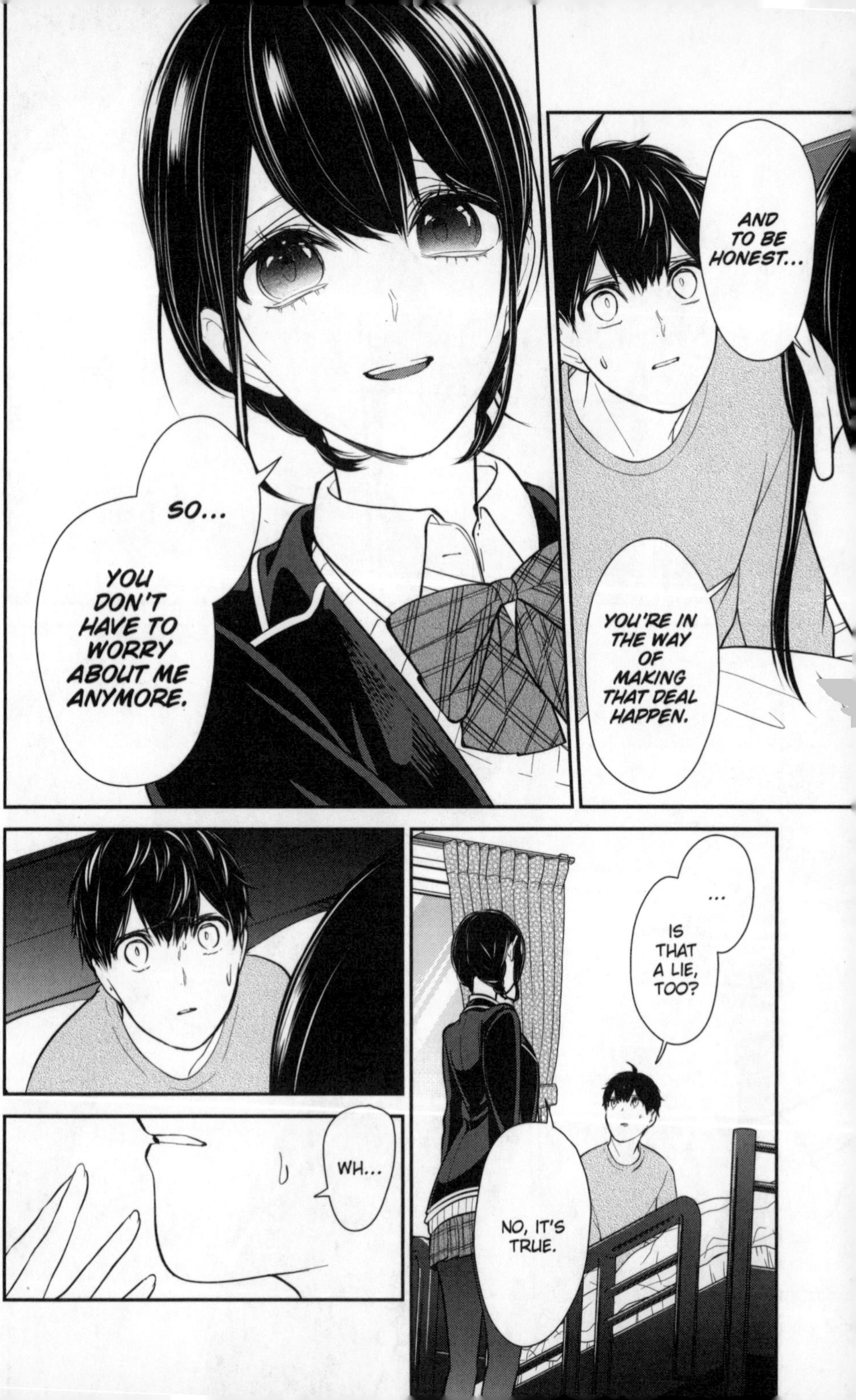
AND TO BE HONEST...
YOU'RE IN THE WAY OF MAKING THAT DEAL HAPPEN.
SO...
YOU DON'T HAVE TO WORRY ABOUT ME ANYMORE.
...
IS THAT A LIE, TOO?
NO, IT'S TRUE.
WH...

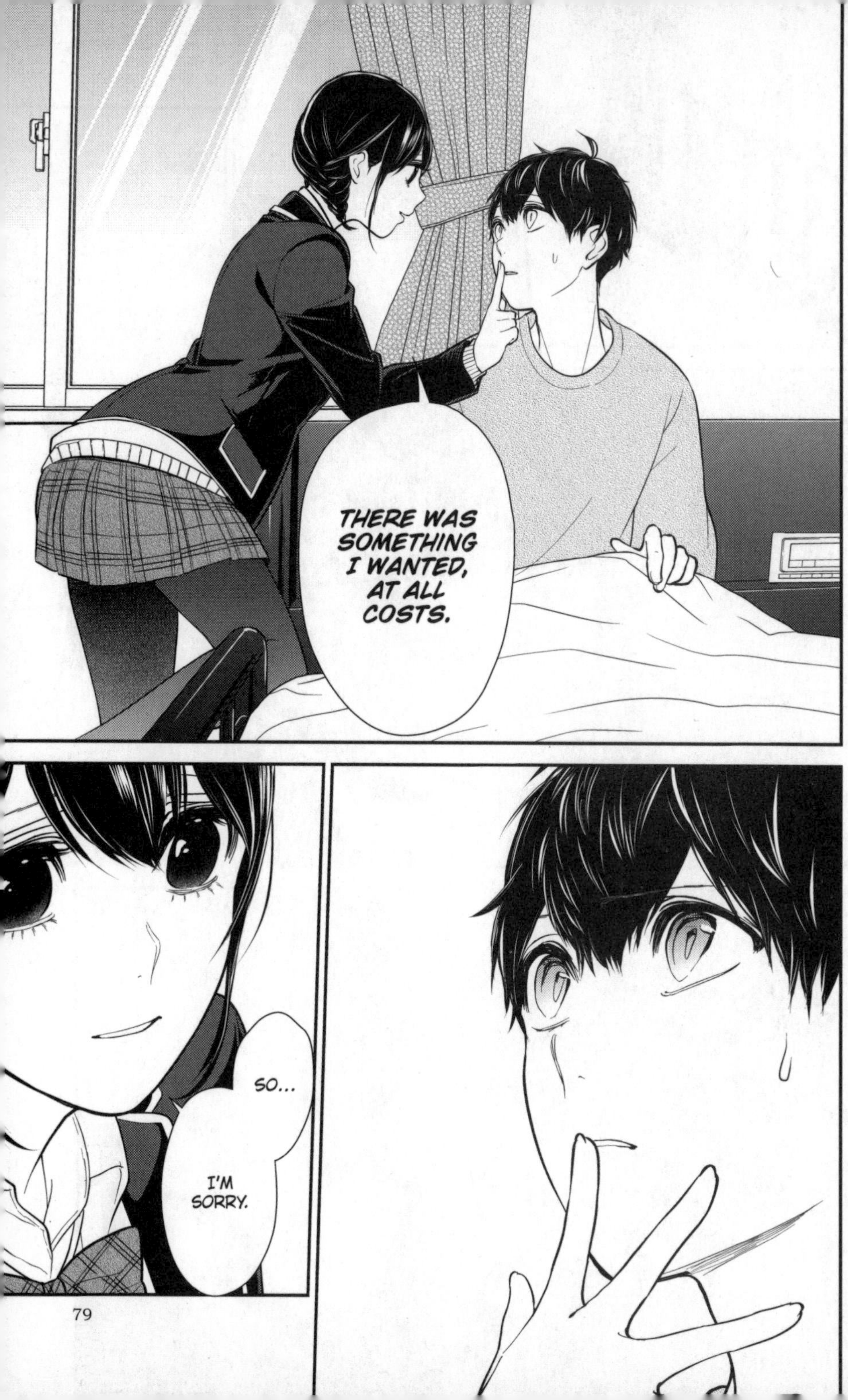
THERE WAS SOMETHING I WANTED, AT ALL COSTS.
SO...
I'M SORRY.

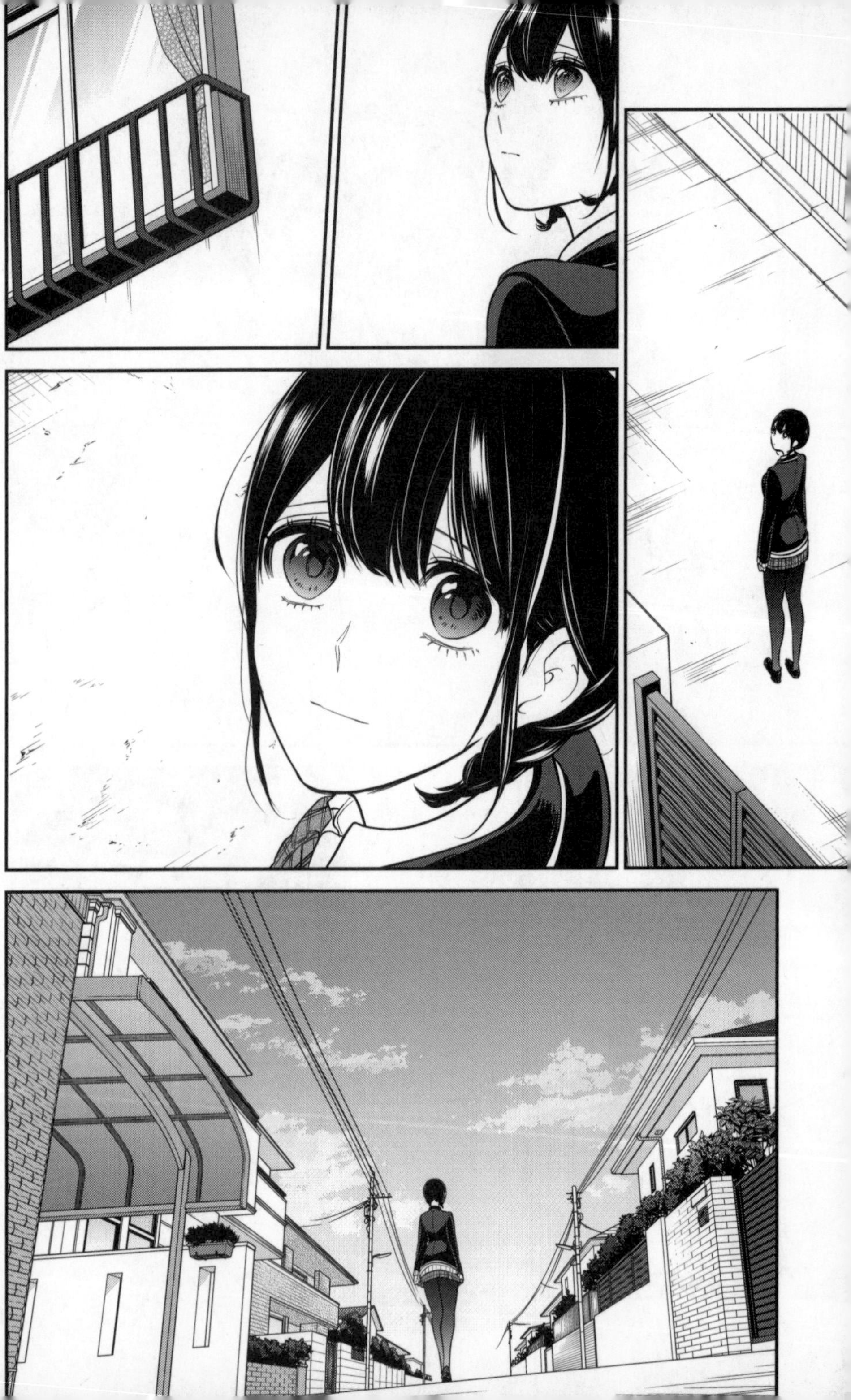

## Chapter 36: Intruder of Love

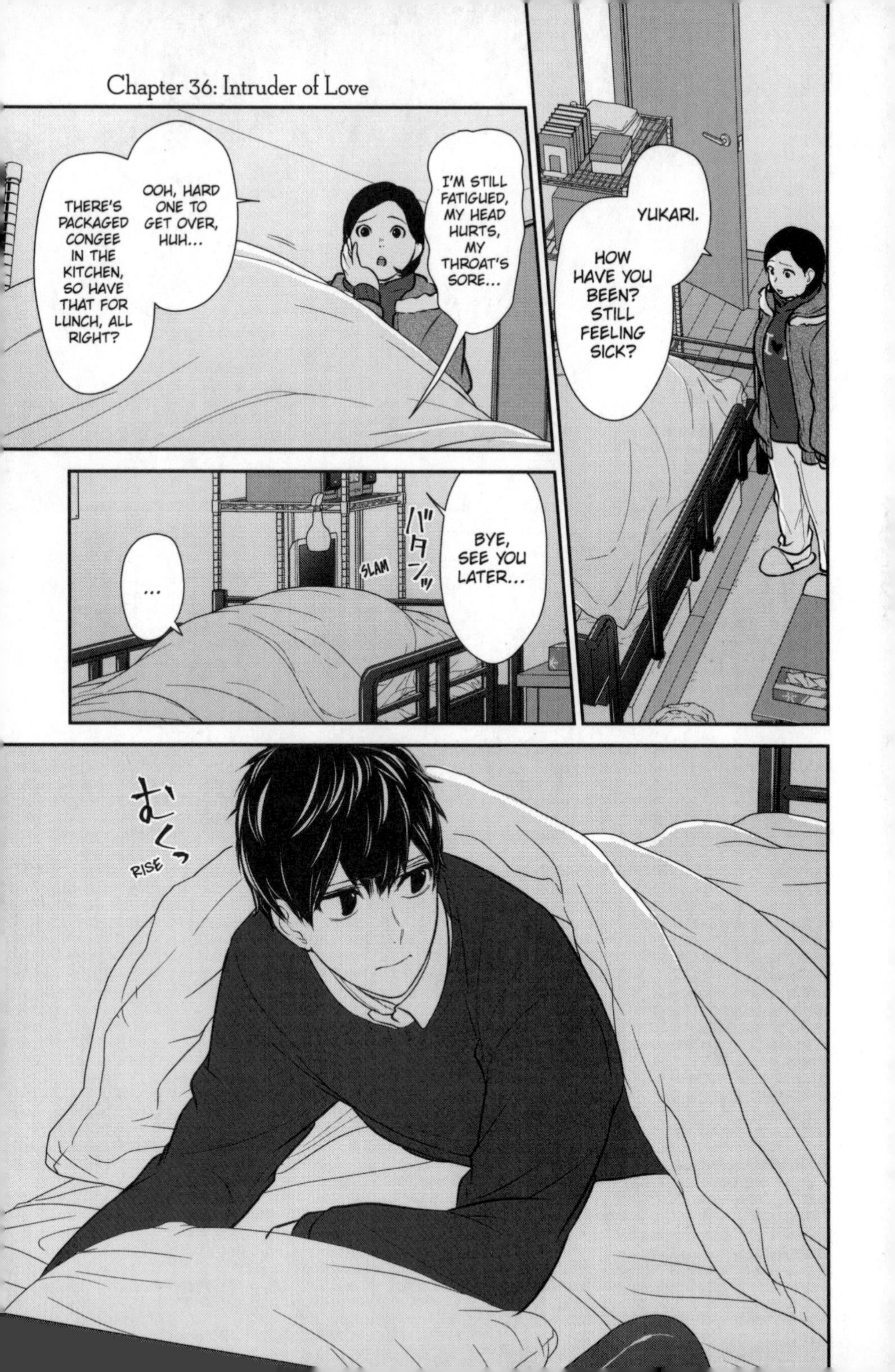
YUKARI.
HOW HAVE YOU BEEN? STILL FEELING SICK?
I'M STILL FATIGUED, MY HEAD HURTS, MY THROAT'S SORE...
OOH, HARD ONE TO GET OVER, HUH...
THERE'S PACKAGED CONGEE IN THE KITCHEN, SO HAVE THAT FOR LUNCH, ALL RIGHT?
BYE, SEE YOU LATER...
バタンッ
SLAM
...
むくっ
RISE

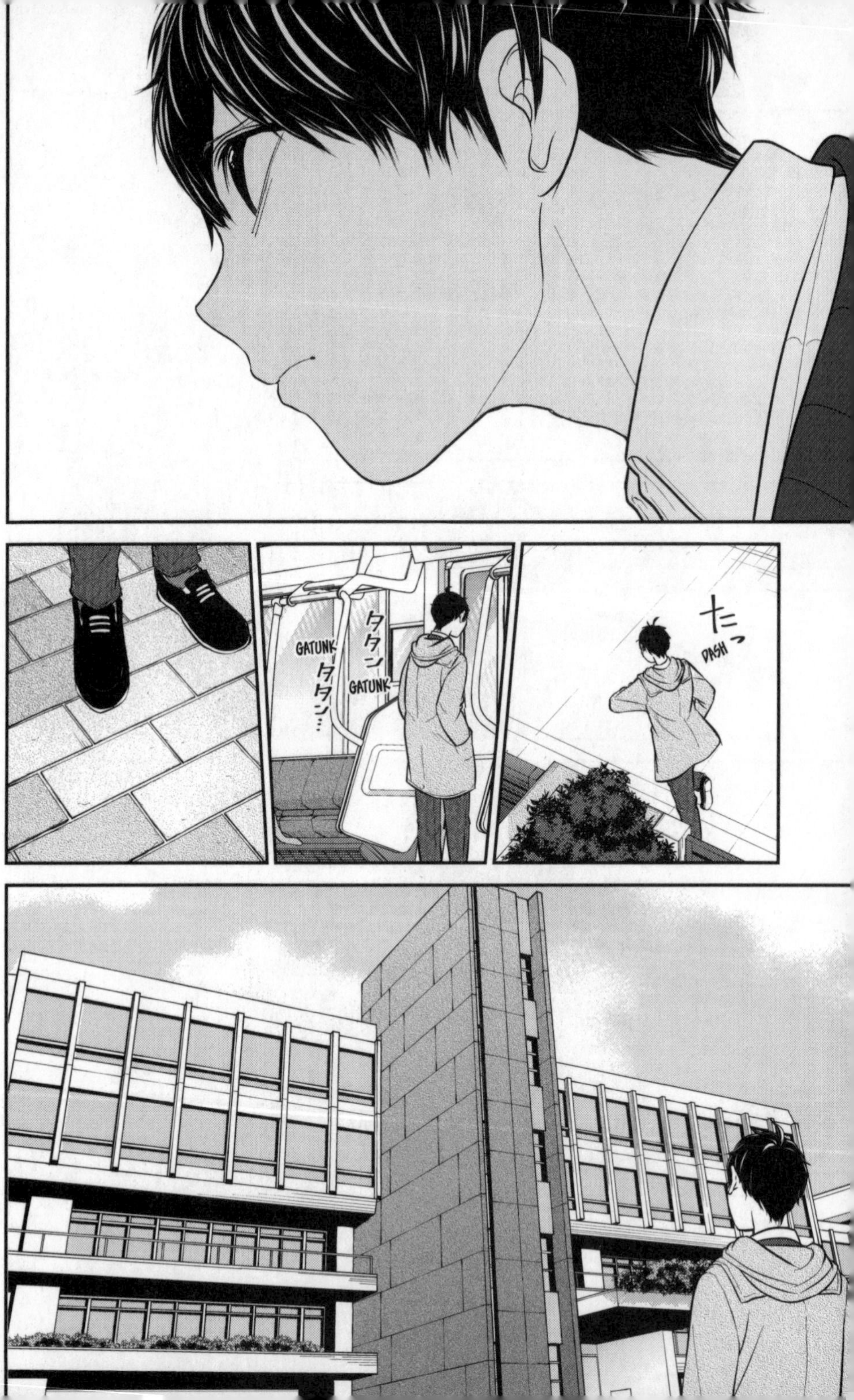
たっ
DASH
タタン
GATUNK
タタン…
GATUNK

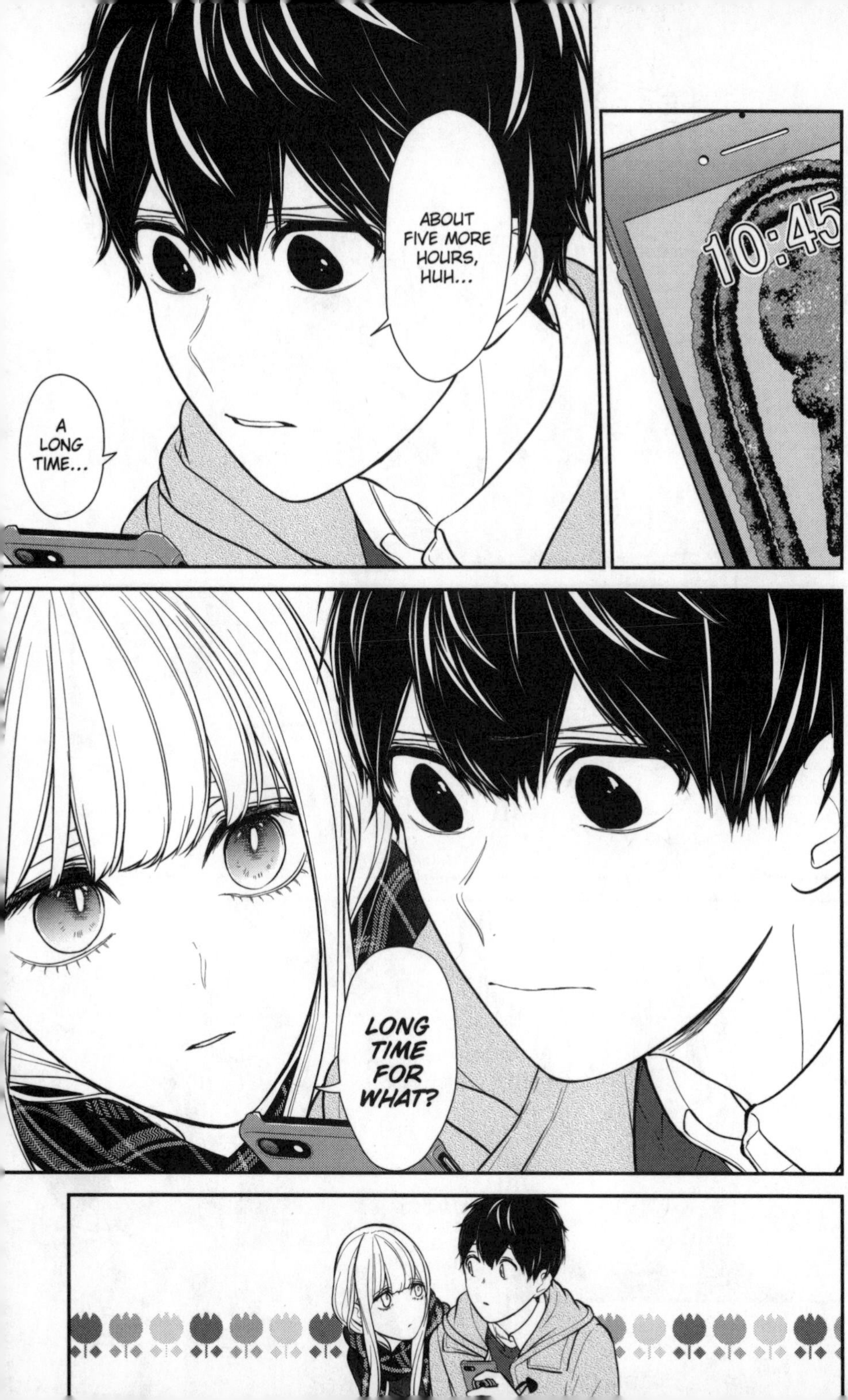
10:45
ABOUT FIVE MORE HOURS, HUH...
A LONG TIME...
LONG TIME FOR WHAT?

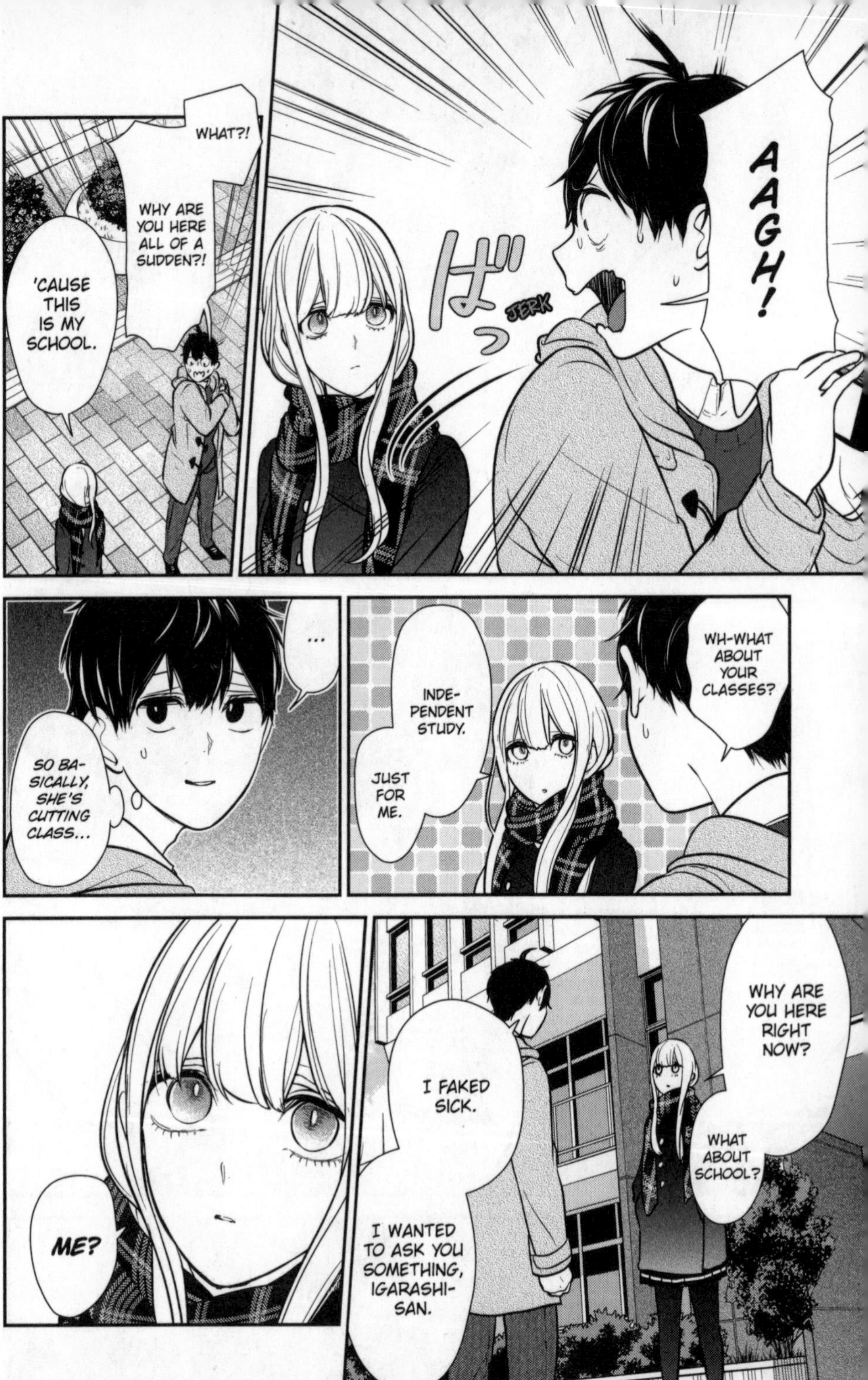
AAGH!
ばっ
JERK
WHAT?!
WHY ARE YOU HERE ALL OF A SUDDEN?!
'CAUSE THIS IS MY SCHOOL.
WH-WHAT ABOUT YOUR CLASSES?
INDE-PENDENT STUDY.
JUST FOR ME.
...
SO BA-SICALLY, SHE'S CUTTING CLASS...
WHY ARE YOU HERE RIGHT NOW?
WHAT ABOUT SCHOOL?
I FAKED SICK.
I WANTED TO ASK YOU SOMETHING, IGARASHI-SAN.
ME?

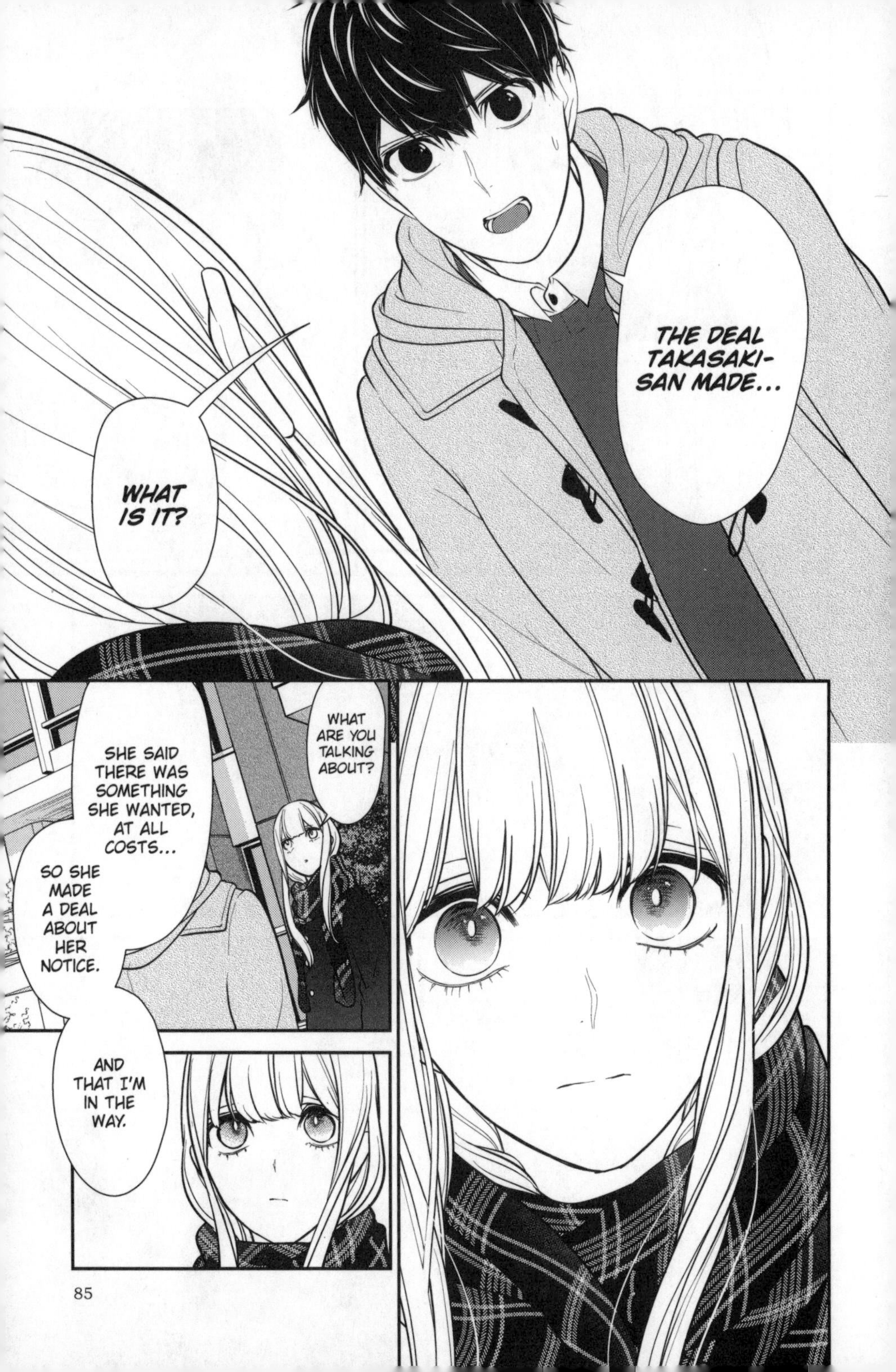
THE DEAL TAKASAKI-SAN MADE...
WHAT IS IT?
WHAT ARE YOU TALKING ABOUT?
SHE SAID THERE WAS SOMETHING SHE WANTED, AT ALL COSTS...
SO SHE MADE A DEAL ABOUT HER NOTICE.
AND THAT I'M IN THE WAY.

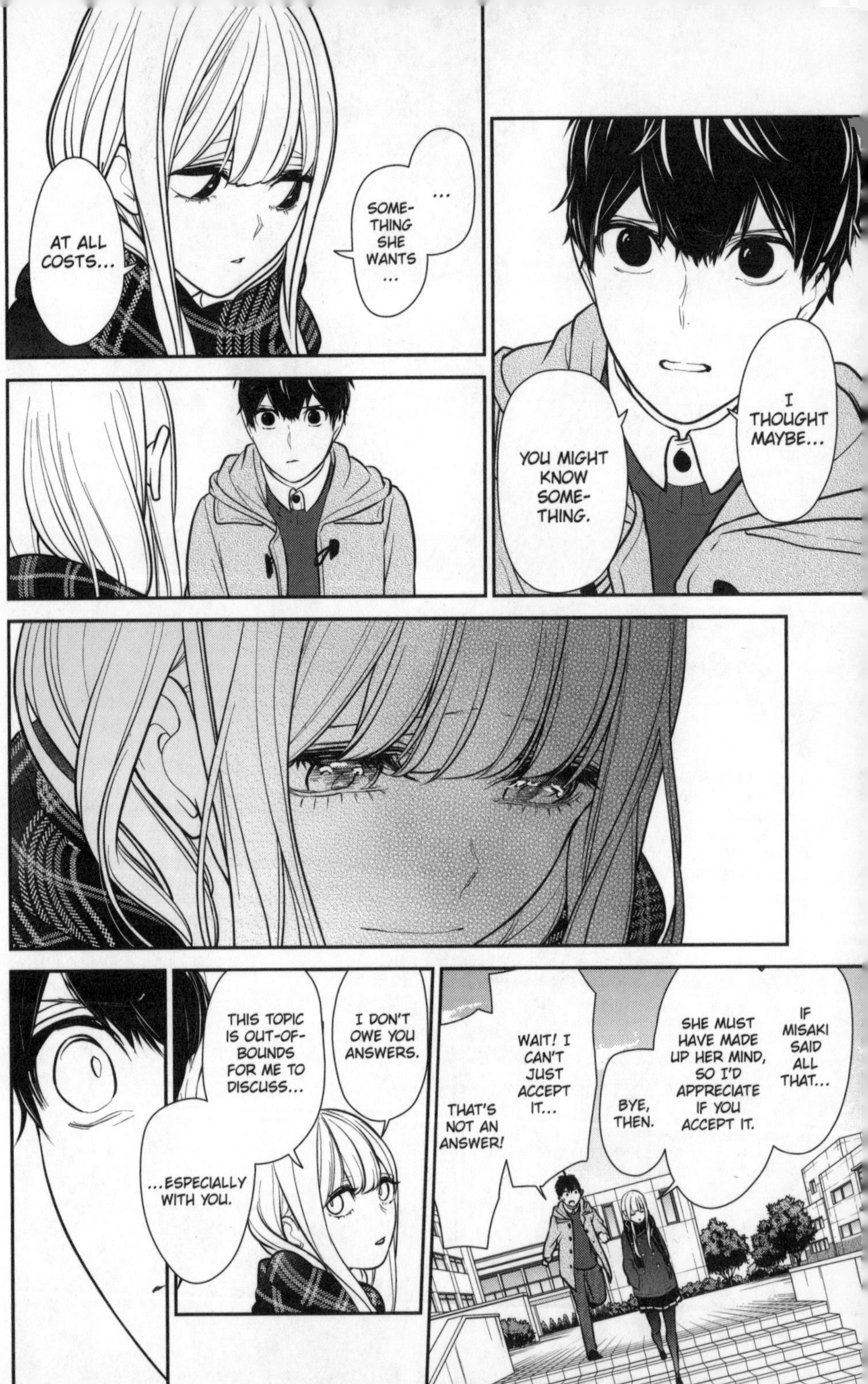
I THOUGHT MAYBE...
YOU MIGHT KNOW SOMETHING.
...
SOMETHING SHE WANTS ...
AT ALL COSTS...
IF MISAKI SAID ALL THAT...
SHE MUST HAVE MADE UP HER MIND, SO I'D APPRECIATE IF YOU ACCEPT IT.
BYE, THEN.
WAIT! I CAN'T JUST ACCEPT IT...
THAT'S NOT AN ANSWER!
I DON'T OWE YOU ANSWERS.
THIS TOPIC IS OUT-OF-BOUNDS FOR ME TO DISCUSS...
...ESPECIALLY WITH YOU.

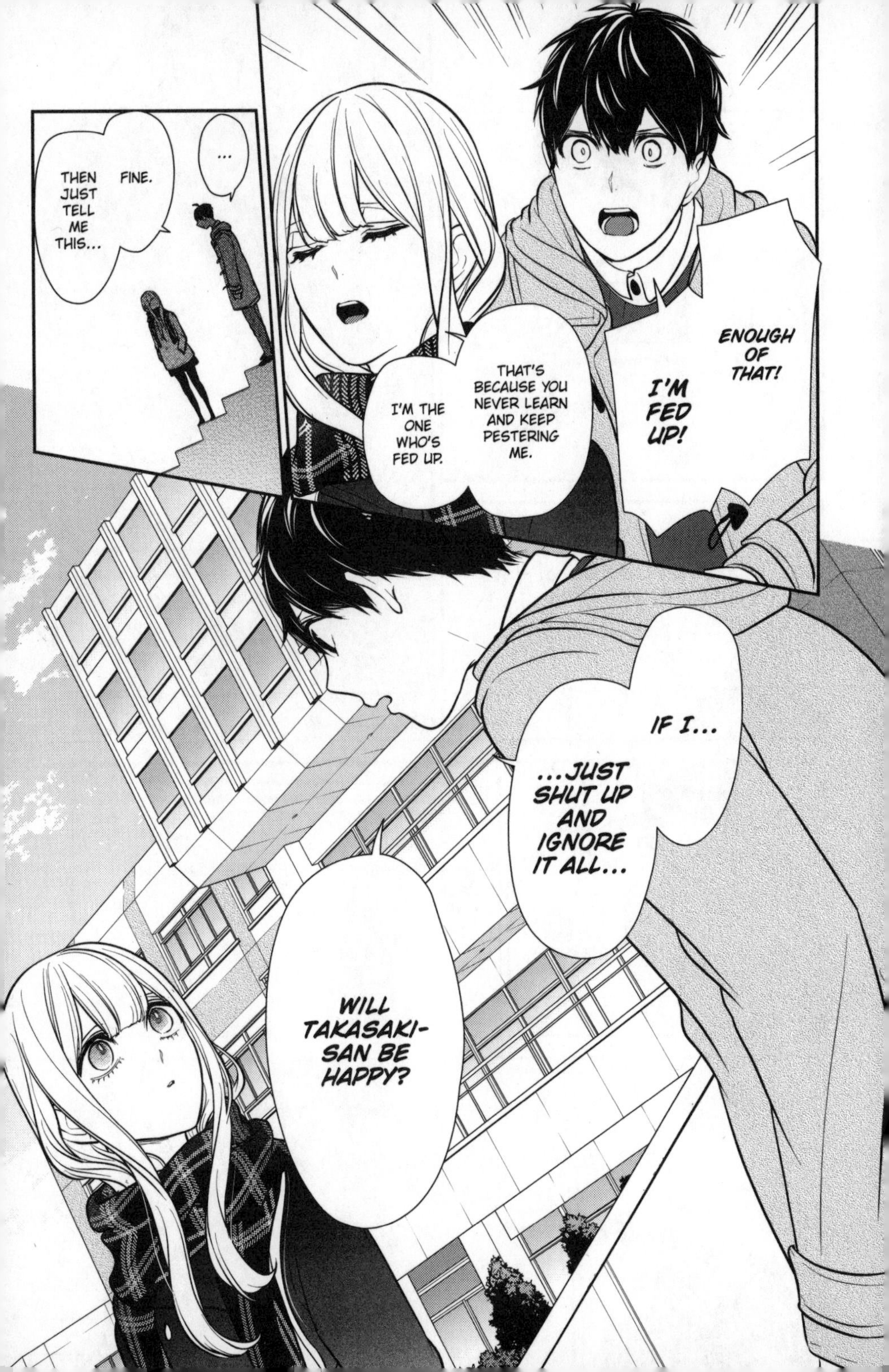
ENOUGH OF THAT!
I'M FED UP!
THAT'S BECAUSE YOU NEVER LEARN AND KEEP PESTERING ME.
I'M THE ONE WHO'S FED UP.
...
FINE.
THEN JUST TELL ME THIS...
IF I...
...JUST SHUT UP AND IGNORE IT ALL...
WILL TAKASAKI-SAN BE HAPPY?

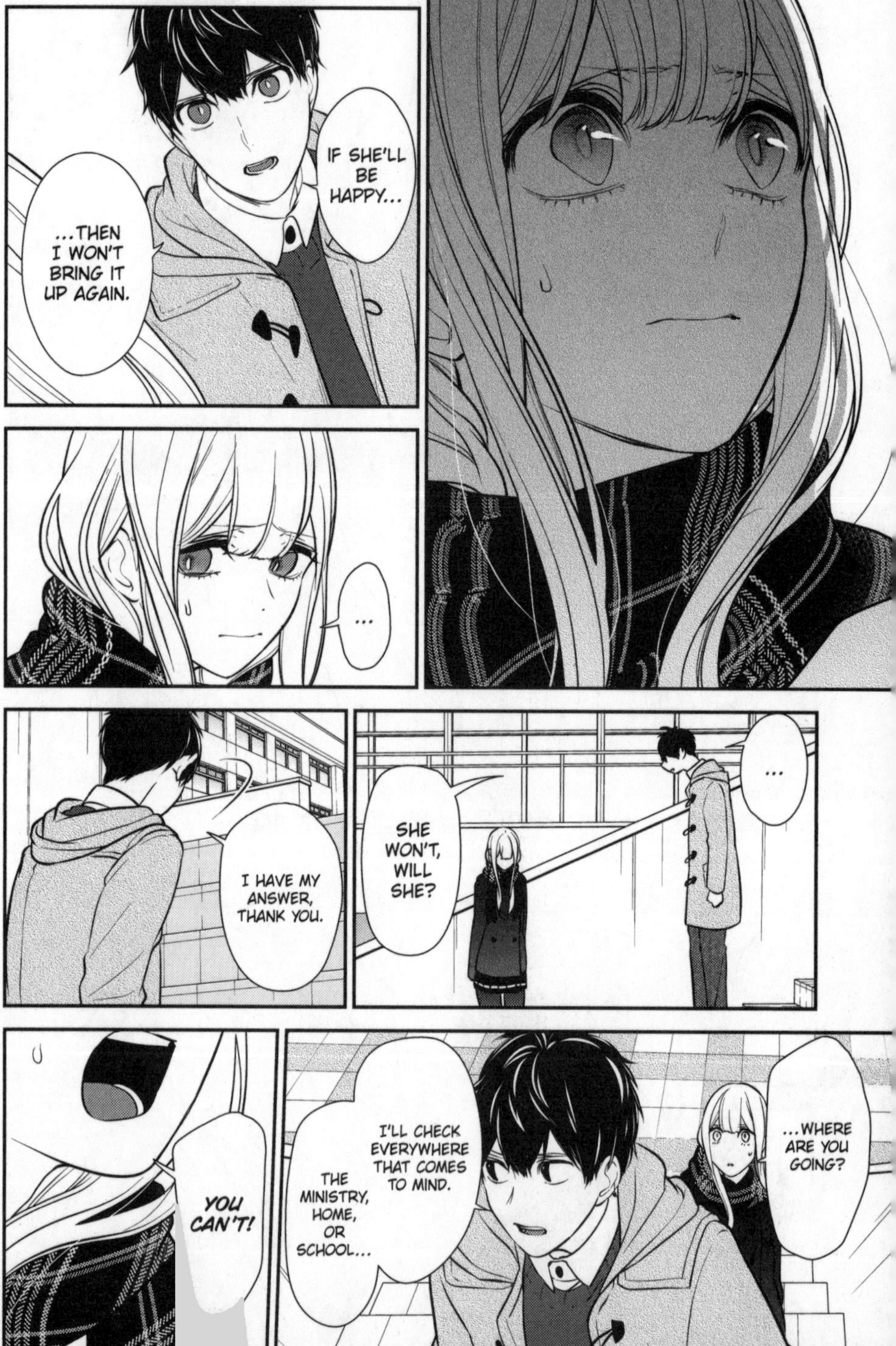
IF SHE'LL BE HAPPY...
...THEN I WON'T BRING IT UP AGAIN.
...
...
SHE WON'T, WILL SHE?
I HAVE MY ANSWER, THANK YOU.
...WHERE ARE YOU GOING?
I'LL CHECK EVERYWHERE THAT COMES TO MIND.
THE MINISTRY, HOME, OR SCHOOL...
YOU CAN'T!

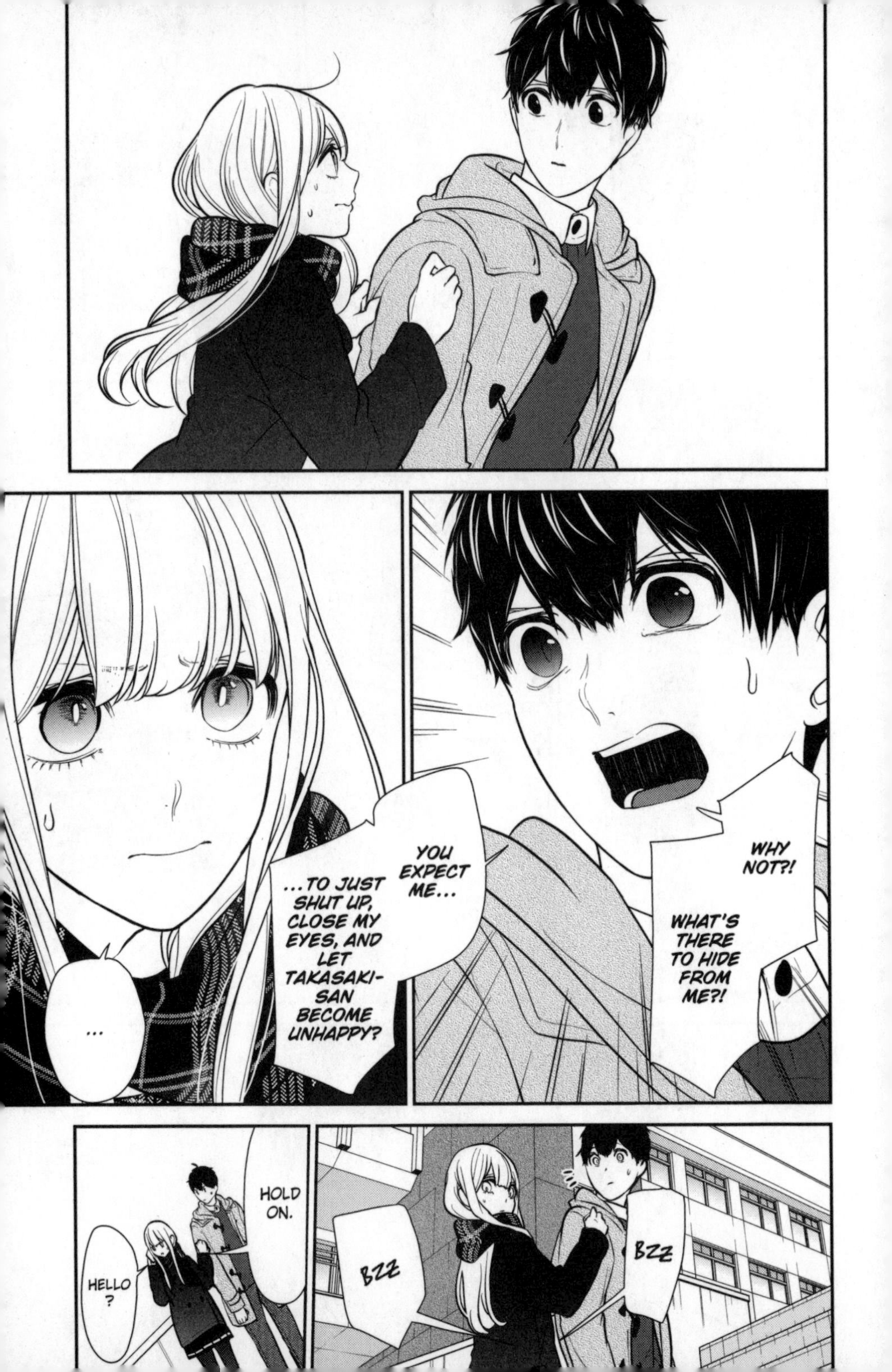
WHY NOT?!
WHAT'S THERE TO HIDE FROM ME?!
YOU EXPECT ME...
...TO JUST SHUT UP, CLOSE MY EYES, AND LET TAKASAKI-SAN BECOME UNHAPPY?
...
BZZ
BZZ
HOLD ON.
HELLO ?

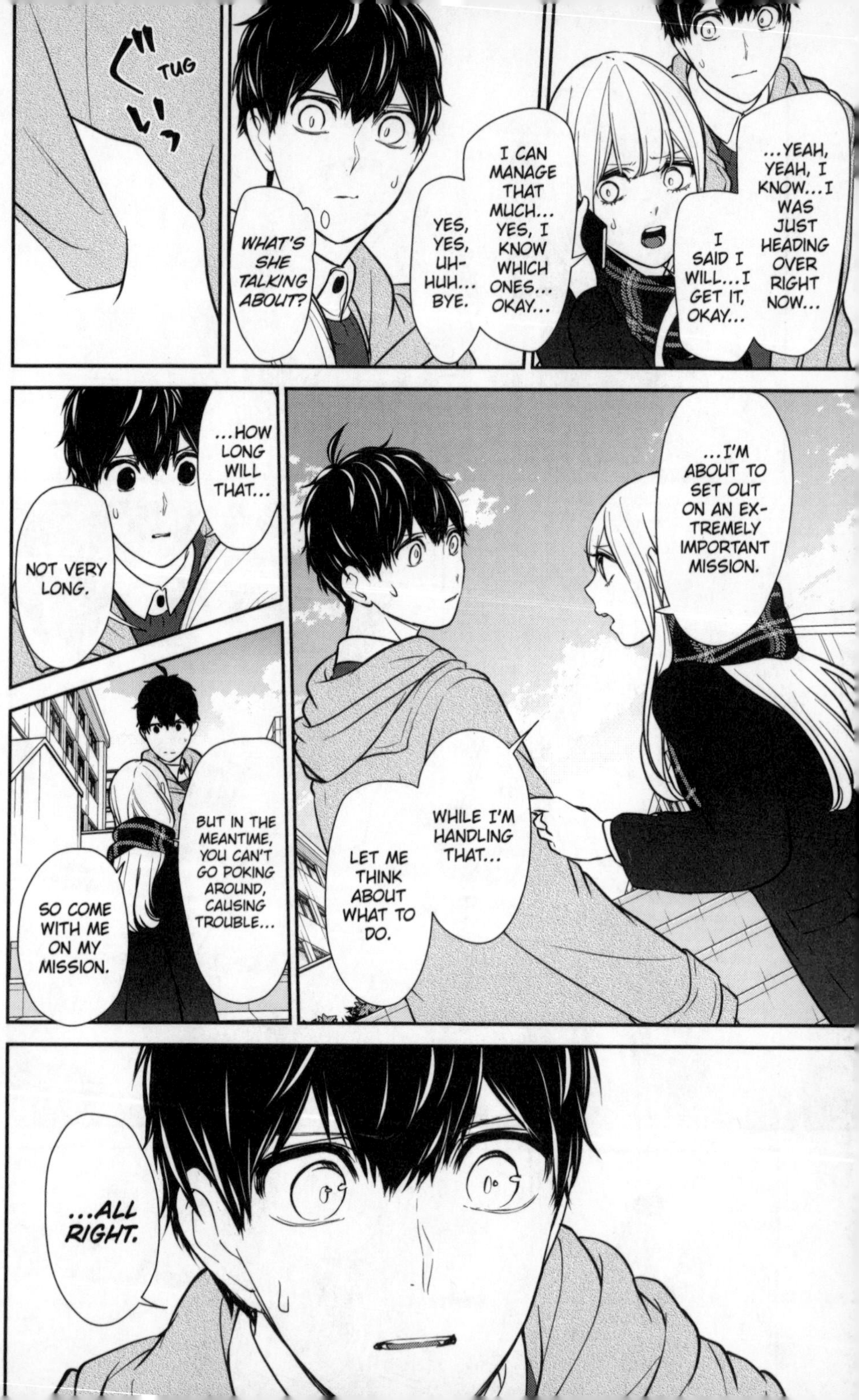
...YEAH, YEAH, I KNOW...I WAS JUST HEADING OVER RIGHT NOW...
I SAID I WILL...I GET IT, OKAY...
I CAN MANAGE THAT MUCH... YES, I KNOW WHICH ONES... OKAY...
YES, YES, UH-HUH... BYE.
WHAT'S SHE TALKING ABOUT?
ぐいっ TUG
...I'M ABOUT TO SET OUT ON AN EXTREMELY IMPORTANT MISSION.
WHILE I'M HANDLING THAT...
LET ME THINK ABOUT WHAT TO DO.
...HOW LONG WILL THAT...
NOT VERY LONG.
BUT IN THE MEANTIME, YOU CAN'T GO POKING AROUND, CAUSING TROUBLE...
SO COME WITH ME ON MY MISSION.
...ALL RIGHT.

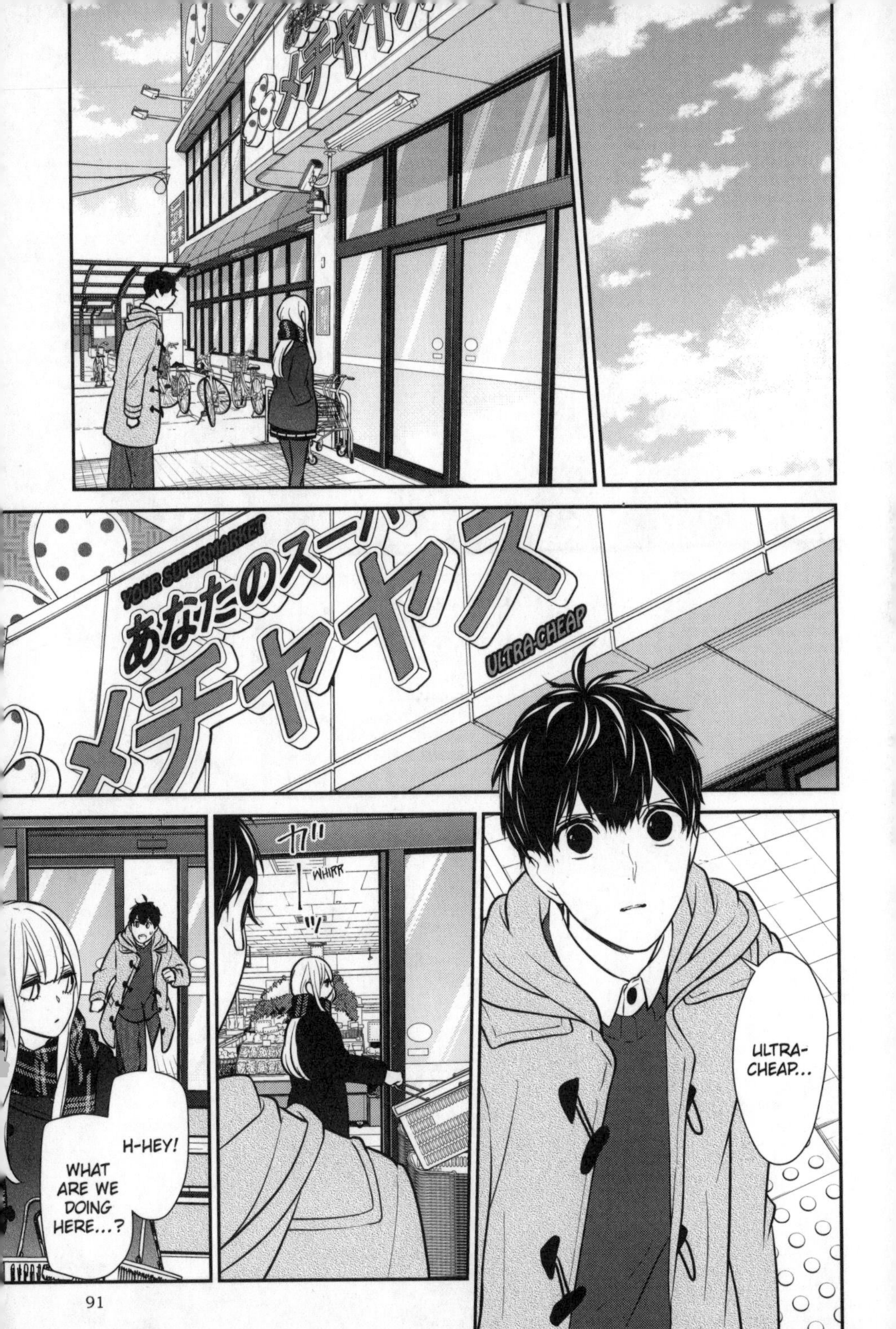
YOUR SUPERMARKET
あなたのスー
チャヤス
ULTRA-CHEAP
ULTRA-CHEAP...
ガ
WHIRR
ツ
H-HEY!
WHAT ARE WE DOING HERE...?

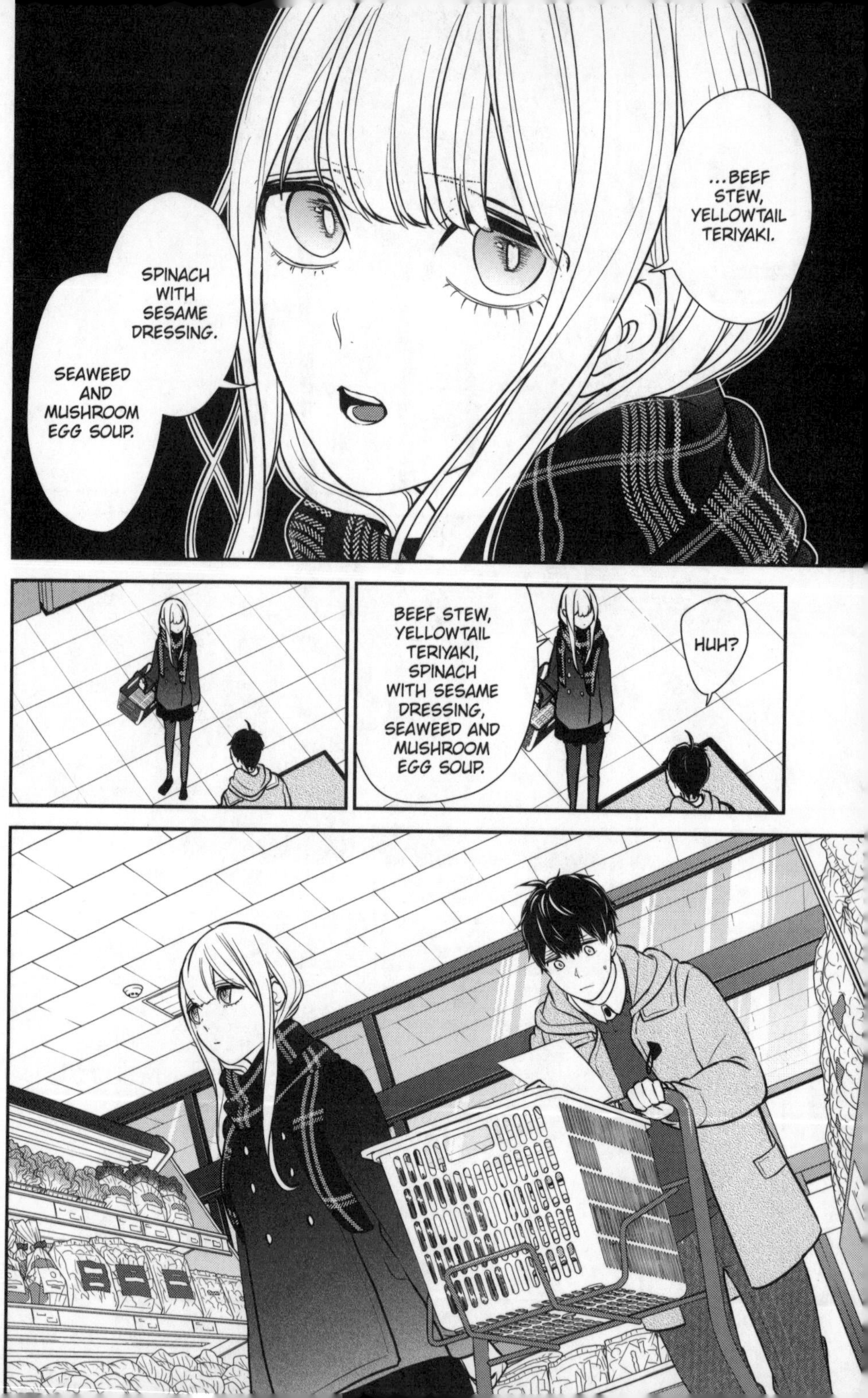
...BEEF STEW, YELLOWTAIL TERIYAKI.
SPINACH WITH SESAME DRESSING.
SEAWEED AND MUSHROOM EGG SOUP.
HUH?
BEEF STEW, YELLOWTAIL TERIYAKI, SPINACH WITH SESAME DRESSING, SEAWEED AND MUSHROOM EGG SOUP.

...MY SCHOOL IS RUN BY RELATIVES OF MINE, AND THE SON OF MY GRANDMOTHER'S OLDER BROTHER IS THE CHAIRMAN...

SO EVEN IF I SKIP OUT A BIT OR DON'T COME TO CLASS, AS LONG AS I PASS THE EXAMS, I CAN GET AWAY WITH IT.

YOUR IMPORTANT MISSION WAS A COOKING ASSIGNMENT?

ISN'T THIS SOMETHING YOU NORMALLY DO WITH A GROUP?

Cooking Assignment: Family Meal

You'll need to buy these ingredients.

| Beef stew | Potatoes |
| | Onions |
| | Carrots |
| | Beef |
| | Soy sauce |
| | cooking sake |
| | sugar |
| | mirin |
| Yellowtail teriyaki | Yellowtail |
| | soy sauce |
| | cooking sake |
| | mirin |
| Spinach with sesame dressing | spinach |
| | ground ses |
| | Soy sauce |
| | sugar |
| Seaweed | wakame |

SHE WAILED ABOUT HOW I WOULDN'T BE A GOOD WIFE, AND SO SHE INSISTED I DO THIS SOLO COOKING ASSIGNMENT TODAY IN ORDER TO PASS.

IT'S A SHAM, BUT I HAVE TO SUCK IT UP.

BUT THE HOME EC TEACHER, MY FIRST COUSIN, TWICE REMOVED, IS VERY OLD-SCHOOL, STUCK IN THE PAST...

MY LACK OF ATTENDANCE IS UNACCEPTABLE TO HER.

...

YOU'RE ACTUALLY SPONGING OFF YOUR FAMILY, HUH?

IGARASHI-SAN...

...

IT'S INCREDIBLY USELESS, WASTEFUL, AND POINTLESS, JUST SPITEFUL.

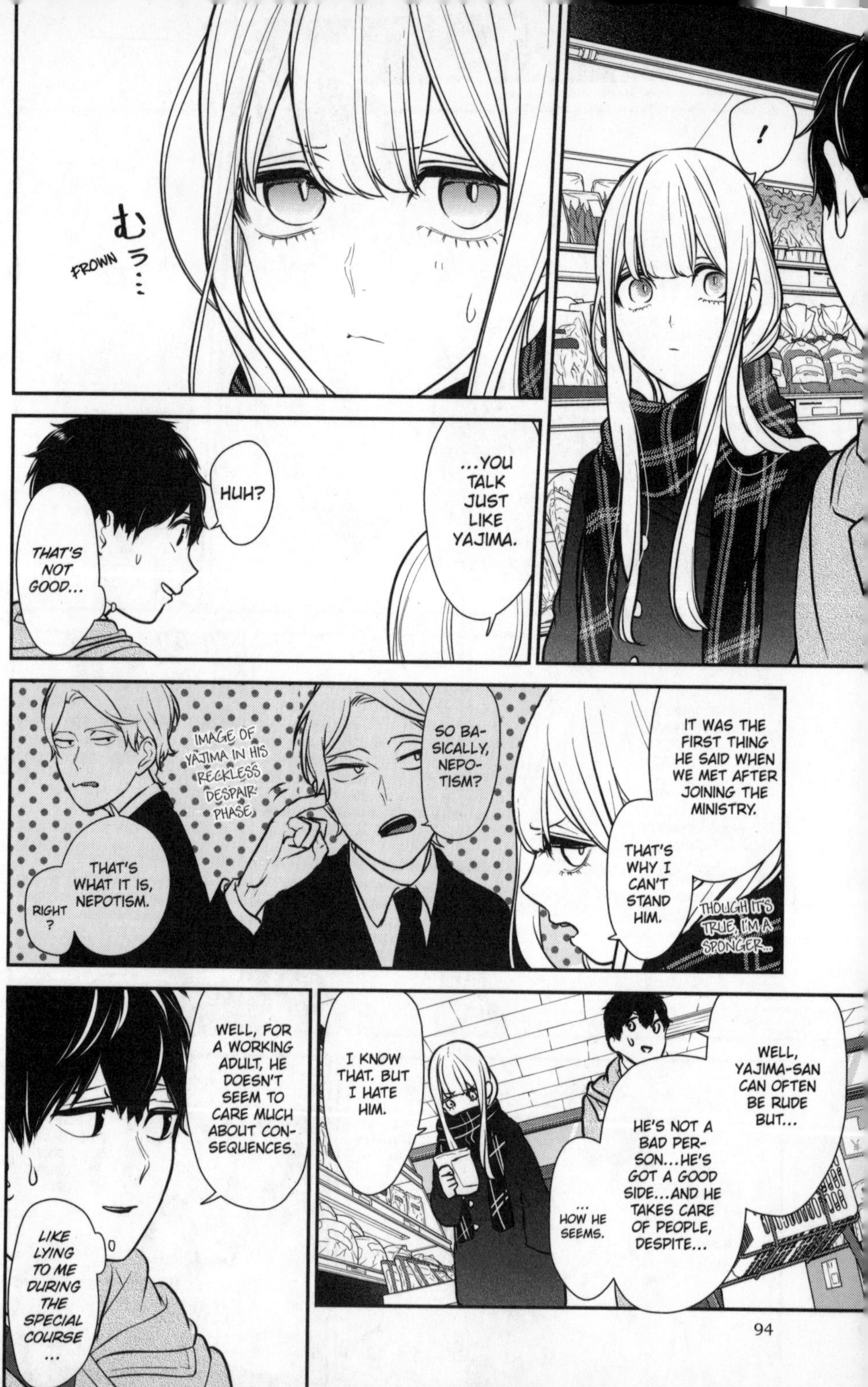

!
むラ…
FROWN
...YOU TALK JUST LIKE YAJIMA.
HUH?
THAT'S NOT GOOD...
IT WAS THE FIRST THING HE SAID WHEN WE MET AFTER JOINING THE MINISTRY.
THAT'S WHY I CAN'T STAND HIM.
THOUGH IT'S TRUE, I'M A SPONGER...
SO BASICALLY, NEPOTISM?
IMAGE OF YAJIMA IN HIS RECKLESS DESPAIR PHASE
THAT'S WHAT IT IS, NEPOTISM.
RIGHT?
WELL, YAJIMA-SAN CAN OFTEN BE RUDE BUT...
HE'S NOT A BAD PERSON...HE'S GOT A GOOD SIDE...AND HE TAKES CARE OF PEOPLE, DESPITE...
...HOW HE SEEMS.
I KNOW THAT. BUT I HATE HIM.
WELL, FOR A WORKING ADULT, HE DOESN'T SEEM TO CARE MUCH ABOUT CONSEQUENCES.
LIKE LYING TO ME DURING THE SPECIAL COURSE...

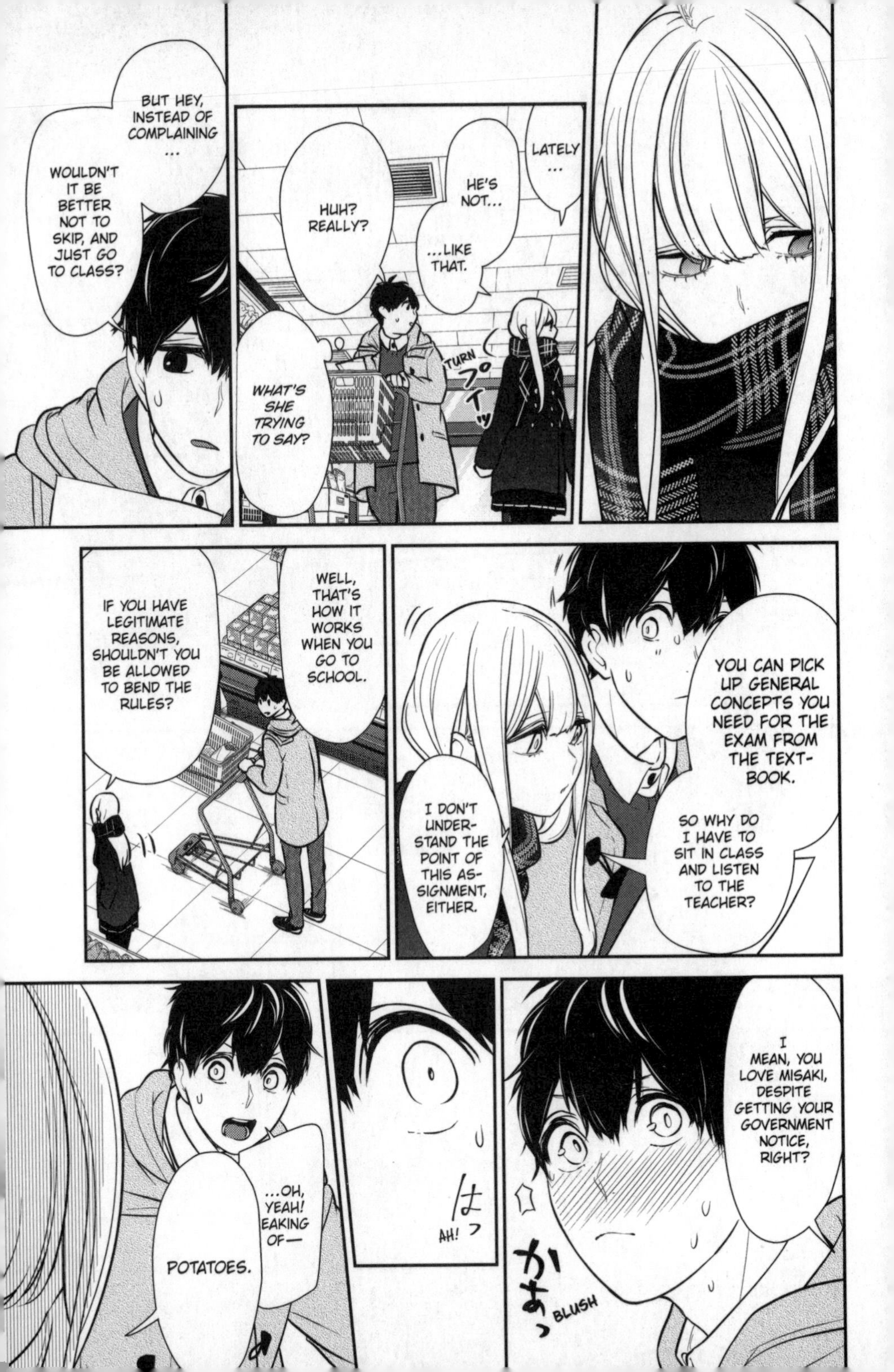

LATELY ...
HE'S NOT...
...LIKE THAT.
HUH? REALLY?
TURN
プイッ
WHAT'S SHE TRYING TO SAY?
BUT HEY, INSTEAD OF COMPLAINING ...
WOULDN'T IT BE BETTER NOT TO SKIP, AND JUST GO TO CLASS?
YOU CAN PICK UP GENERAL CONCEPTS YOU NEED FOR THE EXAM FROM THE TEXT-BOOK.
SO WHY DO I HAVE TO SIT IN CLASS AND LISTEN TO THE TEACHER?
I DON'T UNDER-STAND THE POINT OF THIS AS-SIGNMENT, EITHER.
WELL, THAT'S HOW IT WORKS WHEN YOU GO TO SCHOOL.
IF YOU HAVE LEGITIMATE REASONS, SHOULDN'T YOU BE ALLOWED TO BEND THE RULES?
I MEAN, YOU LOVE MISAKI, DESPITE GETTING YOUR GOVERNMENT NOTICE, RIGHT?
かあっ
BLUSH
はっ
AH!
...OH, YEAH! EAKING OF—
POTATOES.

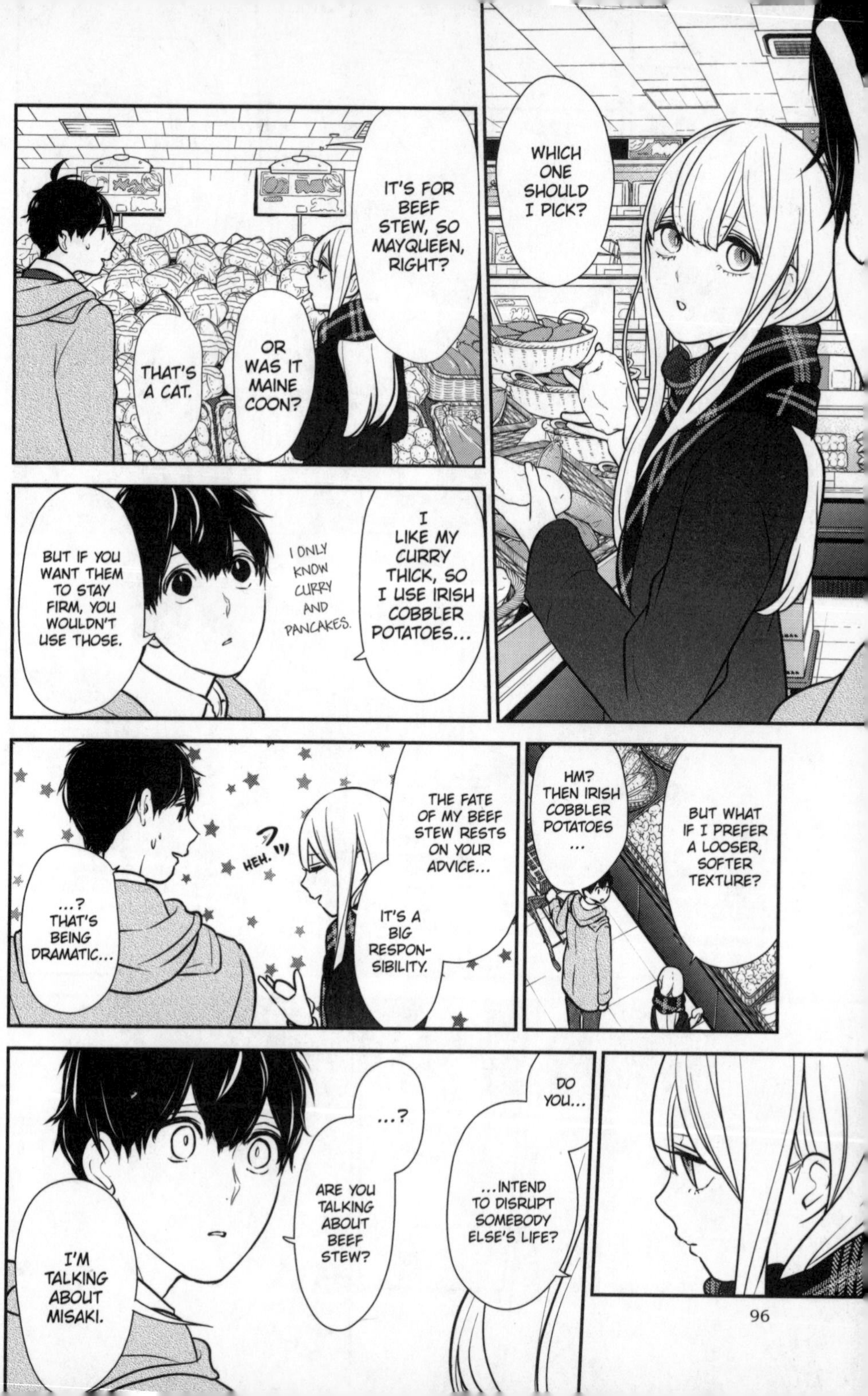
WHICH ONE SHOULD I PICK?
IT'S FOR BEEF STEW, SO MAYQUEEN, RIGHT?
OR WAS IT MAINE COON?
THAT'S A CAT.
I LIKE MY CURRY THICK, SO I USE IRISH COBBLER POTATOES...
I ONLY KNOW CURRY AND PANCAKES.
BUT IF YOU WANT THEM TO STAY FIRM, YOU WOULDN'T USE THOSE.
BUT WHAT IF I PREFER A LOOSER, SOFTER TEXTURE?
HM? THEN IRISH COBBLER POTATOES ...
THE FATE OF MY BEEF STEW RESTS ON YOUR ADVICE...
IT'S A BIG RESPONSIBILITY.
HEH.
...? THAT'S BEING DRAMATIC...
DO YOU...
...INTEND TO DISRUPT SOMEBODY ELSE'S LIFE?
...?
ARE YOU TALKING ABOUT BEEF STEW?
I'M TALKING ABOUT MISAKI.

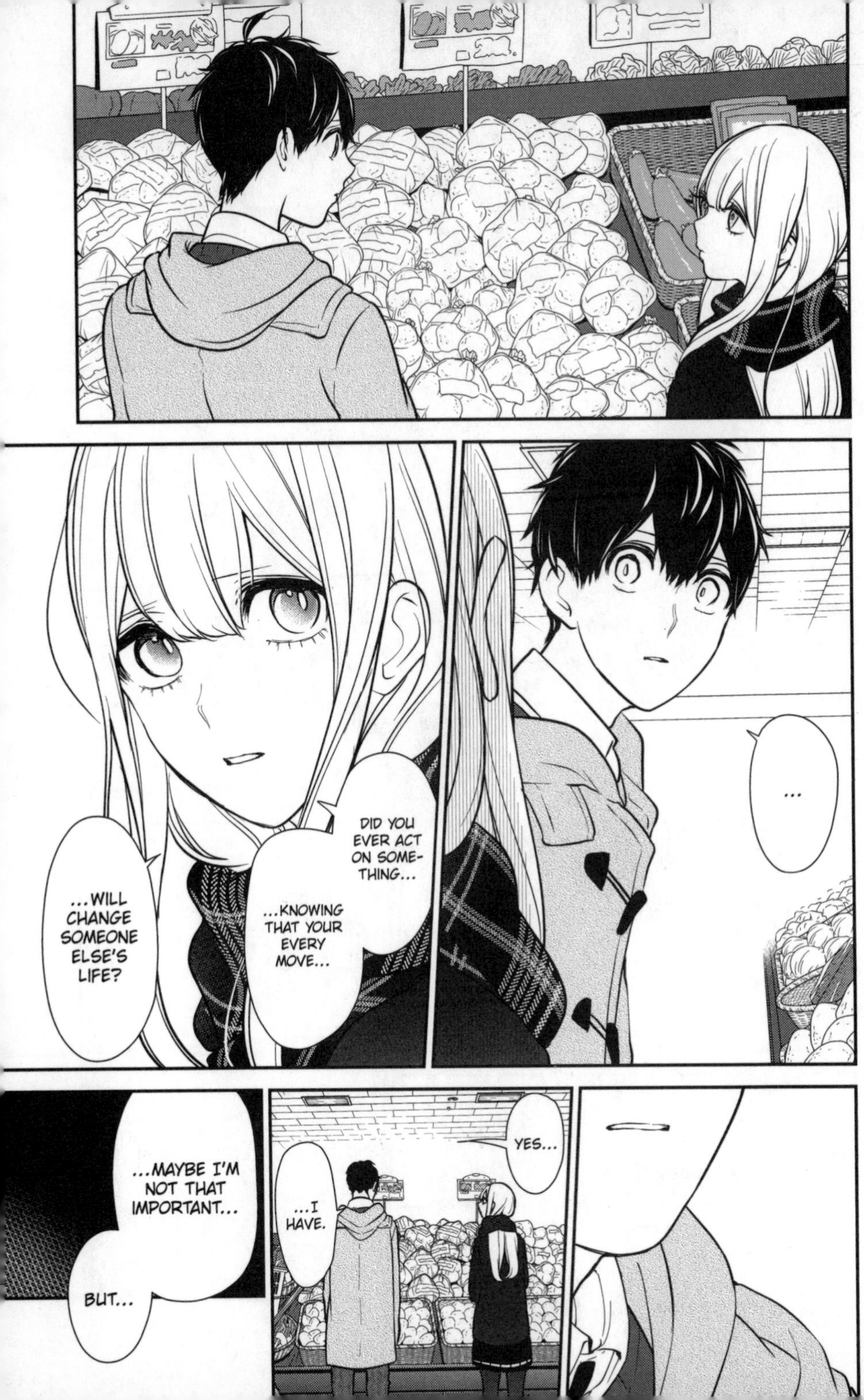
...
DID YOU EVER ACT ON SOME-THING...
...KNOWING THAT YOUR EVERY MOVE...
...WILL CHANGE SOMEONE ELSE'S LIFE?
—
YES...
...I HAVE.
...MAYBE I'M NOT THAT IMPORTANT...
BUT...

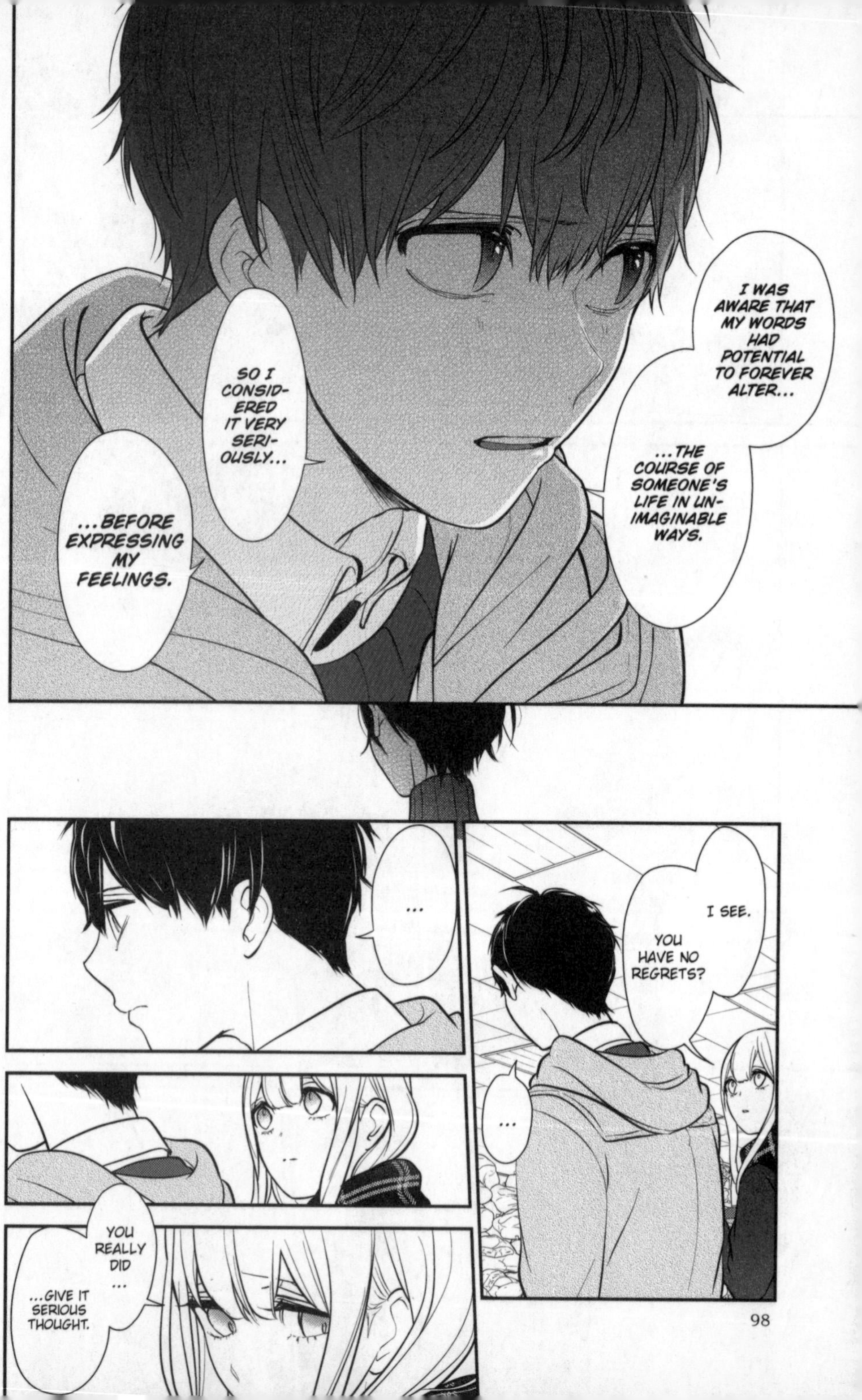
I WAS AWARE THAT MY WORDS HAD POTENTIAL TO FOREVER ALTER...
...THE COURSE OF SOMEONE'S LIFE IN UNIMAGINABLE WAYS.
SO I CONSIDERED IT VERY SERIOUSLY...
...BEFORE EXPRESSING MY FEELINGS.
I SEE.
YOU HAVE NO REGRETS?
...
...
...
YOU REALLY DID ...
...GIVE IT SERIOUS THOUGHT.

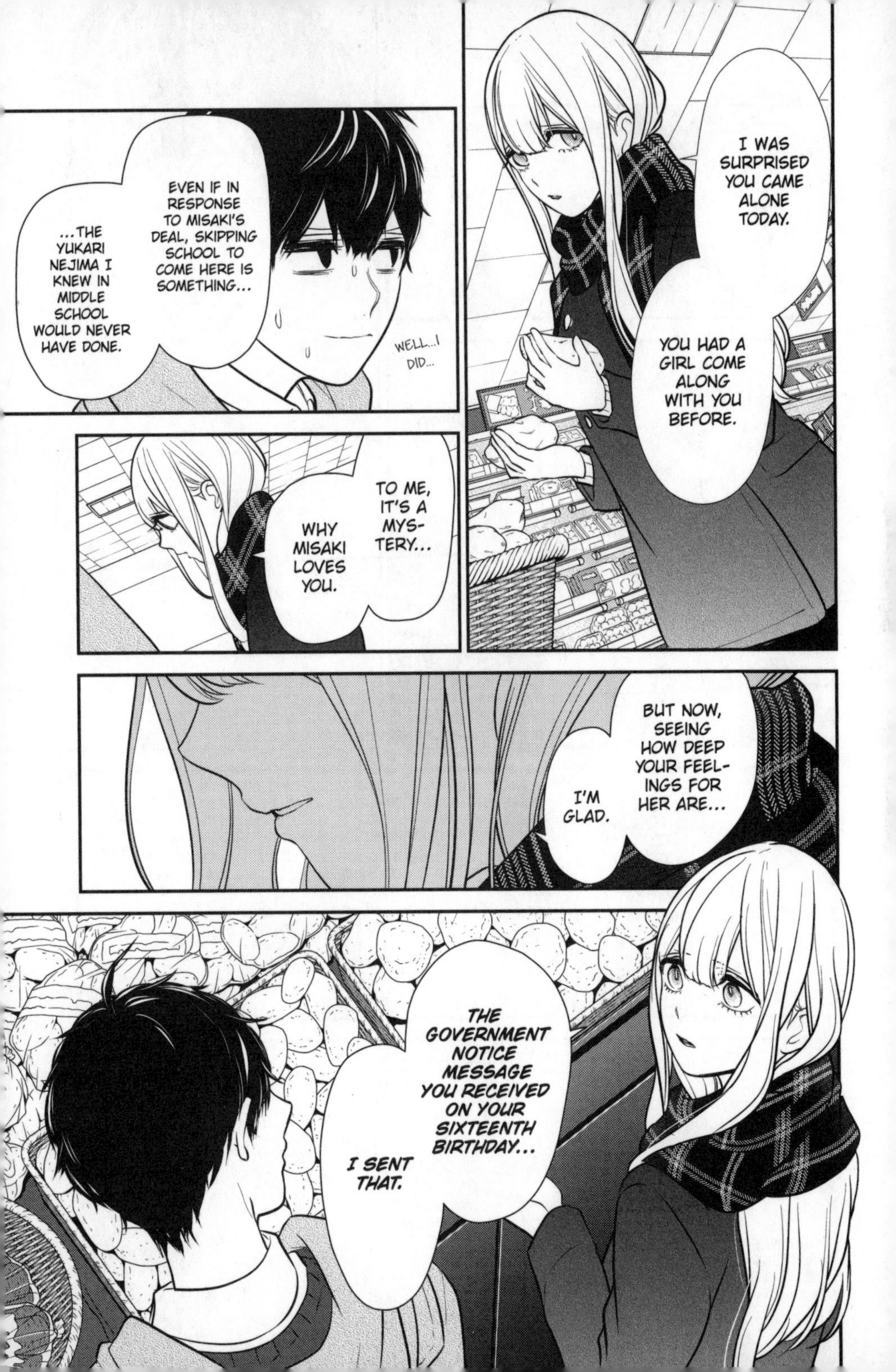
I WAS SURPRISED YOU CAME ALONE TODAY.
YOU HAD A GIRL COME ALONG WITH YOU BEFORE.
EVEN IF IN RESPONSE TO MISAKI'S DEAL, SKIPPING SCHOOL TO COME HERE IS SOMETHING...
...THE YUKARI NEJIMA I KNEW IN MIDDLE SCHOOL WOULD NEVER HAVE DONE.
WELL...I DID...
TO ME, IT'S A MYSTERY...
WHY MISAKI LOVES YOU.
BUT NOW, SEEING HOW DEEP YOUR FEELINGS FOR HER ARE...
I'M GLAD.
THE GOVERNMENT NOTICE MESSAGE YOU RECEIVED ON YOUR SIXTEENTH BIRTHDAY...
I SENT THAT.

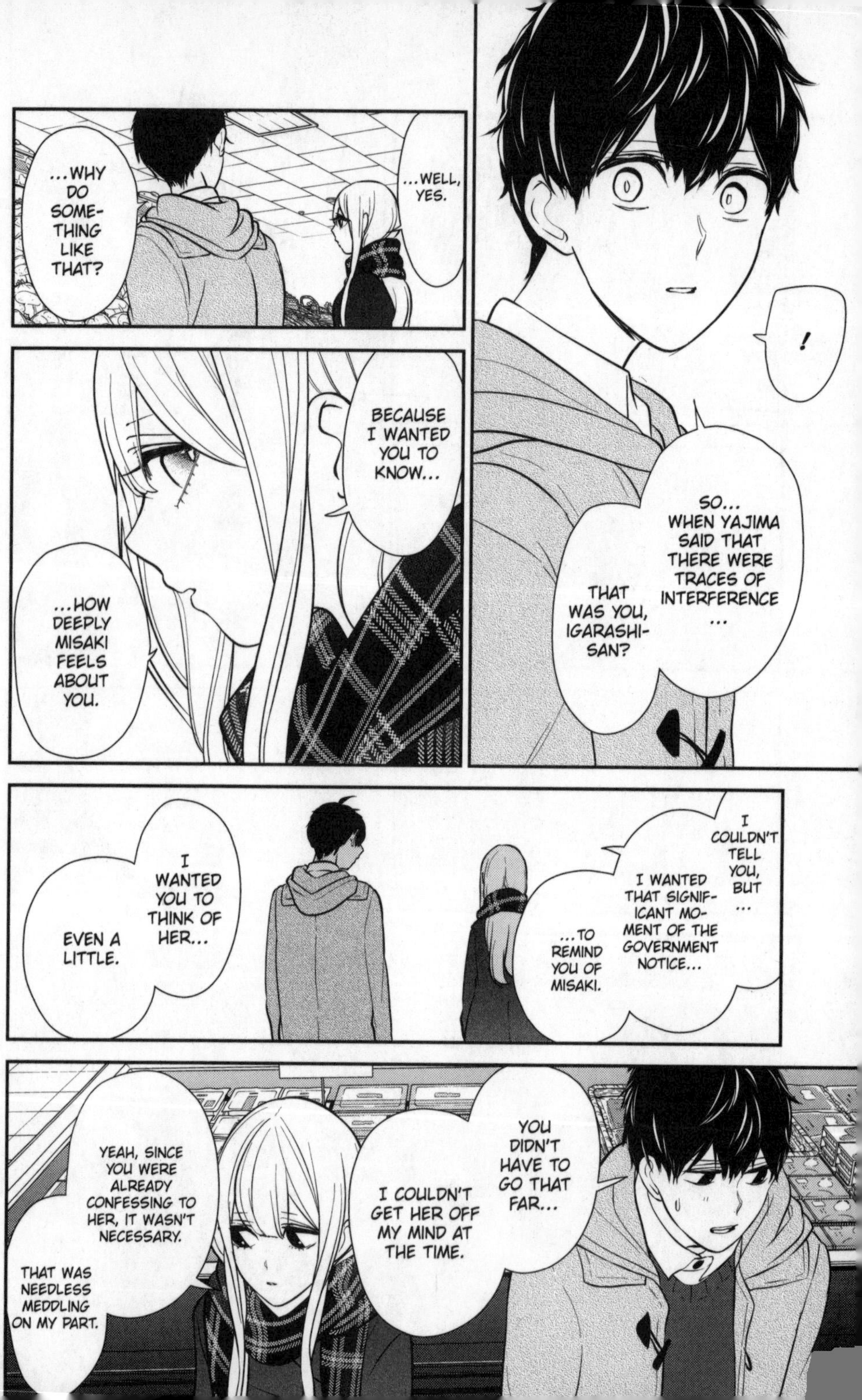
!
SO... WHEN YAJIMA SAID THAT THERE WERE TRACES OF INTERFERENCE...
THAT WAS YOU, IGARASHI-SAN?
...WELL, YES.
...WHY DO SOME-THING LIKE THAT?
BECAUSE I WANTED YOU TO KNOW...
...HOW DEEPLY MISAKI FEELS ABOUT YOU.
I COULDN'T TELL YOU, BUT...
I WANTED THAT SIGNIF-ICANT MO-MENT OF THE GOVERNMENT NOTICE...
...TO REMIND YOU OF MISAKI.
I WANTED YOU TO THINK OF HER...
EVEN A LITTLE.
YOU DIDN'T HAVE TO GO THAT FAR...
I COULDN'T GET HER OFF MY MIND AT THE TIME.
YEAH, SINCE YOU WERE ALREADY CONFESSING TO HER, IT WASN'T NECESSARY.
THAT WAS NEEDLESS MEDDLING ON MY PART.

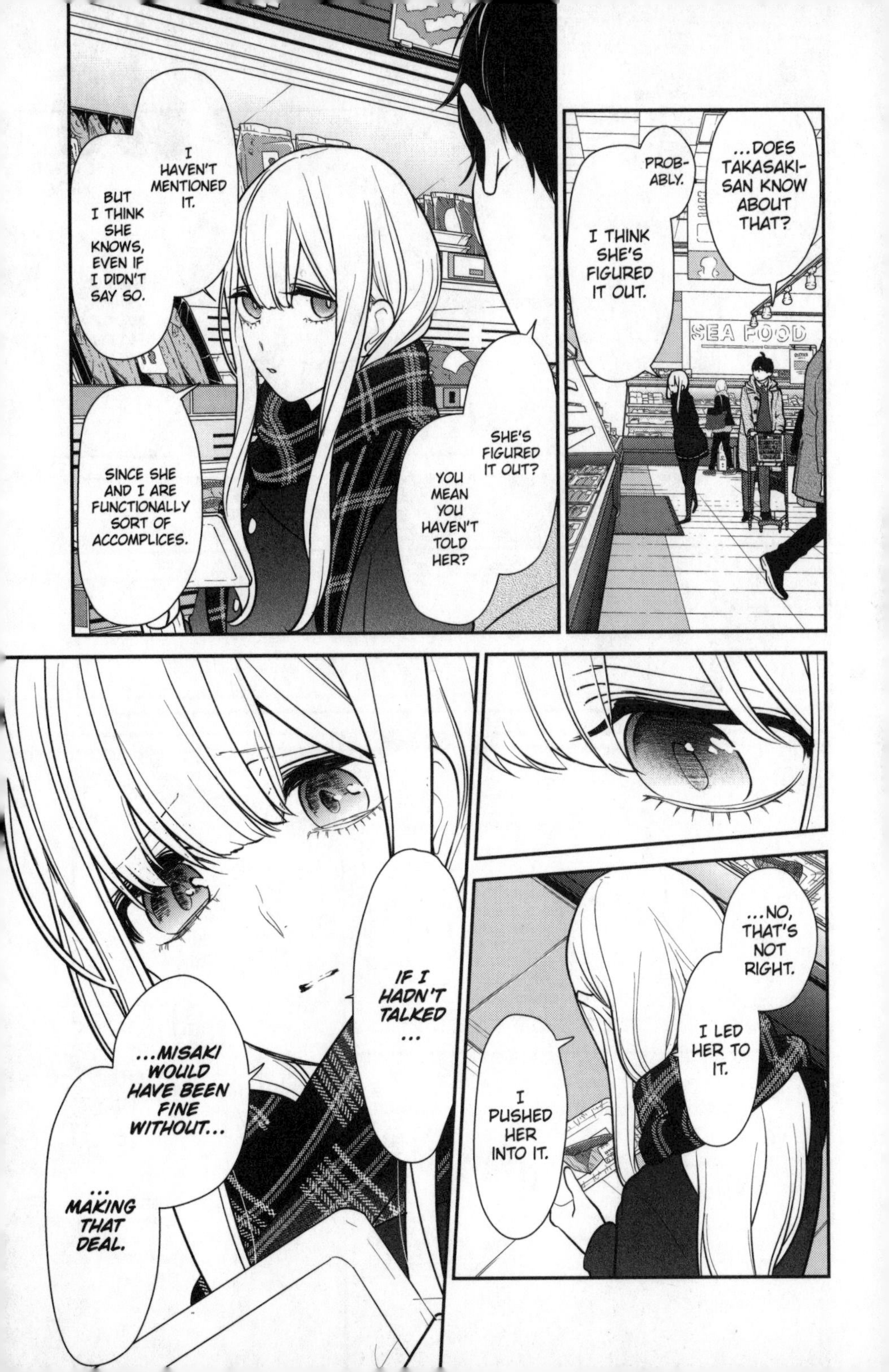
...DOES TAKASAKI-SAN KNOW ABOUT THAT?
PROB-ABLY.
I THINK SHE'S FIGURED IT OUT.
SHE'S FIGURED IT OUT?
YOU MEAN YOU HAVEN'T TOLD HER?
I HAVEN'T MENTIONED IT.
BUT I THINK SHE KNOWS, EVEN IF I DIDN'T SAY SO.
SINCE SHE AND I ARE FUNCTIONALLY SORT OF ACCOMPLICES.
SEA FOOD
...NO, THAT'S NOT RIGHT.
I LED HER TO IT.
I PUSHED HER INTO IT.
IF I HADN'T TALKED...
...MISAKI WOULD HAVE BEEN FINE WITHOUT...
...MAKING THAT DEAL.

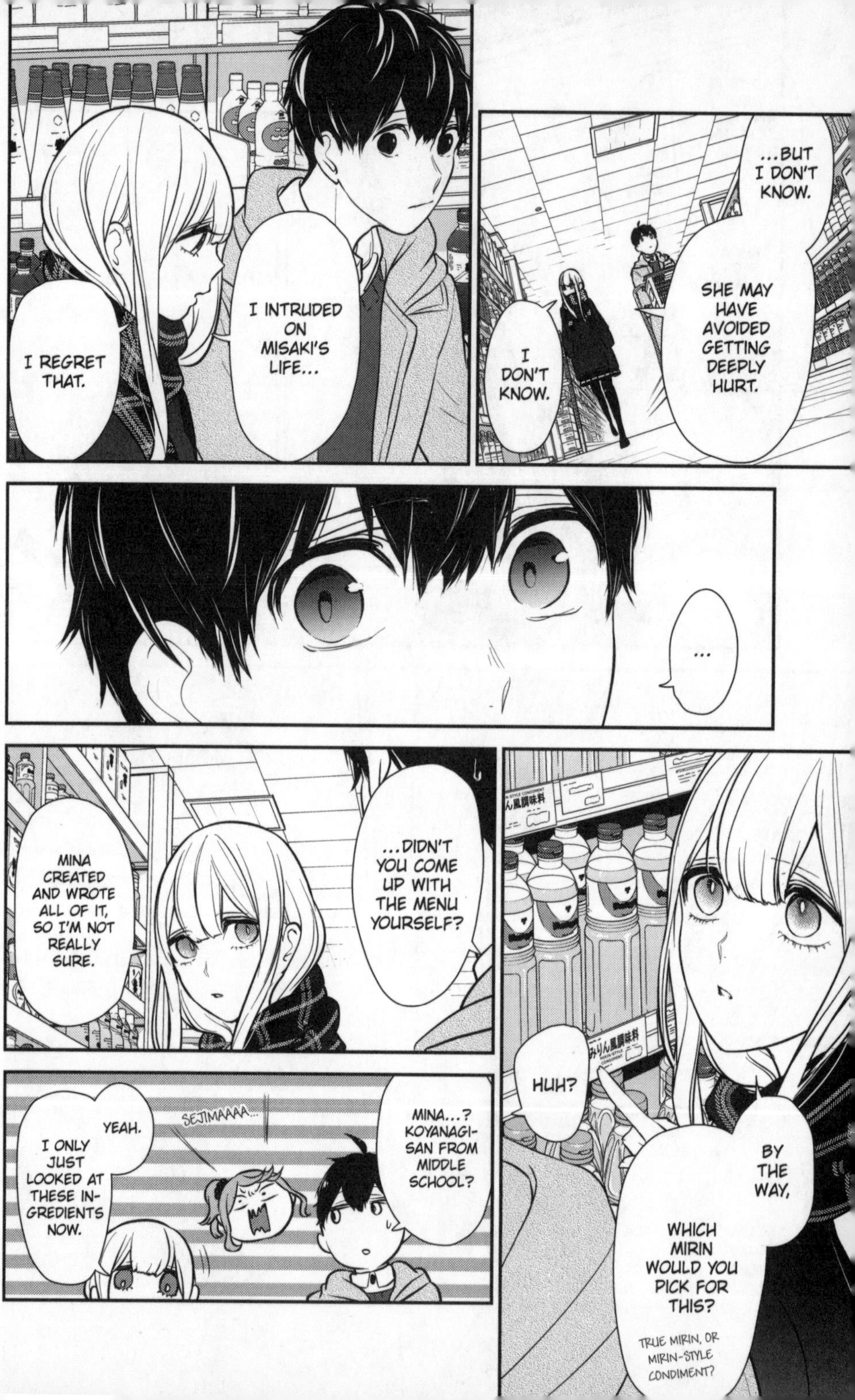
...BUT I DON'T KNOW.
SHE MAY HAVE AVOIDED GETTING DEEPLY HURT.
I DON'T KNOW.
I INTRUDED ON MISAKI'S LIFE...
I REGRET THAT.
...
BY THE WAY,
WHICH MIRIN WOULD YOU PICK FOR THIS?
TRUE MIRIN, OR MIRIN-STYLE CONDIMENT?
HUH?
...DIDN'T YOU COME UP WITH THE MENU YOURSELF?
MINA CREATED AND WROTE ALL OF IT, SO I'M NOT REALLY SURE.
MINA...? KOYANAGI-SAN FROM MIDDLE SCHOOL?
SEJIMAAAA...
YEAH.
I ONLY JUST LOOKED AT THESE IN-GREDIENTS NOW.

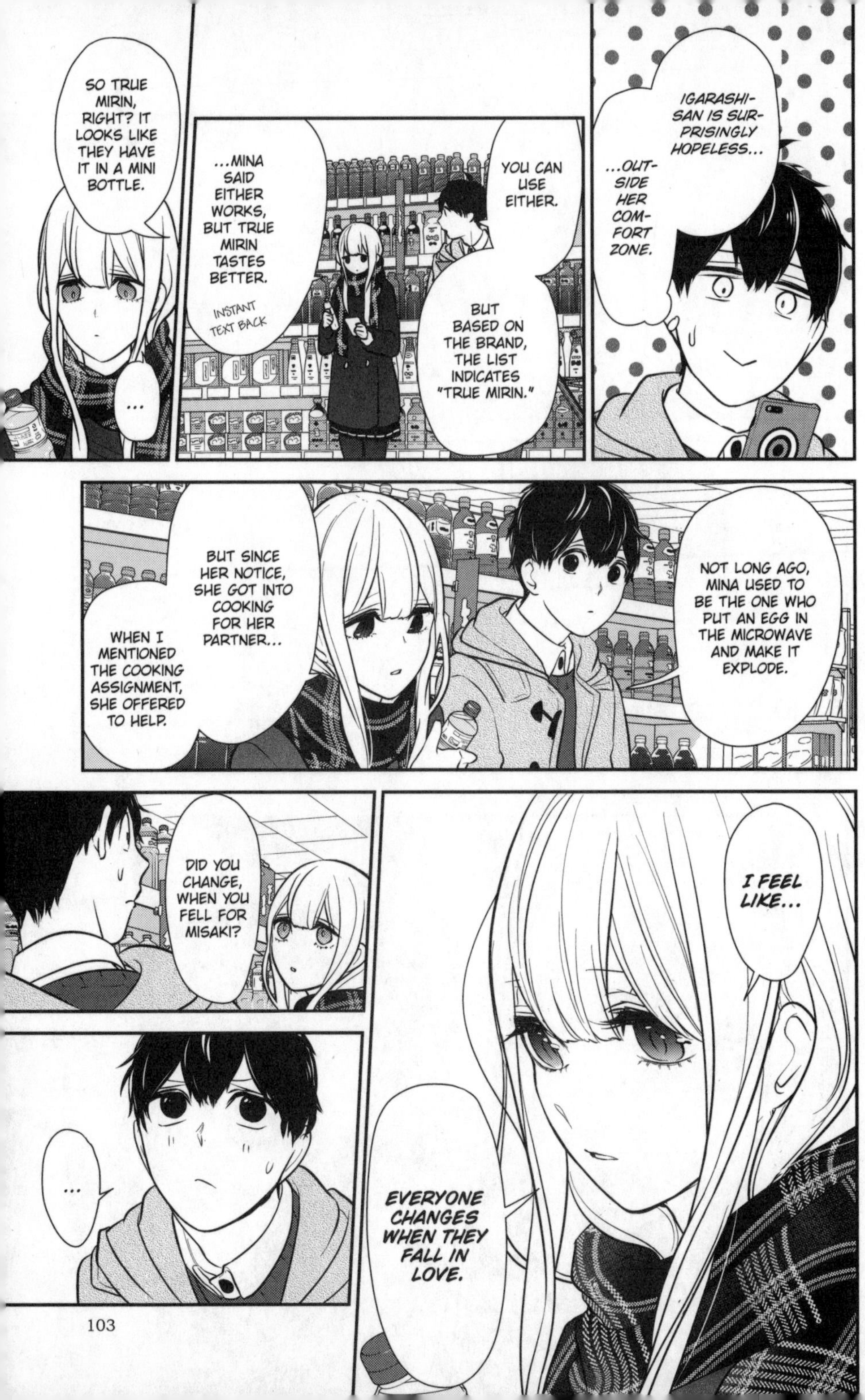
IGARASHI-SAN IS SURPRISINGLY HOPELESS...
...OUTSIDE HER COMFORT ZONE.
YOU CAN USE EITHER.
BUT BASED ON THE BRAND, THE LIST INDICATES "TRUE MIRIN."
...MINA SAID EITHER WORKS, BUT TRUE MIRIN TASTES BETTER.
INSTANT TEXT BACK
SO TRUE MIRIN, RIGHT? IT LOOKS LIKE THEY HAVE IT IN A MINI BOTTLE.
...
NOT LONG AGO, MINA USED TO BE THE ONE WHO PUT AN EGG IN THE MICROWAVE AND MAKE IT EXPLODE.
BUT SINCE HER NOTICE, SHE GOT INTO COOKING FOR HER PARTNER...
WHEN I MENTIONED THE COOKING ASSIGNMENT, SHE OFFERED TO HELP.
I FEEL LIKE...
EVERYONE CHANGES WHEN THEY FALL IN LOVE.
DID YOU CHANGE, WHEN YOU FELL FOR MISAKI?
...

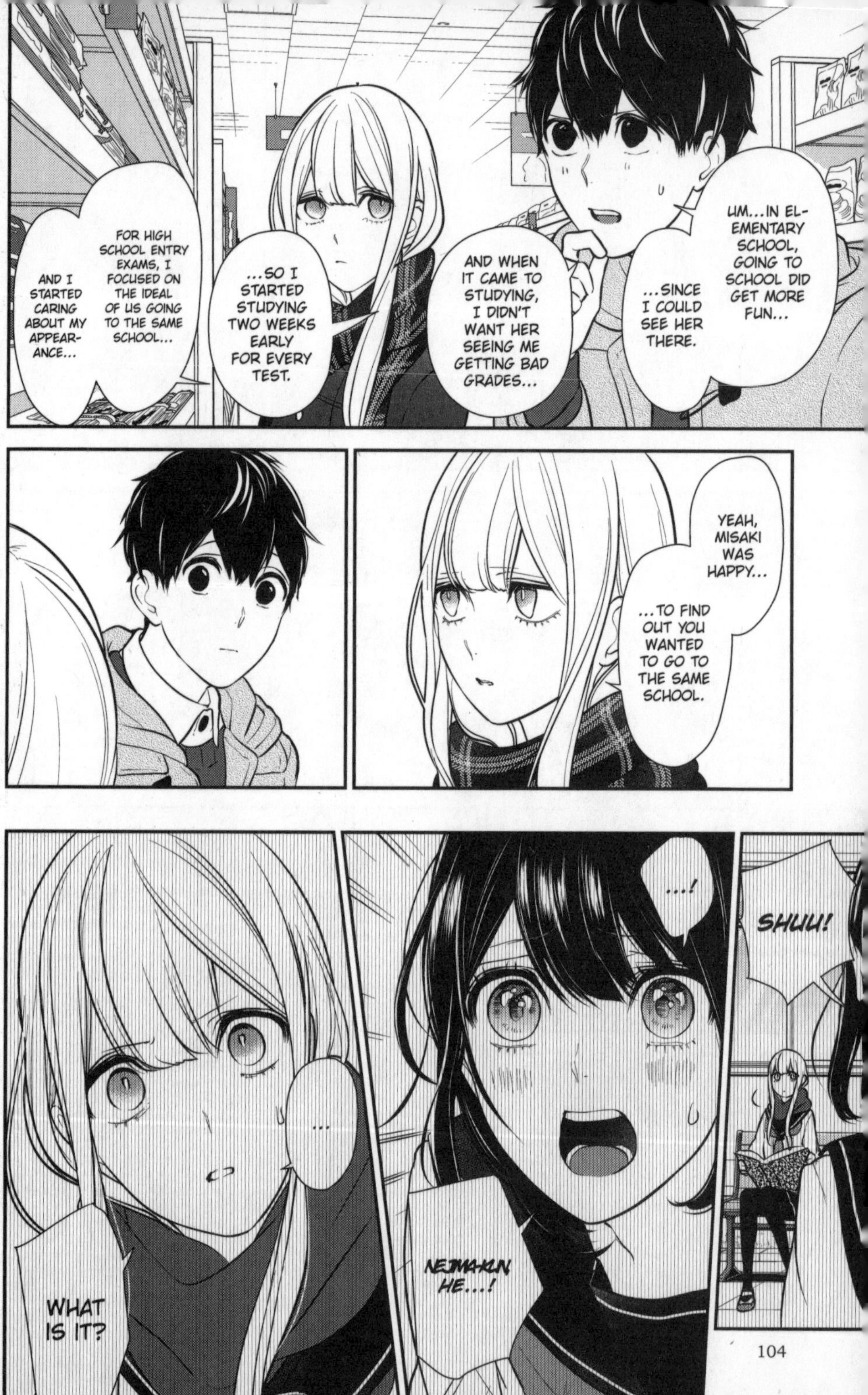
UM...IN ELEMENTARY SCHOOL, GOING TO SCHOOL DID GET MORE FUN...
...SINCE I COULD SEE HER THERE.
AND WHEN IT CAME TO STUDYING, I DIDN'T WANT HER SEEING ME GETTING BAD GRADES...
...SO I STARTED STUDYING TWO WEEKS EARLY FOR EVERY TEST.
FOR HIGH SCHOOL ENTRY EXAMS, I FOCUSED ON THE IDEAL OF US GOING TO THE SAME SCHOOL...
AND I STARTED CARING ABOUT MY APPEARANCE...
YEAH, MISAKI WAS HAPPY...
...TO FIND OUT YOU WANTED TO GO TO THE SAME SCHOOL.
SHUU!
...!
NEJIMA-KUN HE...!
...
WHAT IS IT?

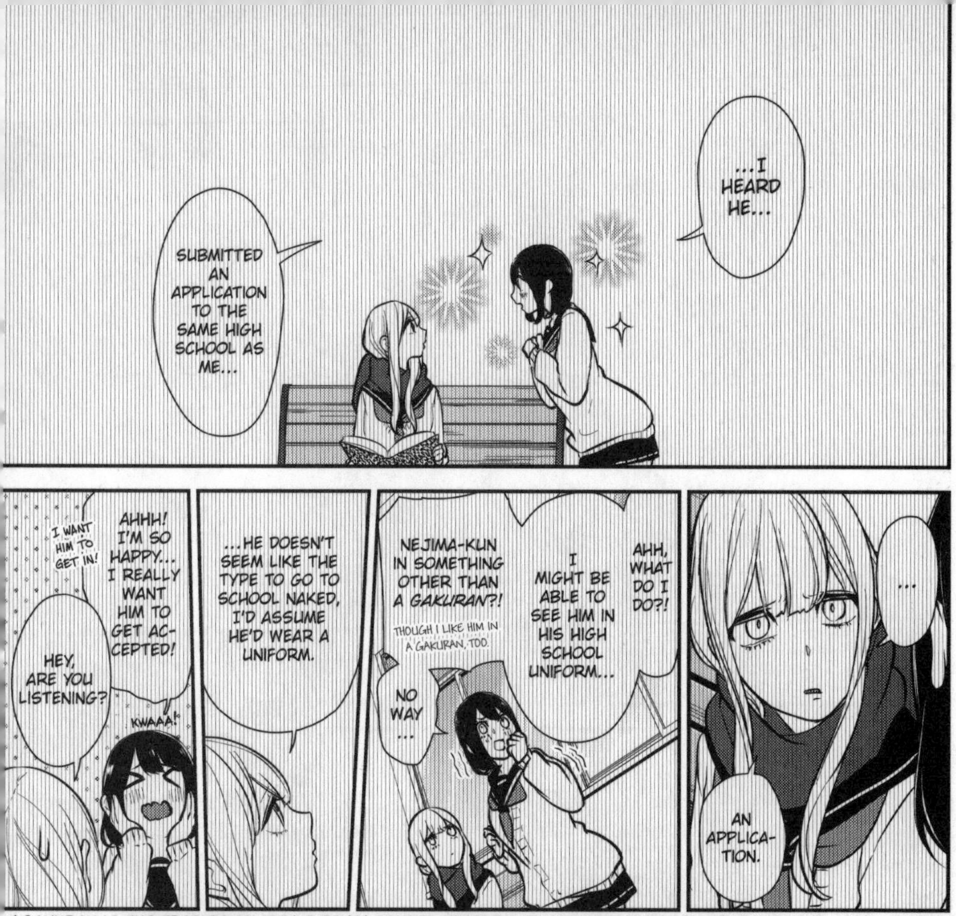
...I HEARD HE...
SUBMITTED AN APPLICATION TO THE SAME HIGH SCHOOL AS ME...
...
AN APPLICATION.
AHH, WHAT DO I DO?!
I MIGHT BE ABLE TO SEE HIM IN HIS HIGH SCHOOL UNIFORM...
NEJIMA-KUN IN SOMETHING OTHER THAN A GAKURAN?!
THOUGH I LIKE HIM IN A GAKURAN, TOO.
NO WAY...
...HE DOESN'T SEEM LIKE THE TYPE TO GO TO SCHOOL NAKED, I'D ASSUME HE'D WEAR A UNIFORM.
AHHH! I'M SO HAPPY... I REALLY WANT HIM TO GET ACCEPTED!
I WANT HIM TO GET IN!
HEY, ARE YOU LISTENING?
KWAAA!

*GAKURAN IS THE TRADITIONAL STYLE BOYS' SCHOOL UNIFORM, BLACK WITH HIGH COLLAR AND ROUND, METAL BUTTONS.

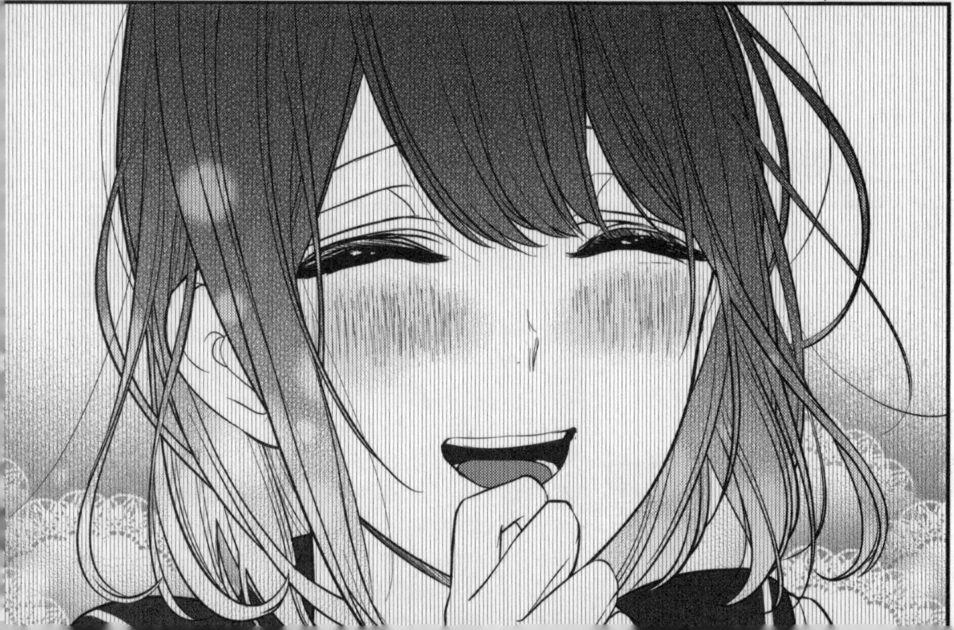

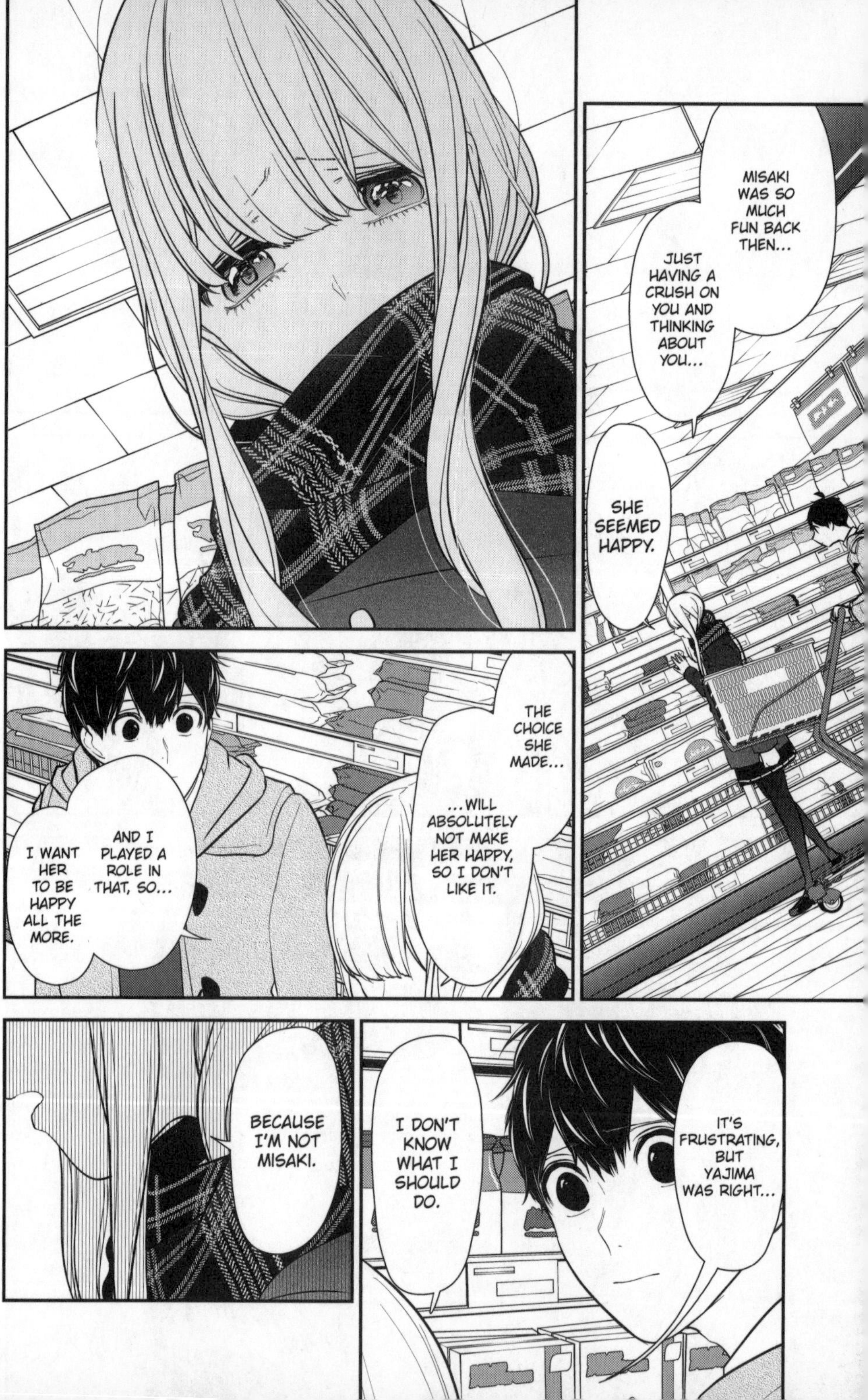
MISAKI WAS SO MUCH FUN BACK THEN…
JUST HAVING A CRUSH ON YOU AND THINKING ABOUT YOU…
SHE SEEMED HAPPY.
THE CHOICE SHE MADE…
…WILL ABSOLUTELY NOT MAKE HER HAPPY, SO I DON'T LIKE IT.
AND I PLAYED A ROLE IN THAT, SO…
I WANT HER TO BE HAPPY ALL THE MORE.
IT'S FRUSTRATING, BUT YAJIMA WAS RIGHT…
I DON'T KNOW WHAT I SHOULD DO.
BECAUSE I'M NOT MISAKI.

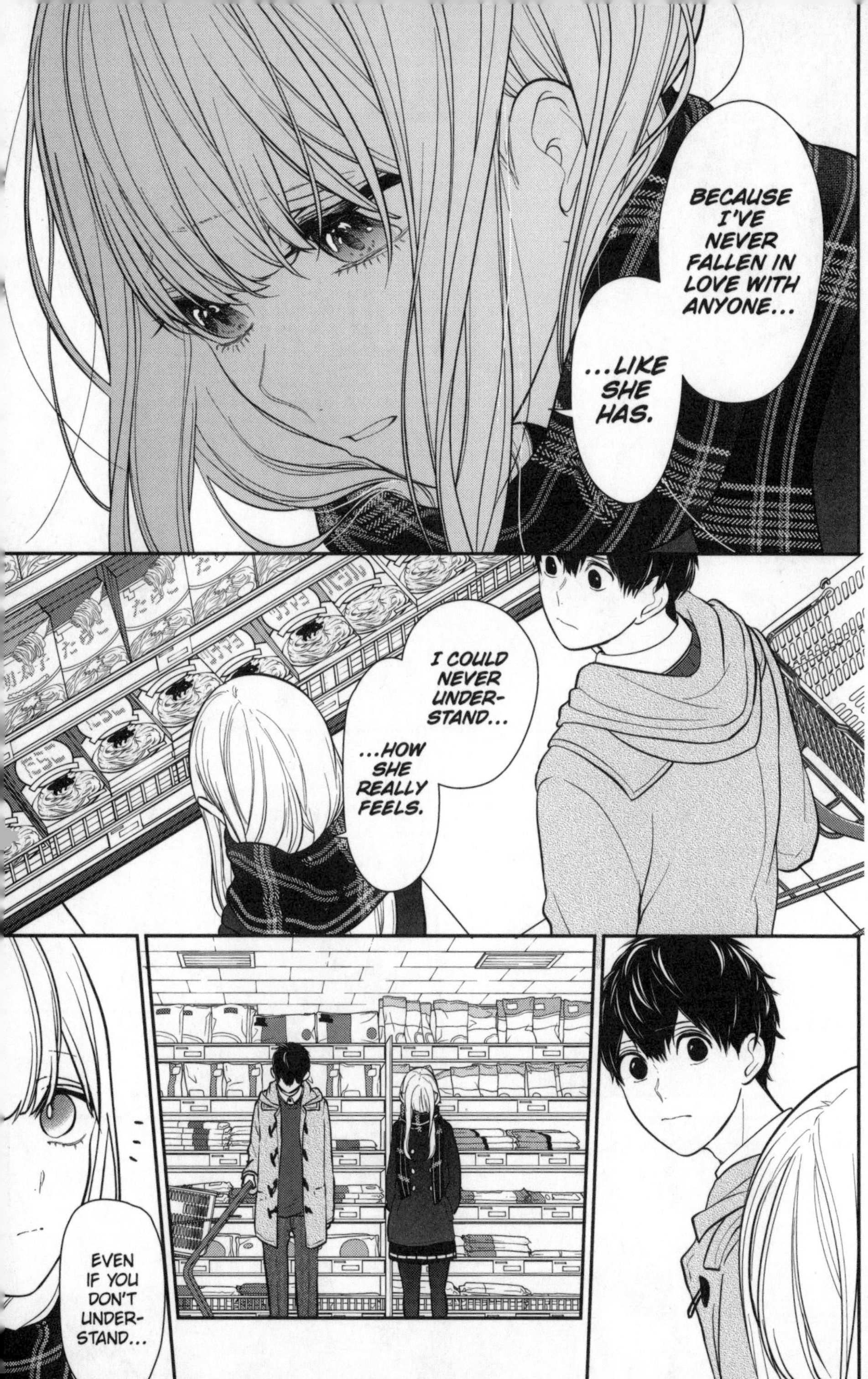
BECAUSE I'VE NEVER FALLEN IN LOVE WITH ANYONE...
...LIKE SHE HAS.
I COULD NEVER UNDER-STAND...
...HOW SHE REALLY FEELS.
EVEN IF YOU DON'T UNDER-STAND...

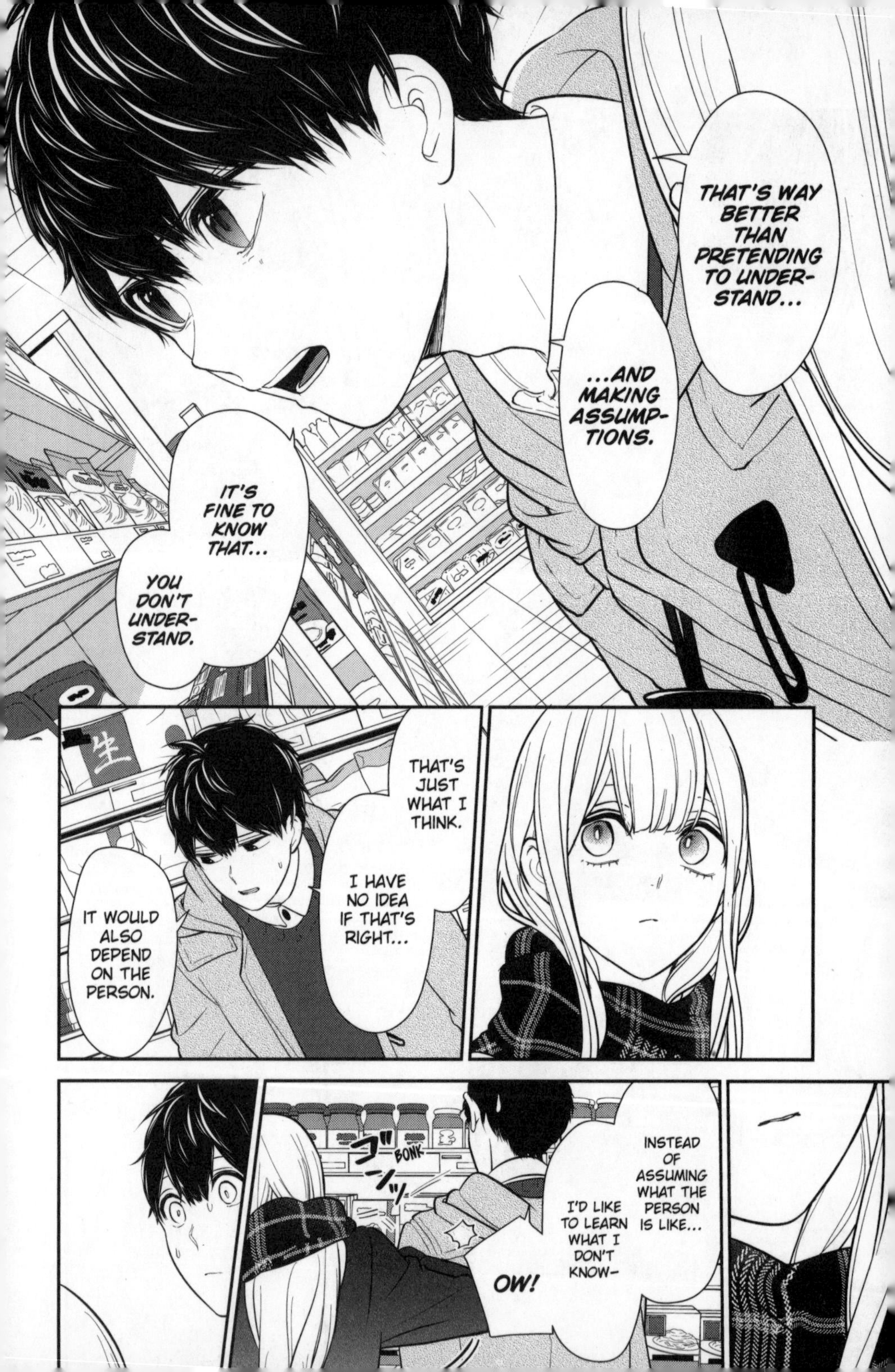
THAT'S WAY BETTER THAN PRETENDING TO UNDER-STAND...
...AND MAKING ASSUMP-TIONS.
IT'S FINE TO KNOW THAT...
YOU DON'T UNDER-STAND.
THAT'S JUST WHAT I THINK.
I HAVE NO IDEA IF THAT'S RIGHT...
IT WOULD ALSO DEPEND ON THE PERSON.
INSTEAD OF ASSUMING WHAT THE PERSON IS LIKE...
I'D LIKE TO LEARN WHAT I DON'T KNOW-
BONK
OW!

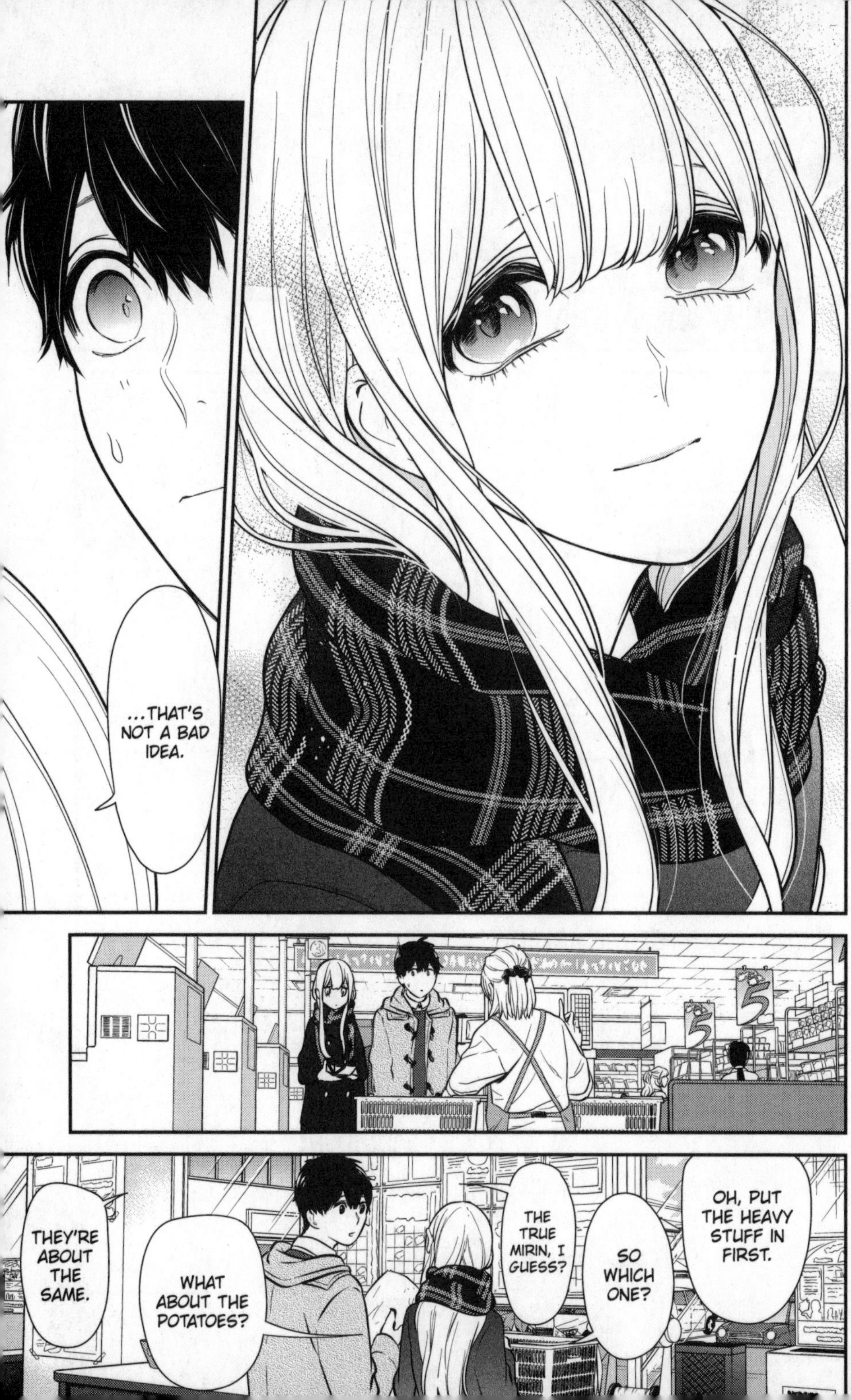
...THAT'S NOT A BAD IDEA.
OH, PUT THE HEAVY STUFF IN FIRST.
SO WHICH ONE?
THE TRUE MIRIN, I GUESS?
WHAT ABOUT THE POTATOES?
THEY'RE ABOUT THE SAME.

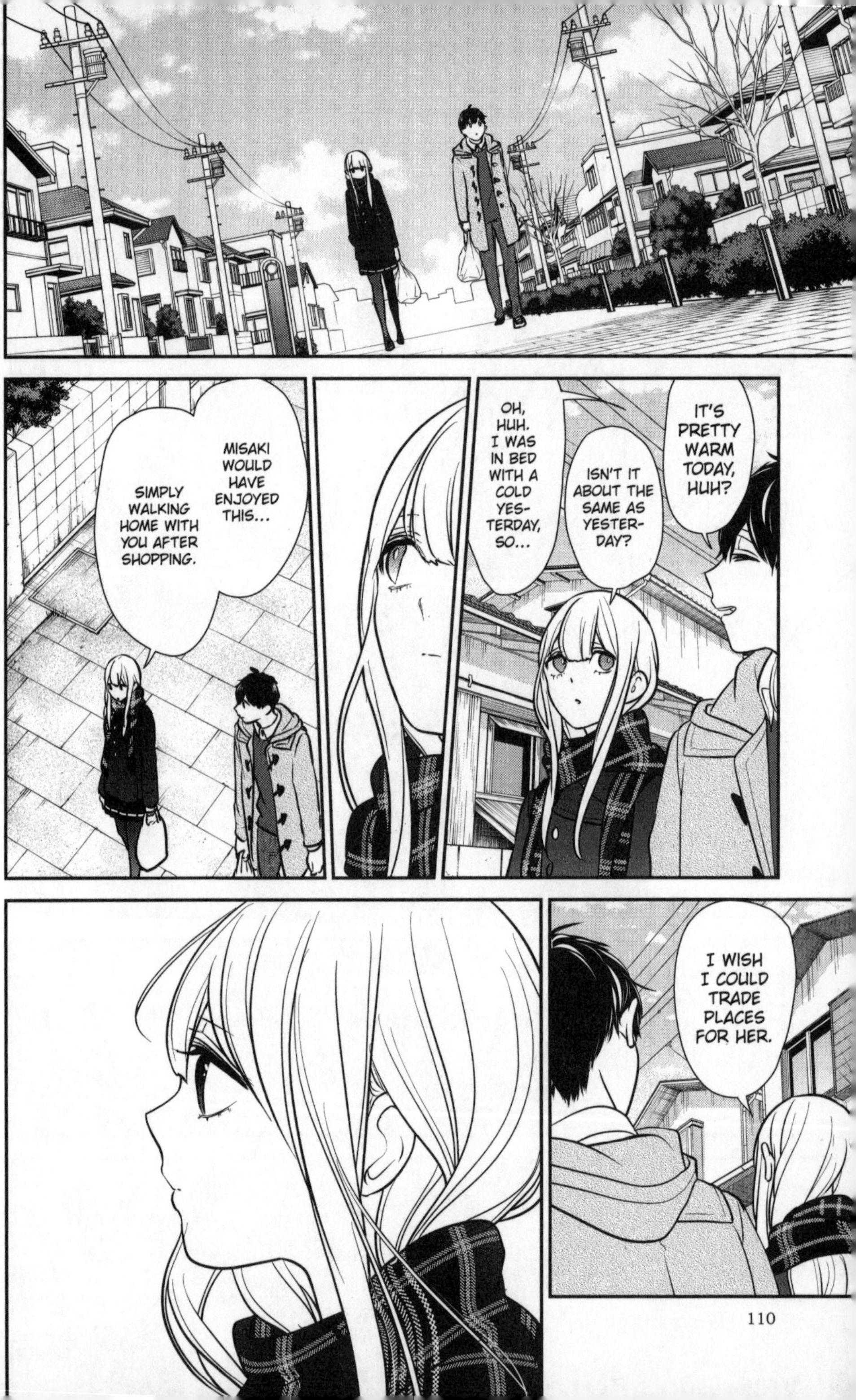
IT'S PRETTY WARM TODAY, HUH?
ISN'T IT ABOUT THE SAME AS YESTERDAY?
OH, HUH. I WAS IN BED WITH A COLD YESTERDAY, SO...
MISAKI WOULD HAVE ENJOYED THIS...
SIMPLY WALKING HOME WITH YOU AFTER SHOPPING.
I WISH I COULD TRADE PLACES FOR HER.

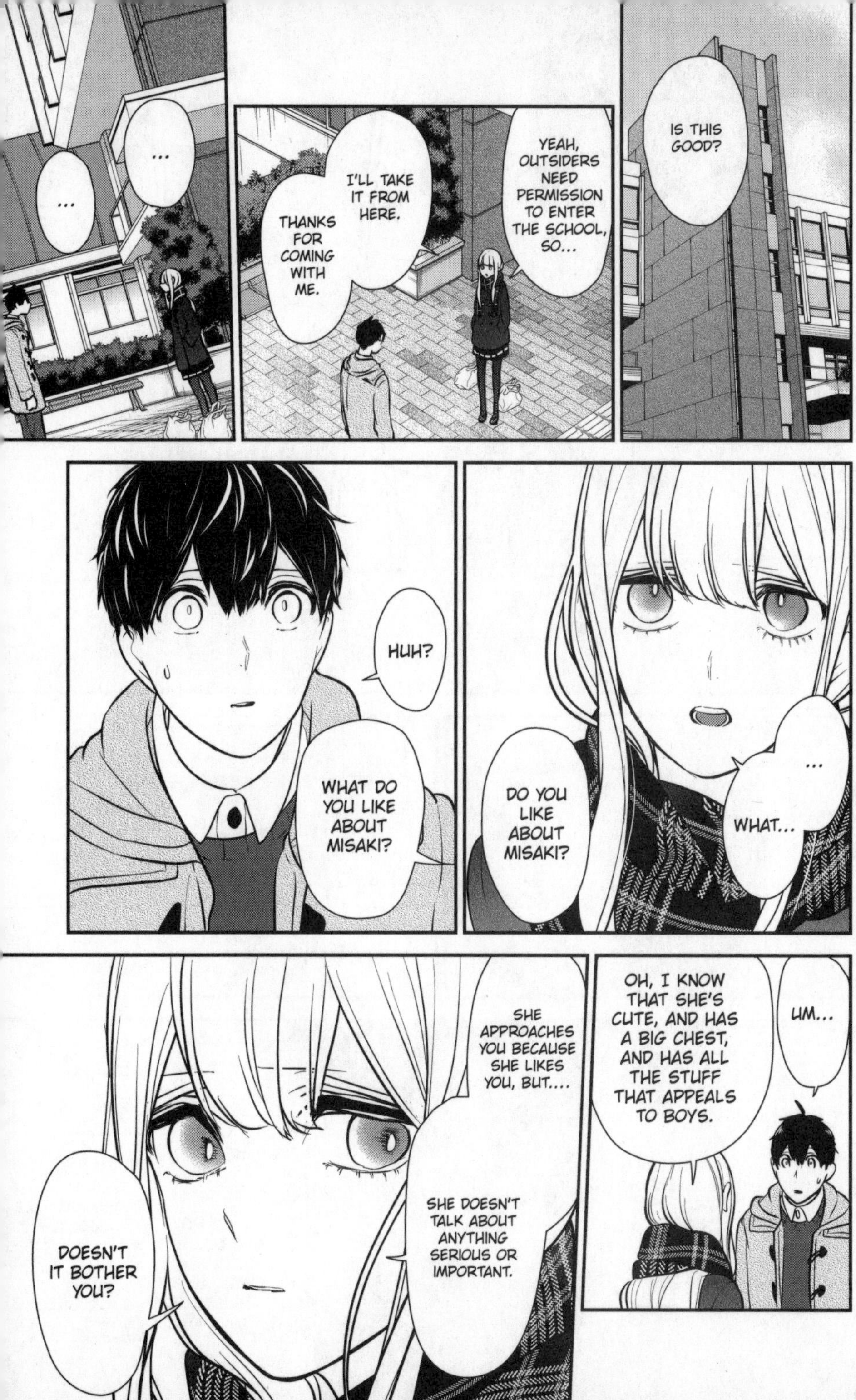
IS THIS GOOD?
YEAH, OUTSIDERS NEED PERMISSION TO ENTER THE SCHOOL, SO…
I'LL TAKE IT FROM HERE.
THANKS FOR COMING WITH ME.
…
…
…
WHAT…
DO YOU LIKE ABOUT MISAKI?
HUH?
WHAT DO YOU LIKE ABOUT MISAKI?
UM…
OH, I KNOW THAT SHE'S CUTE, AND HAS A BIG CHEST, AND HAS ALL THE STUFF THAT APPEALS TO BOYS.
SHE APPROACHES YOU BECAUSE SHE LIKES YOU, BUT….
SHE DOESN'T TALK ABOUT ANYTHING SERIOUS OR IMPORTANT.
DOESN'T IT BOTHER YOU?

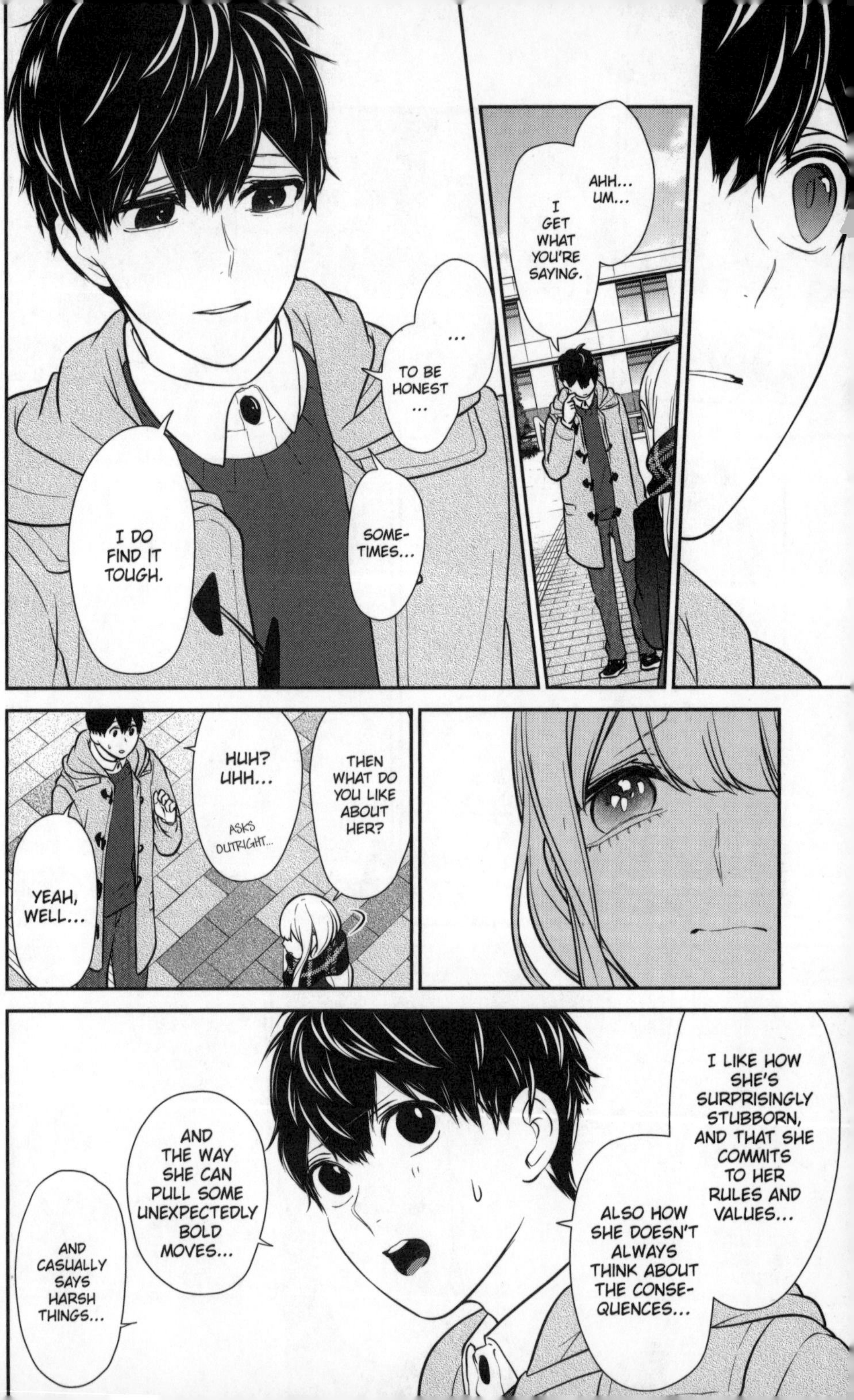
AHH... UM...
I GET WHAT YOU'RE SAYING.
... TO BE HONEST ...
SOMETIMES...
I DO FIND IT TOUGH.
THEN WHAT DO YOU LIKE ABOUT HER?
HUH? UHH...
ASKS OUTRIGHT...
YEAH, WELL...
I LIKE HOW SHE'S SURPRISINGLY STUBBORN, AND THAT SHE COMMITS TO HER RULES AND VALUES...
ALSO HOW SHE DOESN'T ALWAYS THINK ABOUT THE CONSEQUENCES...
AND THE WAY SHE CAN PULL SOME UNEXPECTEDLY BOLD MOVES...
AND CASUALLY SAYS HARSH THINGS...

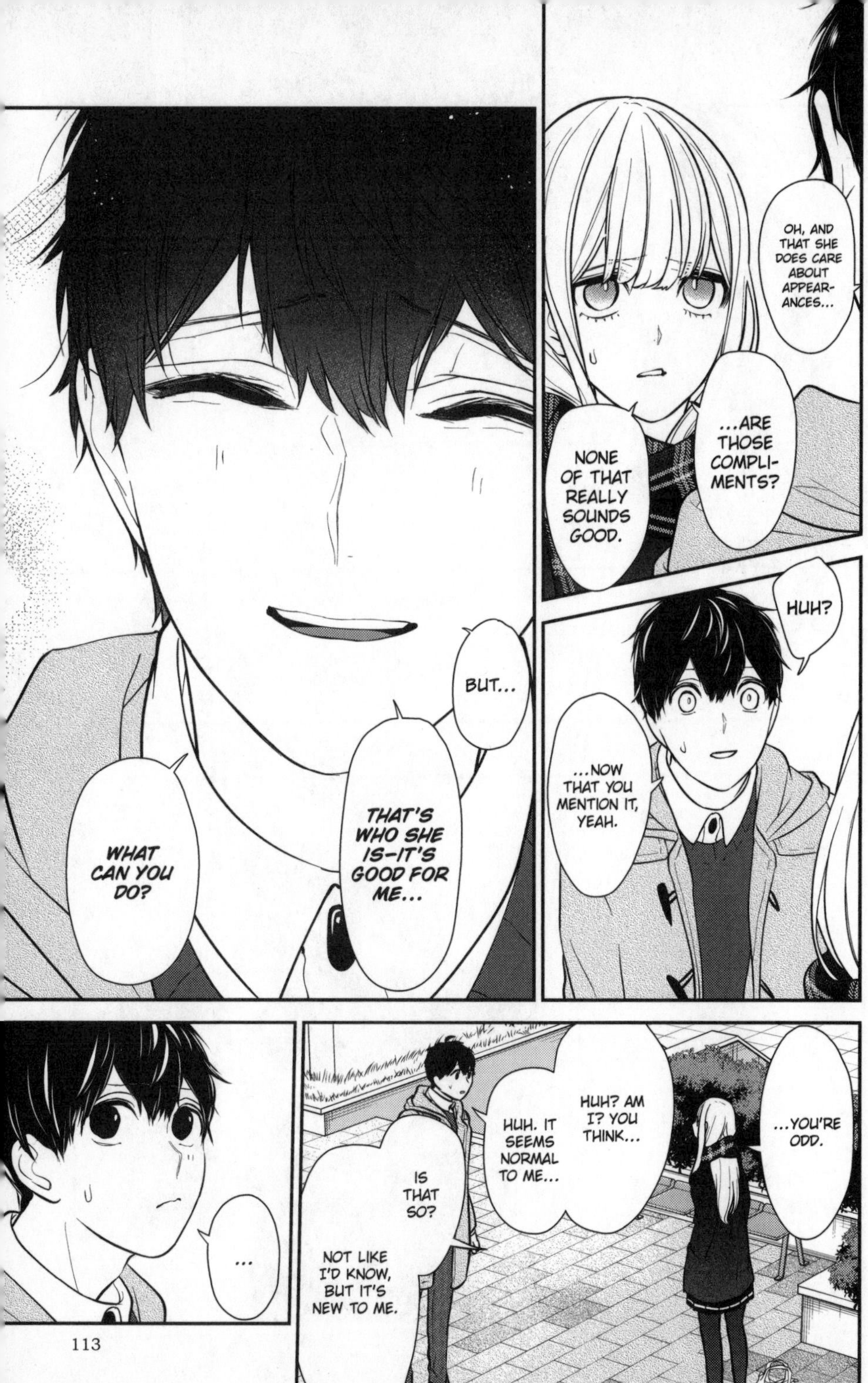
OH, AND THAT SHE DOES CARE ABOUT APPEARANCES...
...ARE THOSE COMPLIMENTS?
NONE OF THAT REALLY SOUNDS GOOD.
HUH?
...NOW THAT YOU MENTION IT, YEAH.
BUT...
THAT'S WHO SHE IS—IT'S GOOD FOR ME...
WHAT CAN YOU DO?
...YOU'RE ODD.
HUH? AM I? YOU THINK...
HUH. IT SEEMS NORMAL TO ME...
IS THAT SO?
NOT LIKE I'D KNOW, BUT IT'S NEW TO ME.
...

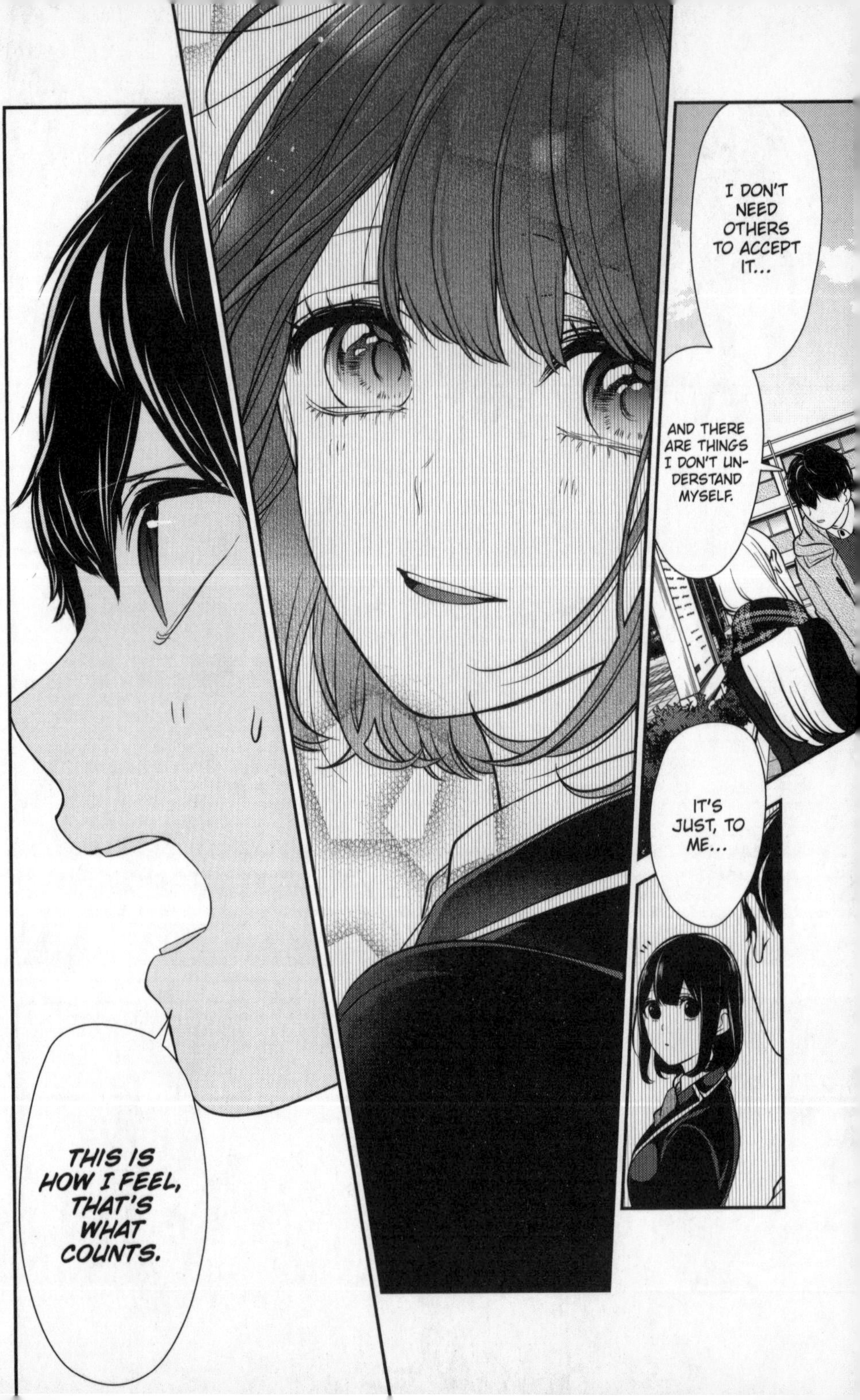
I DON'T NEED OTHERS TO ACCEPT IT...
AND THERE ARE THINGS I DON'T UN-DERSTAND MYSELF.
IT'S JUST, TO ME...
THIS IS HOW I FEEL, THAT'S WHAT COUNTS.

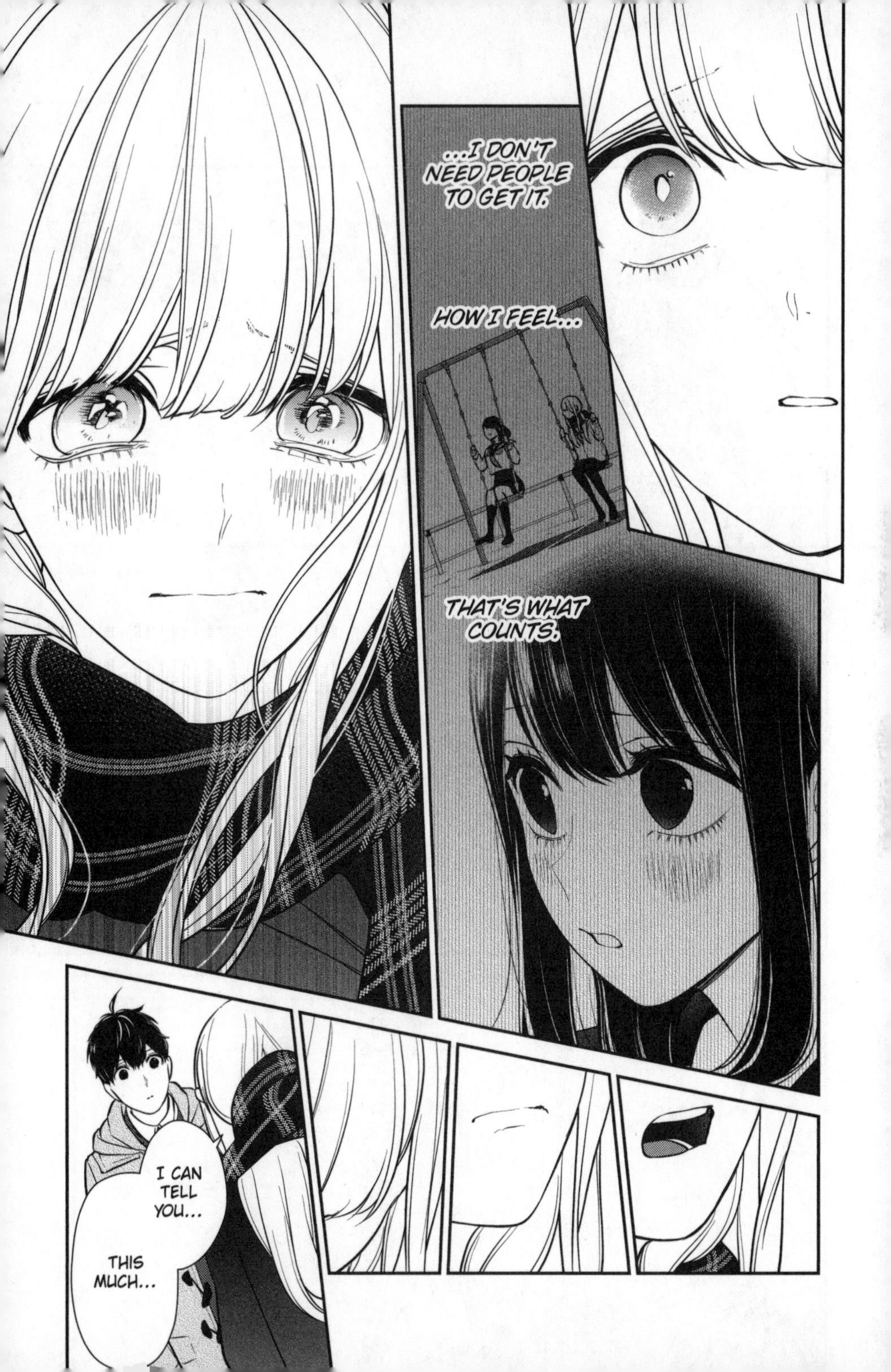
...I DON'T NEED PEOPLE TO GET IT.
HOW I FEEL...
THAT'S WHAT COUNTS.
I CAN TELL YOU...
THIS MUCH...

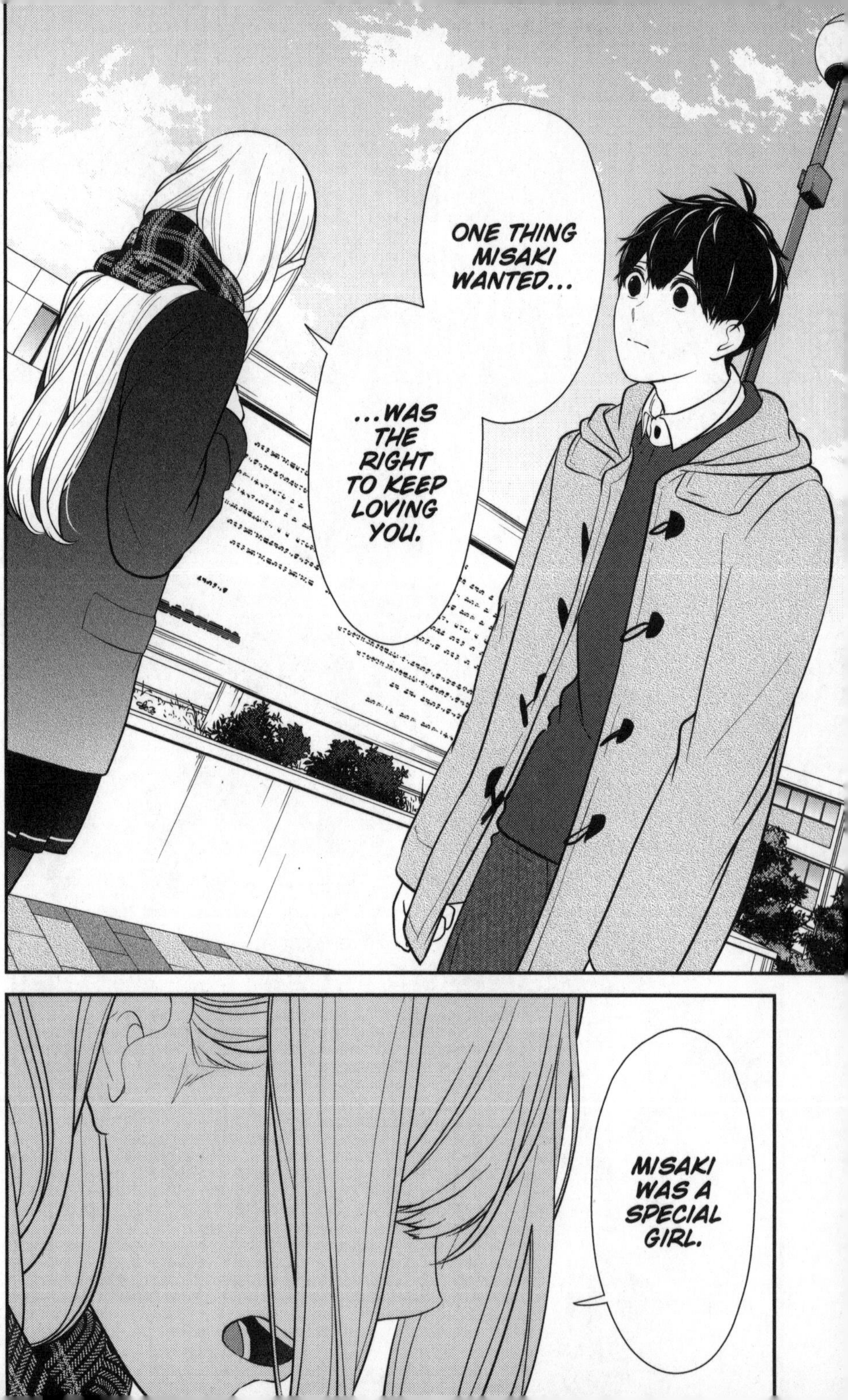
ONE THING MISAKI WANTED...
...WAS THE RIGHT TO KEEP LOVING YOU.
MISAKI WAS A SPECIAL GIRL.

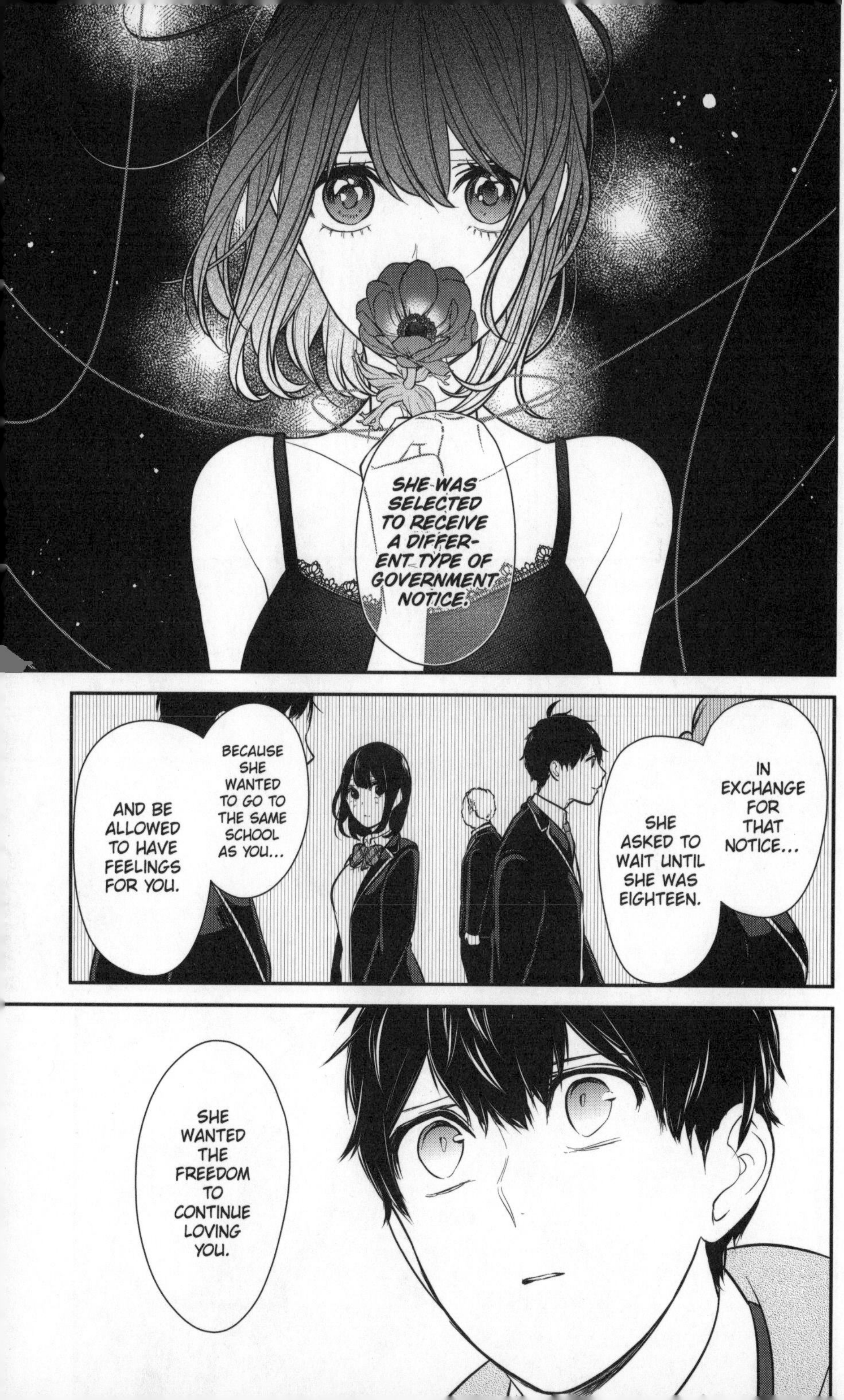
SHE WAS SELECTED TO RECEIVE A DIFFER-ENT TYPE OF GOVERNMENT NOTICE.
IN EXCHANGE FOR THAT NOTICE...
SHE ASKED TO WAIT UNTIL SHE WAS EIGHTEEN.
BECAUSE SHE WANTED TO GO TO THE SAME SCHOOL AS YOU...
AND BE ALLOWED TO HAVE FEELINGS FOR YOU.
SHE WANTED THE FREEDOM TO CONTINUE LOVING YOU.

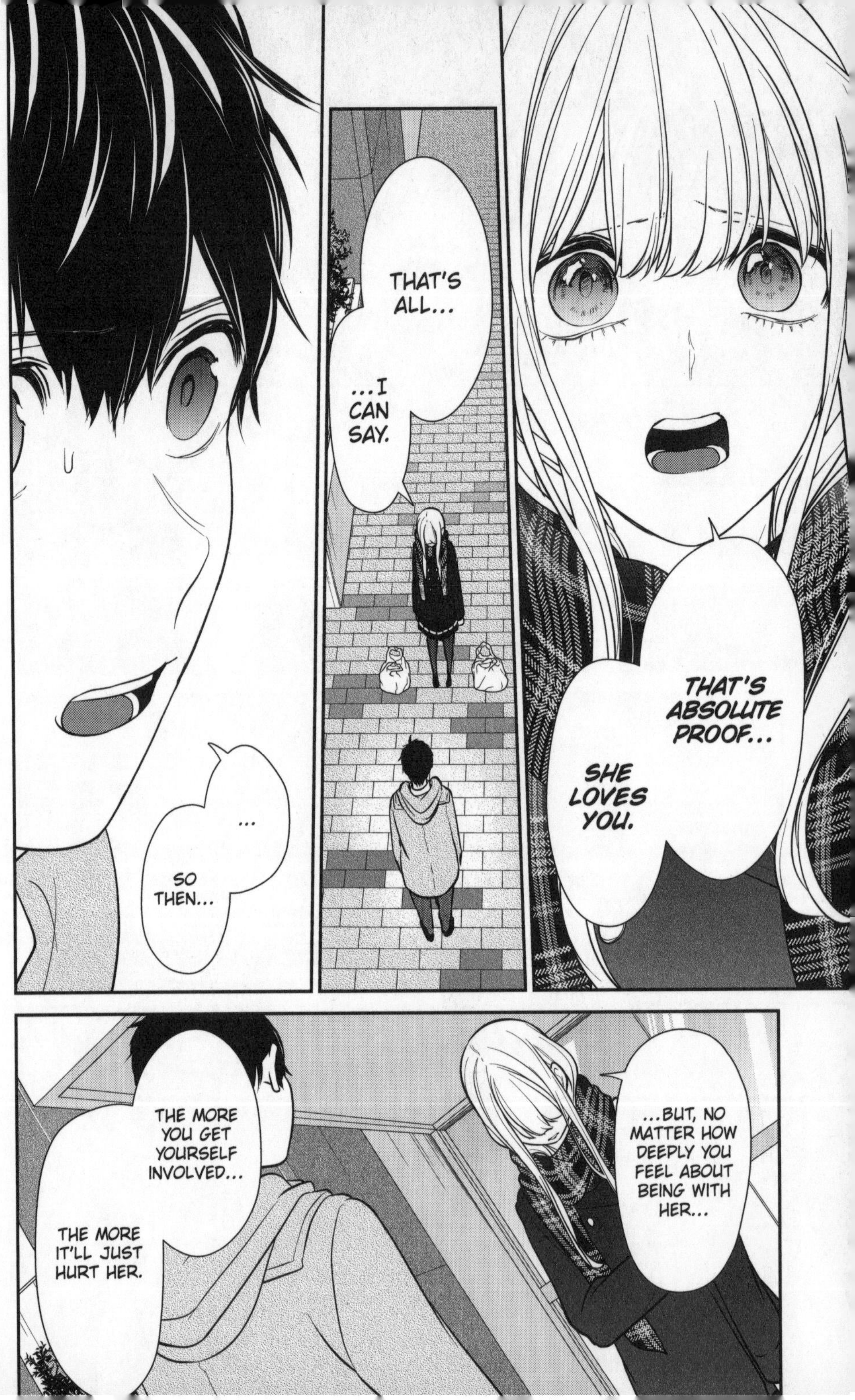
THAT'S ABSOLUTE PROOF...
SHE LOVES YOU.
THAT'S ALL...
...I CAN SAY.
...
SO THEN...
...BUT, NO MATTER HOW DEEPLY YOU FEEL ABOUT BEING WITH HER...
THE MORE YOU GET YOURSELF INVOLVED...
THE MORE IT'LL JUST HURT HER.

IF YOU INTEND TO ABANDON YOUR NOTICE...

I MIGHT TELL YOU THEN.

BECAUSE YOU HAVE A GOVERNMENT NOTICE.

SORRY, I'M BEING UNFAIR.

SO PRETEND YOU NEVER HEARD WHAT I JUST SAID.

AND MISAKI, MORE THAN ANYONE, DOESN'T WANT THAT.

BUT THAT'S NOT A CHOICE FOR YOU.

I...

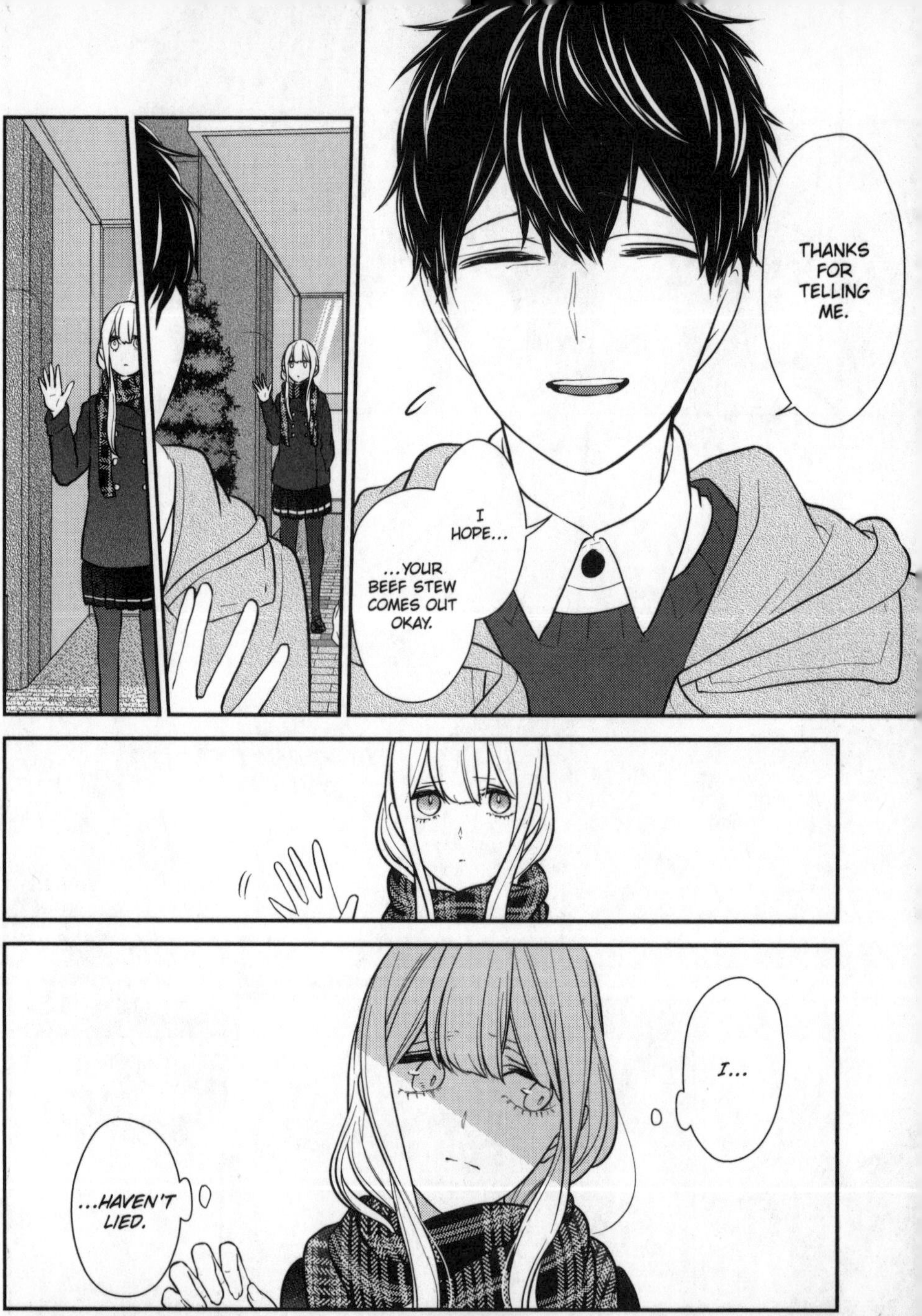
THANKS FOR TELLING ME.
I HOPE...
...YOUR BEEF STEW COMES OUT OKAY.
I...
...HAVEN'T LIED.

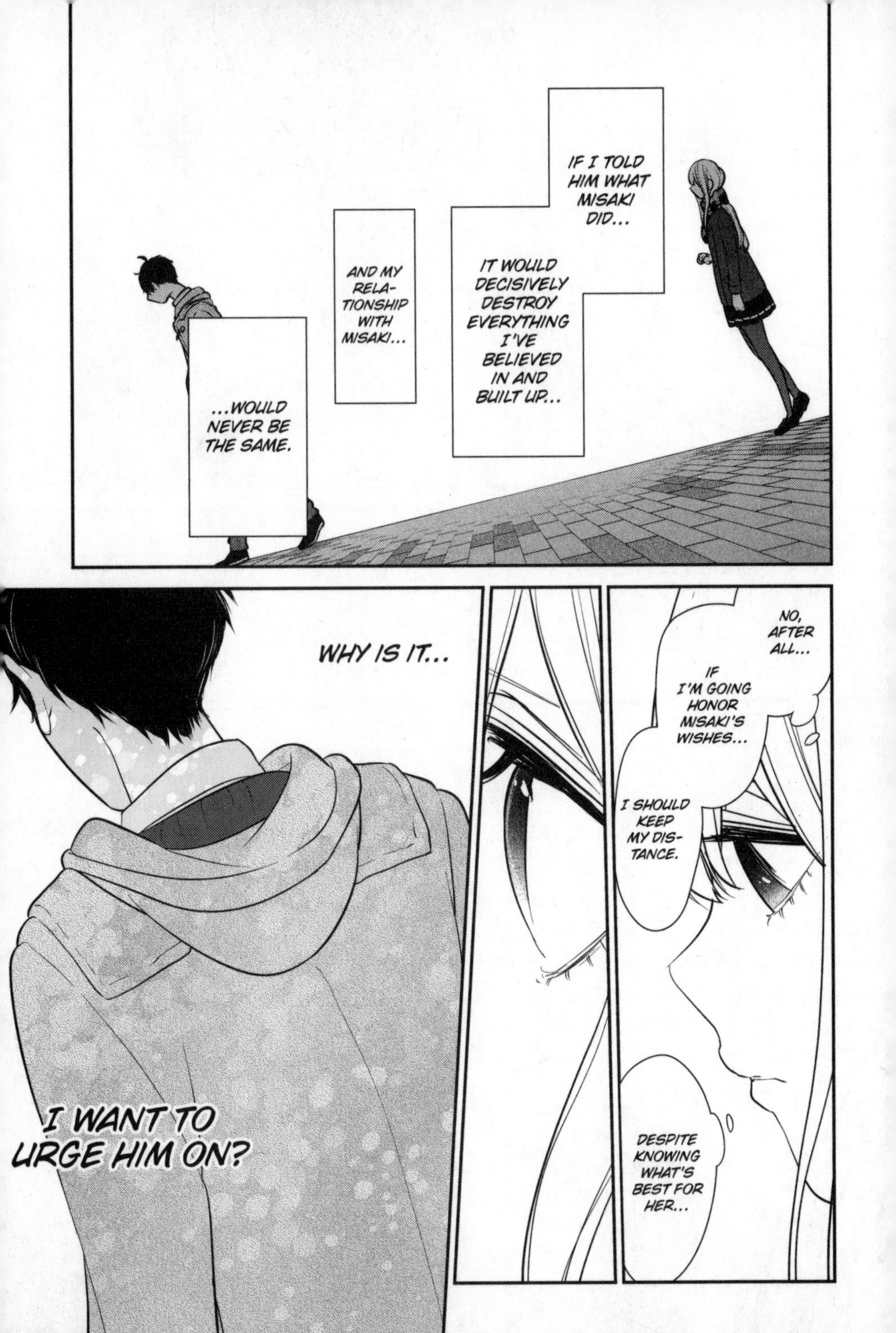
IF I TOLD HIM WHAT MISAKI DID...
IT WOULD DECISIVELY DESTROY EVERYTHING I'VE BELIEVED IN AND BUILT UP...
AND MY RELA-TIONSHIP WITH MISAKI...
...WOULD NEVER BE THE SAME.
NO, AFTER ALL...
IF I'M GOING HONOR MISAKI'S WISHES...
I SHOULD KEEP MY DIS-TANCE.
DESPITE KNOWING WHAT'S BEST FOR HER...
WHY IS IT...
I WANT TO URGE HIM ON?

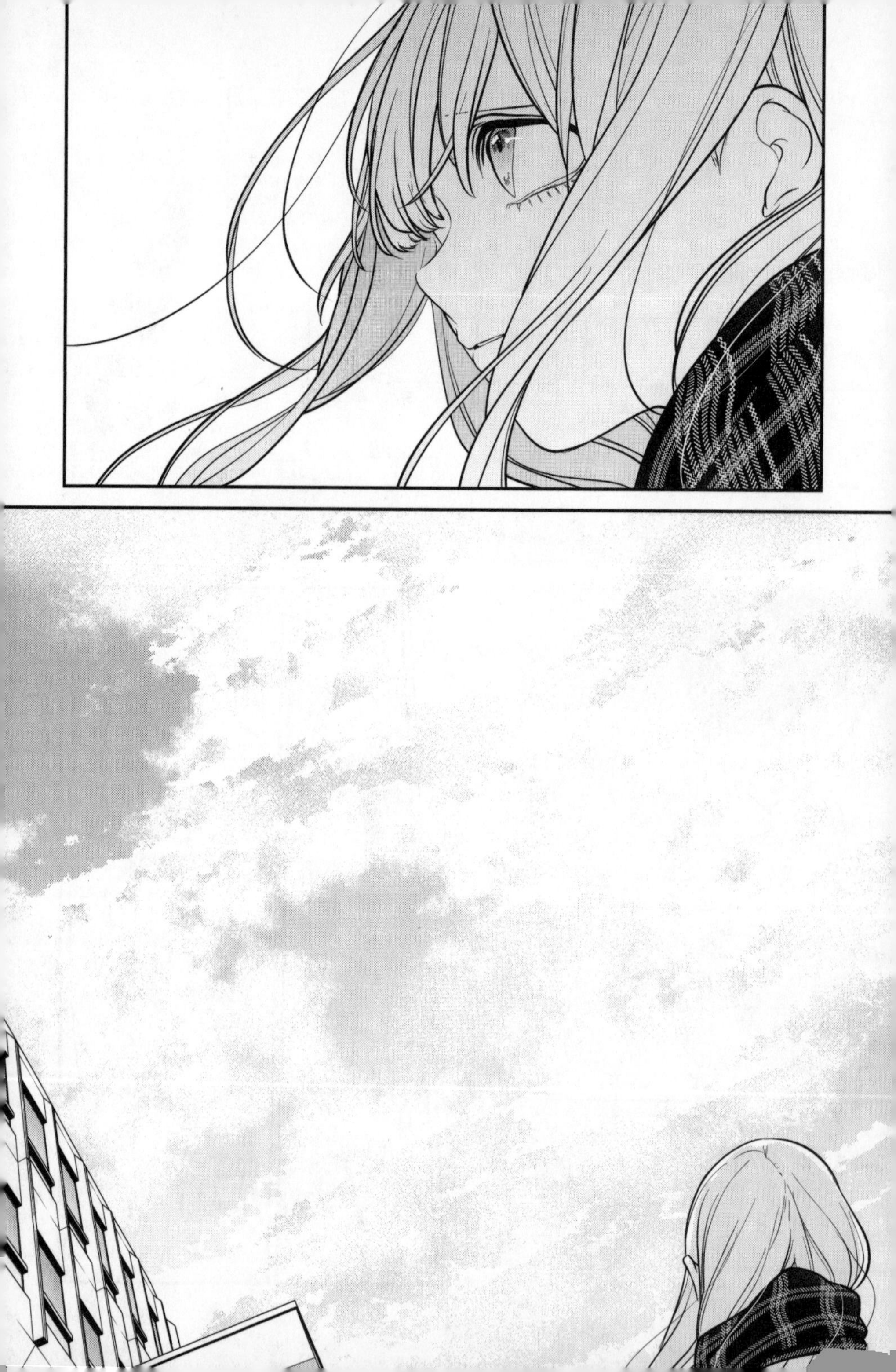

# Chapter 37: The End of the Respite of Lies

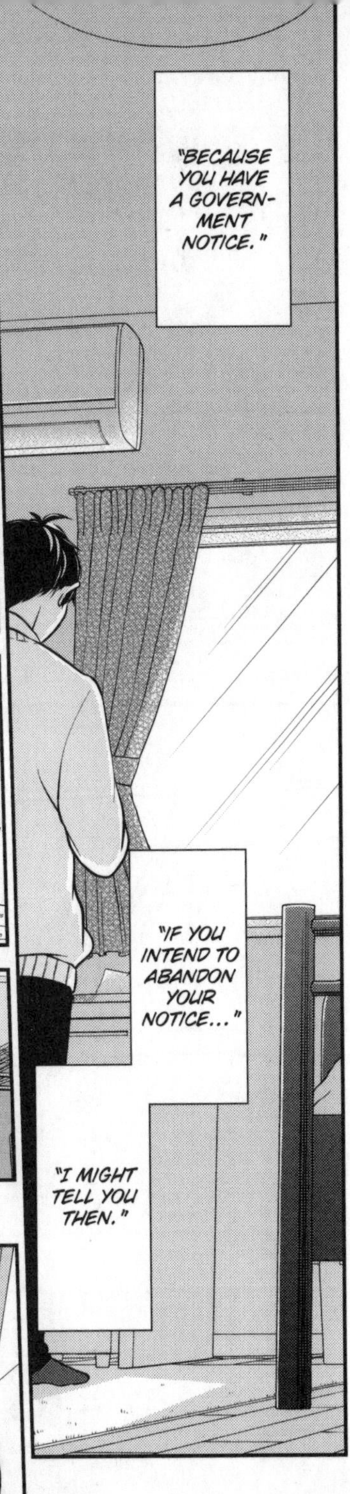
"BECAUSE YOU HAVE A GOVERNMENT NOTICE."
"IF YOU INTEND TO ABANDON YOUR NOTICE..."
"I MIGHT TELL YOU THEN."

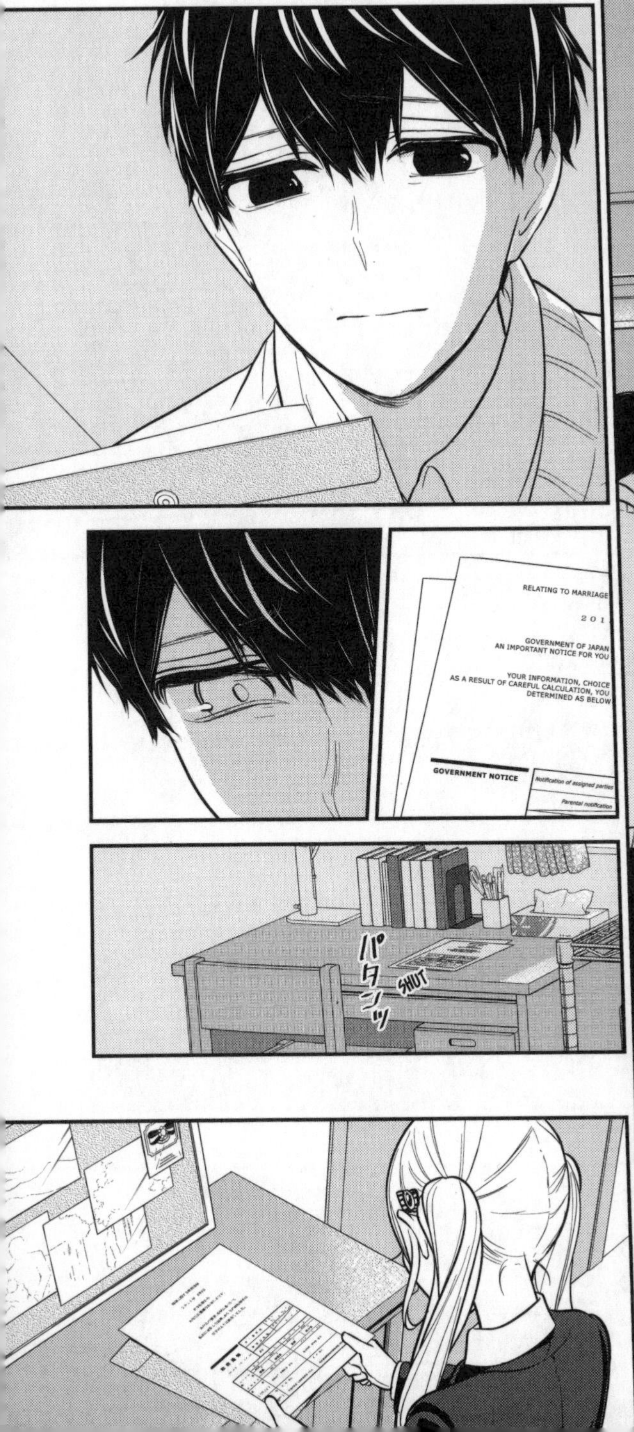
RELATING TO MARRIAGE
201
GOVERNMENT OF JAPAN
AN IMPORTANT NOTICE FOR YOU
YOUR INFORMATION, CHOICE
AS A RESULT OF CAREFUL CALCULATION, YOU
DETERMINED AS BELOW
GOVERNMENT NOTICE
Notification of assigned parties
Parental notification
パタンッ
SHUT

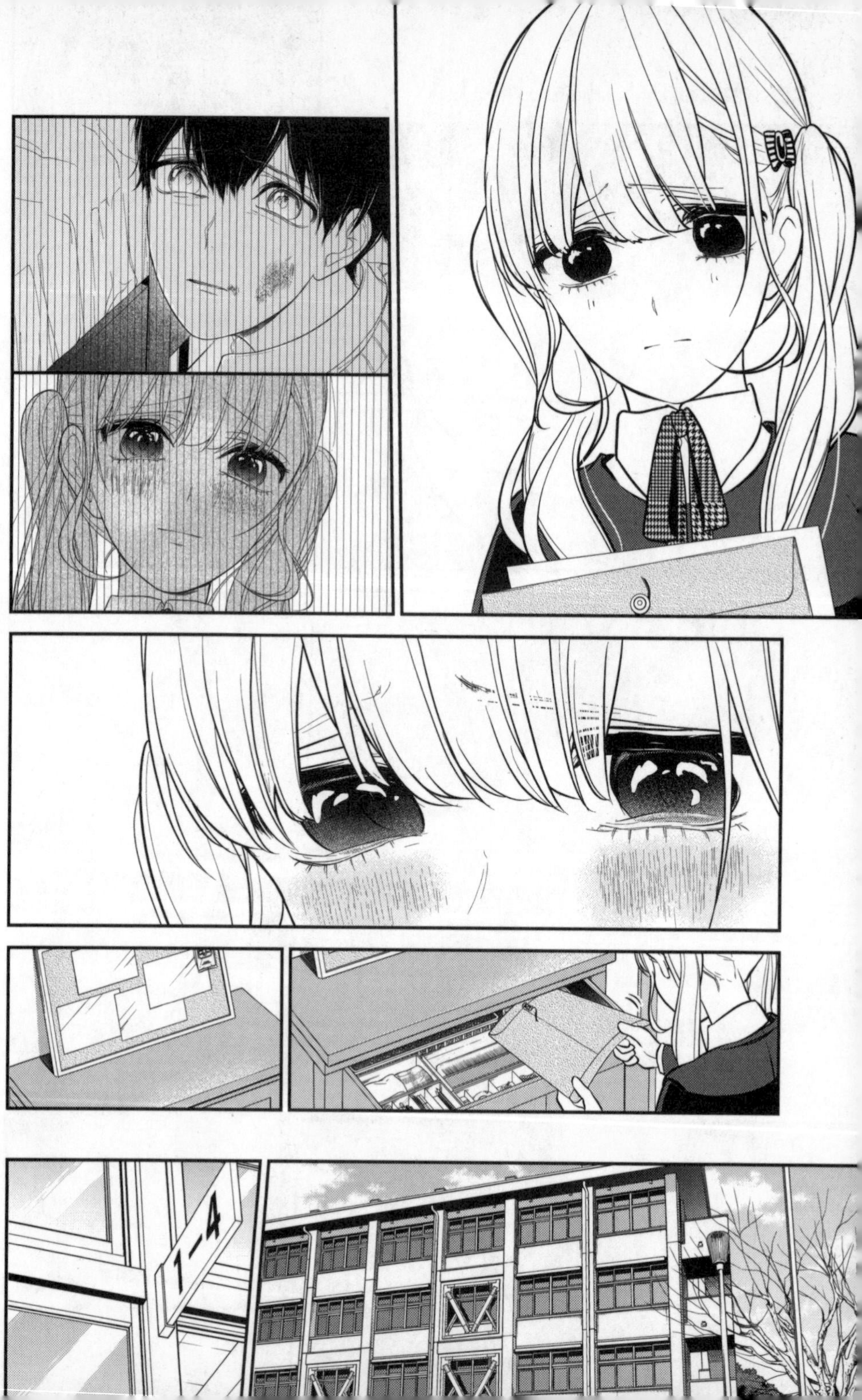
1-4

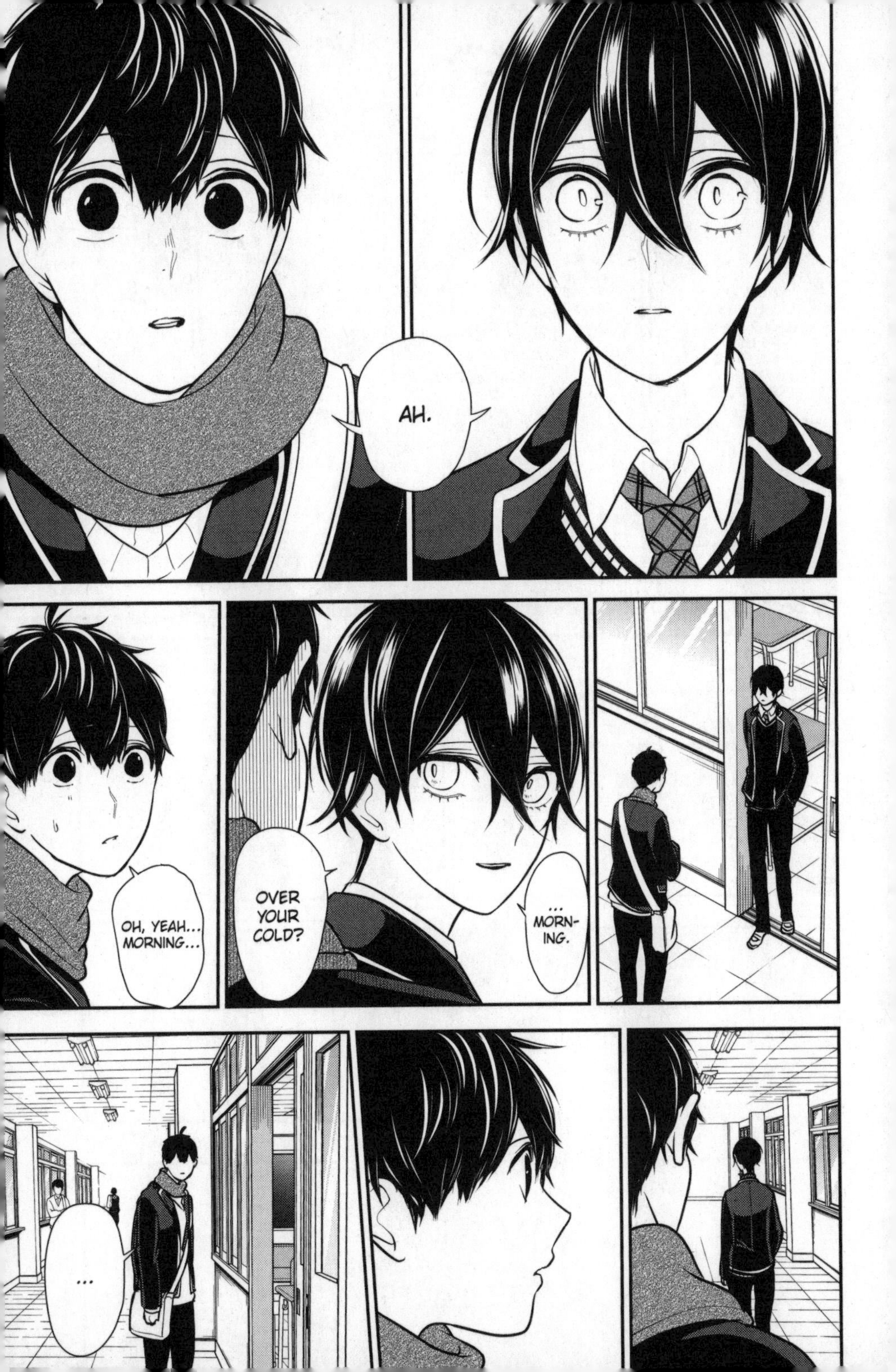
AH.
... MORNING.
OVER YOUR COLD?
OH, YEAH... MORNING...
...

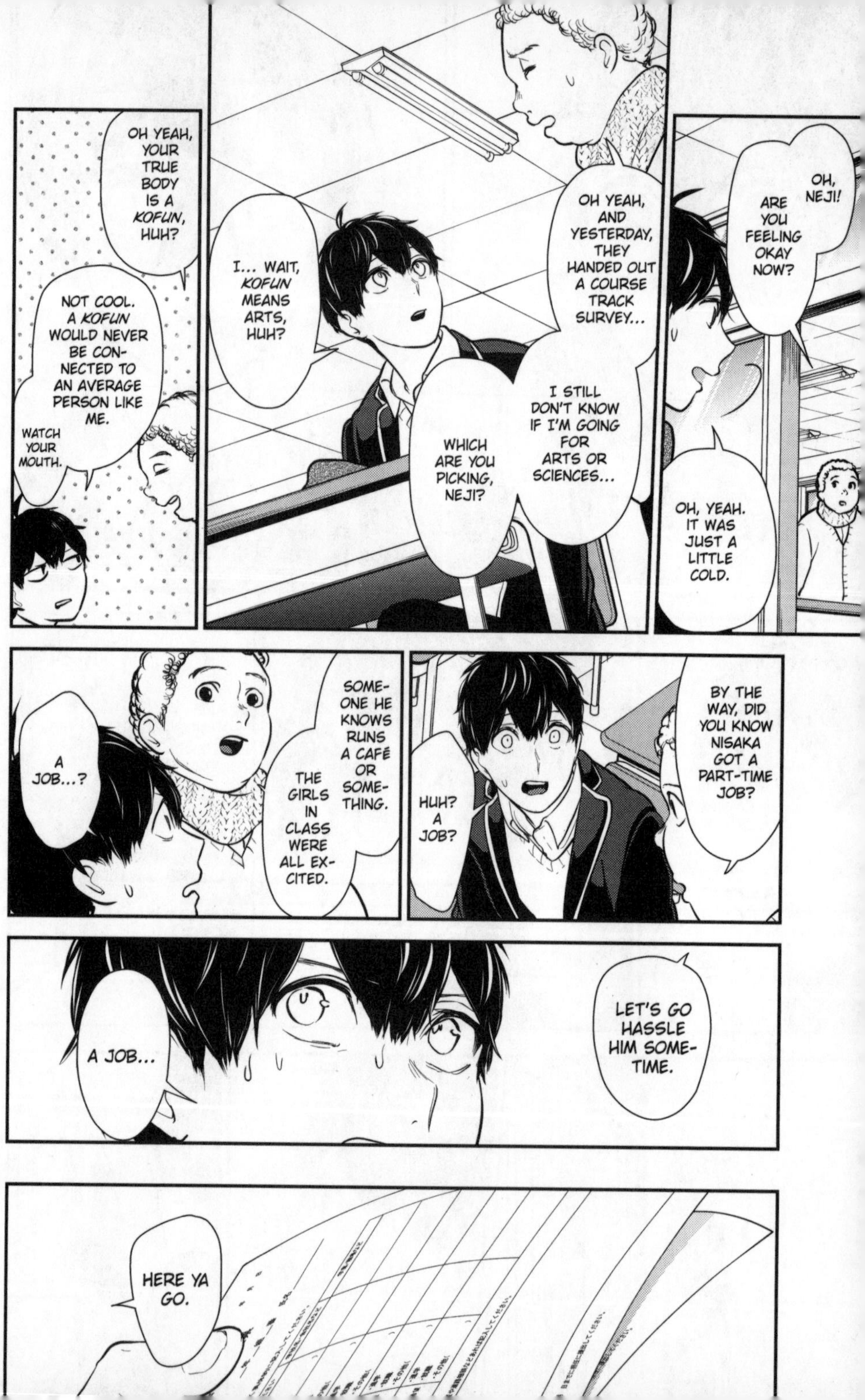
OH, NEJI! ARE YOU FEELING OKAY NOW?
OH, YEAH. IT WAS JUST A LITTLE COLD.
OH YEAH, AND YESTERDAY, THEY HANDED OUT A COURSE TRACK SURVEY...
I STILL DON'T KNOW IF I'M GOING FOR ARTS OR SCIENCES...
WHICH ARE YOU PICKING, NEJI?
I... WAIT, *KOFUN* MEANS ARTS, HUH?
OH YEAH, YOUR TRUE BODY IS A *KOFUN*, HUH?
NOT COOL. A *KOFUN* WOULD NEVER BE CONNECTED TO AN AVERAGE PERSON LIKE ME.
WATCH YOUR MOUTH.
BY THE WAY, DID YOU KNOW NISAKA GOT A PART-TIME JOB?
HUH? A JOB?
SOMEONE HE KNOWS RUNS A CAFÉ OR SOMETHING.
THE GIRLS IN CLASS WERE ALL EXCITED.
A JOB...?
LET'S GO HASSLE HIM SOMETIME.
A JOB...
HERE YA GO.

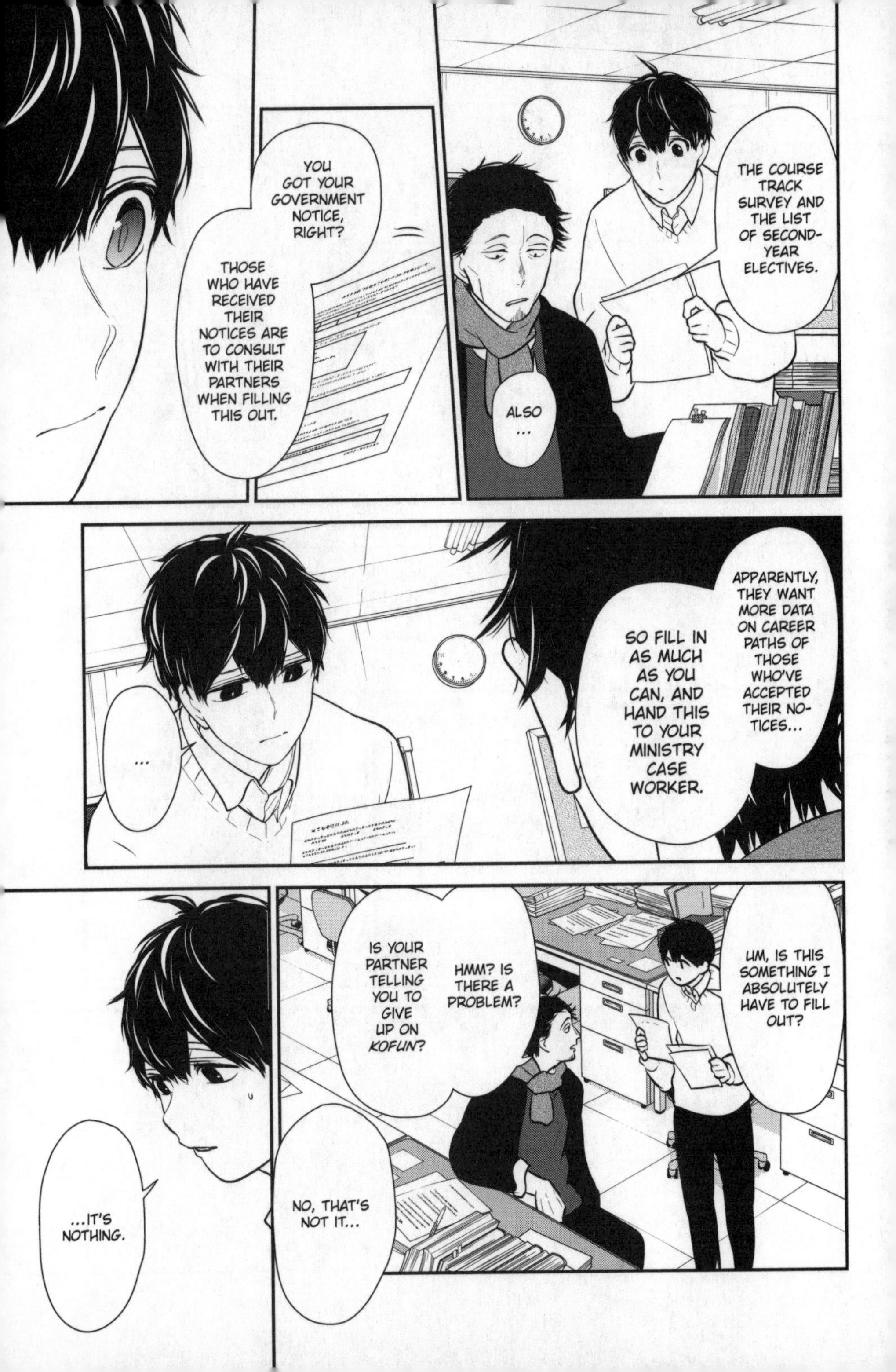
THE COURSE TRACK SURVEY AND THE LIST OF SECOND-YEAR ELECTIVES.
ALSO ...
YOU GOT YOUR GOVERNMENT NOTICE, RIGHT?
THOSE WHO HAVE RECEIVED THEIR NOTICES ARE TO CONSULT WITH THEIR PARTNERS WHEN FILLING THIS OUT.
APPARENTLY, THEY WANT MORE DATA ON CAREER PATHS OF THOSE WHO'VE ACCEPTED THEIR NOTICES...
SO FILL IN AS MUCH AS YOU CAN, AND HAND THIS TO YOUR MINISTRY CASE WORKER.
...
UM, IS THIS SOMETHING I ABSOLUTELY HAVE TO FILL OUT?
HMM? IS THERE A PROBLEM?
IS YOUR PARTNER TELLING YOU TO GIVE UP ON *KOFUN*?
NO, THAT'S NOT IT...
...IT'S NOTHING.

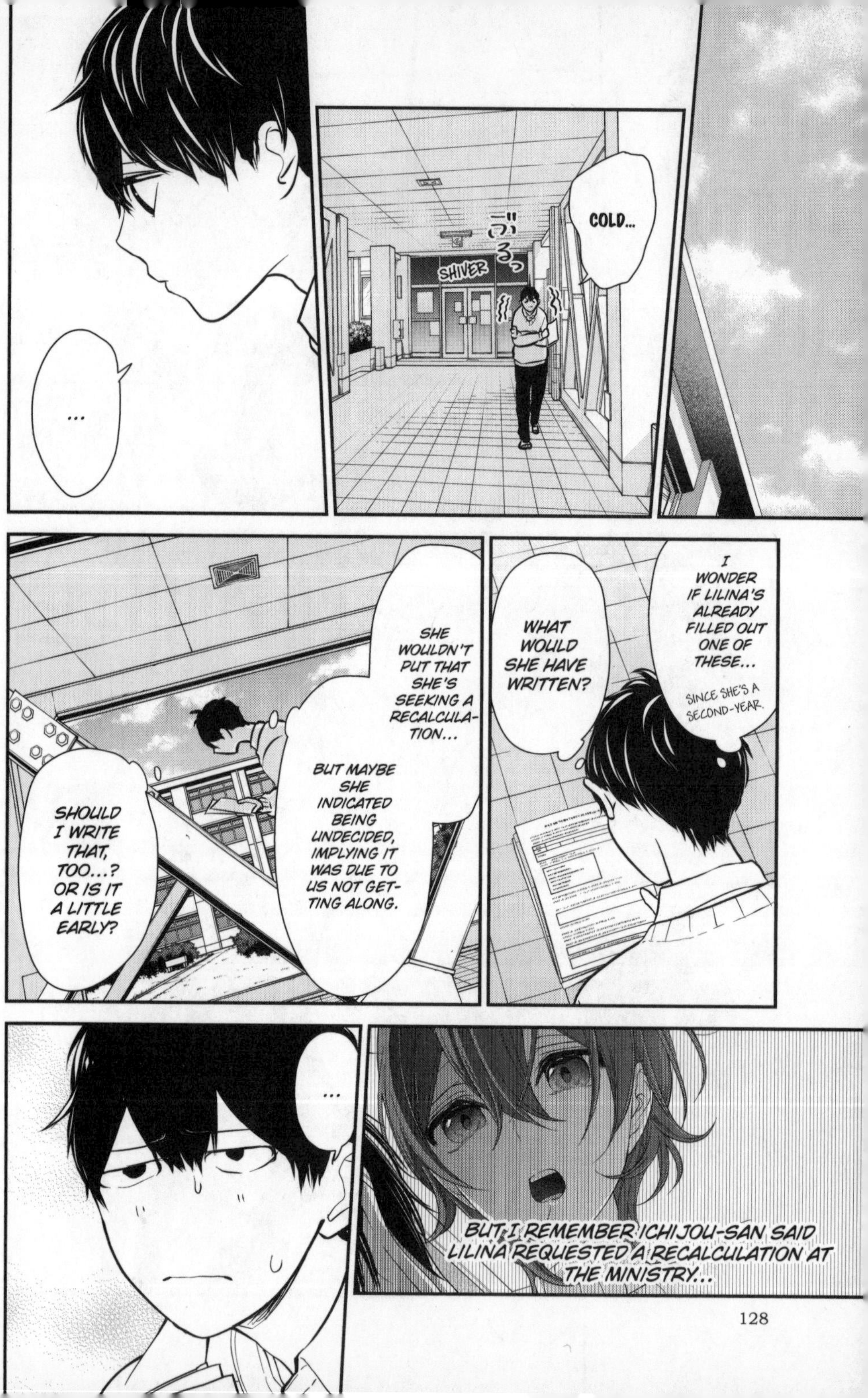
COLD...
ぶるっ
SHIVER
...
I WONDER IF LILINA'S ALREADY FILLED OUT ONE OF THESE...
SINCE SHE'S A SECOND-YEAR.
WHAT WOULD SHE HAVE WRITTEN?
SHE WOULDN'T PUT THAT SHE'S SEEKING A RECALCULA-TION...
BUT MAYBE SHE INDICATED BEING UNDECIDED, IMPLYING IT WAS DUE TO US NOT GET-TING ALONG.
SHOULD I WRITE THAT, TOO...? OR IS IT A LITTLE EARLY?
BUT I REMEMBER ICHIJOU-SAN SAID LILINA REQUESTED A RECALCULATION AT THE MINISTRY...
...

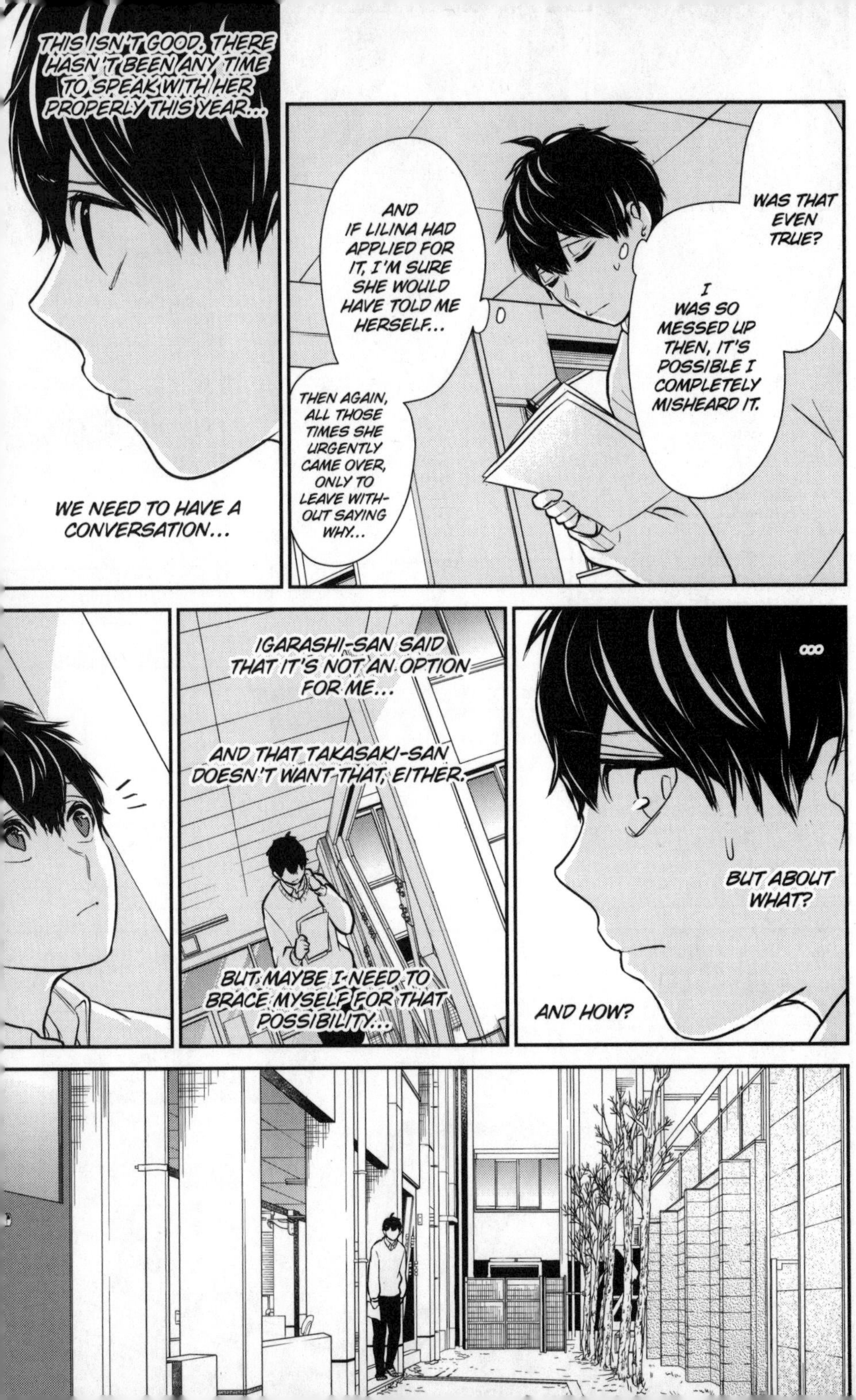
WAS THAT EVEN TRUE?
I WAS SO MESSED UP THEN, IT'S POSSIBLE I COMPLETELY MISHEARD IT.
AND IF LILINA HAD APPLIED FOR IT, I'M SURE SHE WOULD HAVE TOLD ME HERSELF...
THEN AGAIN, ALL THOSE TIMES SHE URGENTLY CAME OVER, ONLY TO LEAVE WITH-OUT SAYING WHY...
THIS ISN'T GOOD. THERE HASN'T BEEN ANY TIME TO SPEAK WITH HER PROPERLY THIS YEAR...
WE NEED TO HAVE A CONVERSATION...
BUT ABOUT WHAT?
AND HOW?
IGARASHI-SAN SAID THAT IT'S NOT AN OPTION FOR ME...
AND THAT TAKASAKI-SAN DOESN'T WANT THAT, EITHER.
BUT MAYBE I NEED TO BRACE MYSELF FOR THAT POSSIBILITY...

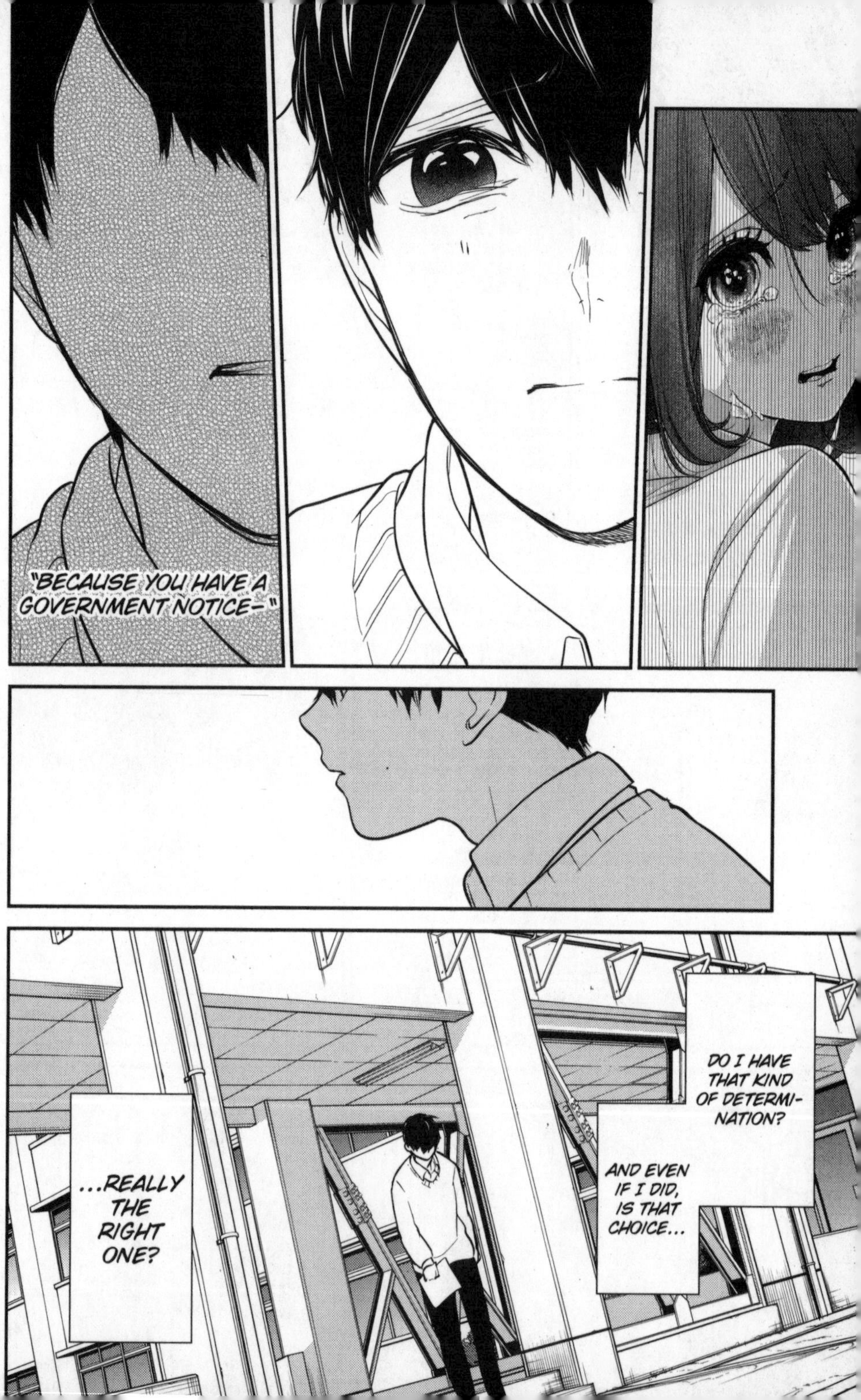
"BECAUSE YOU HAVE A GOVERNMENT NOTICE-"
DO I HAVE THAT KIND OF DETERMI-NATION?
AND EVEN IF I DID, IS THAT CHOICE...
...REALLY THE RIGHT ONE?

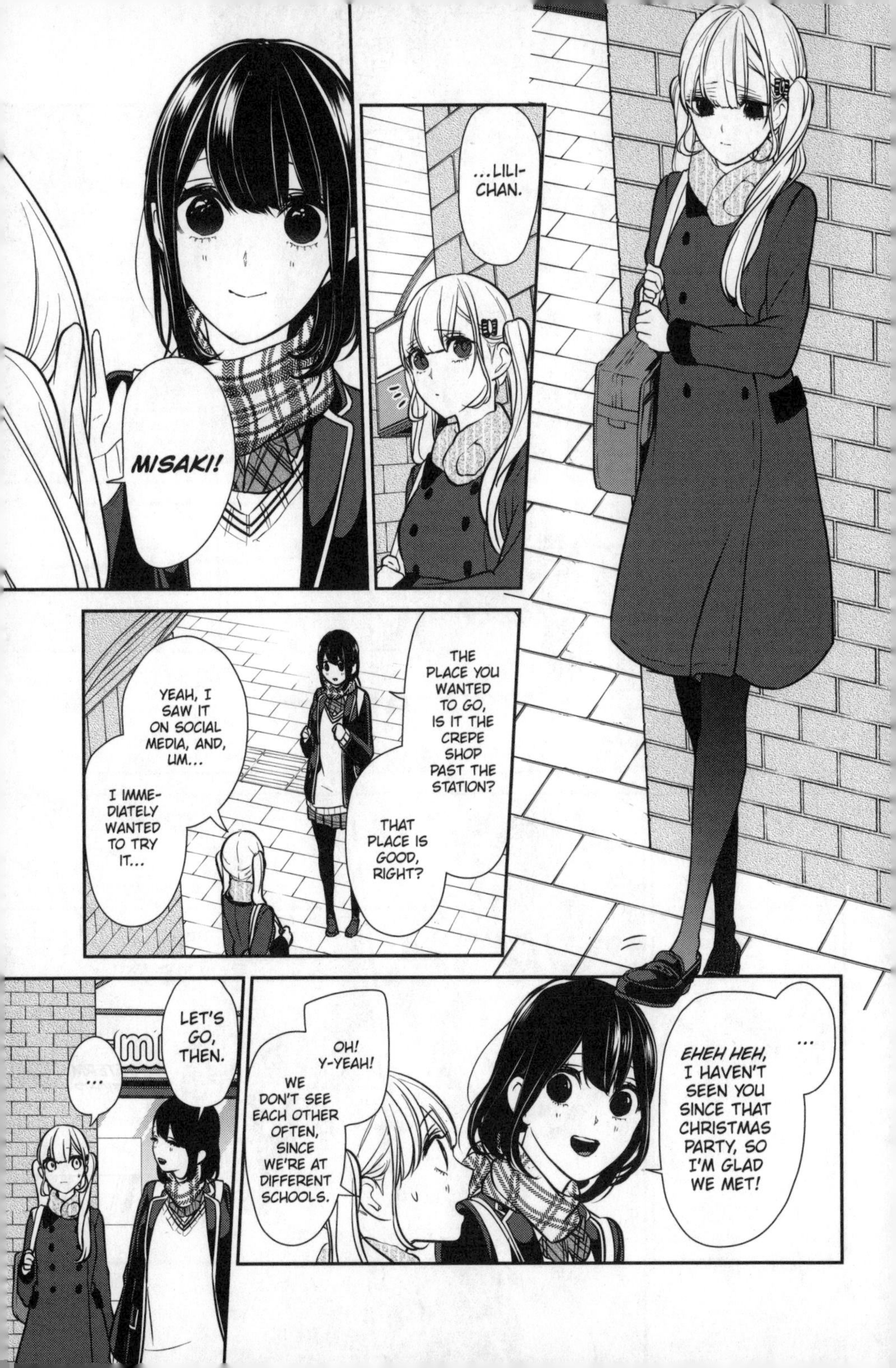
...LILI-CHAN.
MISAKI!
THE PLACE YOU WANTED TO GO, IS IT THE CREPE SHOP PAST THE STATION?
THAT PLACE IS GOOD, RIGHT?
YEAH, I SAW IT ON SOCIAL MEDIA, AND, UM...
I IMMEDIATELY WANTED TO TRY IT...
...
EHEH HEH, I HAVEN'T SEEN YOU SINCE THAT CHRISTMAS PARTY, SO I'M GLAD WE MET!
OH! Y-YEAH!
WE DON'T SEE EACH OTHER OFTEN, SINCE WE'RE AT DIFFERENT SCHOOLS.
LET'S GO, THEN.
...

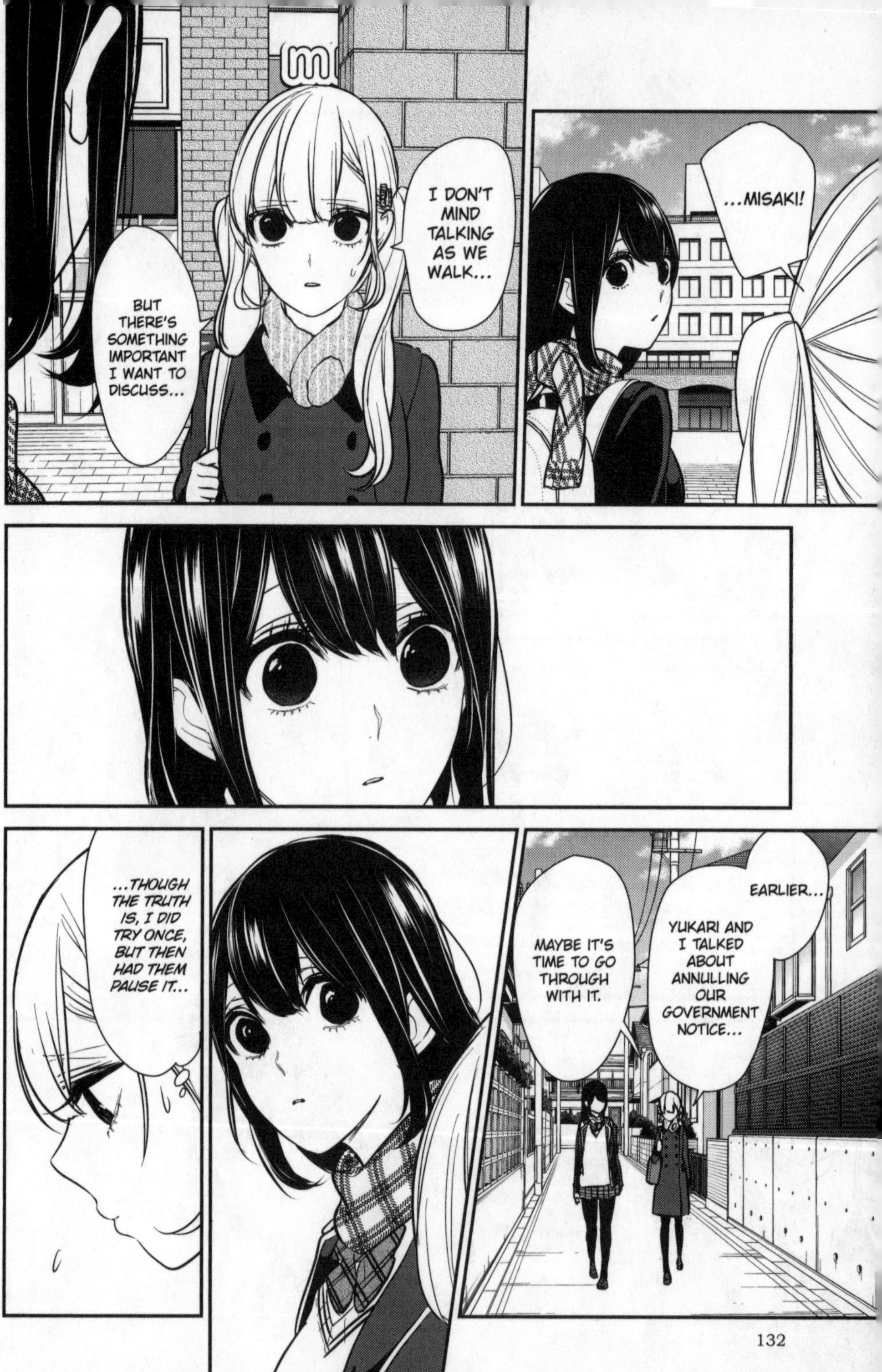
...MISAKI!
I DON'T MIND TALKING AS WE WALK...
BUT THERE'S SOMETHING IMPORTANT I WANT TO DISCUSS...
EARLIER...
YUKARI AND I TALKED ABOUT ANNULLING OUR GOVERNMENT NOTICE...
MAYBE IT'S TIME TO GO THROUGH WITH IT.
...THOUGH THE TRUTH IS, I DID TRY ONCE, BUT THEN HAD THEM PAUSE IT...

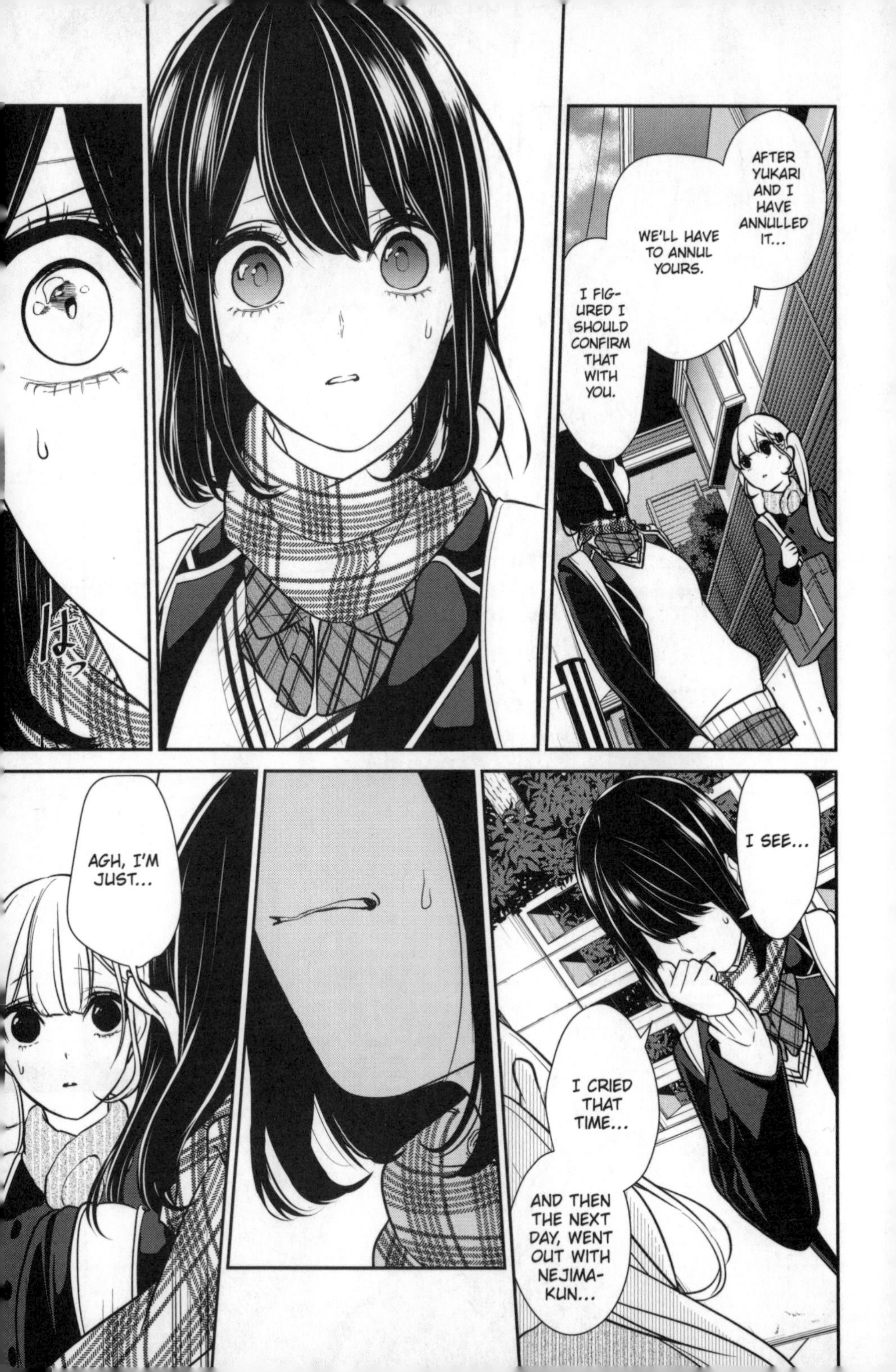
AFTER YUKARI AND I HAVE ANNULLED IT...
WE'LL HAVE TO ANNUL YOURS.
I FIG-URED I SHOULD CONFIRM THAT WITH YOU.
はっ
I SEE...
I CRIED THAT TIME...
AND THEN THE NEXT DAY, WENT OUT WITH NEJIMA-KUN...
AGH, I'M JUST...

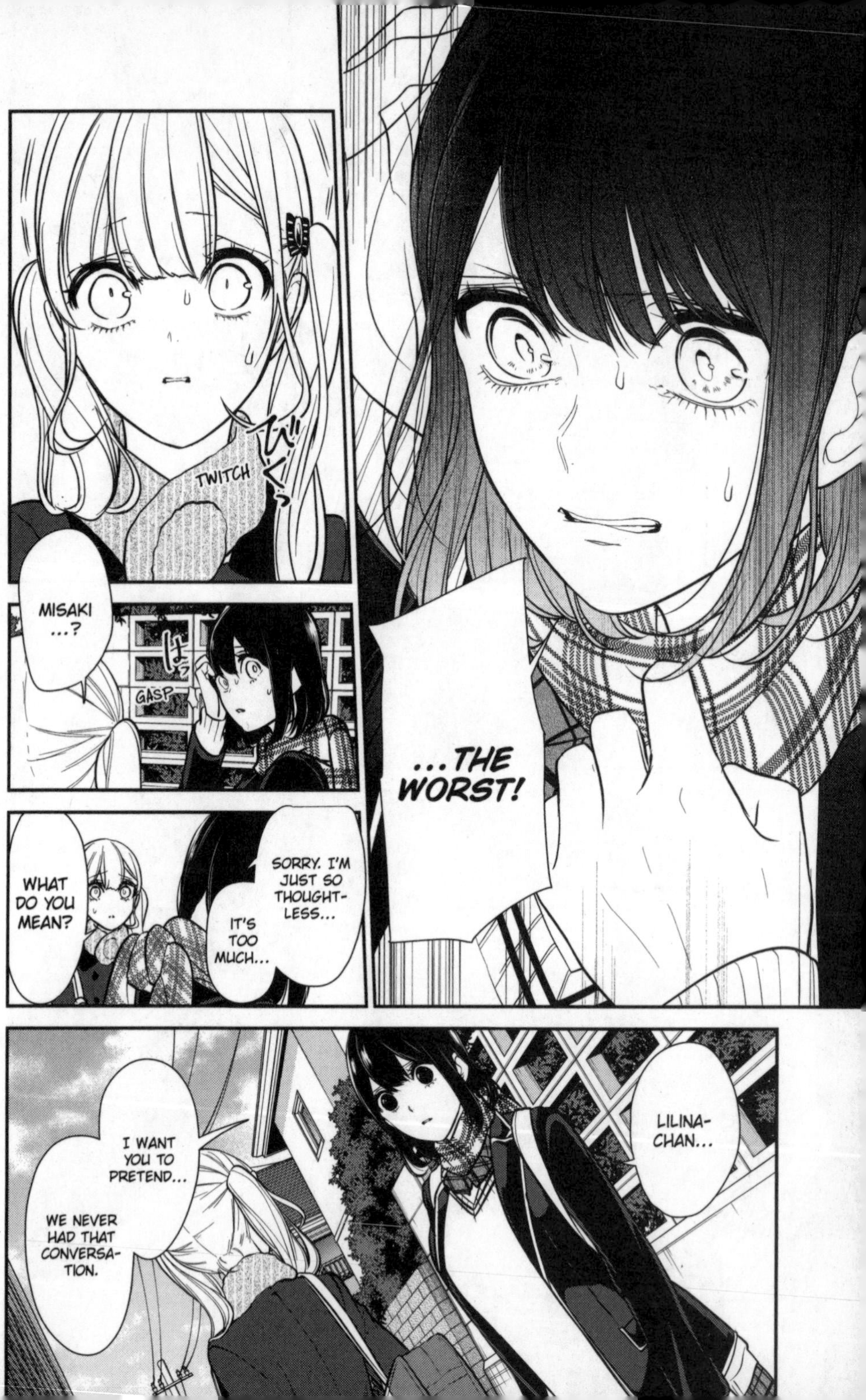
...THE WORST!
TWITCH
びくっ
MISAKI ...?
はっ
GASP
SORRY. I'M JUST SO THOUGHT-LESS...
IT'S TOO MUCH...
WHAT DO YOU MEAN?
LILINA-CHAN...
I WANT YOU TO PRETEND...
WE NEVER HAD THAT CONVERSA-TION.

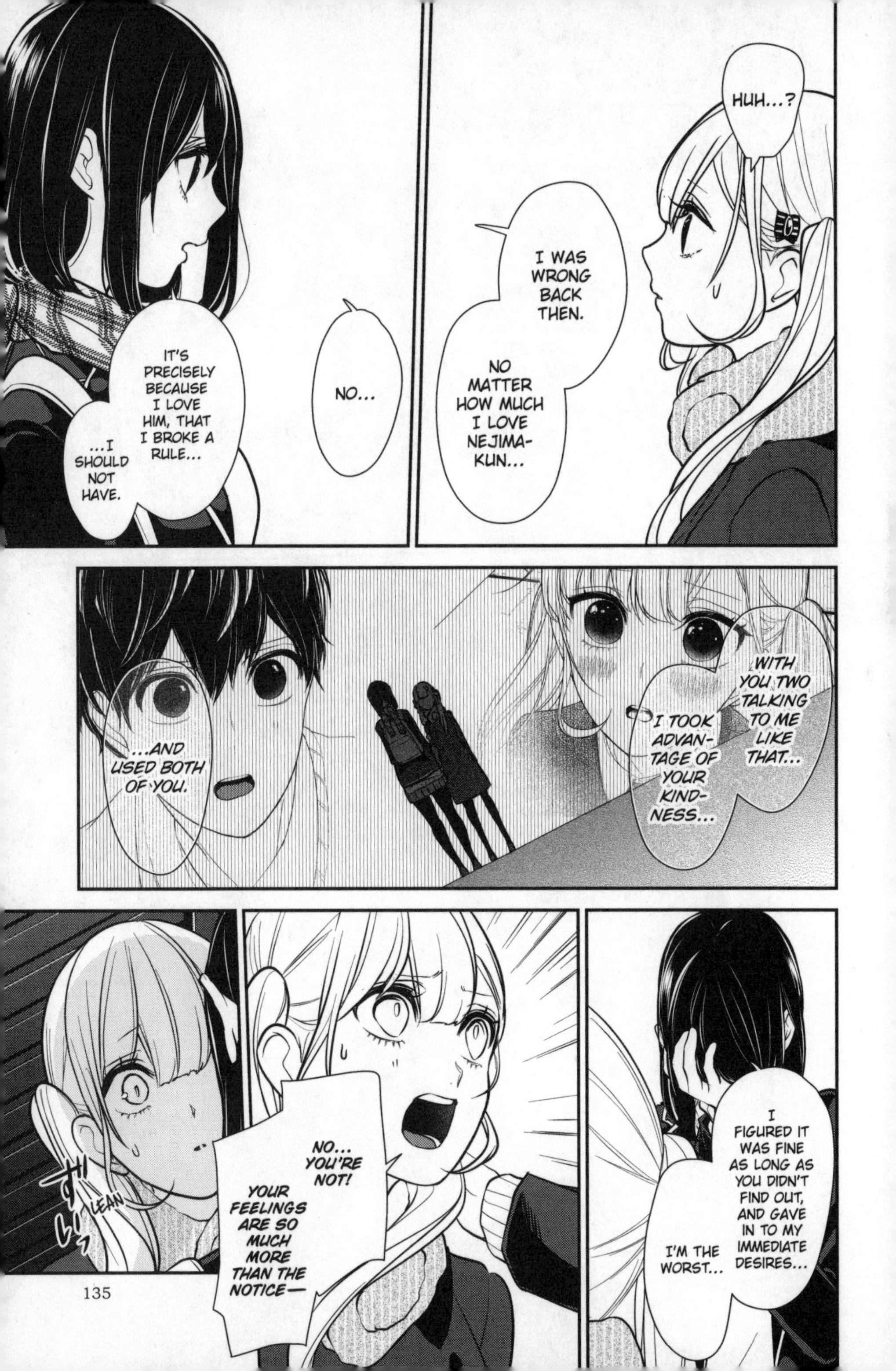
HUH...?
I WAS WRONG BACK THEN.
NO MATTER HOW MUCH I LOVE NEJIMA-KUN...
NO...
IT'S PRECISELY BECAUSE I LOVE HIM, THAT I BROKE A RULE...
...I SHOULD NOT HAVE.
WITH YOU TWO TALKING TO ME LIKE THAT...
I TOOK ADVANTAGE OF YOUR KINDNESS...
...AND USED BOTH OF YOU.
I FIGURED IT WAS FINE AS LONG AS YOU DIDN'T FIND OUT, AND GAVE IN TO MY IMMEDIATE DESIRES...
I'M THE WORST...
NO... YOU'RE NOT!
YOUR FEELINGS ARE SO MUCH MORE THAN THE NOTICE—
LEAN

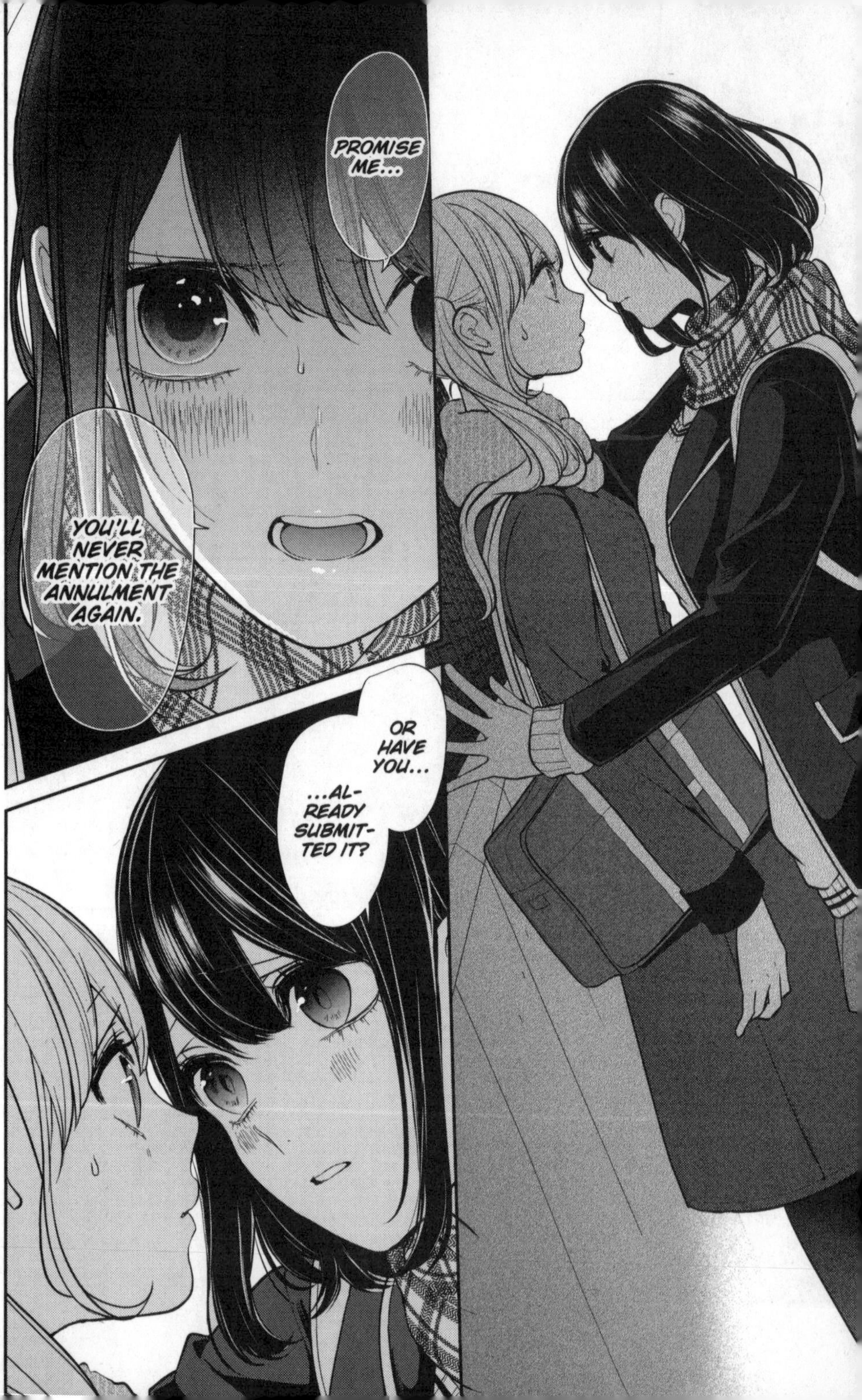
PROMISE ME...
YOU'LL NEVER MENTION THE ANNULMENT AGAIN.
OR HAVE YOU...
...AL-READY SUBMIT-TED IT?

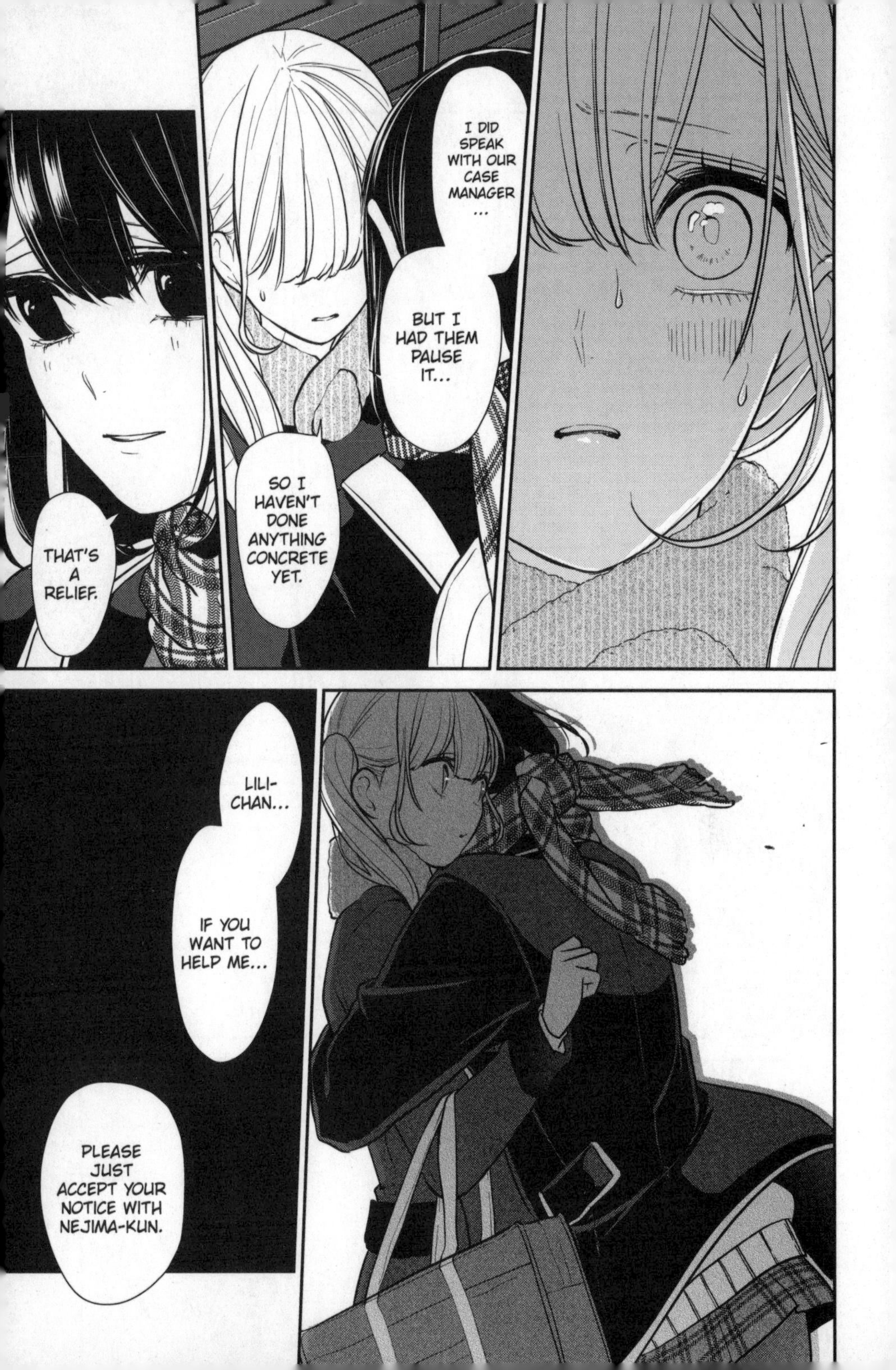
I DID SPEAK WITH OUR CASE MANAGER…
BUT I HAD THEM PAUSE IT…
SO I HAVEN'T DONE ANYTHING CONCRETE YET.
THAT'S A RELIEF.
LILI-CHAN…
IF YOU WANT TO HELP ME…
PLEASE JUST ACCEPT YOUR NOTICE WITH NEJIMA-KUN.

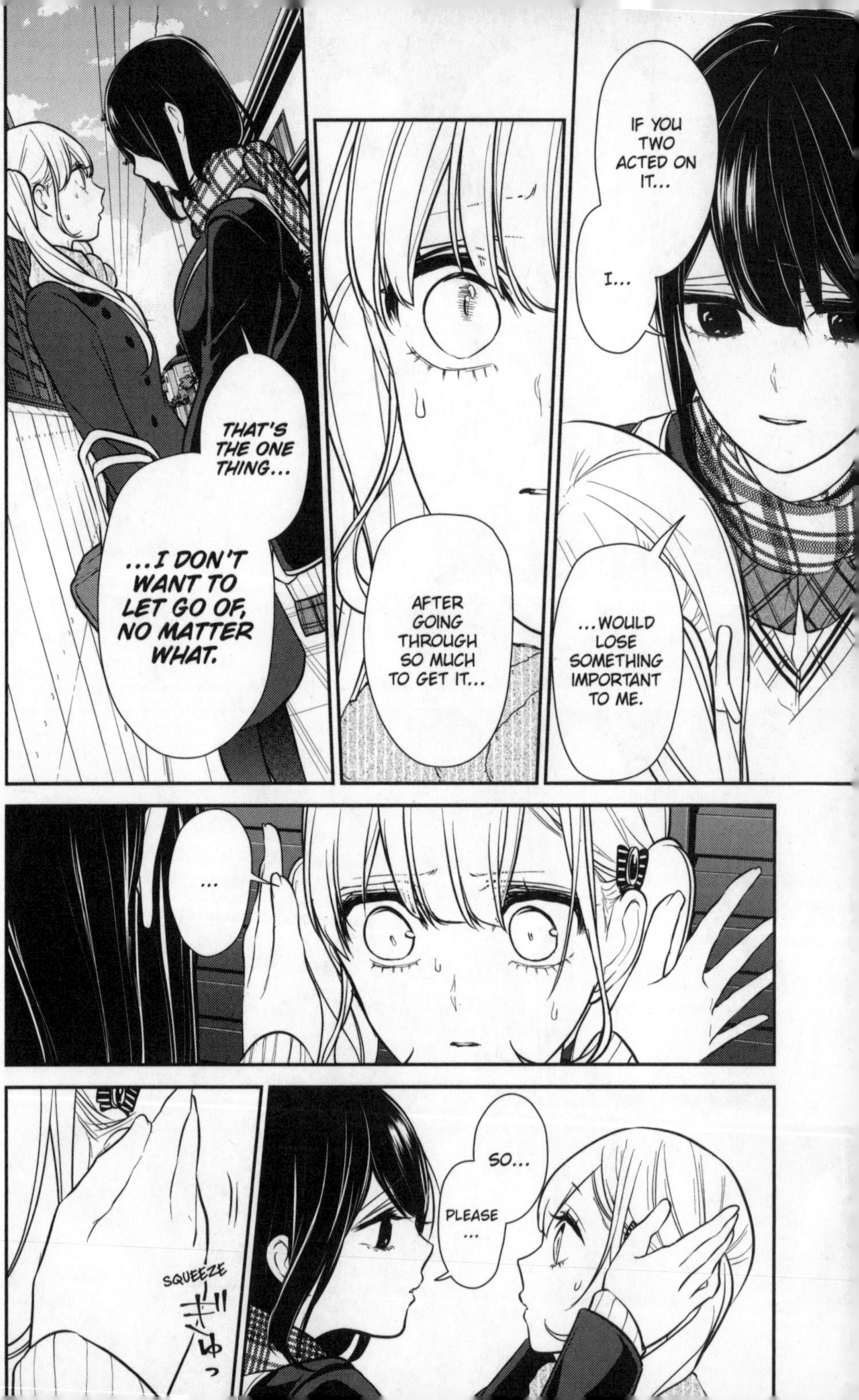
IF YOU TWO ACTED ON IT...
I...
...WOULD LOSE SOMETHING IMPORTANT TO ME.
AFTER GOING THROUGH SO MUCH TO GET IT...
THAT'S THE ONE THING...
...I DON'T WANT TO LET GO OF, NO MATTER WHAT.
...
SO...
PLEASE...
SQUEEZE

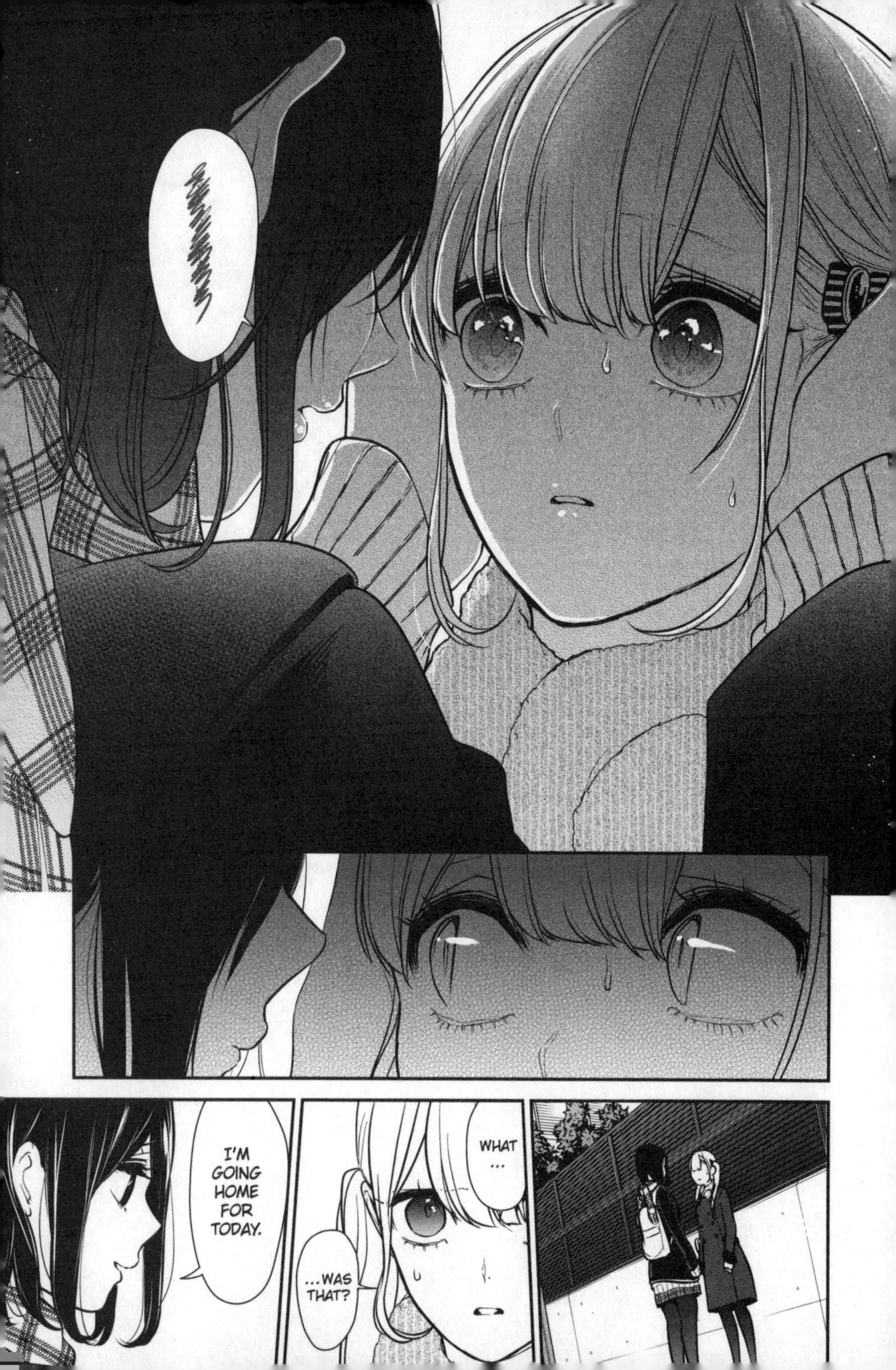
WHAT ...
...WAS THAT?
I'M GOING HOME FOR TODAY.

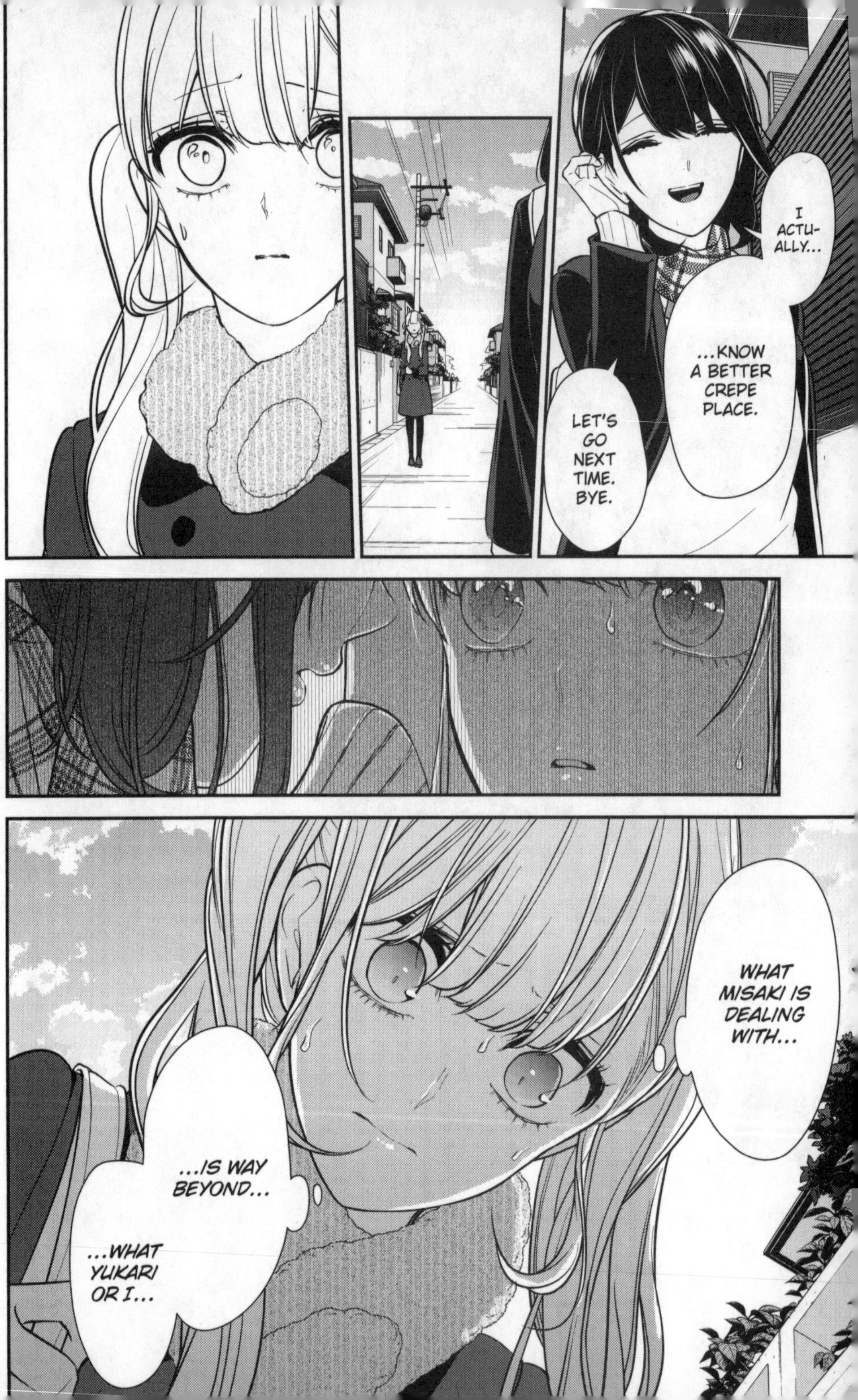
I ACTU-ALLY...
...KNOW A BETTER CREPE PLACE.
LET'S GO NEXT TIME. BYE.
WHAT MISAKI IS DEALING WITH...
...IS WAY BEYOND...
...WHAT YUKARI OR I...

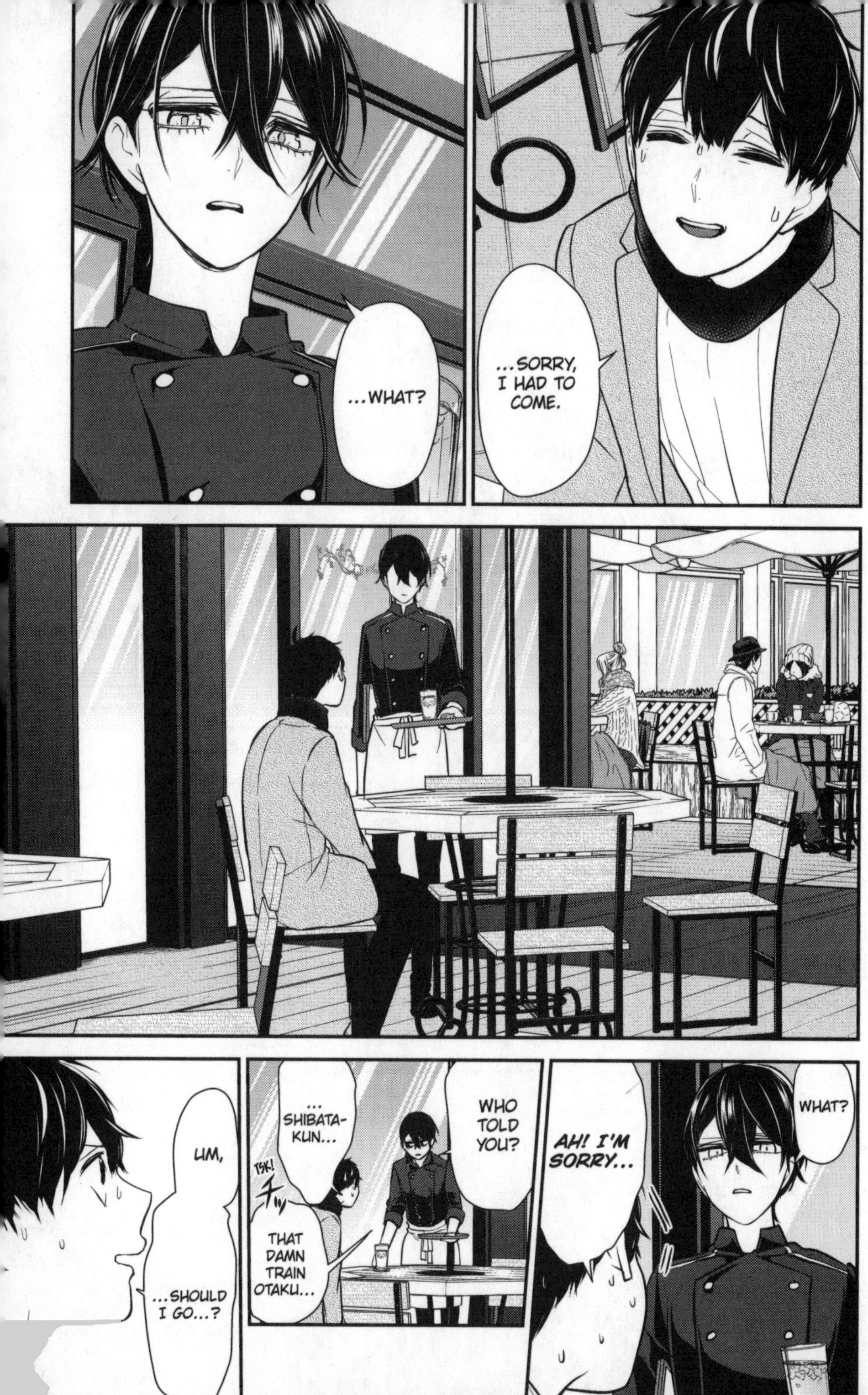
...SORRY, I HAD TO COME.
...WHAT?
WHAT?
AH! I'M SORRY...
WHO TOLD YOU?
... SHIBATA-KUN...
TSK!
チッ
THAT DAMN TRAIN OTAKU...
UM,
...SHOULD I GO...?

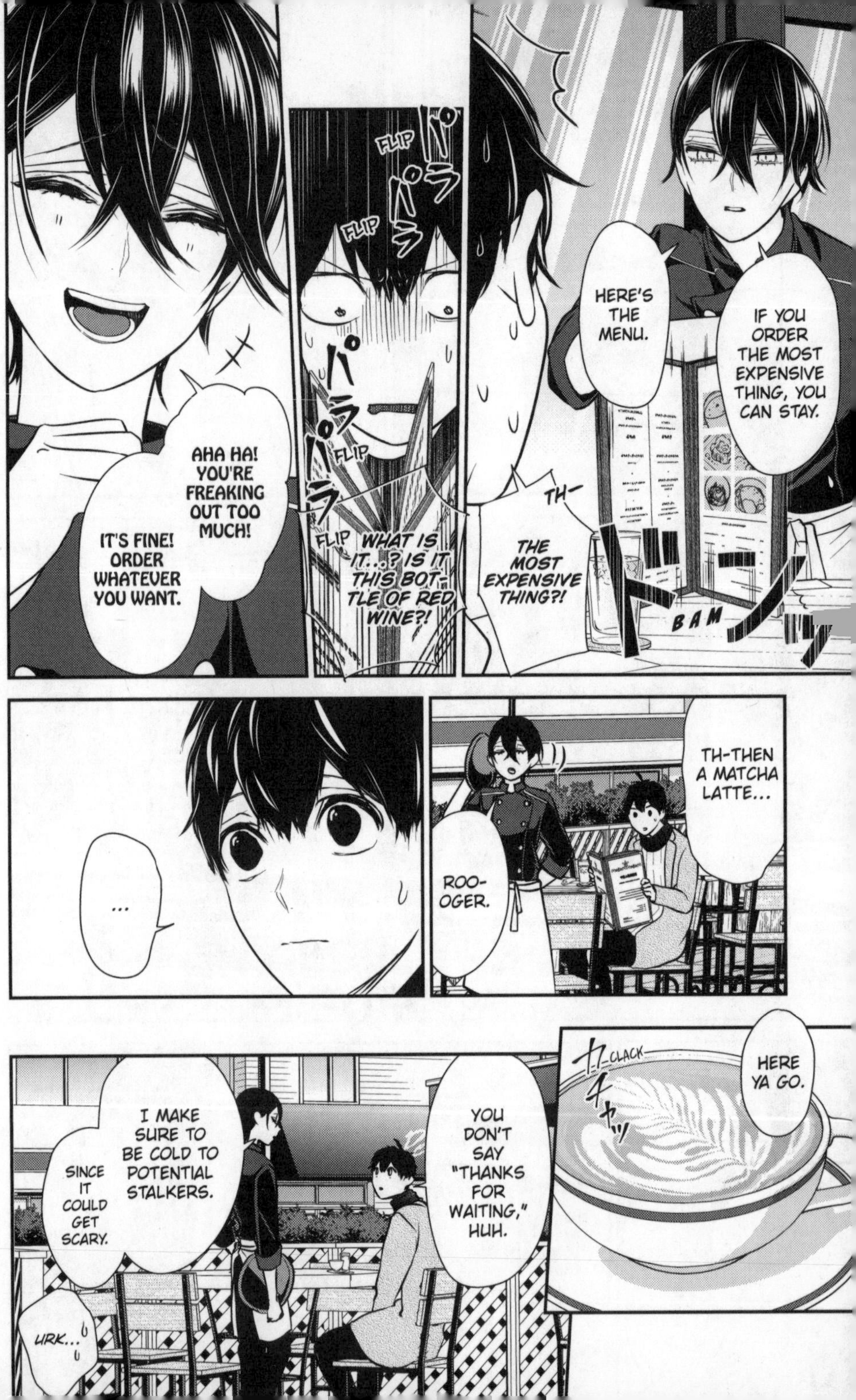
HERE'S THE MENU.
IF YOU ORDER THE MOST EXPENSIVE THING, YOU CAN STAY.
BAM
TH—
THE MOST EXPENSIVE THING?!
FLIP
FLIP
FLIP
FLIP
WHAT IS IT...? IS IT THIS BOT-TLE OF RED WINE?!
AHA HA! YOU'RE FREAKING OUT TOO MUCH!
IT'S FINE! ORDER WHATEVER YOU WANT.
TH-THEN A MATCHA LATTE...
ROO-OGER.
...
CLACK
HERE YA GO.
YOU DON'T SAY "THANKS FOR WAITING," HUH.
I MAKE SURE TO BE COLD TO POTENTIAL STALKERS.
SINCE IT COULD GET SCARY.
URK...

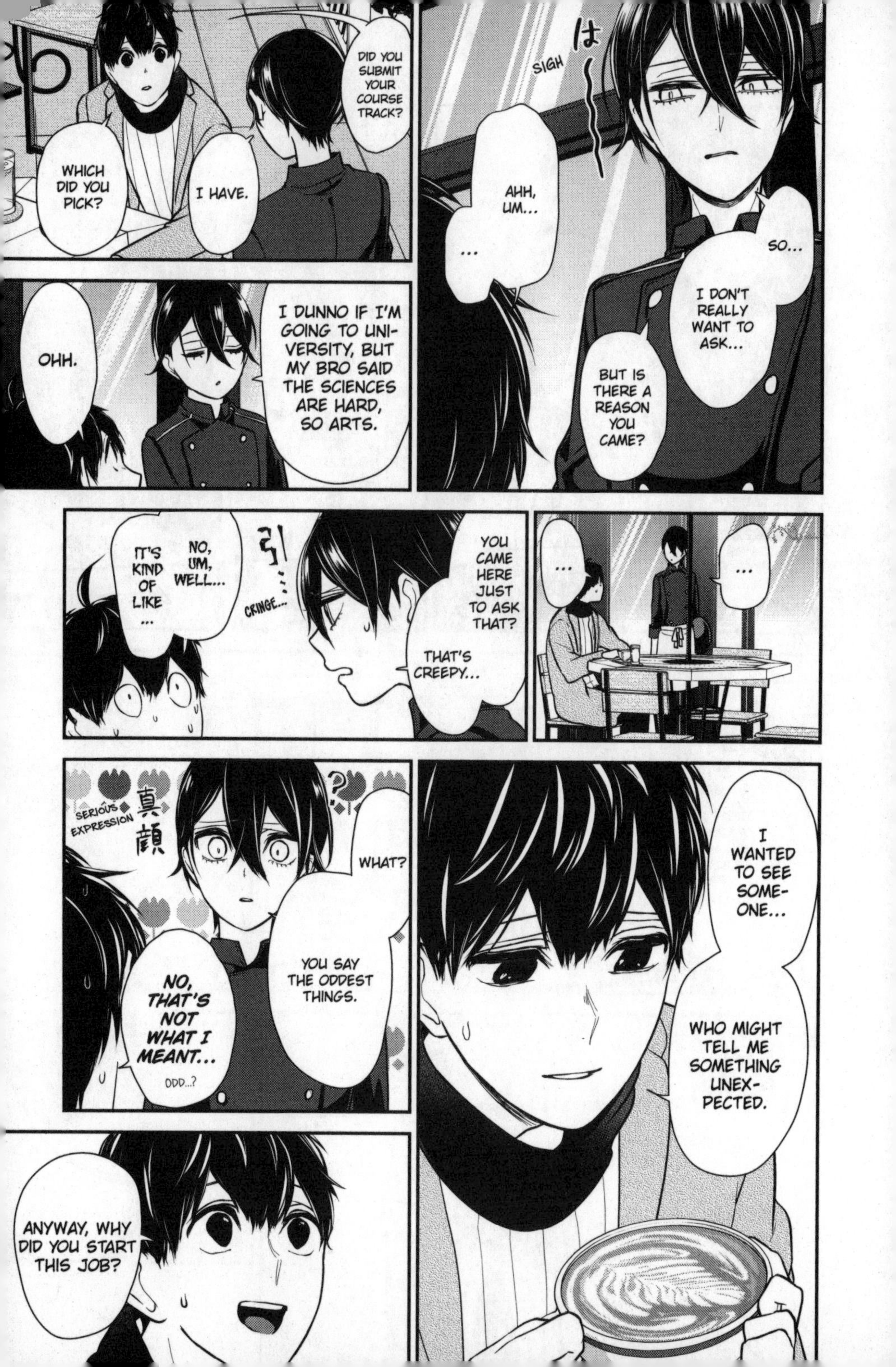
は~
SIGH
AHH, UM...
...
SO...
I DON'T REALLY WANT TO ASK...
BUT IS THERE A REASON YOU CAME?
DID YOU SUBMIT YOUR COURSE TRACK?
I HAVE.
WHICH DID YOU PICK?
I DUNNO IF I'M GOING TO UNIVERSITY, BUT MY BRO SAID THE SCIENCES ARE HARD, SO ARTS.
OHH.
...
...
YOU CAME HERE JUST TO ASK THAT?
THAT'S CREEPY...
CRINGE...
NO, UM, WELL...
IT'S KIND OF LIKE...
I WANTED TO SEE SOMEONE...
WHO MIGHT TELL ME SOMETHING UNEXPECTED.
WHAT?
真顔
SERIOUS EXPRESSION
YOU SAY THE ODDEST THINGS.
NO, THAT'S NOT WHAT I MEANT...
ODD...?
ANYWAY, WHY DID YOU START THIS JOB?

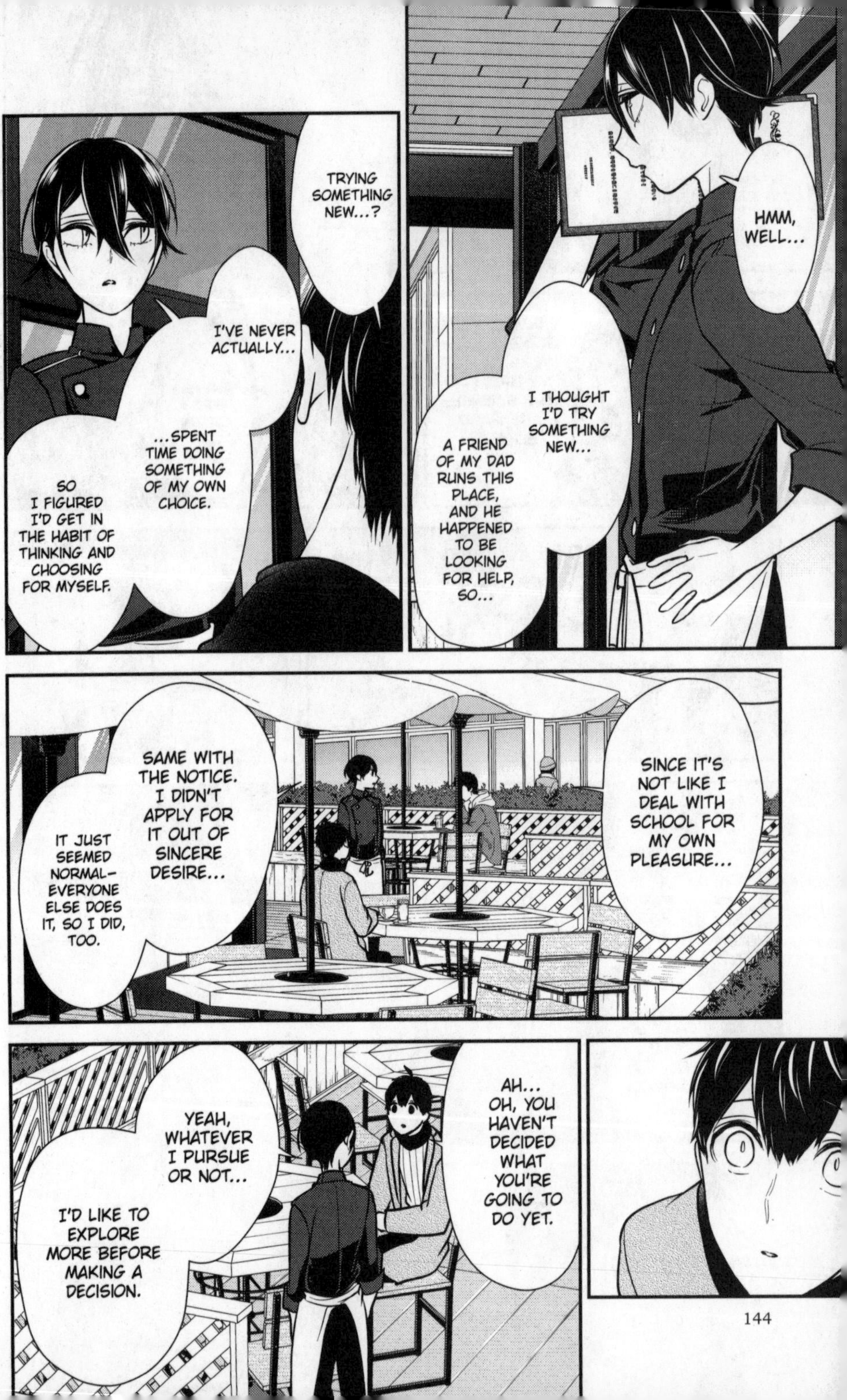
HMM, WELL...
I THOUGHT I'D TRY SOMETHING NEW...
A FRIEND OF MY DAD RUNS THIS PLACE, AND HE HAPPENED TO BE LOOKING FOR HELP, SO...
TRYING SOMETHING NEW...?
I'VE NEVER ACTUALLY...
...SPENT TIME DOING SOMETHING OF MY OWN CHOICE.
SO I FIGURED I'D GET IN THE HABIT OF THINKING AND CHOOSING FOR MYSELF.
SINCE IT'S NOT LIKE I DEAL WITH SCHOOL FOR MY OWN PLEASURE...
SAME WITH THE NOTICE. I DIDN'T APPLY FOR IT OUT OF SINCERE DESIRE...
IT JUST SEEMED NORMAL– EVERYONE ELSE DOES IT, SO I DID, TOO.
AH... OH, YOU HAVEN'T DECIDED WHAT YOU'RE GOING TO DO YET.
YEAH, WHATEVER I PURSUE OR NOT...
I'D LIKE TO EXPLORE MORE BEFORE MAKING A DECISION.

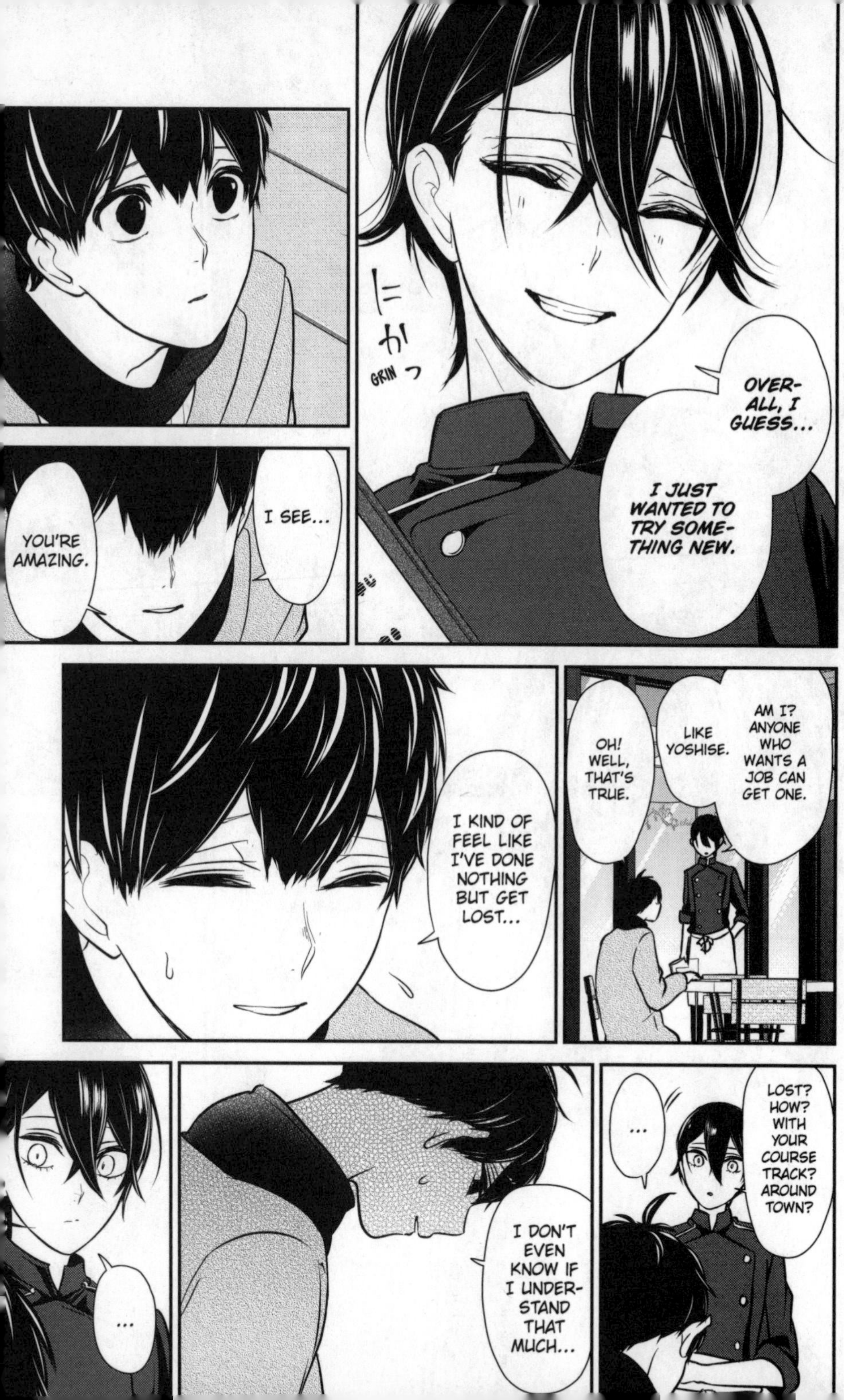
にかっ
GRIN
OVER-ALL, I GUESS...
I JUST WANTED TO TRY SOME-THING NEW.
I SEE...
YOU'RE AMAZING.
AM I? ANYONE WHO WANTS A JOB CAN GET ONE.
LIKE YOSHISE.
OH! WELL, THAT'S TRUE.
I KIND OF FEEL LIKE I'VE DONE NOTHING BUT GET LOST...
LOST? HOW? WITH YOUR COURSE TRACK? AROUND TOWN?
...
I DON'T EVEN KNOW IF I UNDER-STAND THAT MUCH...
...

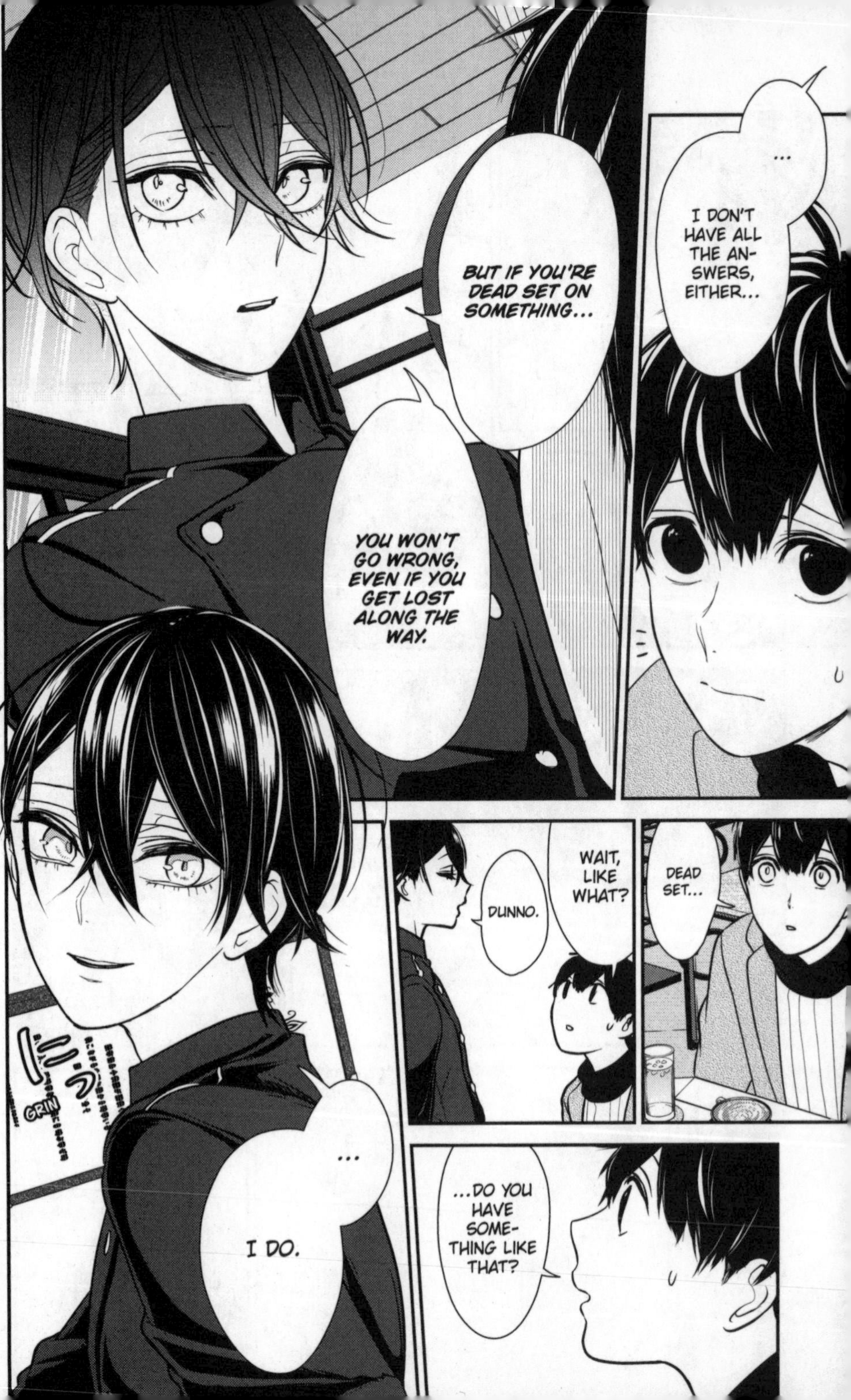
...
I DON'T HAVE ALL THE ANSWERS, EITHER...
BUT IF YOU'RE DEAD SET ON SOMETHING...
YOU WON'T GO WRONG, EVEN IF YOU GET LOST ALONG THE WAY.
DEAD SET...
WAIT, LIKE WHAT?
DUNNO.
...DO YOU HAVE SOMETHING LIKE THAT?
...
I DO.
GRIN

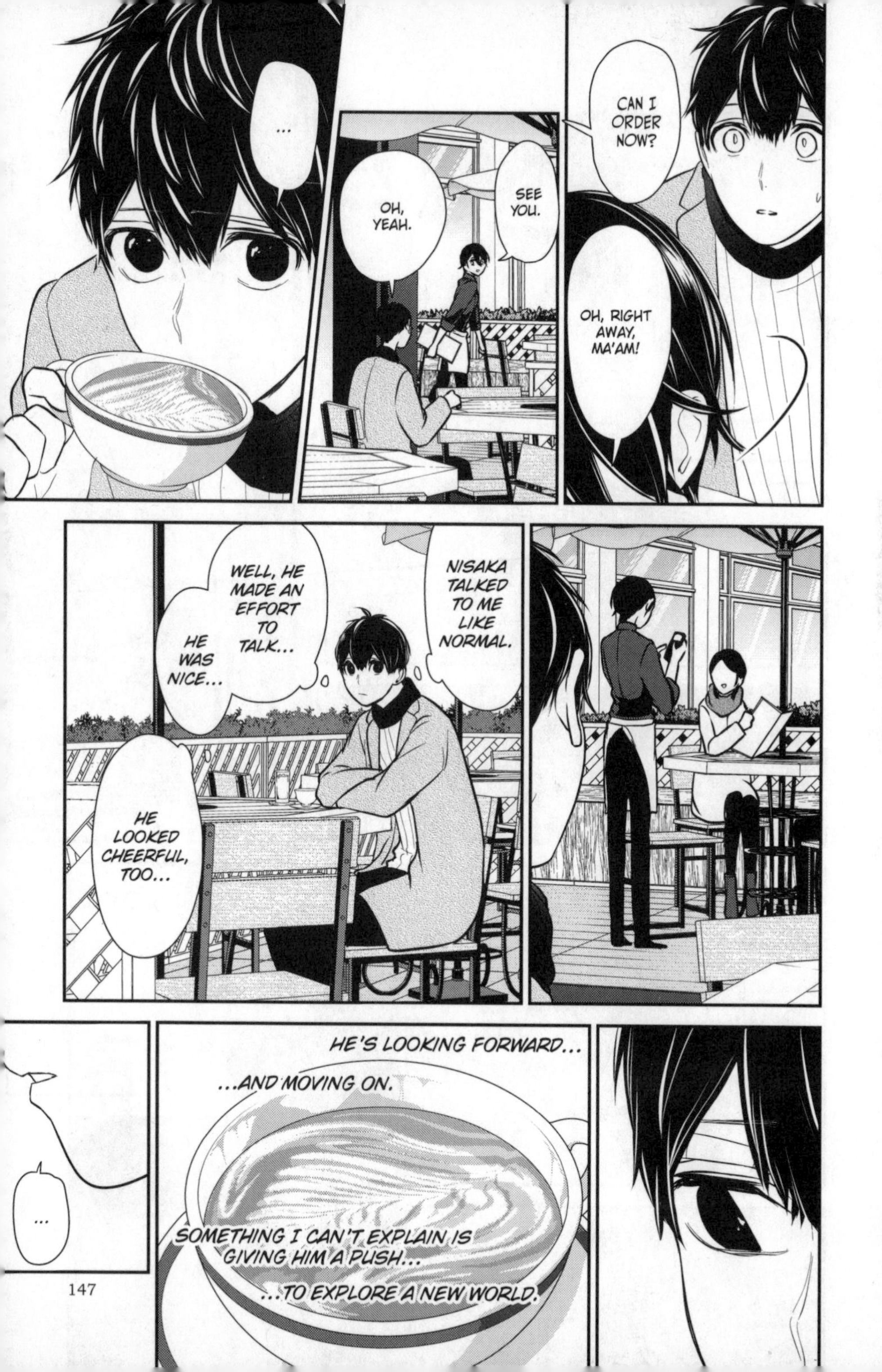
CAN I ORDER NOW?
OH, RIGHT AWAY, MA'AM!
SEE YOU.
OH, YEAH.
...
NISAKA TALKED TO ME LIKE NORMAL.
WELL, HE MADE AN EFFORT TO TALK...
HE WAS NICE...
HE LOOKED CHEERFUL, TOO...
HE'S LOOKING FORWARD...
...AND MOVING ON.
SOMETHING I CAN'T EXPLAIN IS GIVING HIM A PUSH...
...TO EXPLORE A NEW WORLD.
...

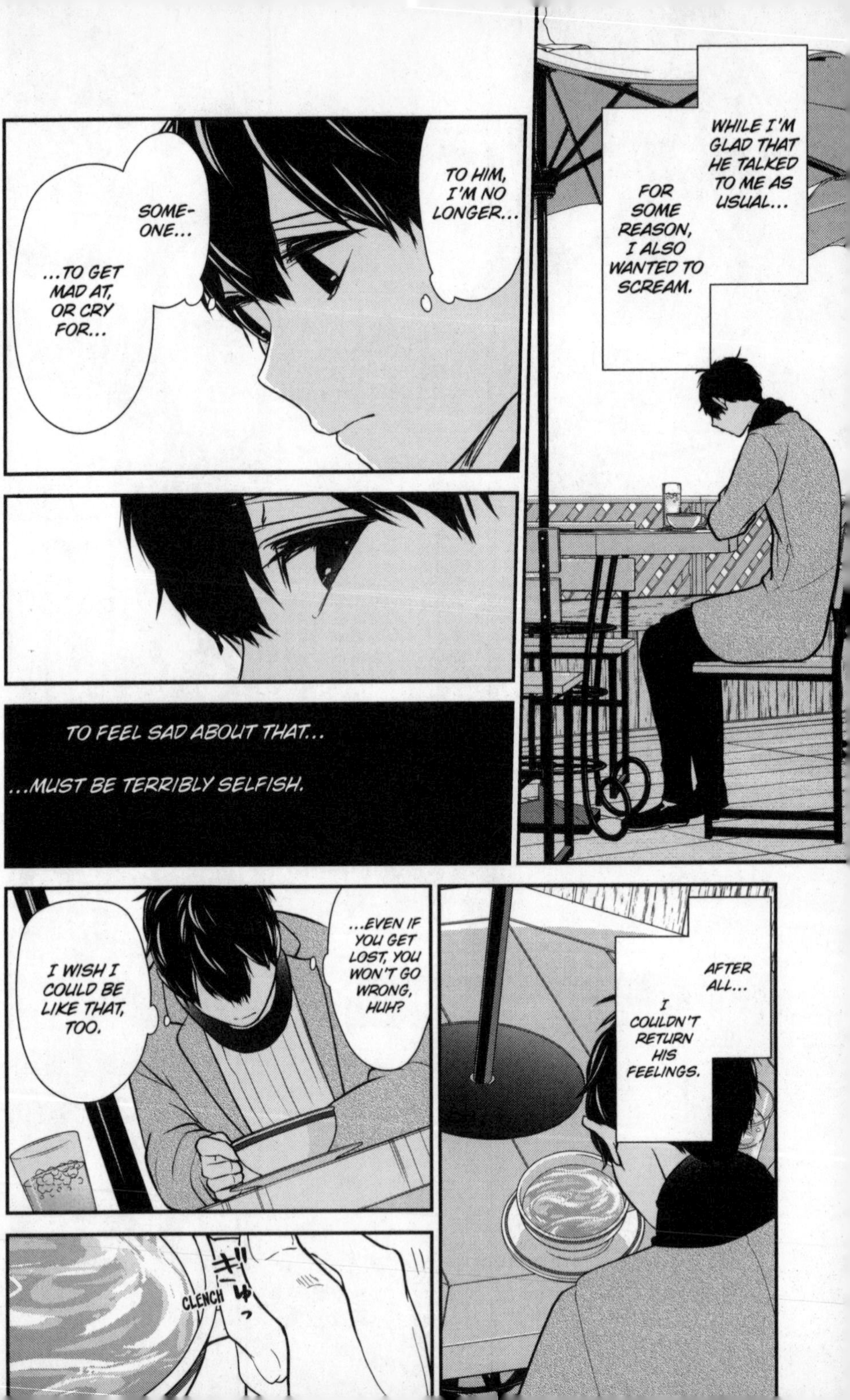
WHILE I'M GLAD THAT HE TALKED TO ME AS USUAL...
FOR SOME REASON, I ALSO WANTED TO SCREAM.
TO HIM, I'M NO LONGER...
SOME-ONE...
...TO GET MAD AT, OR CRY FOR...
TO FEEL SAD ABOUT THAT...
...MUST BE TERRIBLY SELFISH.
AFTER ALL...
I COULDN'T RETURN HIS FEELINGS.
...EVEN IF YOU GET LOST, YOU WON'T GO WRONG, HUH?
I WISH I COULD BE LIKE THAT, TOO.
ぎゅっ
CLENCH

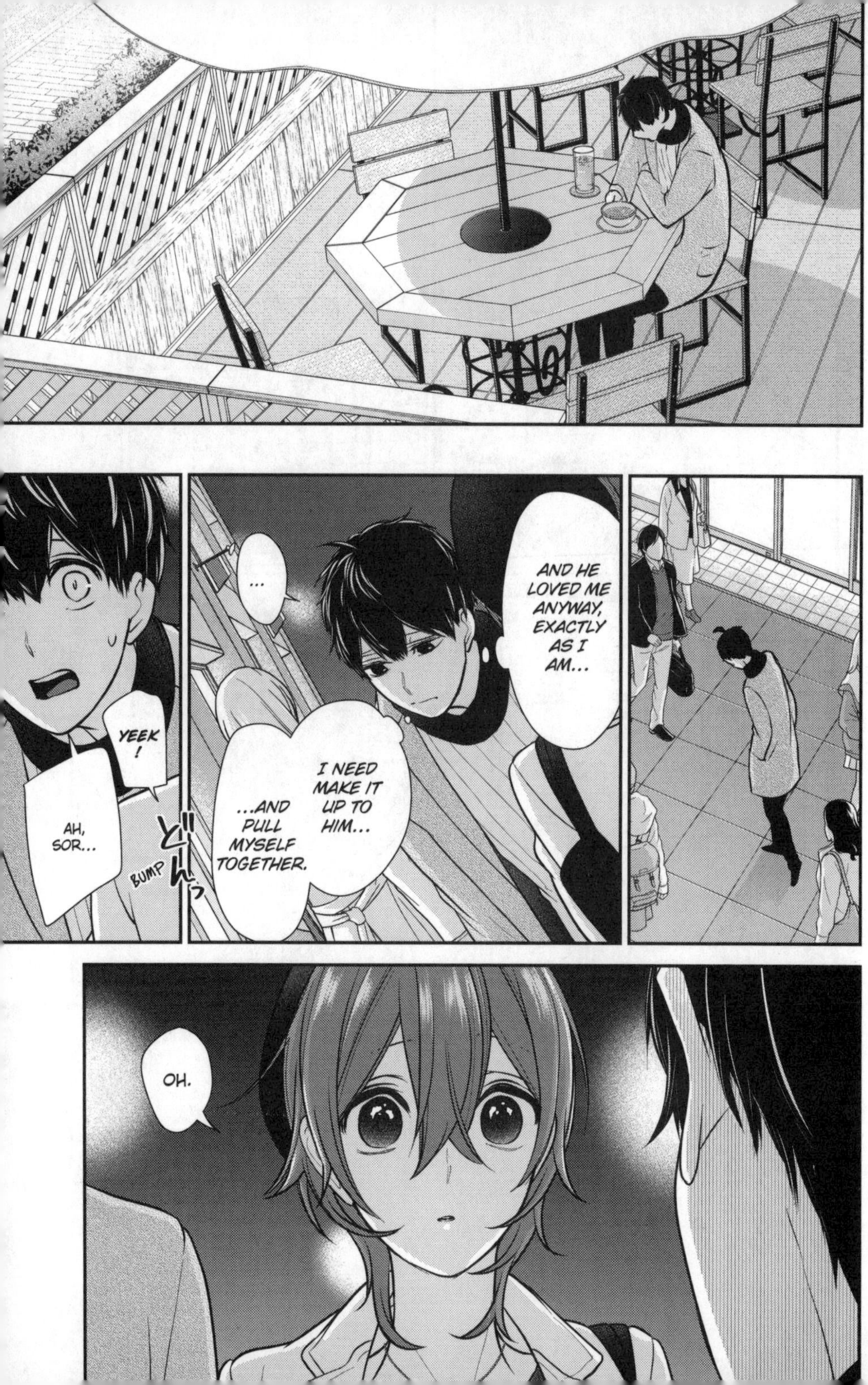
AND HE LOVED ME ANYWAY, EXACTLY AS I AM...
...
I NEED MAKE IT UP TO HIM...
...AND PULL MYSELF TOGETHER.
YEEK!
BUMP
AH, SOR...
OH.

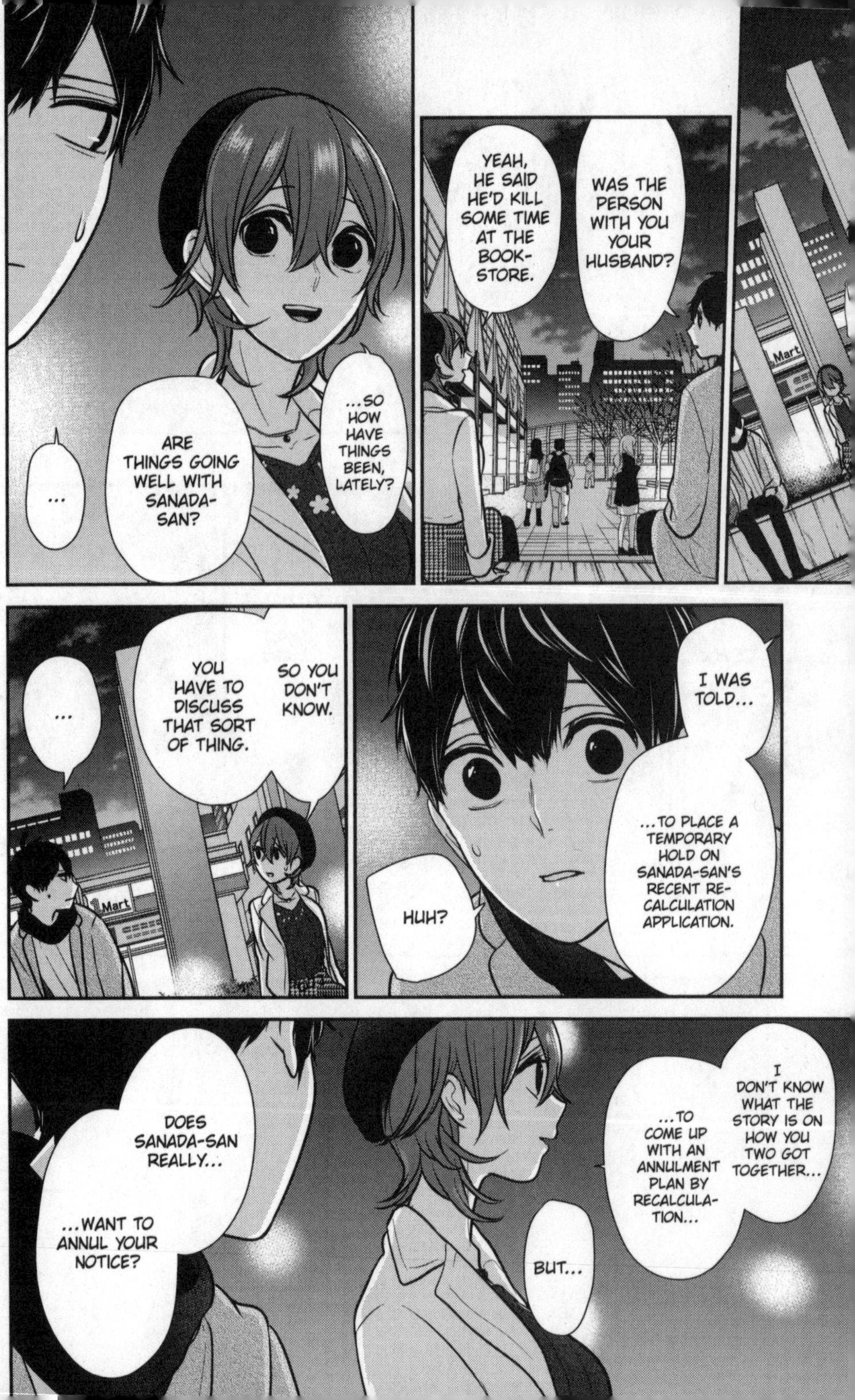
WAS THE PERSON WITH YOU YOUR HUSBAND?
YEAH, HE SAID HE'D KILL SOME TIME AT THE BOOK-STORE.
...SO HOW HAVE THINGS BEEN, LATELY?
ARE THINGS GOING WELL WITH SANADA-SAN?
...
I WAS TOLD...
...TO PLACE A TEMPORARY HOLD ON SANADA-SAN'S RECENT RE-CALCULATION APPLICATION.
HUH?
SO YOU DON'T KNOW.
YOU HAVE TO DISCUSS THAT SORT OF THING.
...
I DON'T KNOW WHAT THE STORY IS ON HOW YOU TWO GOT TOGETHER...
...TO COME UP WITH AN ANNULMENT PLAN BY RECALCULA-TION...
BUT...
DOES SANADA-SAN REALLY...
...WANT TO ANNUL YOUR NOTICE?

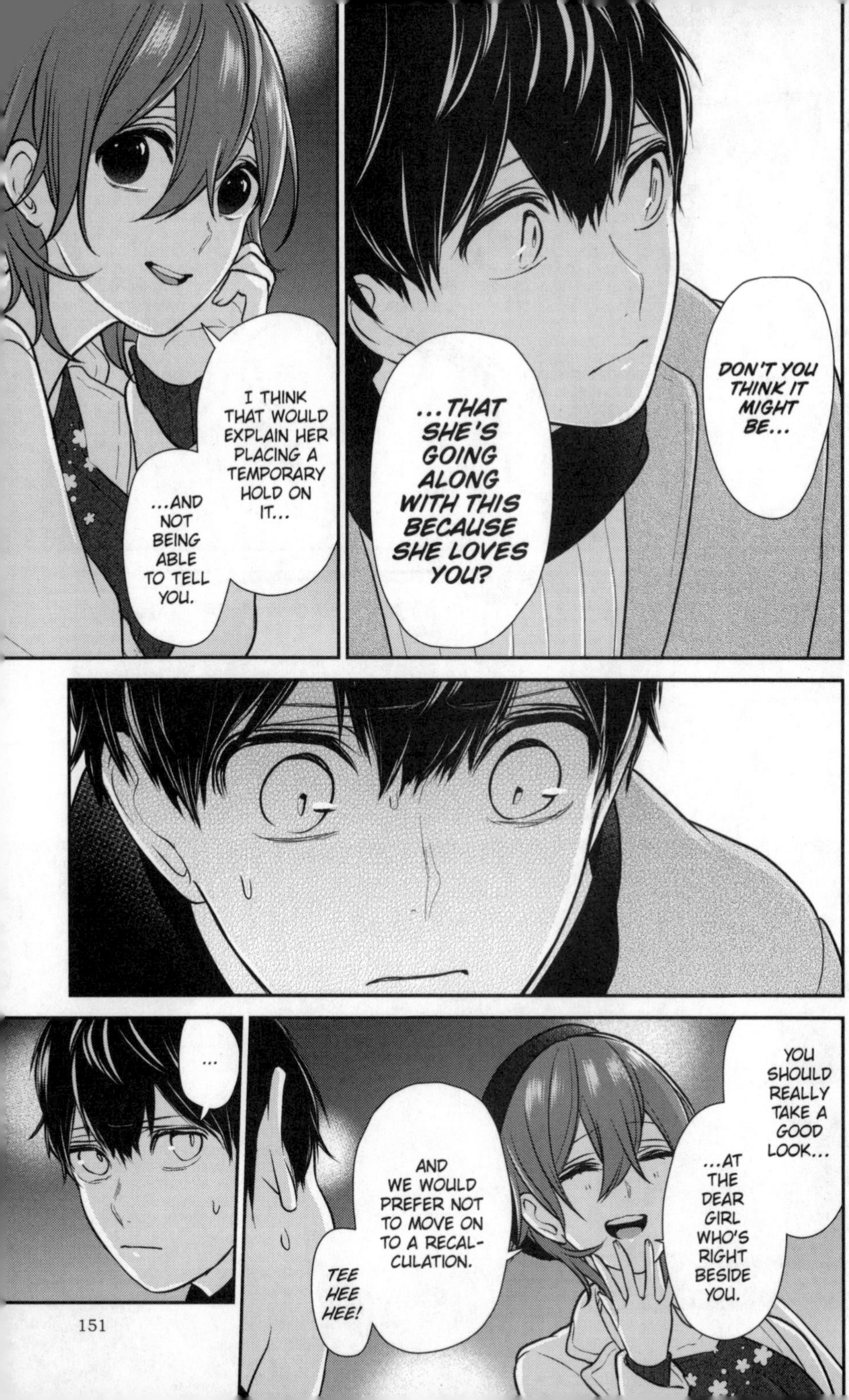
DON'T YOU THINK IT MIGHT BE...
...THAT SHE'S GOING ALONG WITH THIS BECAUSE SHE LOVES YOU?
I THINK THAT WOULD EXPLAIN HER PLACING A TEMPORARY HOLD ON IT...
...AND NOT BEING ABLE TO TELL YOU.
YOU SHOULD REALLY TAKE A GOOD LOOK...
...AT THE DEAR GIRL WHO'S RIGHT BESIDE YOU.
AND WE WOULD PREFER NOT TO MOVE ON TO A RECAL-CULATION.
TEE HEE HEE!
...

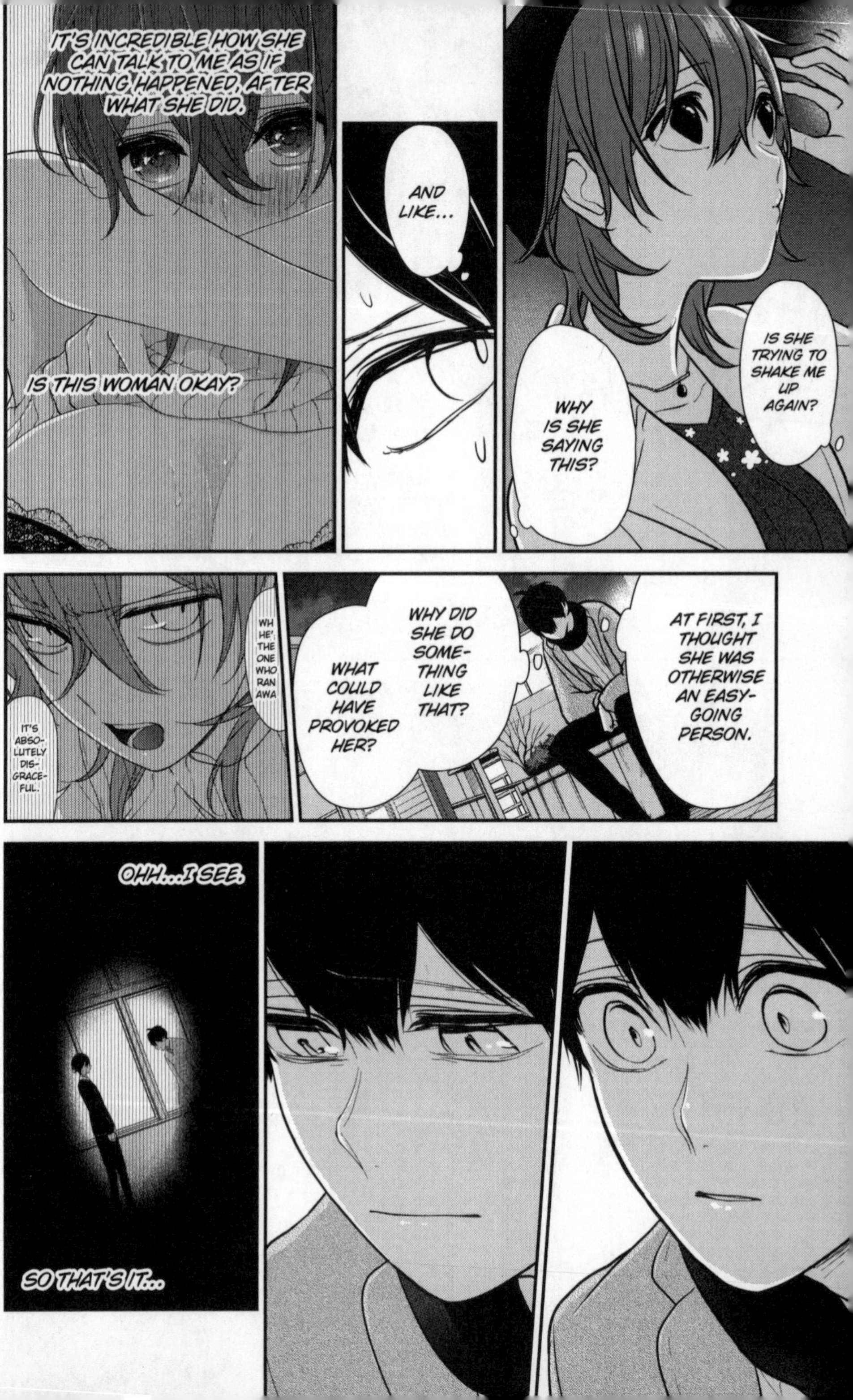
IS SHE TRYING TO SHAKE ME UP AGAIN?
WHY IS SHE SAYING THIS?
AND LIKE...
IT'S INCREDIBLE HOW SHE CAN TALK TO ME AS IF NOTHING HAPPENED, AFTER WHAT SHE DID.
IS THIS WOMAN OKAY?
AT FIRST, I THOUGHT SHE WAS OTHERWISE AN EASY-GOING PERSON.
WHY DID SHE DO SOMETHING LIKE THAT?
WHAT COULD HAVE PROVOKED HER?
WH HE' THE ONE WHO RAN AWA
IT'S ABSOLUTELY DISGRACEFUL.
OHH...I SEE.
SO THAT'S IT...

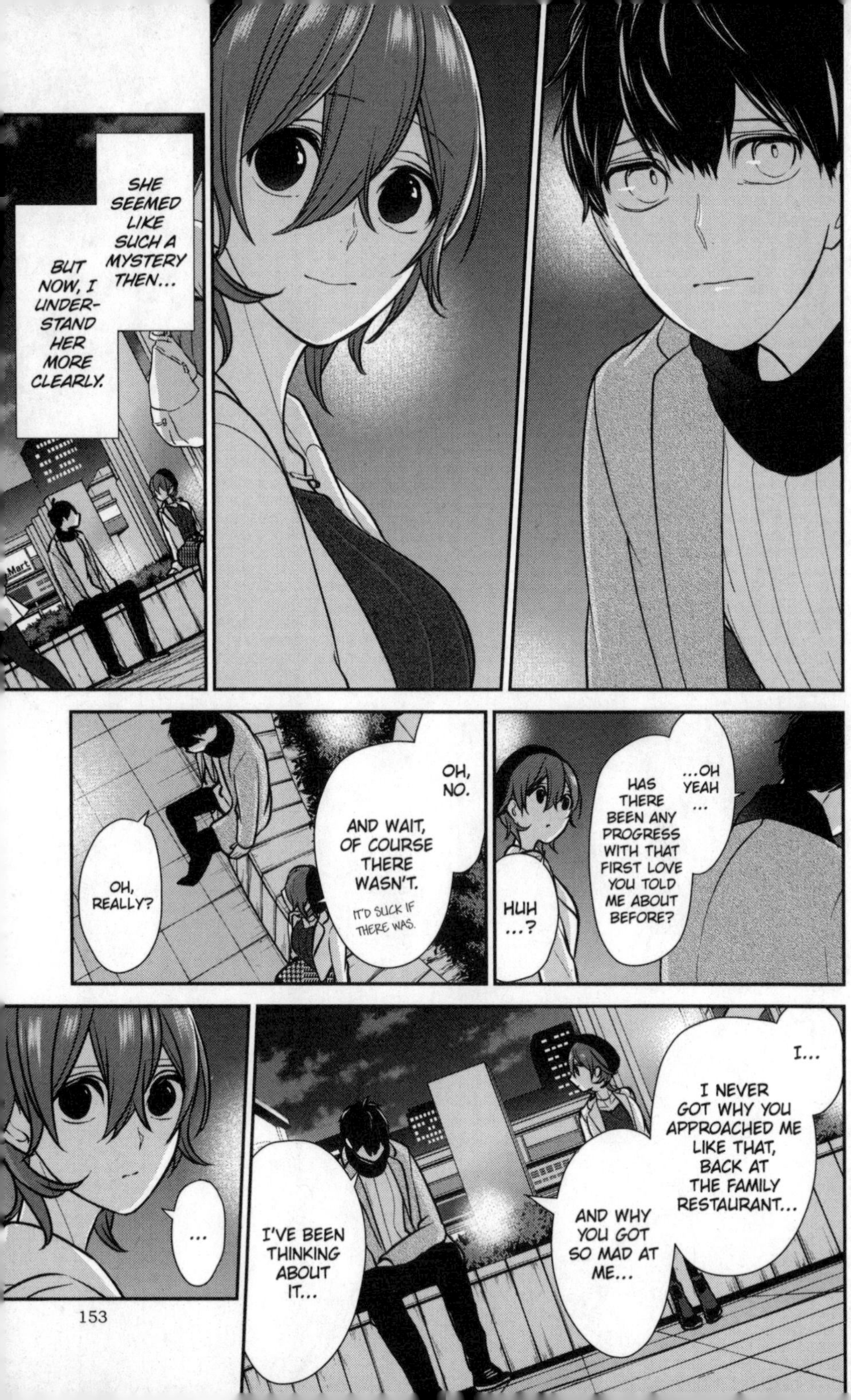
SHE SEEMED LIKE SUCH A MYSTERY THEN...
BUT NOW, I UNDERSTAND HER MORE CLEARLY.
...OH YEAH...
HAS THERE BEEN ANY PROGRESS WITH THAT FIRST LOVE YOU TOLD ME ABOUT BEFORE?
HUH...?
OH, NO.
AND WAIT, OF COURSE THERE WASN'T.
IT'D SUCK IF THERE WAS.
OH, REALLY?
I...
I NEVER GOT WHY YOU APPROACHED ME LIKE THAT, BACK AT THE FAMILY RESTAURANT...
AND WHY YOU GOT SO MAD AT ME...
I'VE BEEN THINKING ABOUT IT...
...

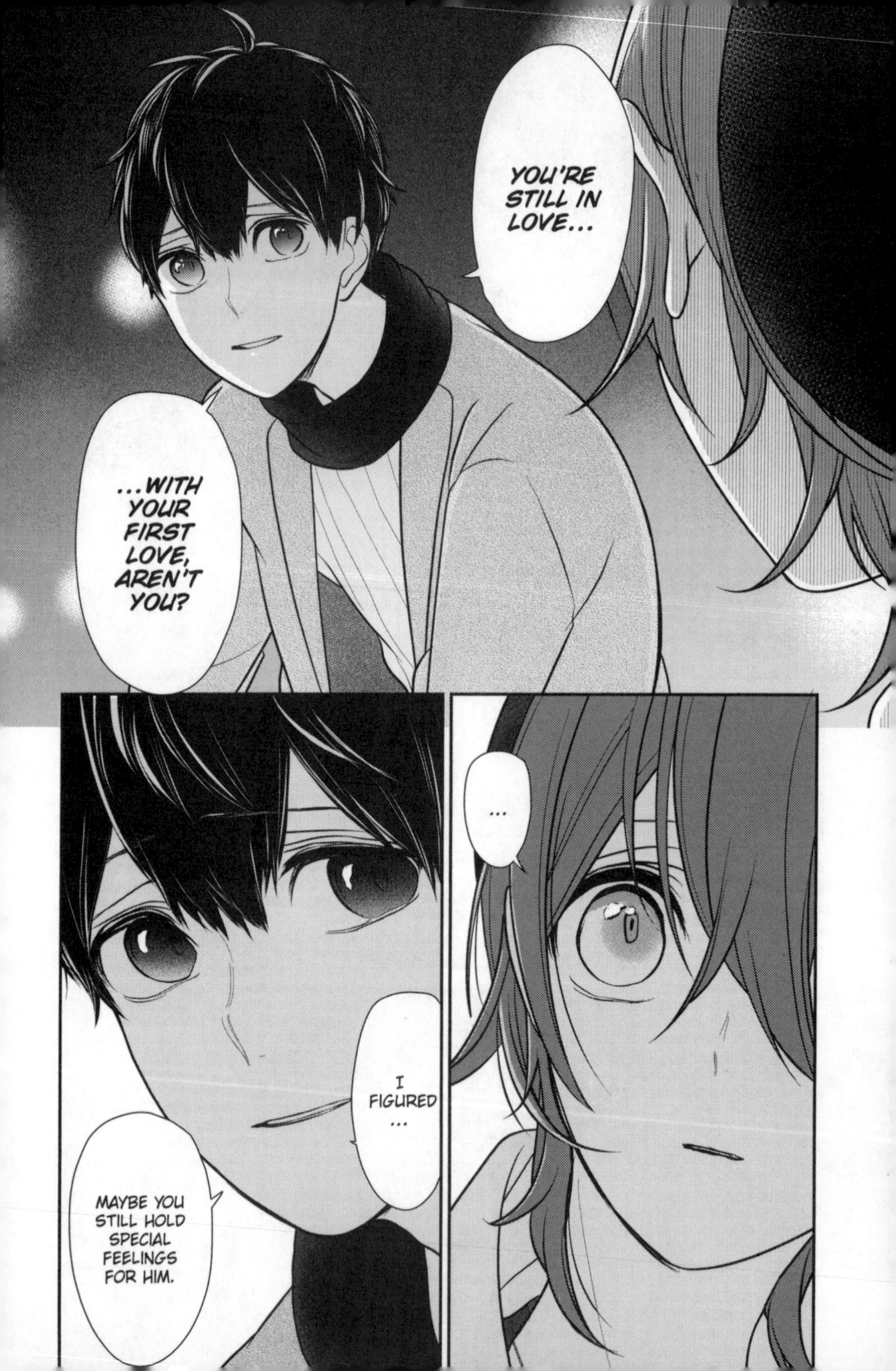
YOU'RE STILL IN LOVE...
...WITH YOUR FIRST LOVE, AREN'T YOU?
...
I FIGURED...
MAYBE YOU STILL HOLD SPECIAL FEELINGS FOR HIM.

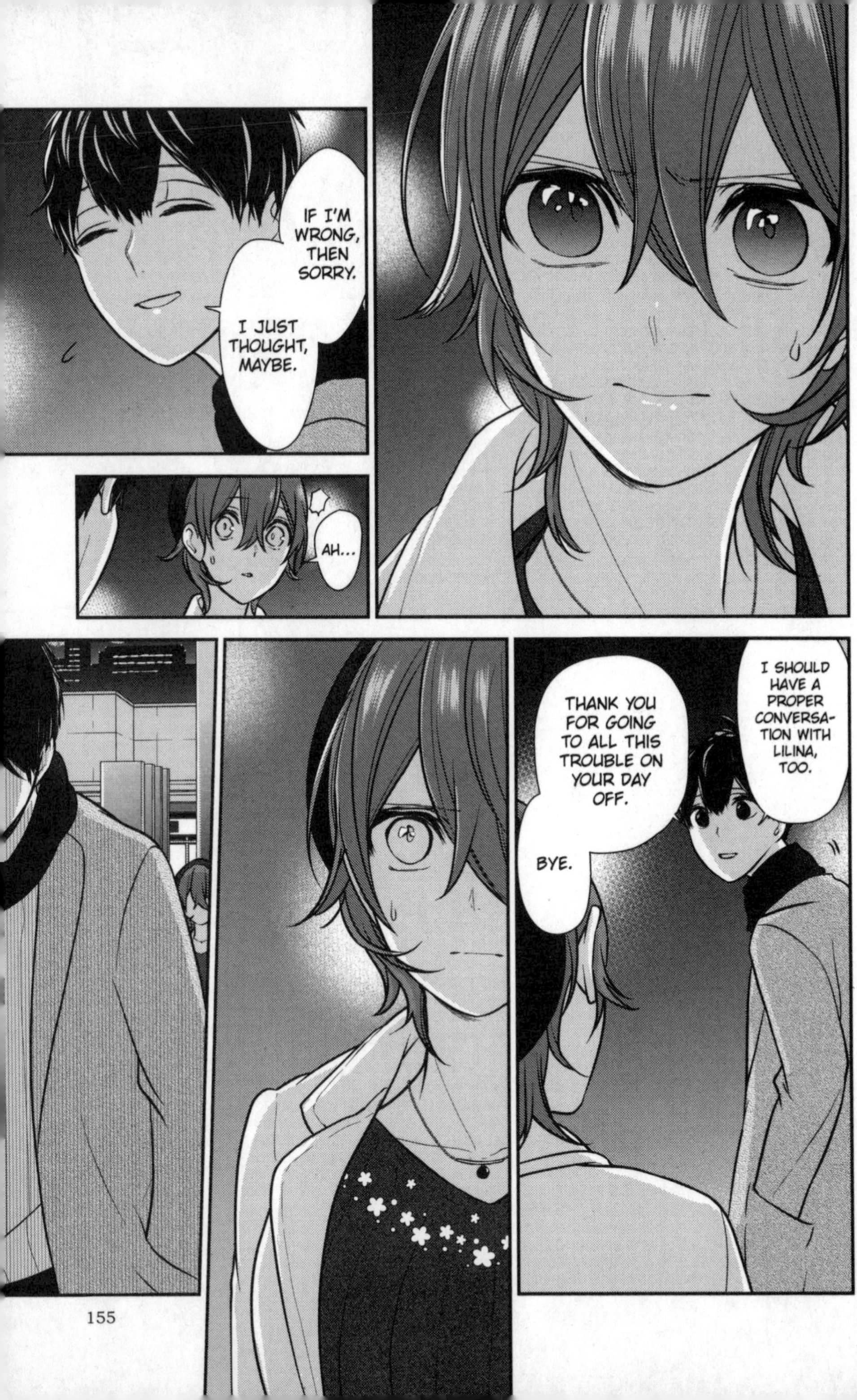
IF I'M WRONG, THEN SORRY.
I JUST THOUGHT, MAYBE.
AH...
I SHOULD HAVE A PROPER CONVERSATION WITH LILINA, TOO.
THANK YOU FOR GOING TO ALL THIS TROUBLE ON YOUR DAY OFF.
BYE.

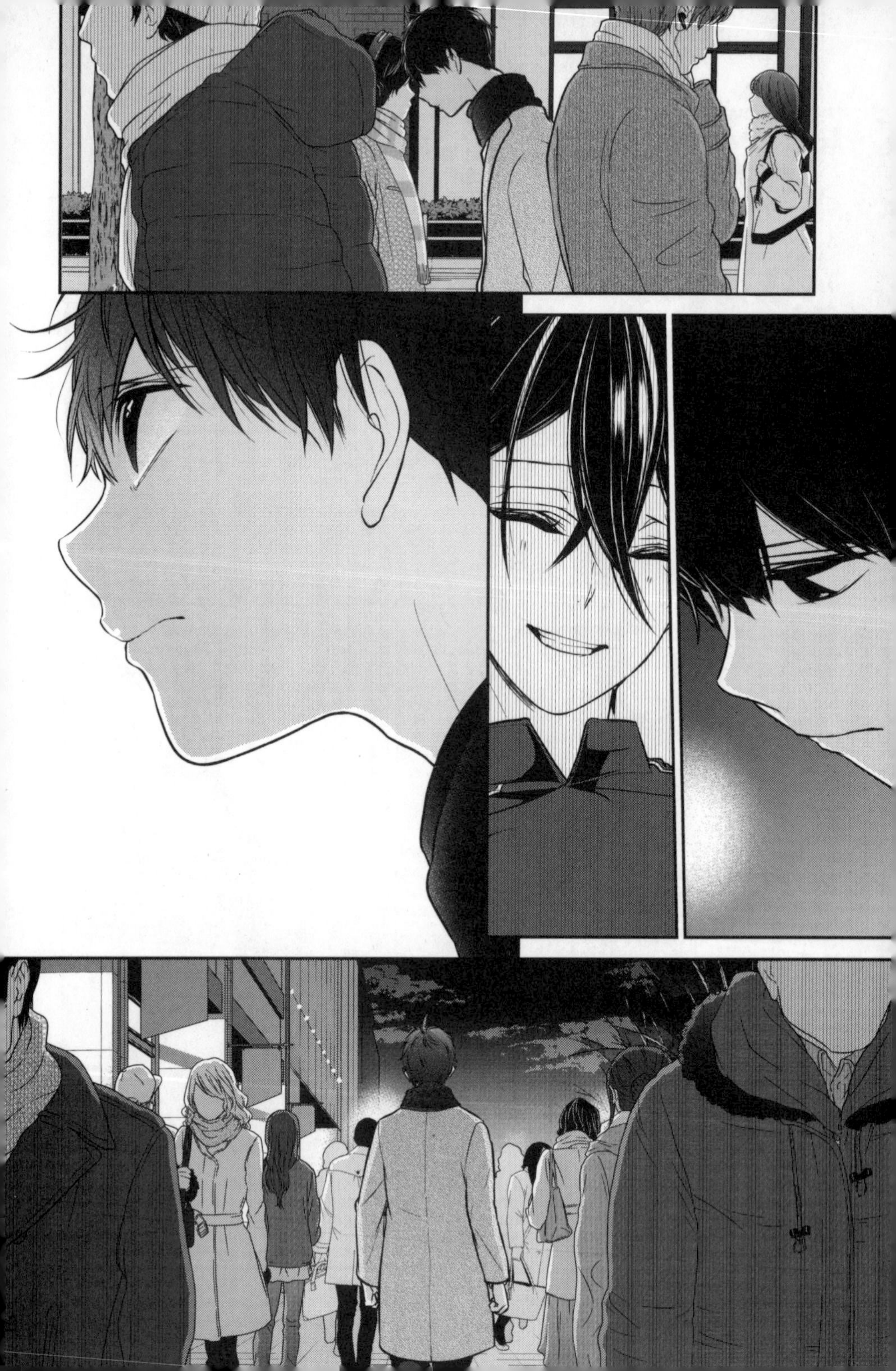

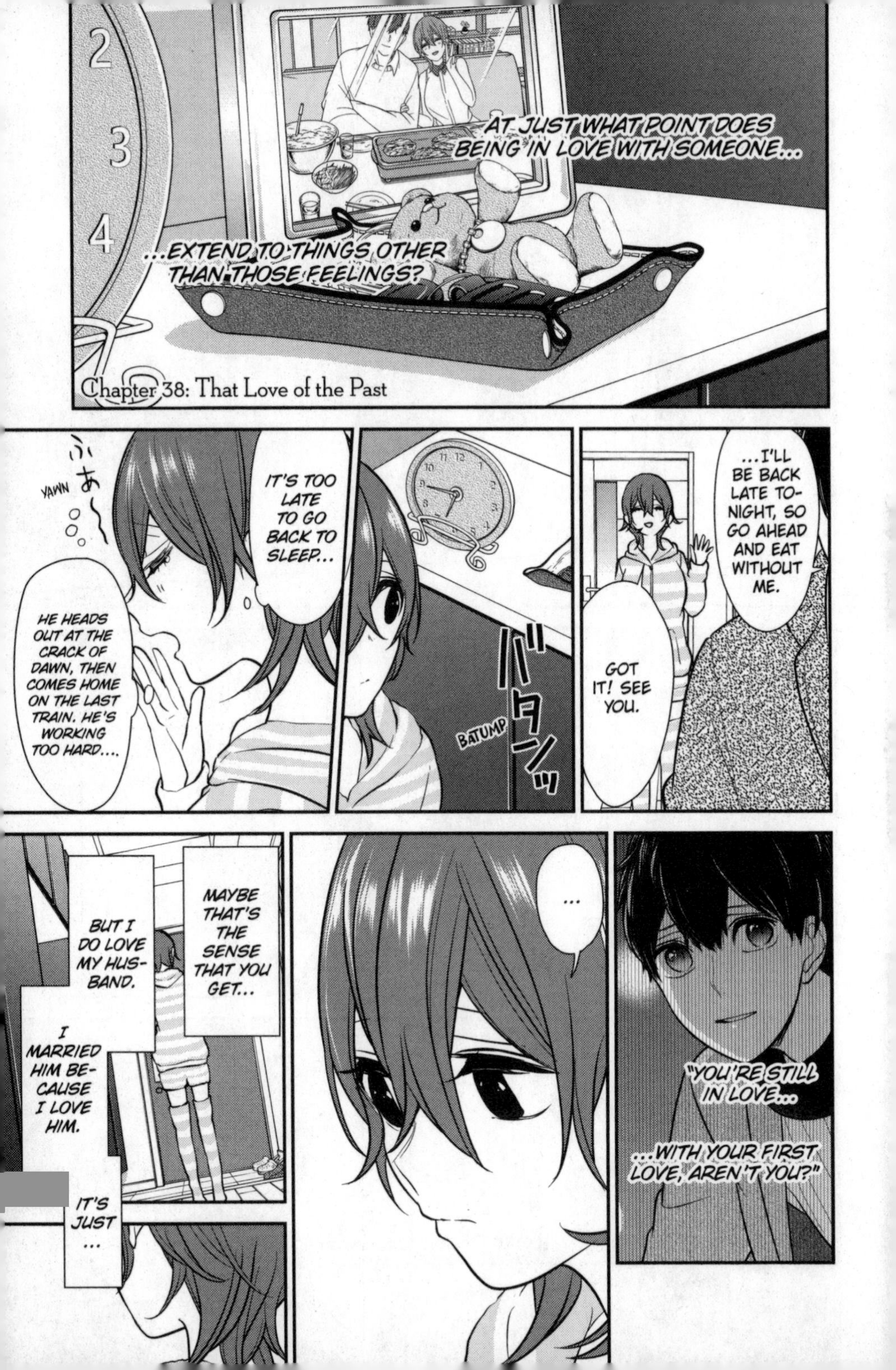
AT JUST WHAT POINT DOES BEING IN LOVE WITH SOMEONE...
...EXTEND TO THINGS OTHER THAN THOSE FEELINGS?
Chapter 38: That Love of the Past
...I'LL BE BACK LATE TO-NIGHT, SO GO AHEAD AND EAT WITHOUT ME.
GOT IT! SEE YOU.
バタンッ
BATUMP
ふあ〜
YAWN
IT'S TOO LATE TO GO BACK TO SLEEP...
HE HEADS OUT AT THE CRACK OF DAWN, THEN COMES HOME ON THE LAST TRAIN. HE'S WORKING TOO HARD....
"YOU'RE STILL IN LOVE...
...WITH YOUR FIRST LOVE, AREN'T YOU?"
...
MAYBE THAT'S THE SENSE THAT YOU GET...
BUT I DO LOVE MY HUS-BAND.
I MARRIED HIM BE-CAUSE I LOVE HIM.
IT'S JUST...

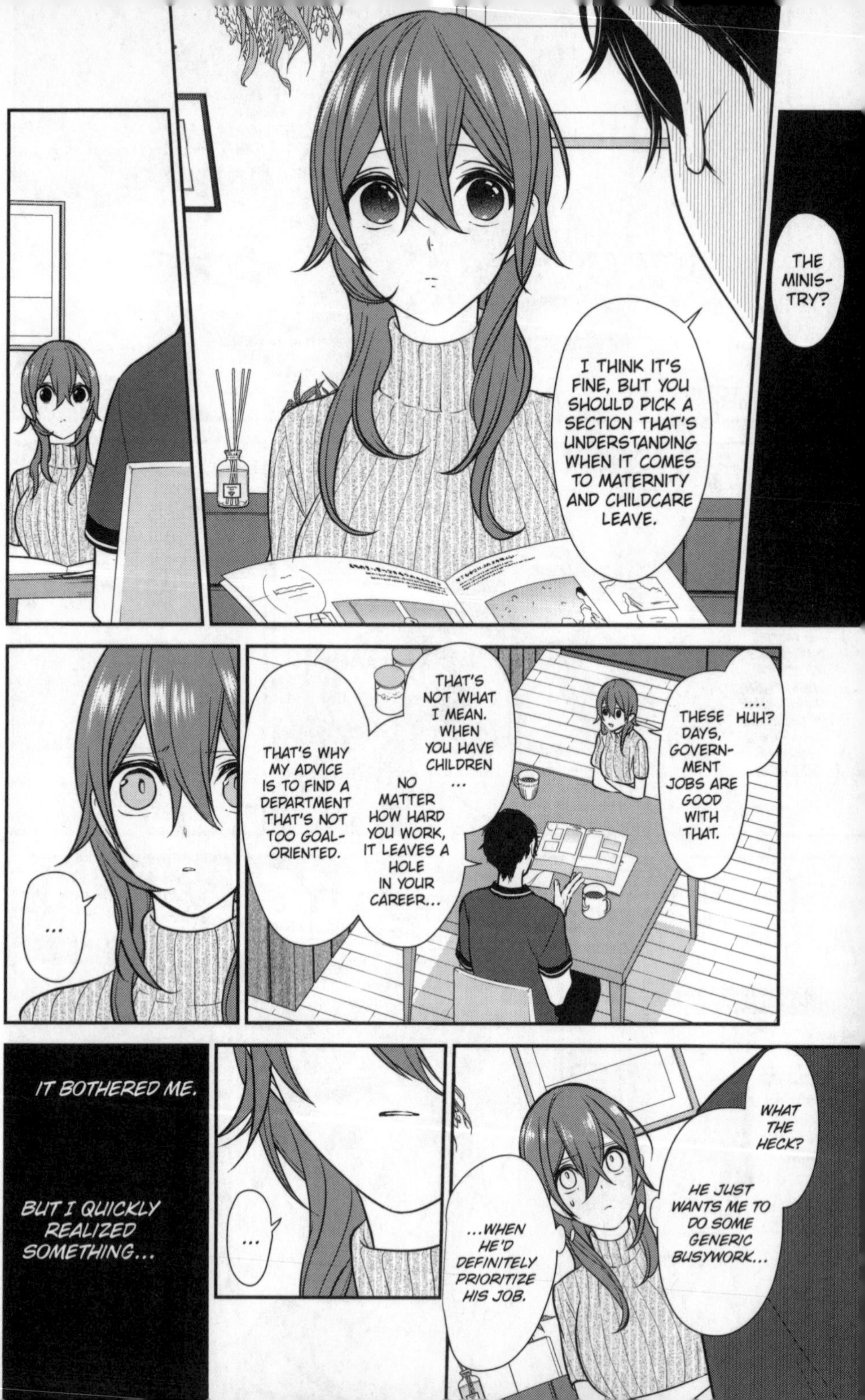
THE MINISTRY?
I THINK IT'S FINE, BUT YOU SHOULD PICK A SECTION THAT'S UNDERSTANDING WHEN IT COMES TO MATERNITY AND CHILDCARE LEAVE.
....HUH?
THESE DAYS, GOVERNMENT JOBS ARE GOOD WITH THAT.
THAT'S NOT WHAT I MEAN. WHEN YOU HAVE CHILDREN...
NO MATTER HOW HARD YOU WORK, IT LEAVES A HOLE IN YOUR CAREER...
THAT'S WHY MY ADVICE IS TO FIND A DEPARTMENT THAT'S NOT TOO GOAL-ORIENTED.
...
WHAT THE HECK?
HE JUST WANTS ME TO DO SOME GENERIC BUSYWORK...
...WHEN HE'D DEFINITELY PRIORITIZE HIS JOB.
...
IT BOTHERED ME.
BUT I QUICKLY REALIZED SOMETHING...

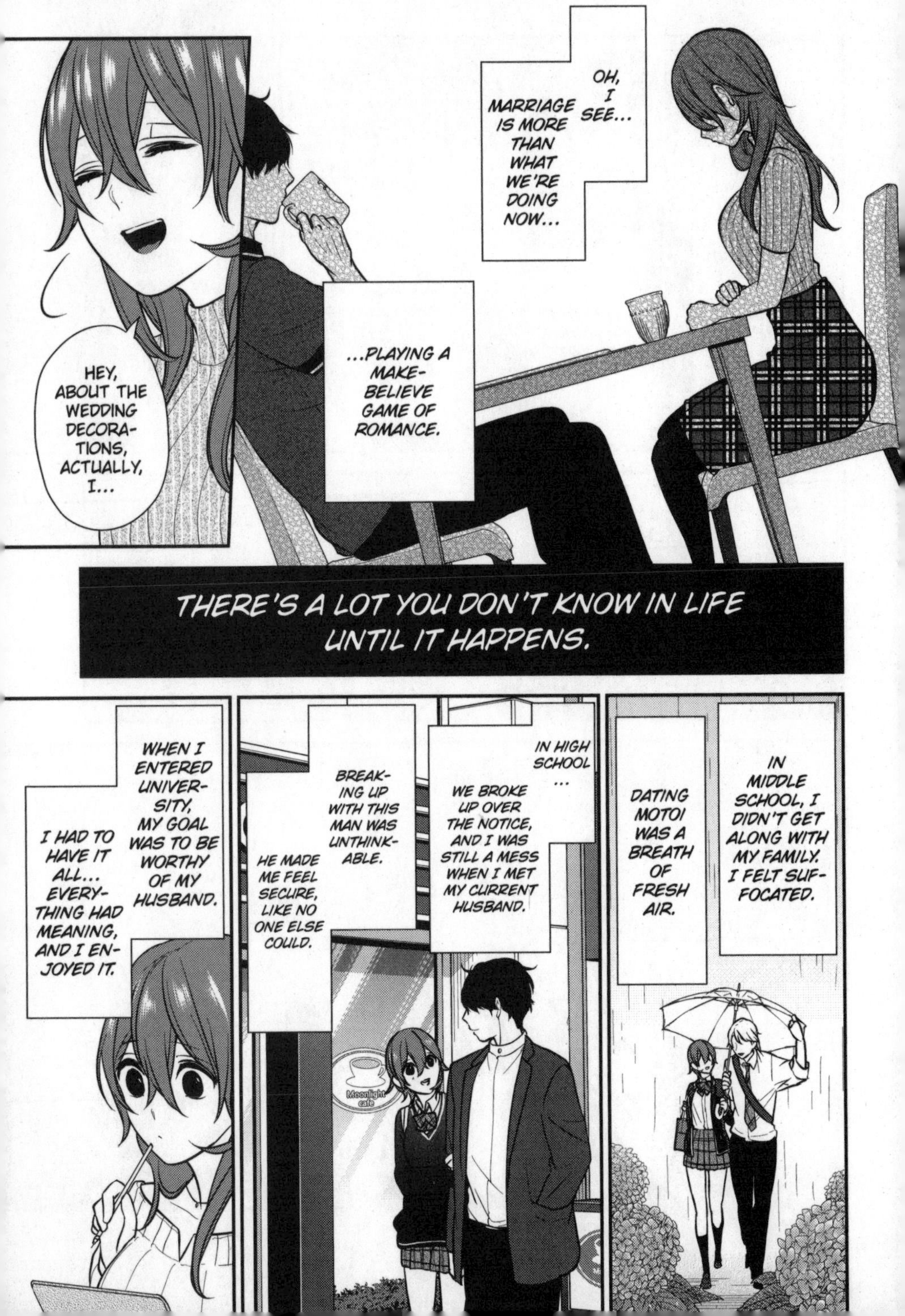
OH, I SEE... MARRIAGE IS MORE THAN WHAT WE'RE DOING NOW...
...PLAYING A MAKE-BELIEVE GAME OF ROMANCE.
HEY, ABOUT THE WEDDING DECORATIONS, ACTUALLY, I...
THERE'S A LOT YOU DON'T KNOW IN LIFE UNTIL IT HAPPENS.
IN MIDDLE SCHOOL, I DIDN'T GET ALONG WITH MY FAMILY. I FELT SUFFOCATED.
DATING MOTOI WAS A BREATH OF FRESH AIR.
IN HIGH SCHOOL...
WE BROKE UP OVER THE NOTICE, AND I WAS STILL A MESS WHEN I MET MY CURRENT HUSBAND.
BREAKING UP WITH THIS MAN WAS UNTHINKABLE.
HE MADE ME FEEL SECURE, LIKE NO ONE ELSE COULD.
Moonlight cafe
WHEN I ENTERED UNIVERSITY, MY GOAL WAS TO BE WORTHY OF MY HUSBAND.
I HAD TO HAVE IT ALL... EVERYTHING HAD MEANING, AND I ENJOYED IT.

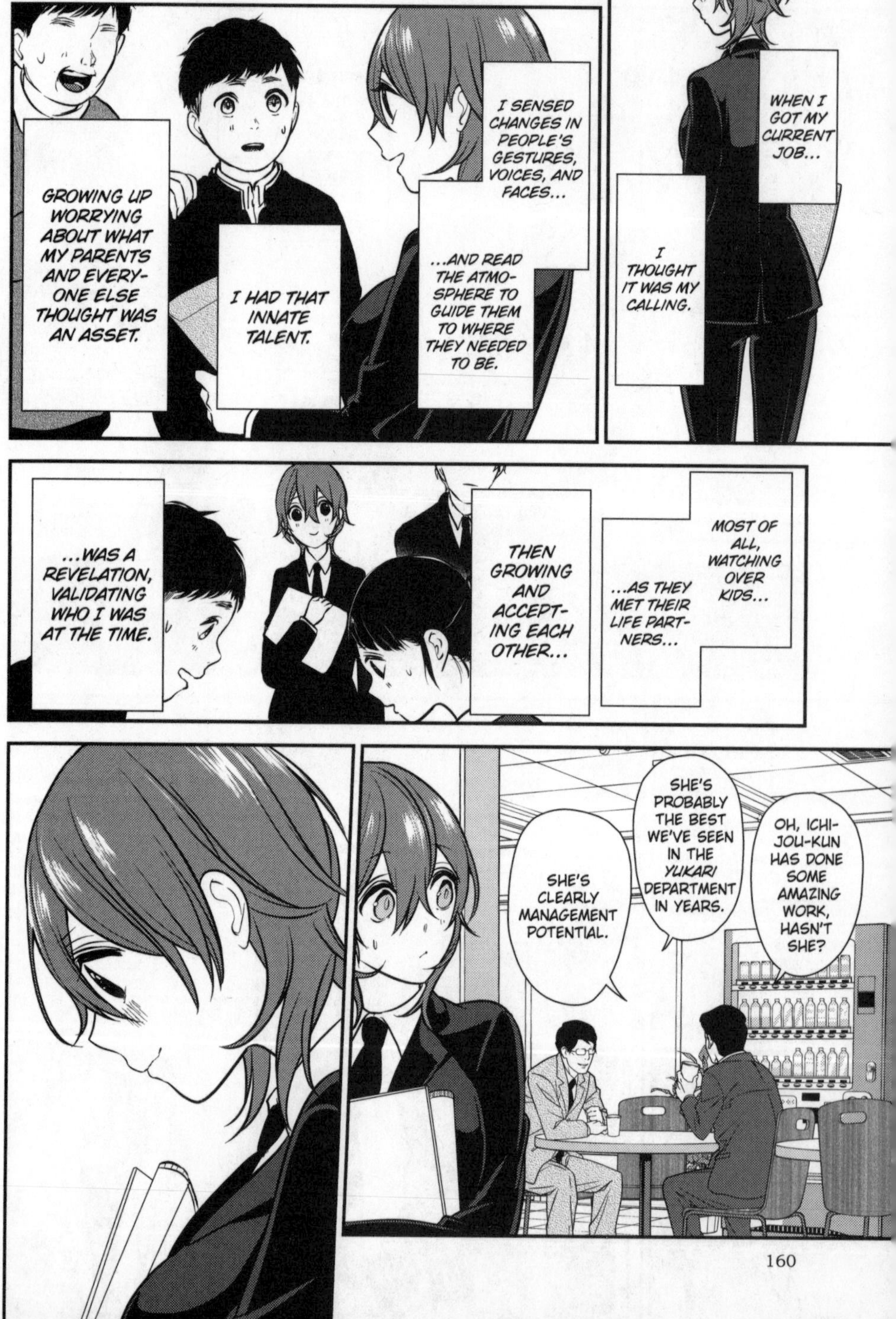
WHEN I GOT MY CURRENT JOB...
I THOUGHT IT WAS MY CALLING.
I SENSED CHANGES IN PEOPLE'S GESTURES, VOICES, AND FACES...
...AND READ THE ATMOSPHERE TO GUIDE THEM TO WHERE THEY NEEDED TO BE.
I HAD THAT INNATE TALENT.
GROWING UP WORRYING ABOUT WHAT MY PARENTS AND EVERYONE ELSE THOUGHT WAS AN ASSET.
MOST OF ALL, WATCHING OVER KIDS...
...AS THEY MET THEIR LIFE PARTNERS...
THEN GROWING AND ACCEPTING EACH OTHER...
...WAS A REVELATION, VALIDATING WHO I WAS AT THE TIME.
OH, ICHIJOU-KUN HAS DONE SOME AMAZING WORK, HASN'T SHE?
SHE'S PROBABLY THE BEST WE'VE SEEN IN THE *YUKARI* DEPARTMENT IN YEARS.
SHE'S CLEARLY MANAGEMENT POTENTIAL.

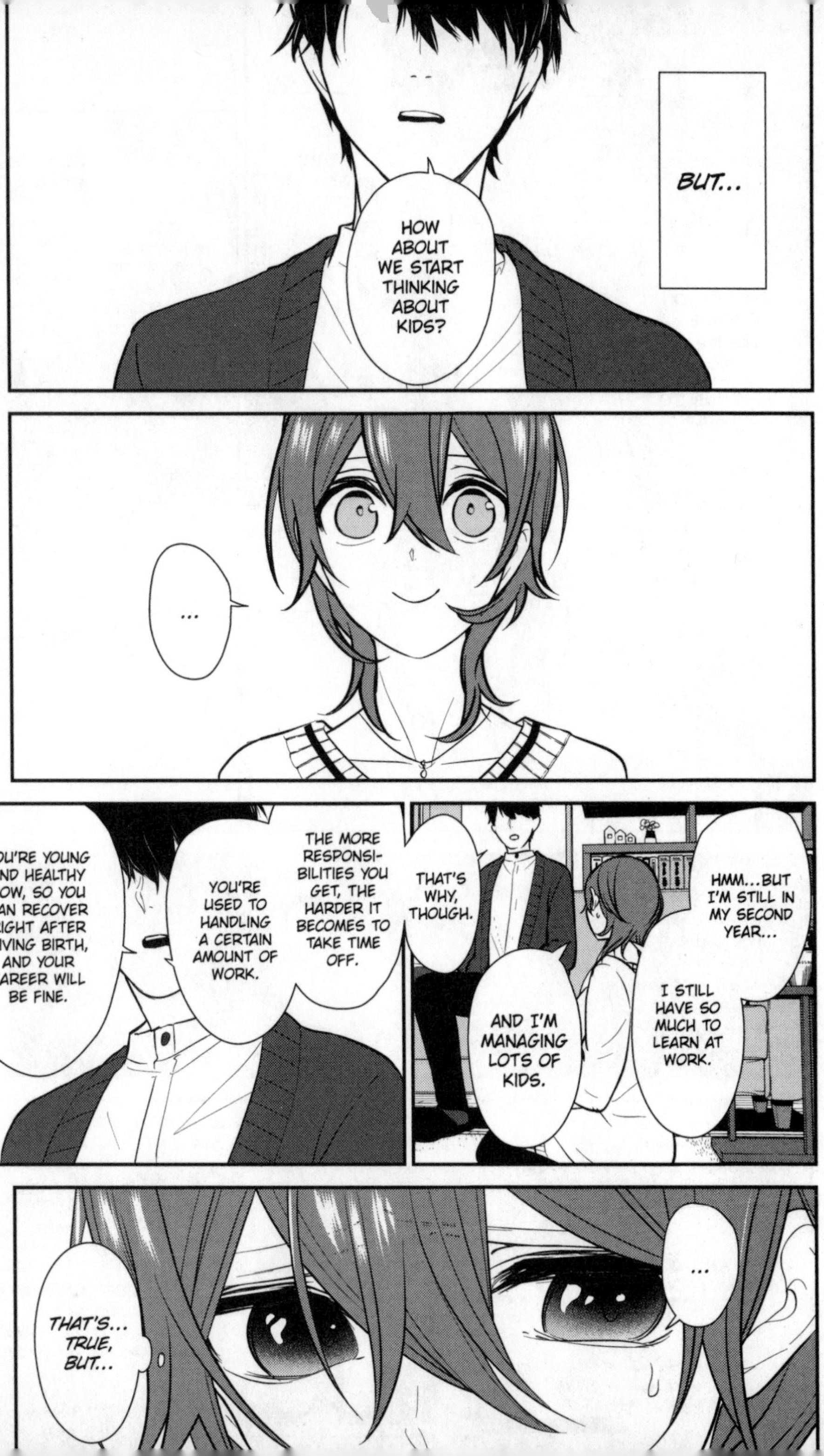
BUT...
HOW ABOUT WE START THINKING ABOUT KIDS?
...
HMM...BUT I'M STILL IN MY SECOND YEAR...
I STILL HAVE SO MUCH TO LEARN AT WORK.
AND I'M MANAGING LOTS OF KIDS.
THAT'S WHY, THOUGH.
THE MORE RESPONSI-BILITIES YOU GET, THE HARDER IT BECOMES TO TAKE TIME OFF.
YOU'RE USED TO HANDLING A CERTAIN AMOUNT OF WORK.
YOU'RE YOUNG AND HEALTHY NOW, SO YOU CAN RECOVER RIGHT AFTER GIVING BIRTH, AND YOUR CAREER WILL BE FINE.
...
THAT'S... TRUE, BUT...

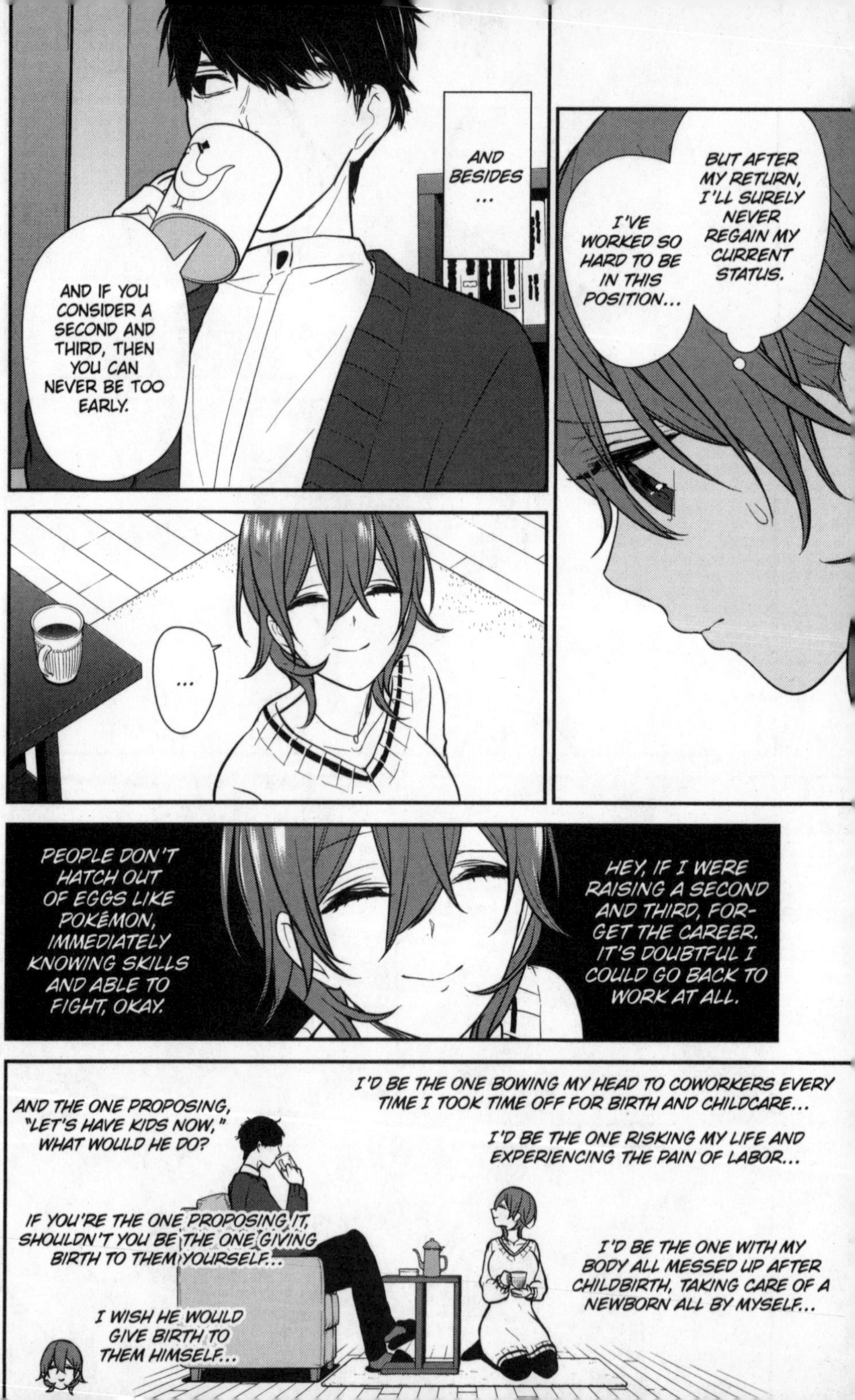
BUT AFTER MY RETURN, I'LL SURELY NEVER REGAIN MY CURRENT STATUS.
I'VE WORKED SO HARD TO BE IN THIS POSITION...
AND BESIDES ...
AND IF YOU CONSIDER A SECOND AND THIRD, THEN YOU CAN NEVER BE TOO EARLY.
...
HEY, IF I WERE RAISING A SECOND AND THIRD, FOR-GET THE CAREER. IT'S DOUBTFUL I COULD GO BACK TO WORK AT ALL.
PEOPLE DON'T HATCH OUT OF EGGS LIKE POKÉMON, IMMEDIATELY KNOWING SKILLS AND ABLE TO FIGHT, OKAY.
I'D BE THE ONE BOWING MY HEAD TO COWORKERS EVERY TIME I TOOK TIME OFF FOR BIRTH AND CHILDCARE...
I'D BE THE ONE RISKING MY LIFE AND EXPERIENCING THE PAIN OF LABOR...
I'D BE THE ONE WITH MY BODY ALL MESSED UP AFTER CHILDBIRTH, TAKING CARE OF A NEWBORN ALL BY MYSELF...
AND THE ONE PROPOSING, "LET'S HAVE KIDS NOW," WHAT WOULD HE DO?
IF YOU'RE THE ONE PROPOSING IT, SHOULDN'T YOU BE THE ONE GIVING BIRTH TO THEM YOURSELF...
I WISH HE WOULD GIVE BIRTH TO THEM HIMSELF...

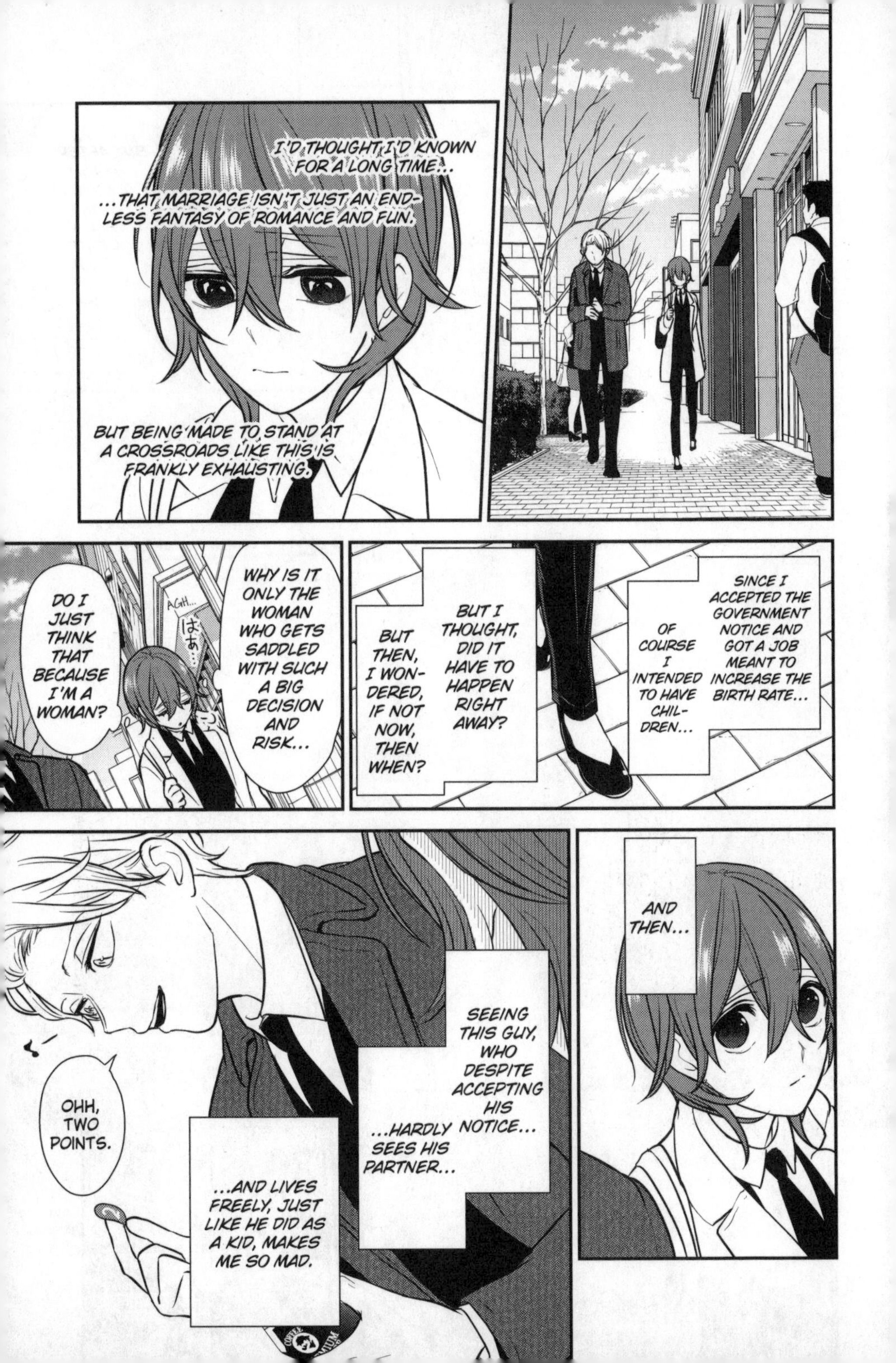

I'D THOUGHT I'D KNOWN FOR A LONG TIME...
...THAT MARRIAGE ISN'T JUST AN ENDLESS FANTASY OF ROMANCE AND FUN.
BUT BEING MADE TO STAND AT A CROSSROADS LIKE THIS IS FRANKLY EXHAUSTING.
SINCE I ACCEPTED THE GOVERNMENT NOTICE AND GOT A JOB MEANT TO INCREASE THE BIRTH RATE...
OF COURSE I INTENDED TO HAVE CHILDREN...
BUT I THOUGHT, DID IT HAVE TO HAPPEN RIGHT AWAY?
BUT THEN, I WONDERED, IF NOT NOW, THEN WHEN?
WHY IS IT ONLY THE WOMAN WHO GETS SADDLED WITH SUCH A BIG DECISION AND RISK...
AGH...
はぁ...
DO I JUST THINK THAT BECAUSE I'M A WOMAN?
AND THEN...
SEEING THIS GUY, WHO DESPITE ACCEPTING HIS NOTICE...
...HARDLY SEES HIS PARTNER...
OHH, TWO POINTS.
...AND LIVES FREELY, JUST LIKE HE DID AS A KID, MAKES ME SO MAD.

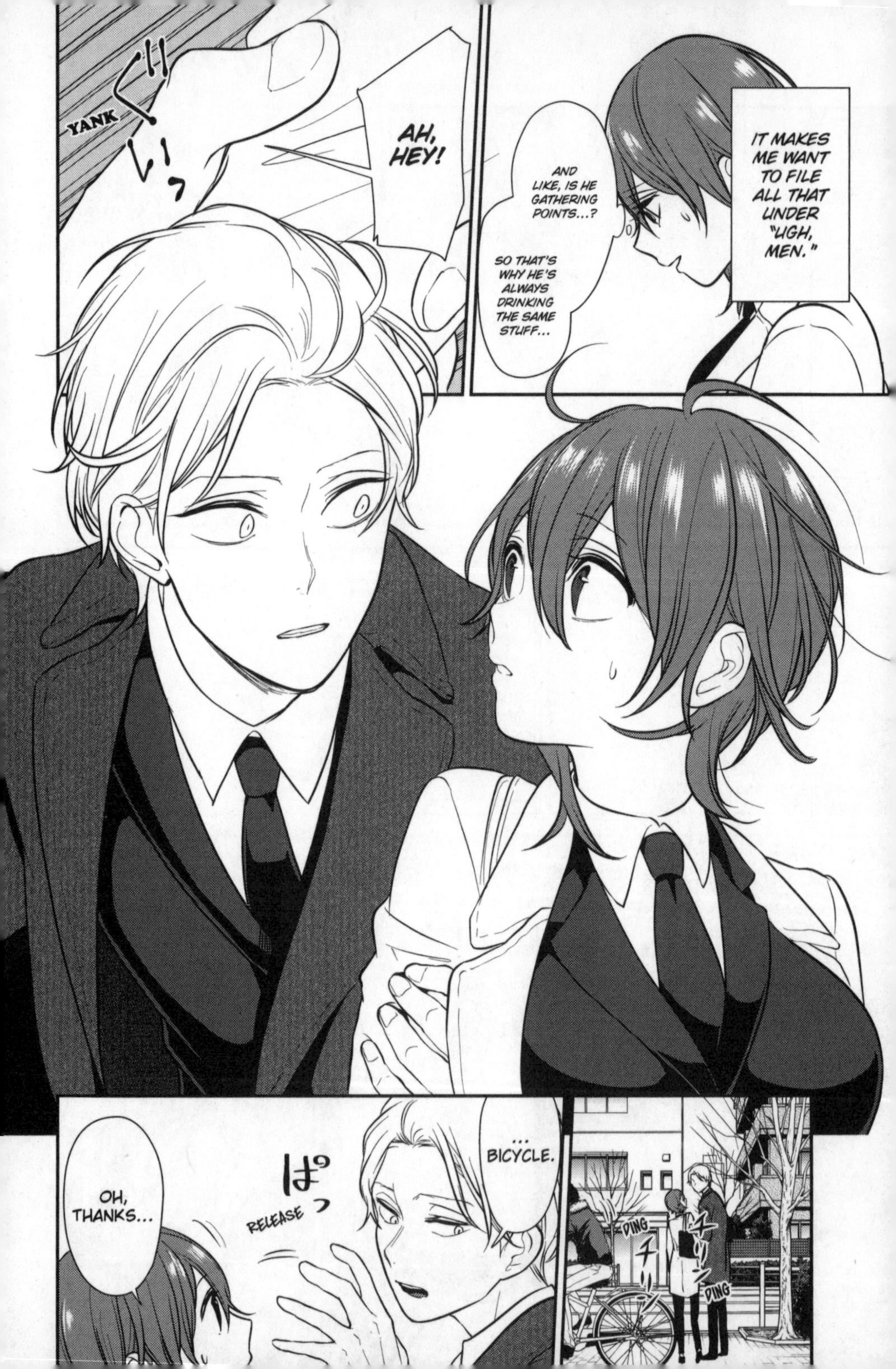
IT MAKES ME WANT TO FILE ALL THAT UNDER "UGH, MEN."
AND LIKE, IS HE GATHERING POINTS...?
SO THAT'S WHY HE'S ALWAYS DRINKING THE SAME STUFF...
AH, HEY!
YANK
DING
DING
...BICYCLE.
RELEASE
OH, THANKS...

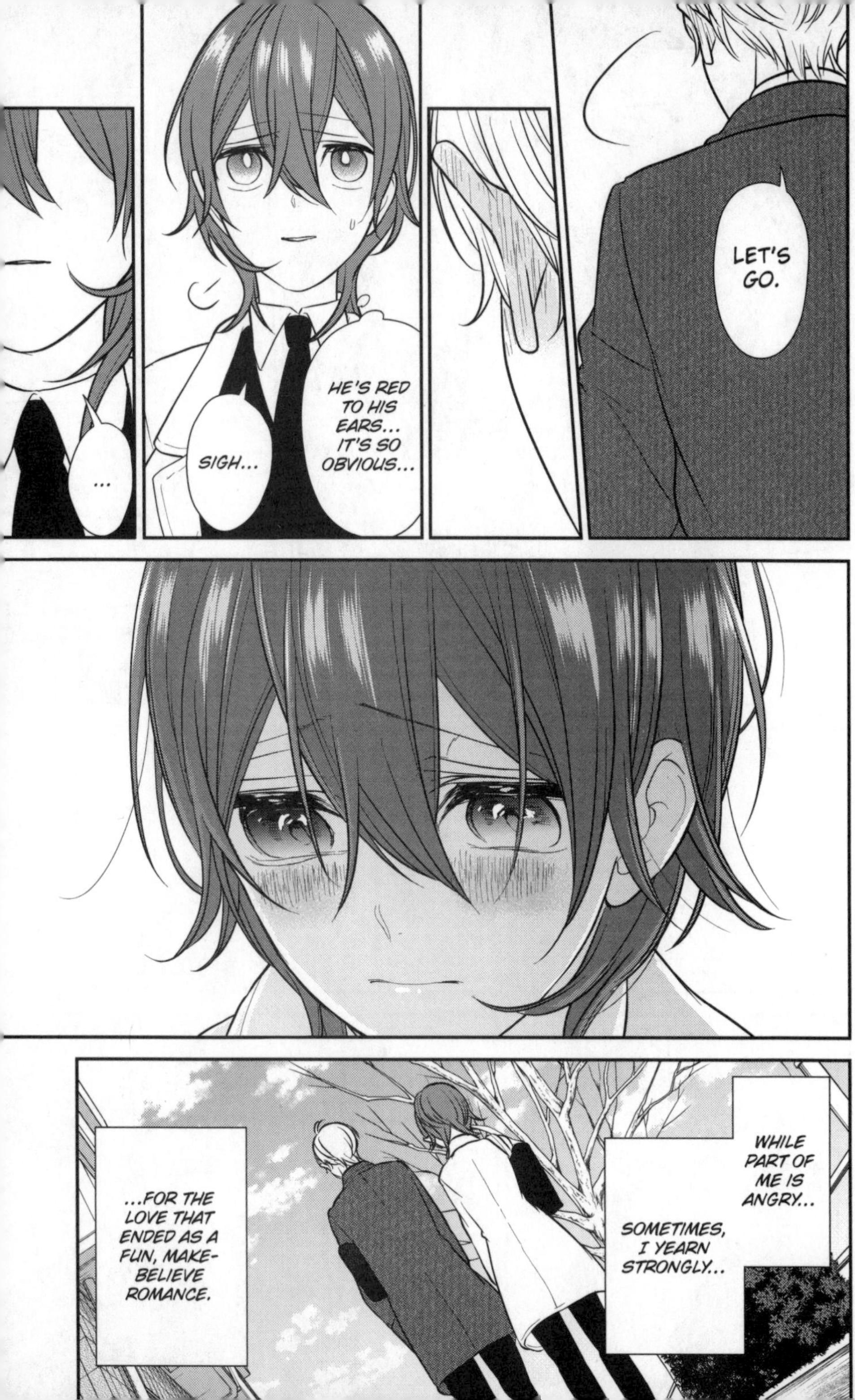
LET'S GO.
HE'S RED TO HIS EARS... IT'S SO OBVIOUS...
SIGH...
...
WHILE PART OF ME IS ANGRY...
SOMETIMES, I YEARN STRONGLY...
...FOR THE LOVE THAT ENDED AS A FUN, MAKE-BELIEVE ROMANCE.

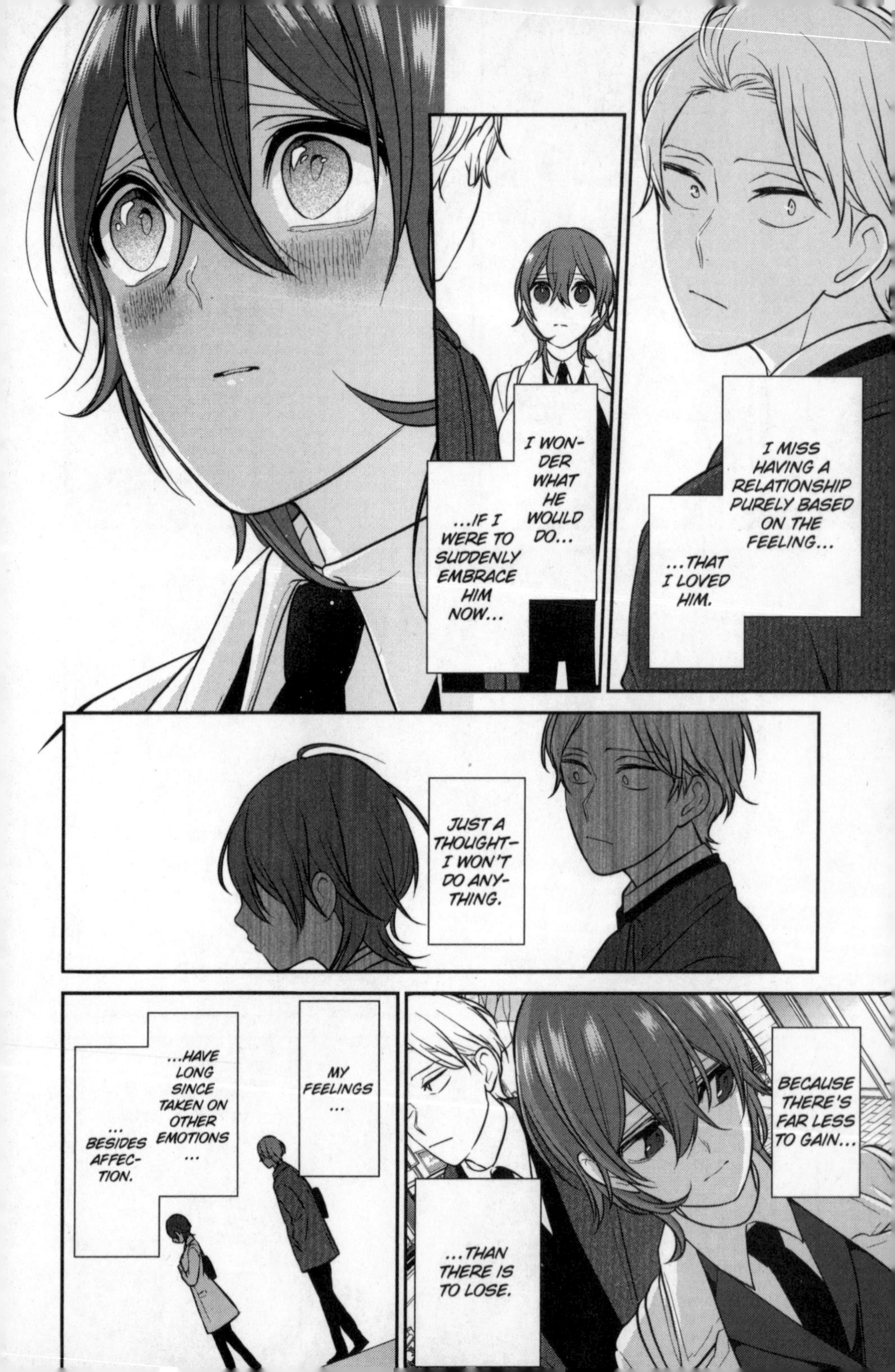
I MISS HAVING A RELATIONSHIP PURELY BASED ON THE FEELING...
...THAT I LOVED HIM.
I WONDER WHAT HE WOULD DO...
...IF I WERE TO SUDDENLY EMBRACE HIM NOW...
JUST A THOUGHT–I WON'T DO ANYTHING.
BECAUSE THERE'S FAR LESS TO GAIN...
...THAN THERE IS TO LOSE.
MY FEELINGS...
...HAVE LONG SINCE TAKEN ON OTHER EMOTIONS...
...BESIDES AFFECTION.

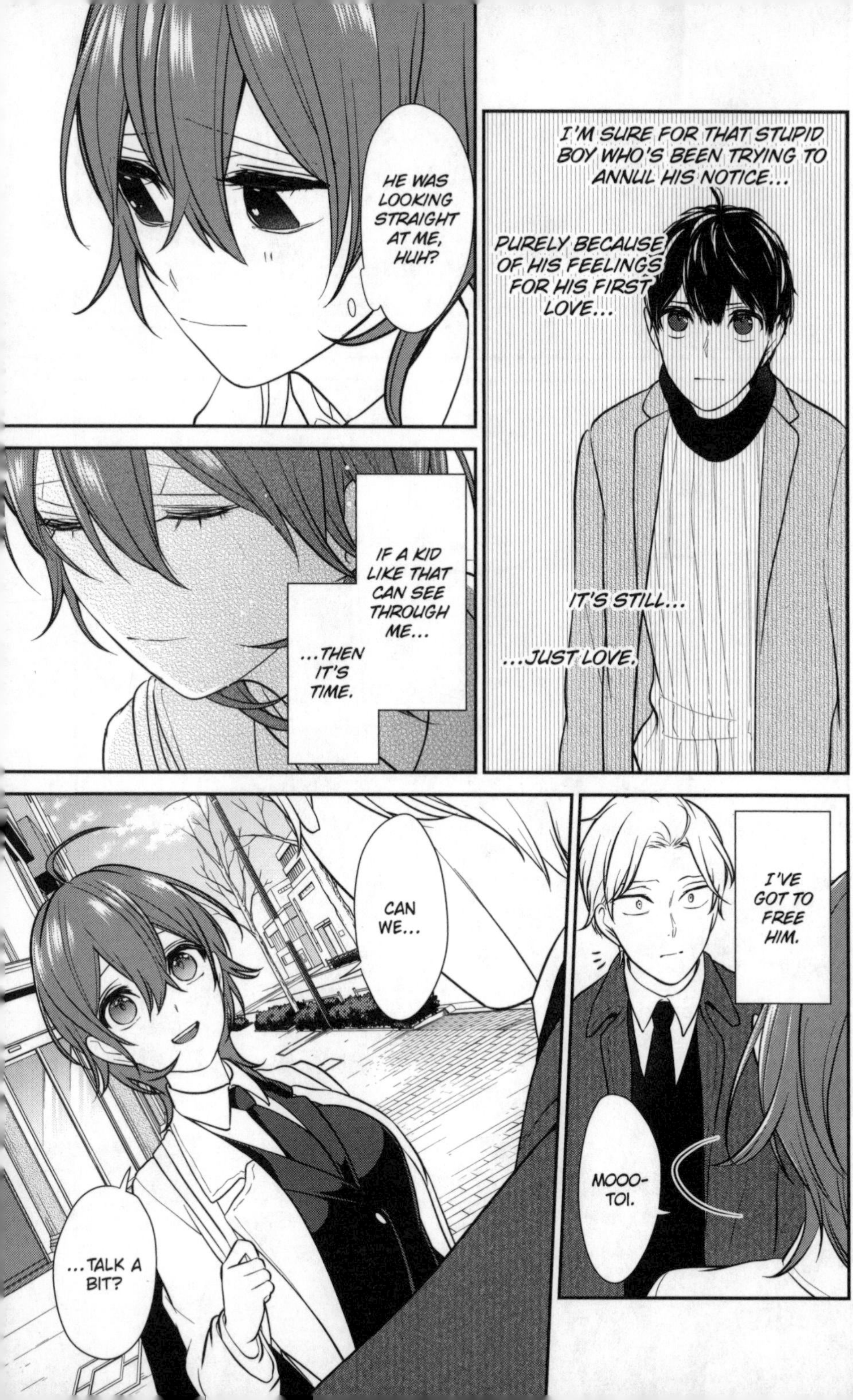
I'M SURE FOR THAT STUPID BOY WHO'S BEEN TRYING TO ANNUL HIS NOTICE...
PURELY BECAUSE OF HIS FEELINGS FOR HIS FIRST LOVE...
IT'S STILL...
...JUST LOVE.
HE WAS LOOKING STRAIGHT AT ME, HUH?
IF A KID LIKE THAT CAN SEE THROUGH ME...
...THEN IT'S TIME.
I'VE GOT TO FREE HIM.
MOOO-TOI.
CAN WE...
...TALK A BIT?

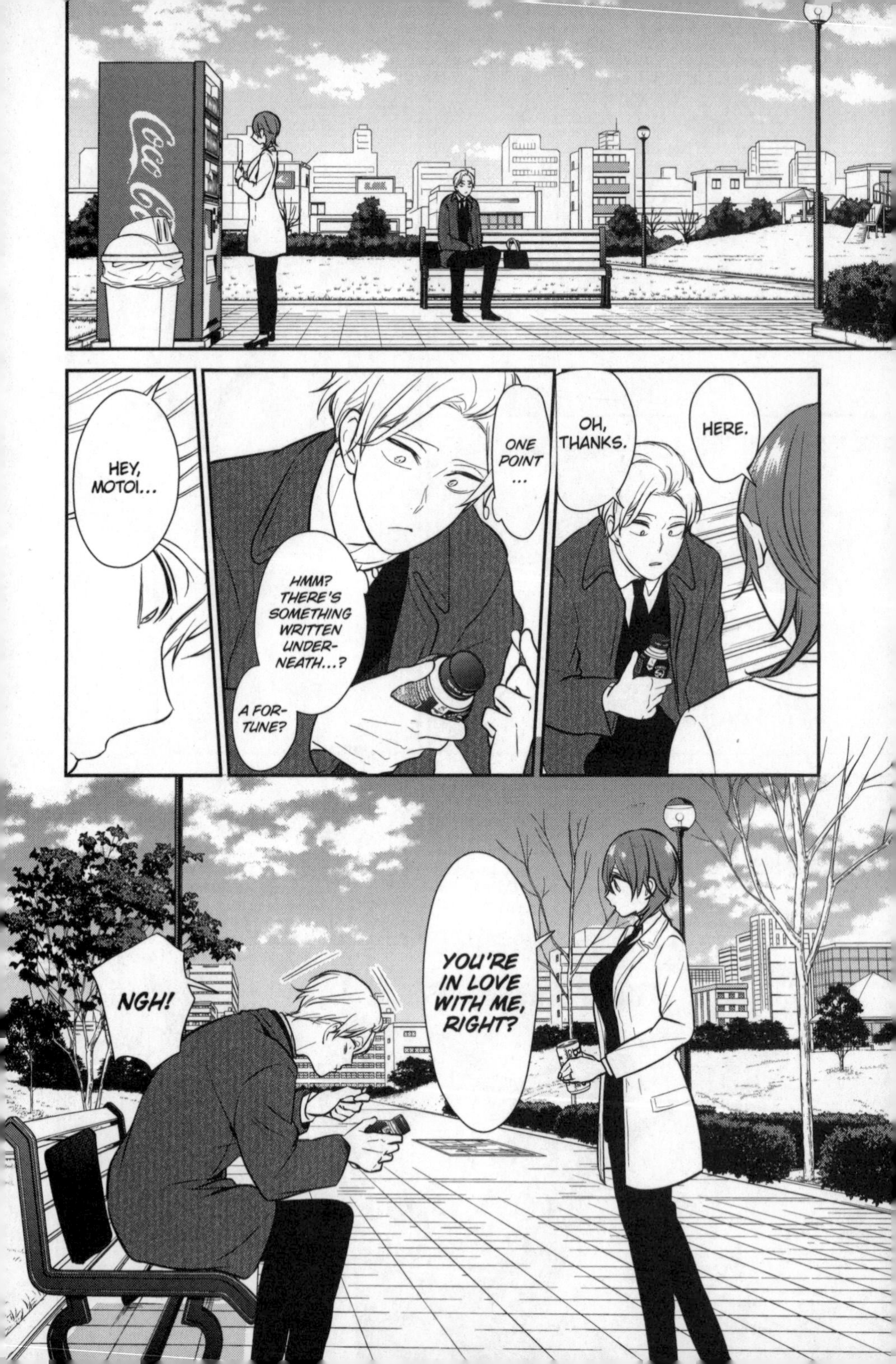
HERE.
OH, THANKS.
ONE POINT ...
HMM? THERE'S SOMETHING WRITTEN UNDER-NEATH...?
A FOR-TUNE?
HEY, MOTOI...
YOU'RE IN LOVE WITH ME, RIGHT?
NGH!

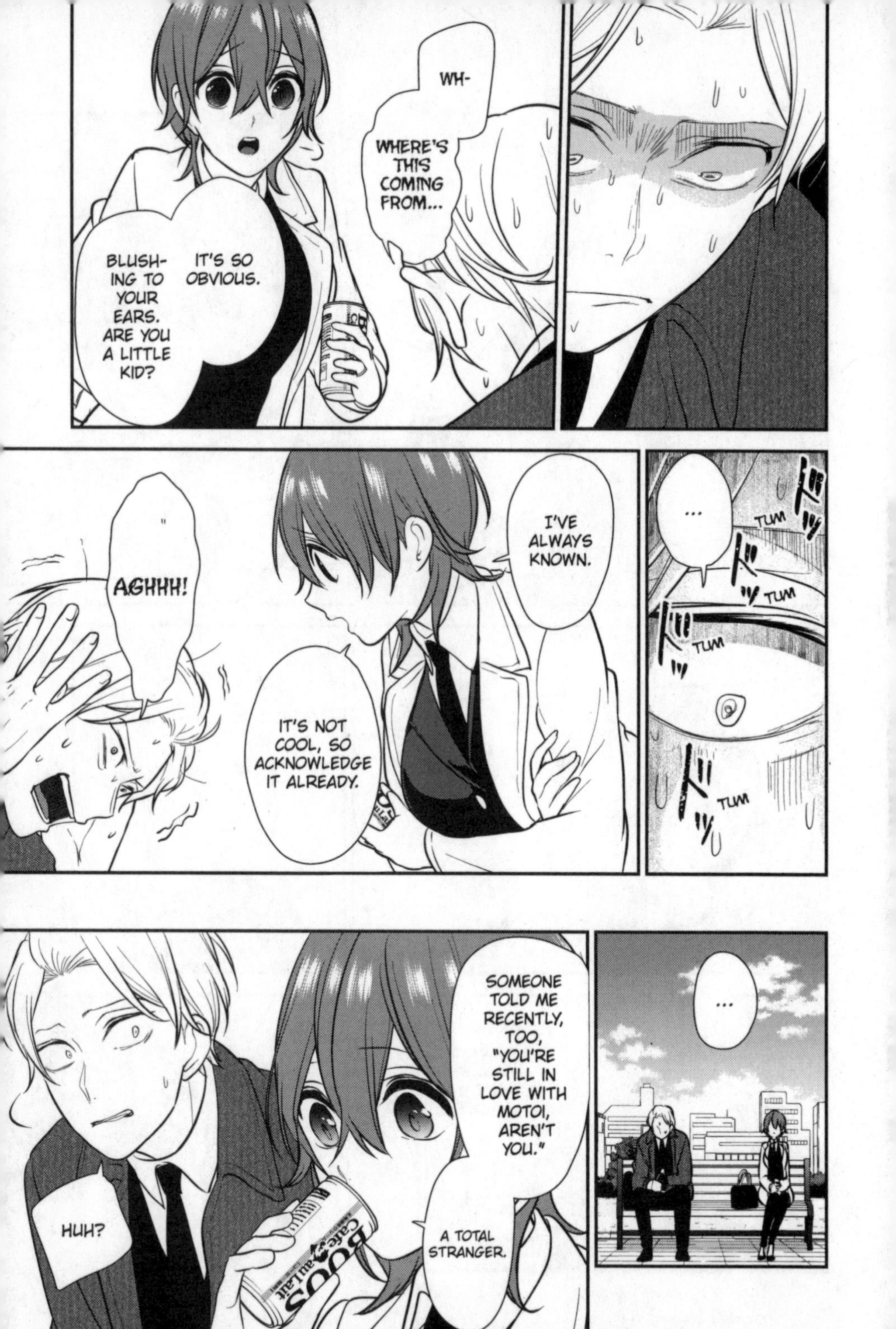
WH-
WHERE'S THIS COMING FROM...
IT'S SO OBVIOUS.
BLUSHING TO YOUR EARS. ARE YOU A LITTLE KID?
...
TUM
TUM
TUM
TUM
I'VE ALWAYS KNOWN.
IT'S NOT COOL, SO ACKNOWLEDGE IT ALREADY.
"
AGHHH!
...
SOMEONE TOLD ME RECENTLY, TOO, "YOU'RE STILL IN LOVE WITH MOTOI, AREN'T YOU."
A TOTAL STRANGER.
HUH?
BOSS Cafe au Lait

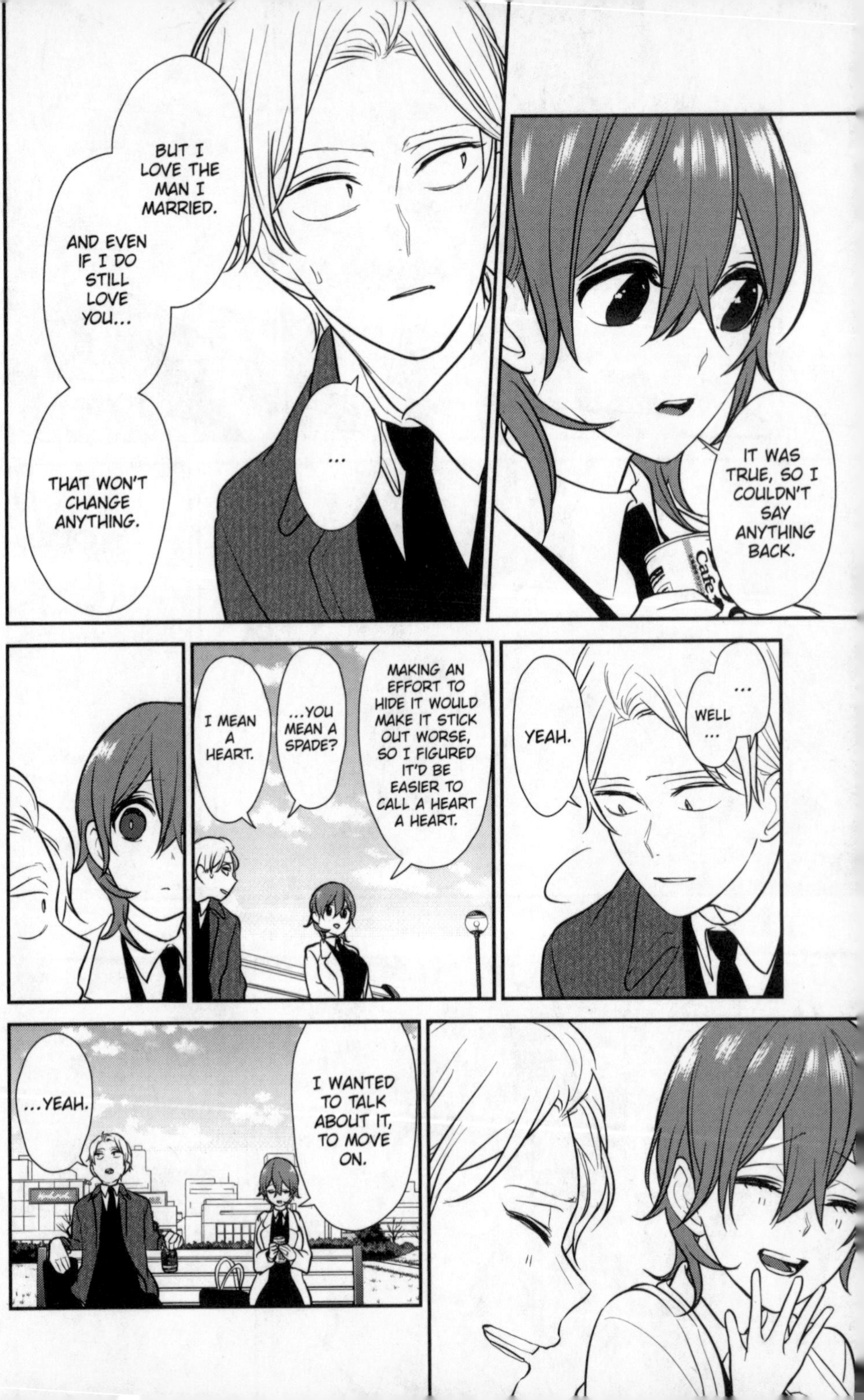
IT WAS TRUE, SO I COULDN'T SAY ANYTHING BACK.
BUT I LOVE THE MAN I MARRIED.
AND EVEN IF I DO STILL LOVE YOU...
THAT WON'T CHANGE ANYTHING.
...
...WELL...
YEAH.
MAKING AN EFFORT TO HIDE IT WOULD MAKE IT STICK OUT WORSE, SO I FIGURED IT'D BE EASIER TO CALL A HEART A HEART.
...YOU MEAN A SPADE?
I MEAN A HEART.
I WANTED TO TALK ABOUT IT, TO MOVE ON.
...YEAH.

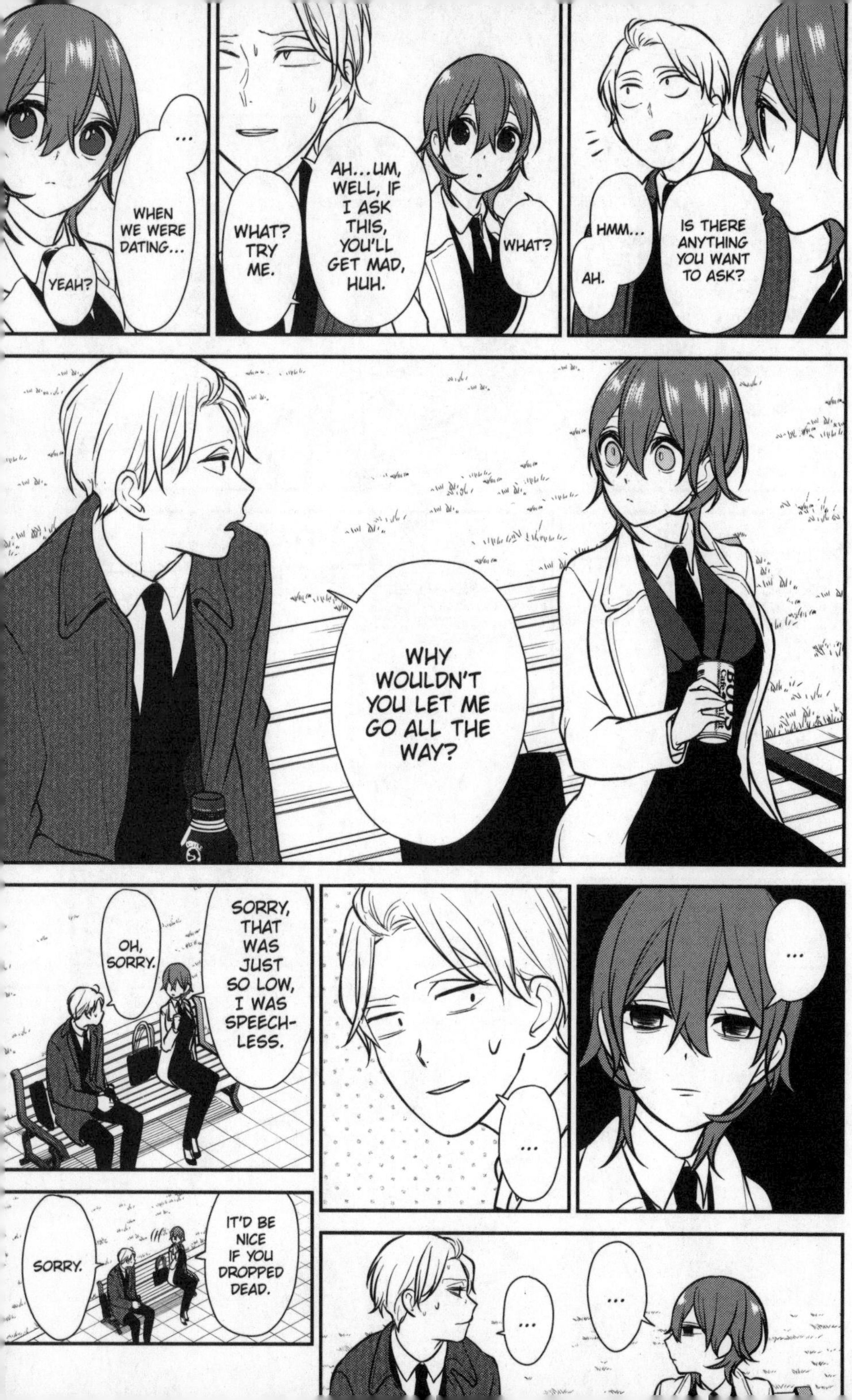
IS THERE ANYTHING YOU WANT TO ASK?
HMM...
AH.
WHAT?
AH...UM, WELL, IF I ASK THIS, YOU'LL GET MAD, HUH.
WHAT? TRY ME.
...
WHEN WE WERE DATING...
YEAH?
WHY WOULDN'T YOU LET ME GO ALL THE WAY?
...
...
...
...
SORRY, THAT WAS JUST SO LOW, I WAS SPEECH-LESS.
OH, SORRY.
IT'D BE NICE IF YOU DROPPED DEAD.
SORRY.

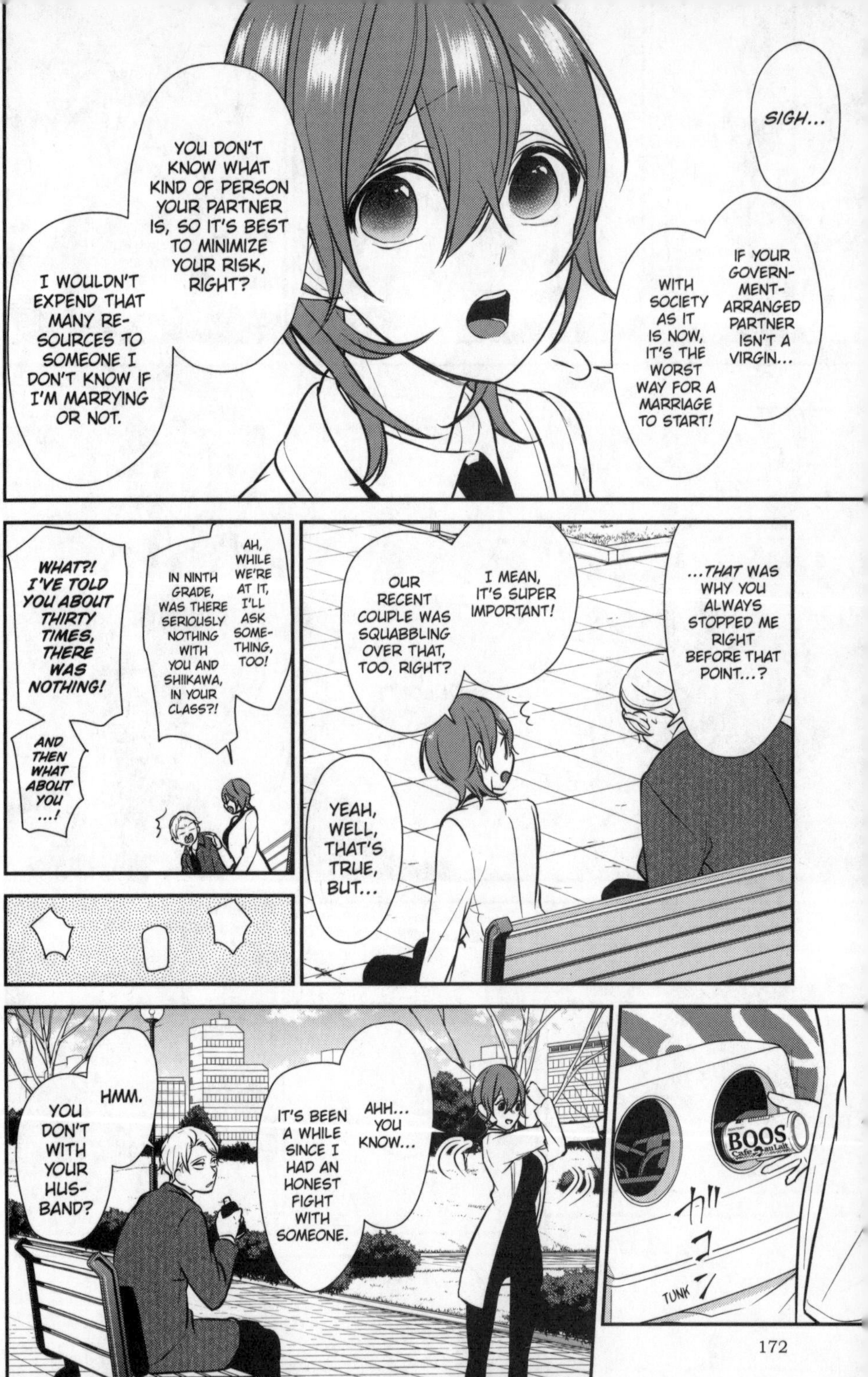
SIGH...
IF YOUR GOVERNMENT-ARRANGED PARTNER ISN'T A VIRGIN...
WITH SOCIETY AS IT IS NOW, IT'S THE WORST WAY FOR A MARRIAGE TO START!
YOU DON'T KNOW WHAT KIND OF PERSON YOUR PARTNER IS, SO IT'S BEST TO MINIMIZE YOUR RISK, RIGHT?
I WOULDN'T EXPEND THAT MANY RESOURCES TO SOMEONE I DON'T KNOW IF I'M MARRYING OR NOT.
...THAT WAS WHY YOU ALWAYS STOPPED ME RIGHT BEFORE THAT POINT...?
I MEAN, IT'S SUPER IMPORTANT!
OUR RECENT COUPLE WAS SQUABBLING OVER THAT, TOO, RIGHT?
YEAH, WELL, THAT'S TRUE, BUT...
AH, WHILE WE'RE AT IT, I'LL ASK SOMETHING, TOO!
IN NINTH GRADE, WAS THERE SERIOUSLY NOTHING WITH YOU AND SHIIKAWA, IN YOUR CLASS?!
WHAT?! I'VE TOLD YOU ABOUT THIRTY TIMES, THERE WAS NOTHING!
AND THEN WHAT ABOUT YOU...!
TUNK
BOOS
Cafe au Lait
AHH... YOU KNOW...
IT'S BEEN A WHILE SINCE I HAD AN HONEST FIGHT WITH SOMEONE.
HMM.
YOU DON'T WITH YOUR HUSBAND?

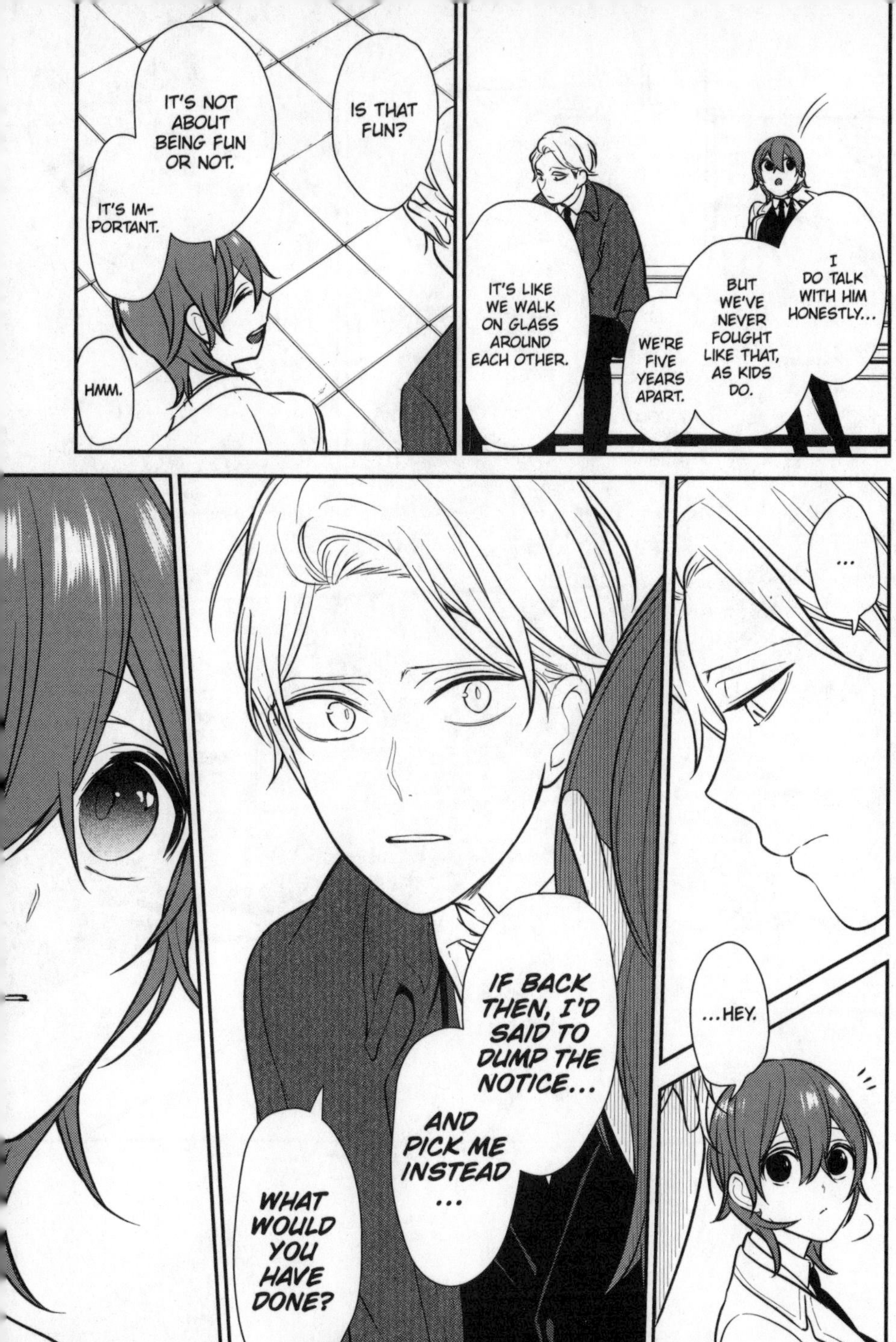

I DO TALK WITH HIM HONESTLY...
BUT WE'VE NEVER FOUGHT LIKE THAT, AS KIDS DO.
WE'RE FIVE YEARS APART.
IT'S LIKE WE WALK ON GLASS AROUND EACH OTHER.
IS THAT FUN?
IT'S NOT ABOUT BEING FUN OR NOT.
IT'S IM-PORTANT.
HMM.
...
...HEY.
IF BACK THEN, I'D SAID TO DUMP THE NOTICE...
AND PICK ME INSTEAD...
WHAT WOULD YOU HAVE DONE?

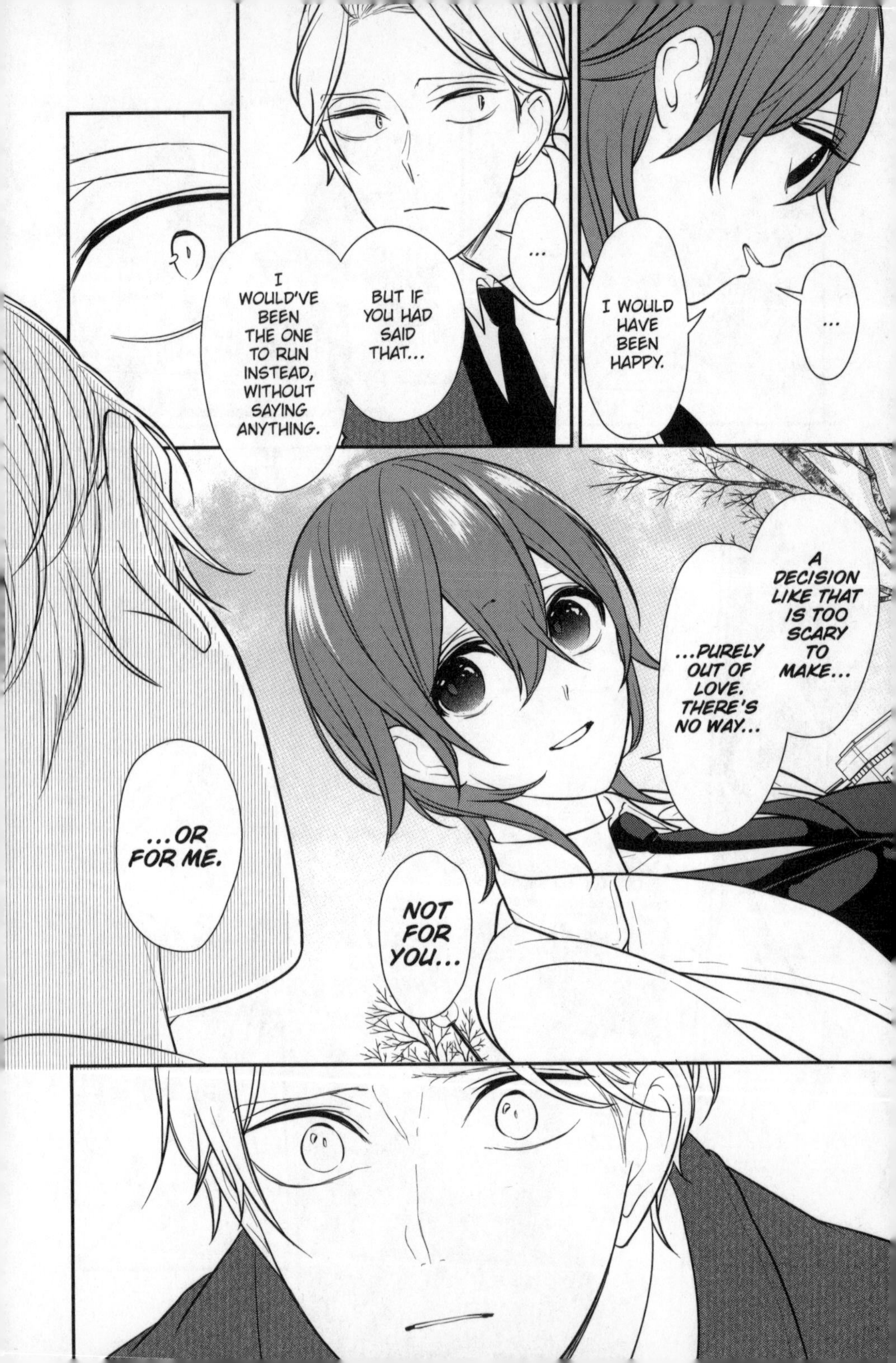
...
I WOULD HAVE BEEN HAPPY.
...
BUT IF YOU HAD SAID THAT...
I WOULD'VE BEEN THE ONE TO RUN INSTEAD, WITHOUT SAYING ANYTHING.
A DECISION LIKE THAT IS TOO SCARY TO MAKE...
...PURELY OUT OF LOVE. THERE'S NO WAY...
NOT FOR YOU...
...OR FOR ME.

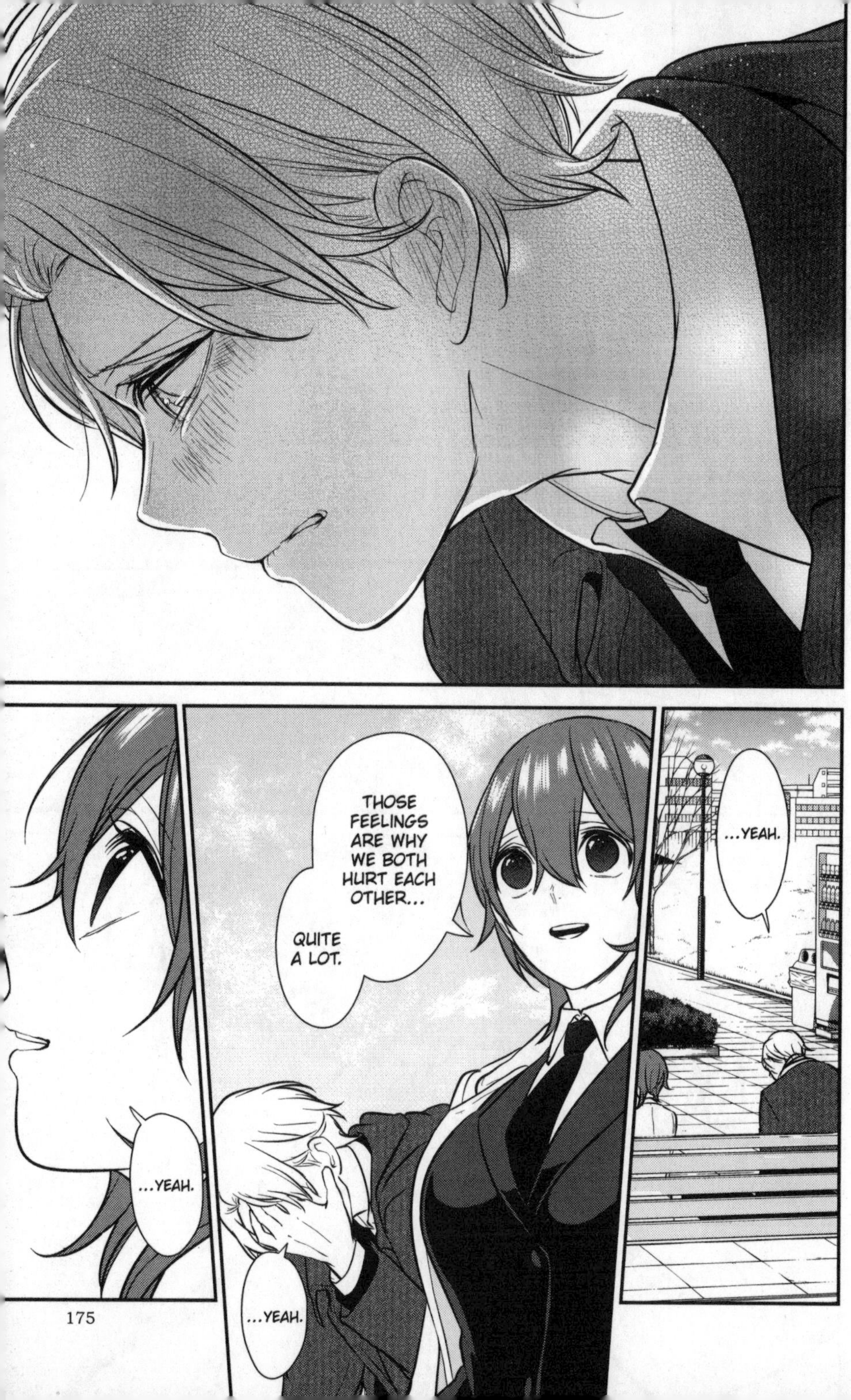
...YEAH.
THOSE FEELINGS ARE WHY WE BOTH HURT EACH OTHER...
QUITE A LOT.
...YEAH.
...YEAH.

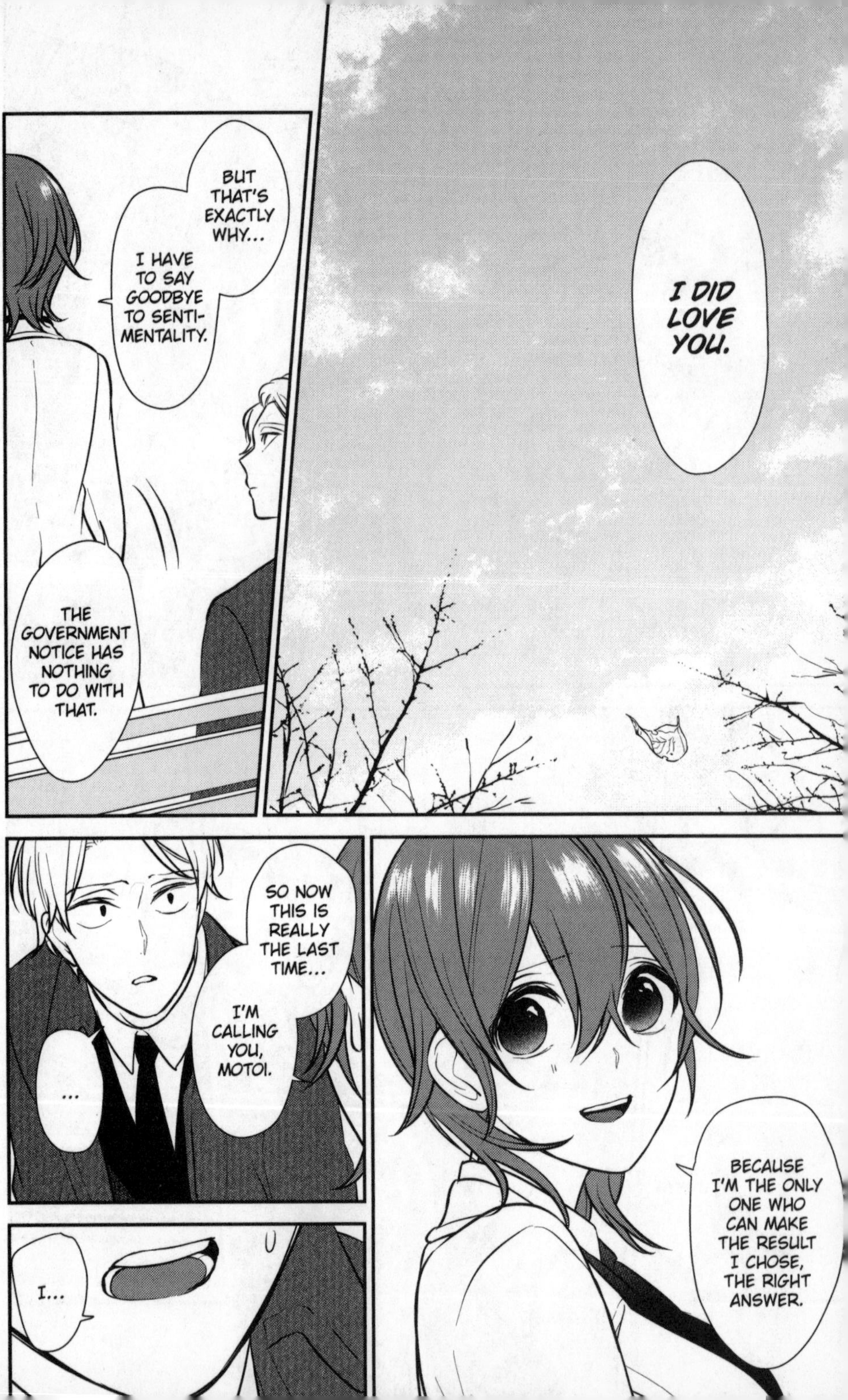
I DID LOVE YOU.
BUT THAT'S EXACTLY WHY...
I HAVE TO SAY GOODBYE TO SENTI- MENTALITY.
THE GOVERNMENT NOTICE HAS NOTHING TO DO WITH THAT.
BECAUSE I'M THE ONLY ONE WHO CAN MAKE THE RESULT I CHOSE, THE RIGHT ANSWER.
SO NOW THIS IS REALLY THE LAST TIME...
I'M CALLING YOU, MOTOI.
...
I...

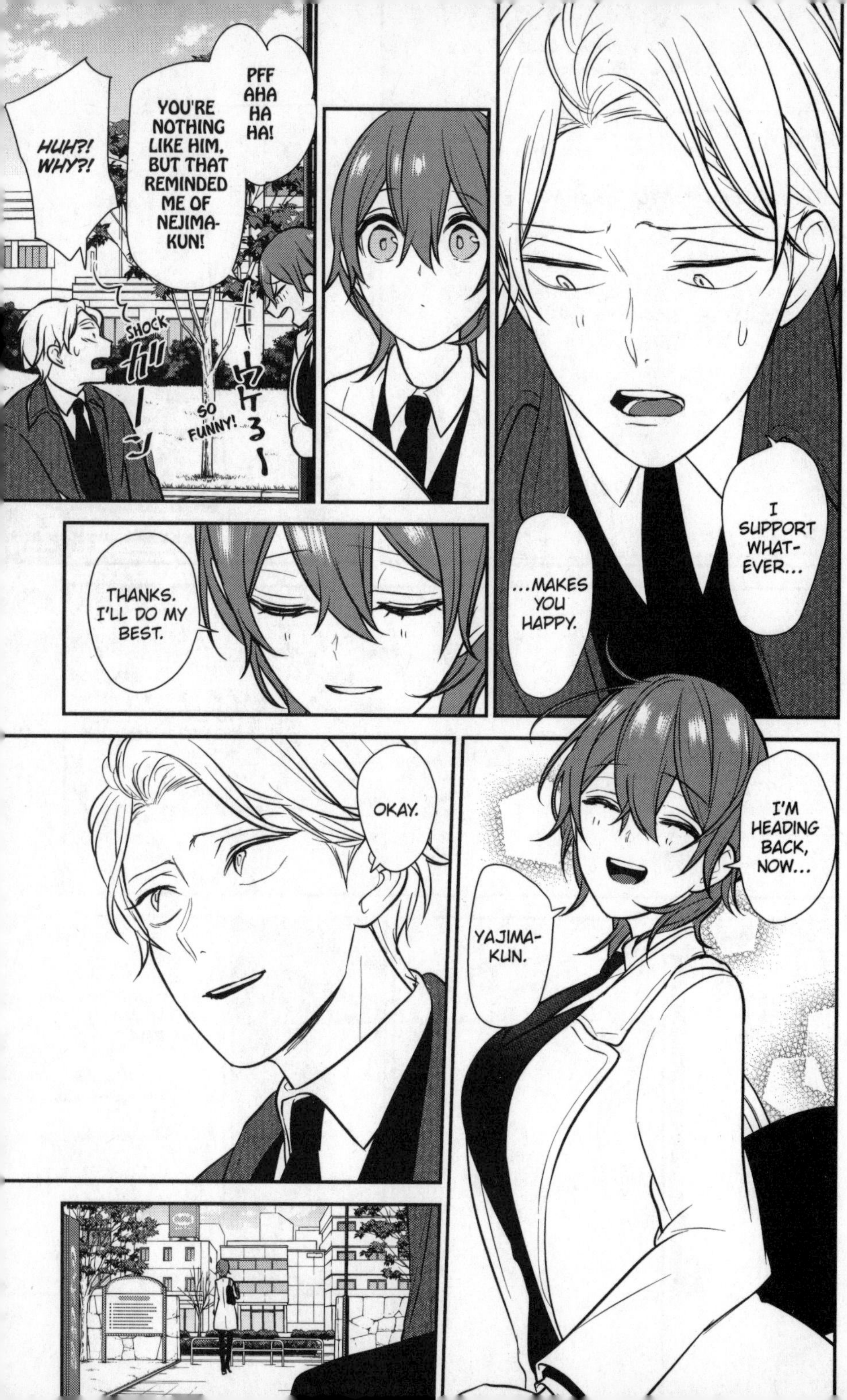
I SUPPORT WHAT-EVER...
...MAKES YOU HAPPY.
PFF AHA HA HA!
YOU'RE NOTHING LIKE HIM, BUT THAT REMINDED ME OF NEJIMA-KUN!
HUH?! WHY?!
SHOCK
SO FUNNY!
THANKS. I'LL DO MY BEST.
I'M HEADING BACK, NOW...
YAJIMA-KUN.
OKAY.

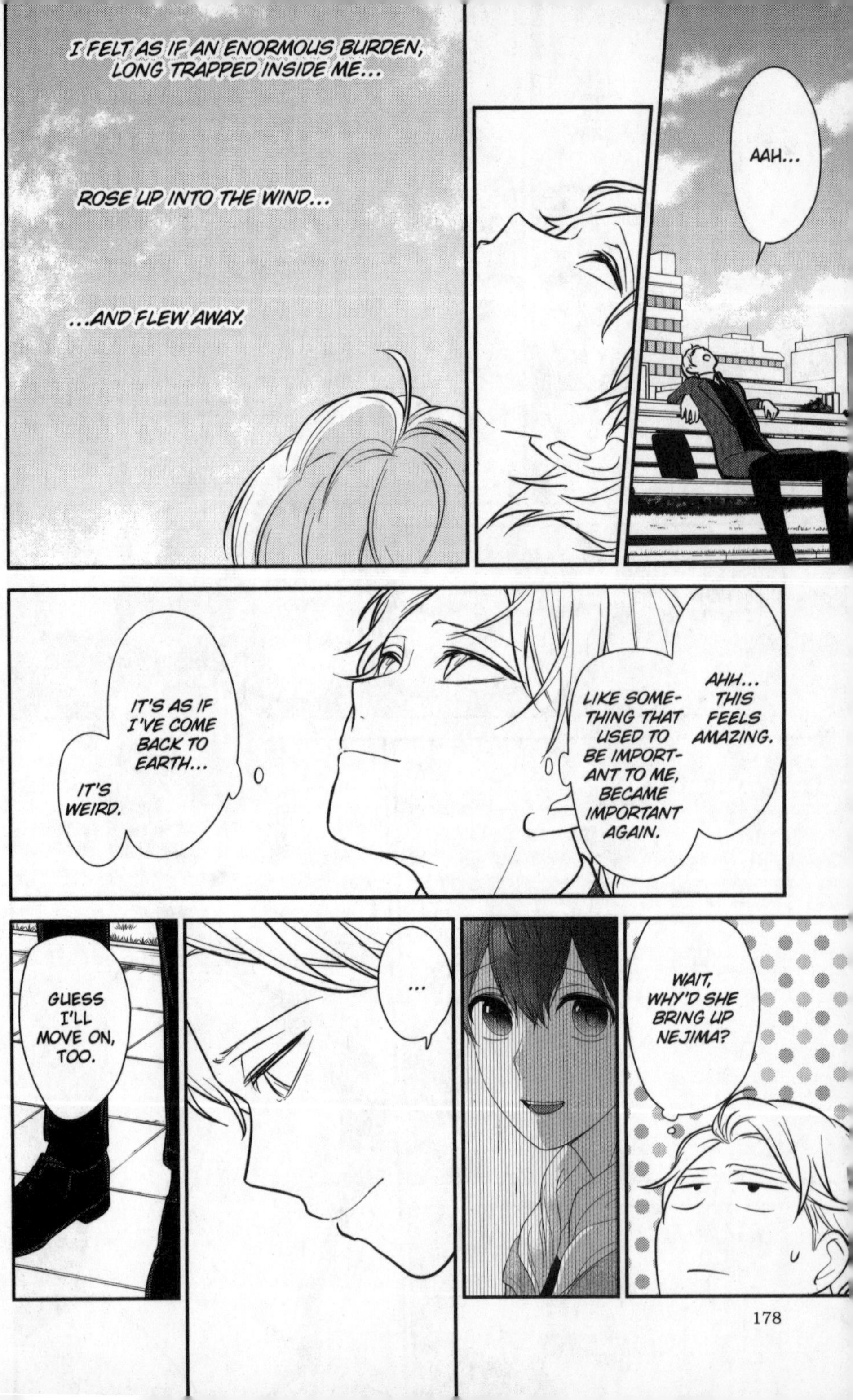
AAH...
I FELT AS IF AN ENORMOUS BURDEN, LONG TRAPPED INSIDE ME...
ROSE UP INTO THE WIND...
...AND FLEW AWAY.
AHH... THIS FEELS AMAZING.
LIKE SOMETHING THAT USED TO BE IMPORTANT TO ME, BECAME IMPORTANT AGAIN.
IT'S AS IF I'VE COME BACK TO EARTH...
IT'S WEIRD.
WAIT, WHY'D SHE BRING UP NEJIMA?
...
GUESS I'LL MOVE ON, TOO.

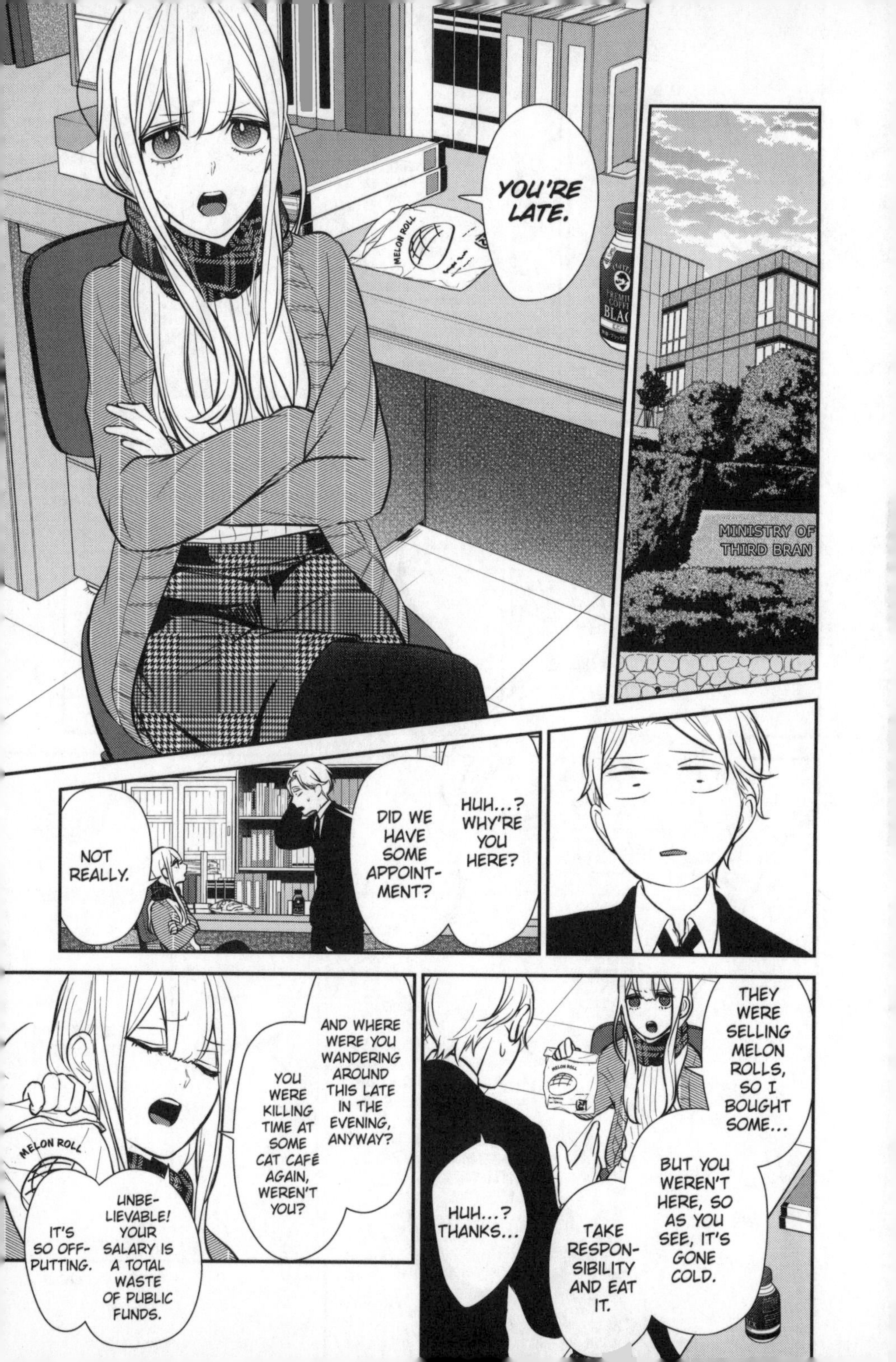
MINISTRY OF THIRD BRAN
YOU'RE LATE.
MELON ROLL
HUH...? WHY'RE YOU HERE?
DID WE HAVE SOME APPOINTMENT?
NOT REALLY.
THEY WERE SELLING MELON ROLLS, SO I BOUGHT SOME...
BUT YOU WEREN'T HERE, SO AS YOU SEE, IT'S GONE COLD.
TAKE RESPONSIBILITY AND EAT IT.
HUH...? THANKS...
AND WHERE WERE YOU WANDERING AROUND THIS LATE IN THE EVENING, ANYWAY?
YOU WERE KILLING TIME AT SOME CAT CAFÉ AGAIN, WEREN'T YOU?
UNBELIEVABLE! YOUR SALARY IS A TOTAL WASTE OF PUBLIC FUNDS.
IT'S SO OFF-PUTTING.
MELON ROLL

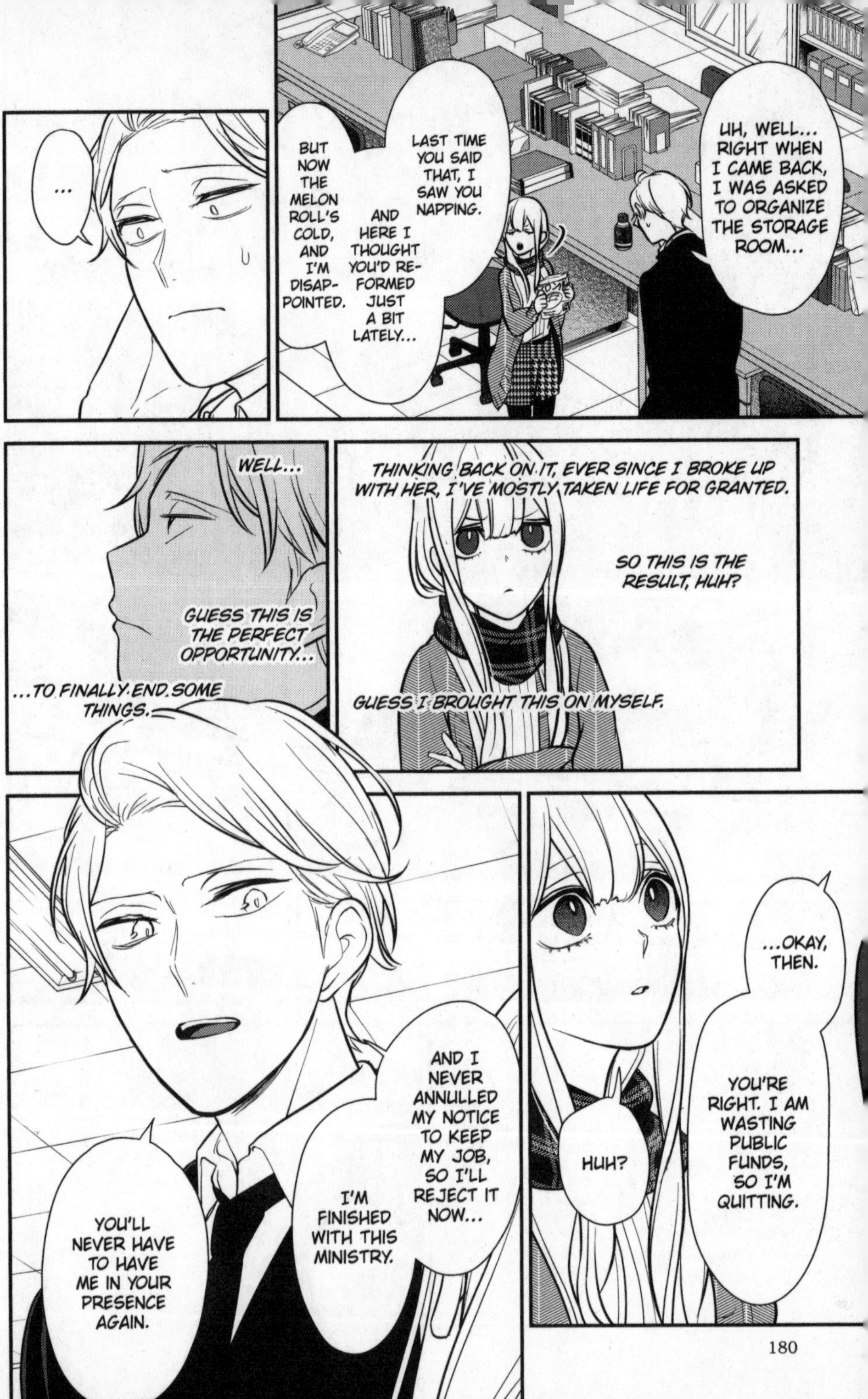
UH, WELL... RIGHT WHEN I CAME BACK, I WAS ASKED TO ORGANIZE THE STORAGE ROOM...
LAST TIME YOU SAID THAT, I SAW YOU NAPPING.
AND HERE I THOUGHT YOU'D RE-FORMED JUST A BIT LATELY...
BUT NOW THE MELON ROLL'S COLD, AND I'M DISAP-POINTED.
...
THINKING BACK ON IT, EVER SINCE I BROKE UP WITH HER, I'VE MOSTLY TAKEN LIFE FOR GRANTED.
SO THIS IS THE RESULT, HUH?
GUESS I BROUGHT THIS ON MYSELF.
WELL...
GUESS THIS IS THE PERFECT OPPORTUNITY...
...TO FINALLY END SOME THINGS.
...OKAY, THEN.
YOU'RE RIGHT. I AM WASTING PUBLIC FUNDS, SO I'M QUITTING.
HUH?
AND I NEVER ANNULLED MY NOTICE TO KEEP MY JOB, SO I'LL REJECT IT NOW...
I'M FINISHED WITH THIS MINISTRY.
YOU'LL NEVER HAVE TO HAVE ME IN YOUR PRESENCE AGAIN.

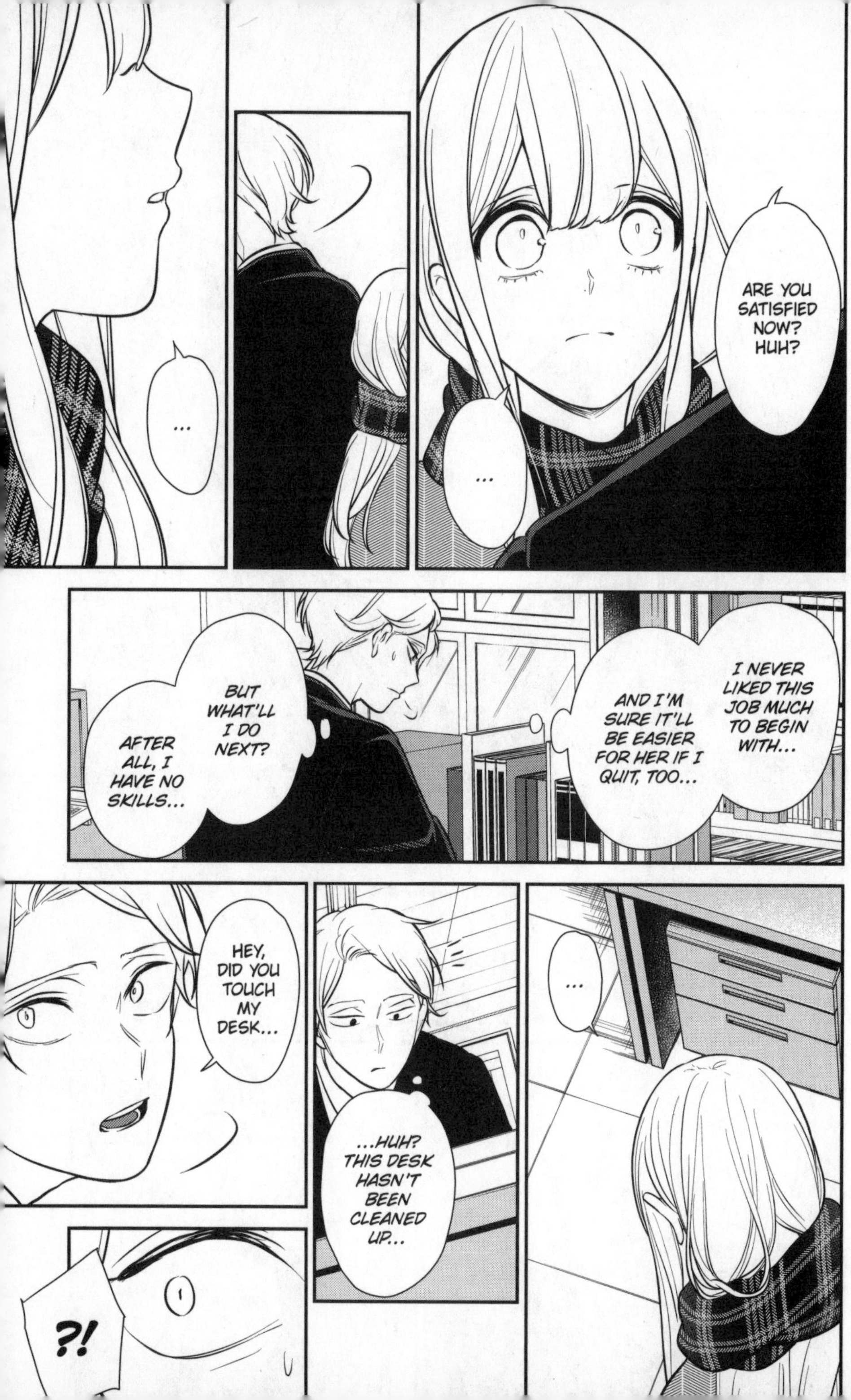
ARE YOU SATISFIED NOW? HUH?
...
...
I NEVER LIKED THIS JOB MUCH TO BEGIN WITH...
AND I'M SURE IT'LL BE EASIER FOR HER IF I QUIT, TOO...
BUT WHAT'LL I DO NEXT?
AFTER ALL, I HAVE NO SKILLS...
...
...HUH? THIS DESK HASN'T BEEN CLEANED UP...
HEY, DID YOU TOUCH MY DESK...
?!

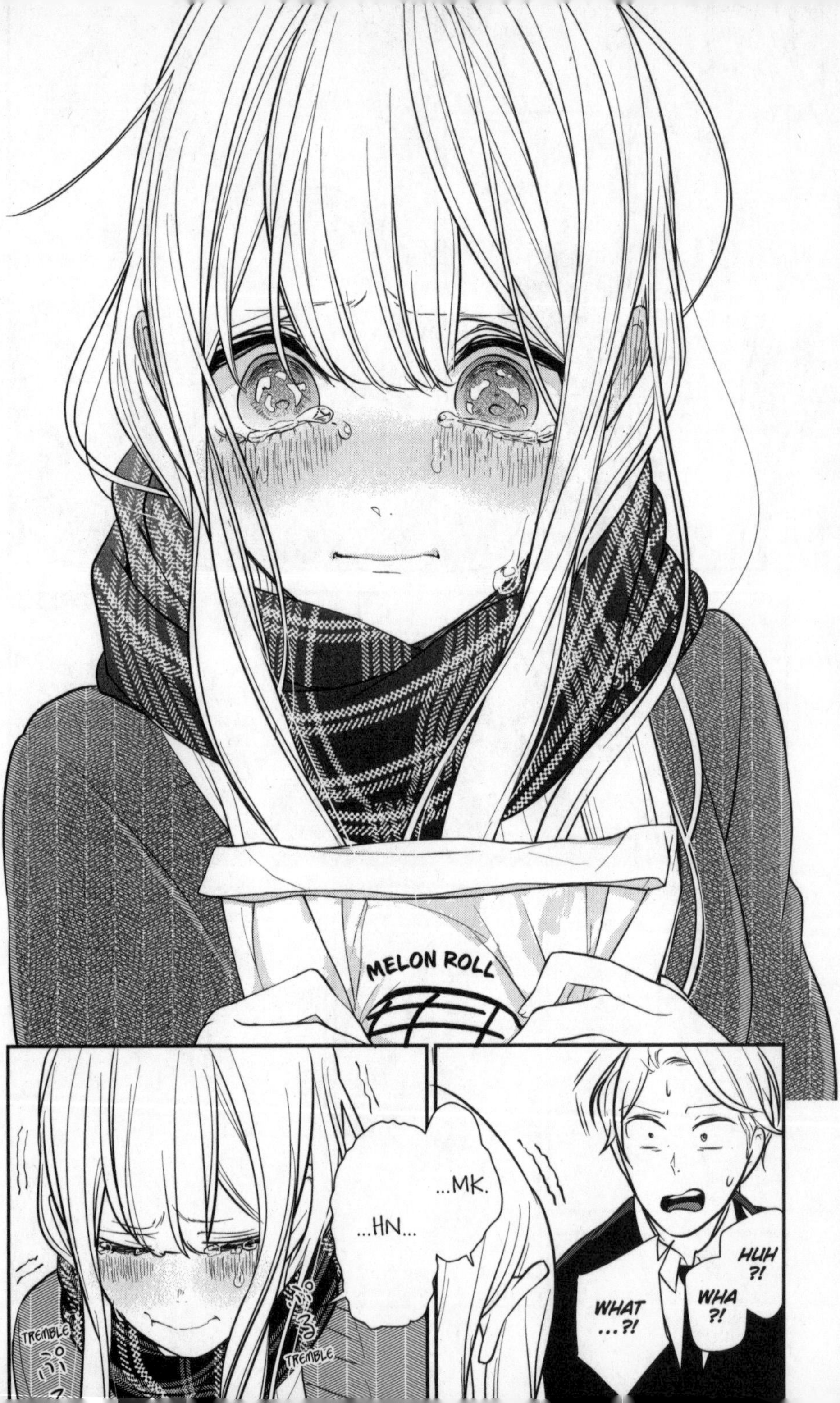
MELON ROLL
...MK.
...HN...
HUH ?!
WHA ?!
WHAT ...?!
TREMBLE
TREMBLE

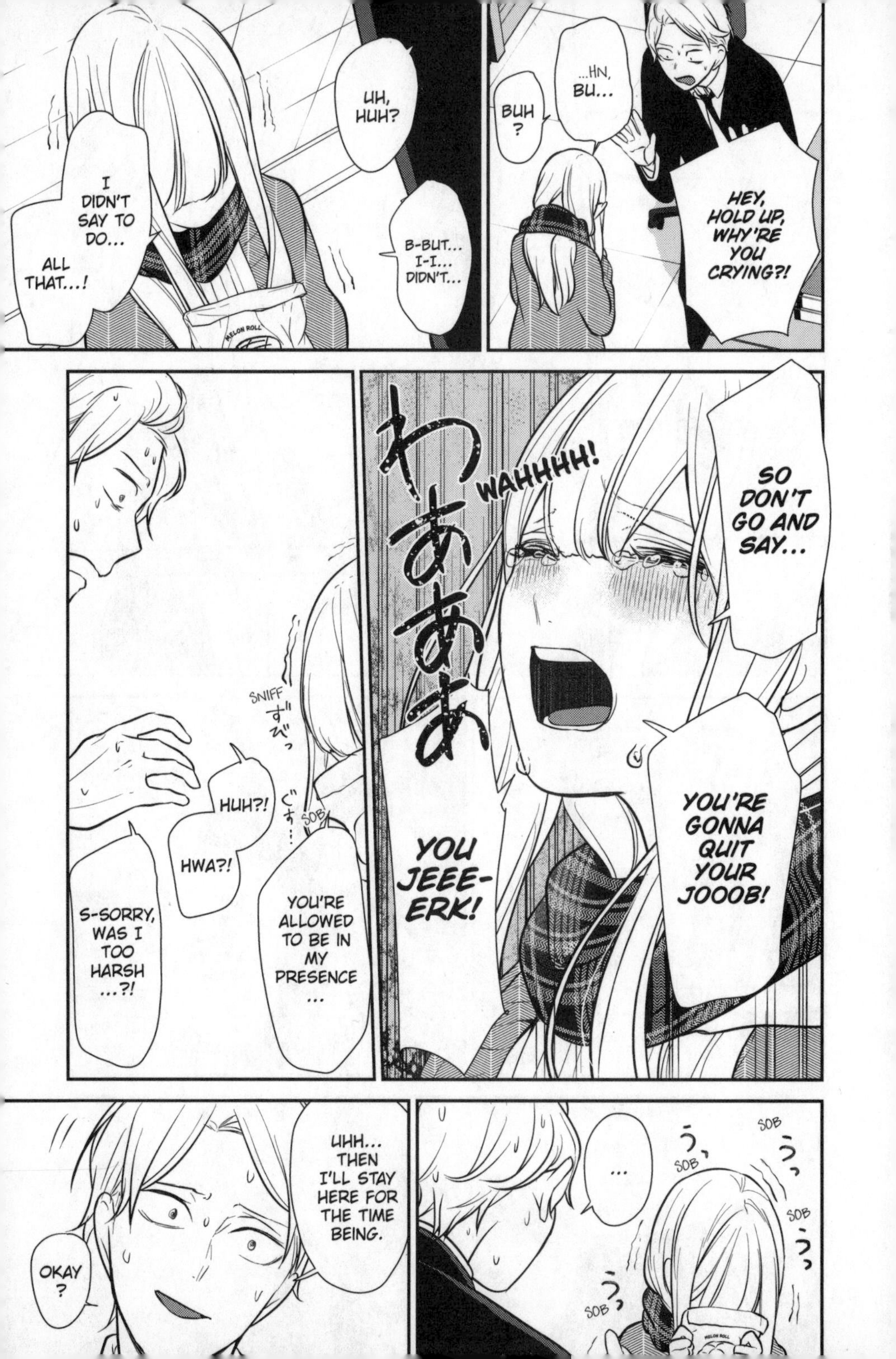
...HN, BU...
BUH?
HEY, HOLD UP, WHY'RE YOU CRYING?!
UH, HUH?
B-BUT... I-I... DIDN'T...
I DIDN'T SAY TO DO... ALL THAT...!
MELON ROLL
SO DON'T GO AND SAY...
わあああ
WAHHHH!
YOU'RE GONNA QUIT YOUR JOOOB!
YOU JEEE-ERK!
SNIFF ずびっ
HUH?!
ぐす…
SOB
HWA?!
YOU'RE ALLOWED TO BE IN MY PRESENCE...
S-SORRY, WAS I TOO HARSH...?!
SOB うっ
SOB う、
SOB うっ
SOB うっ
...
MELON ROLL
UHH... THEN I'LL STAY HERE FOR THE TIME BEING.
OKAY?

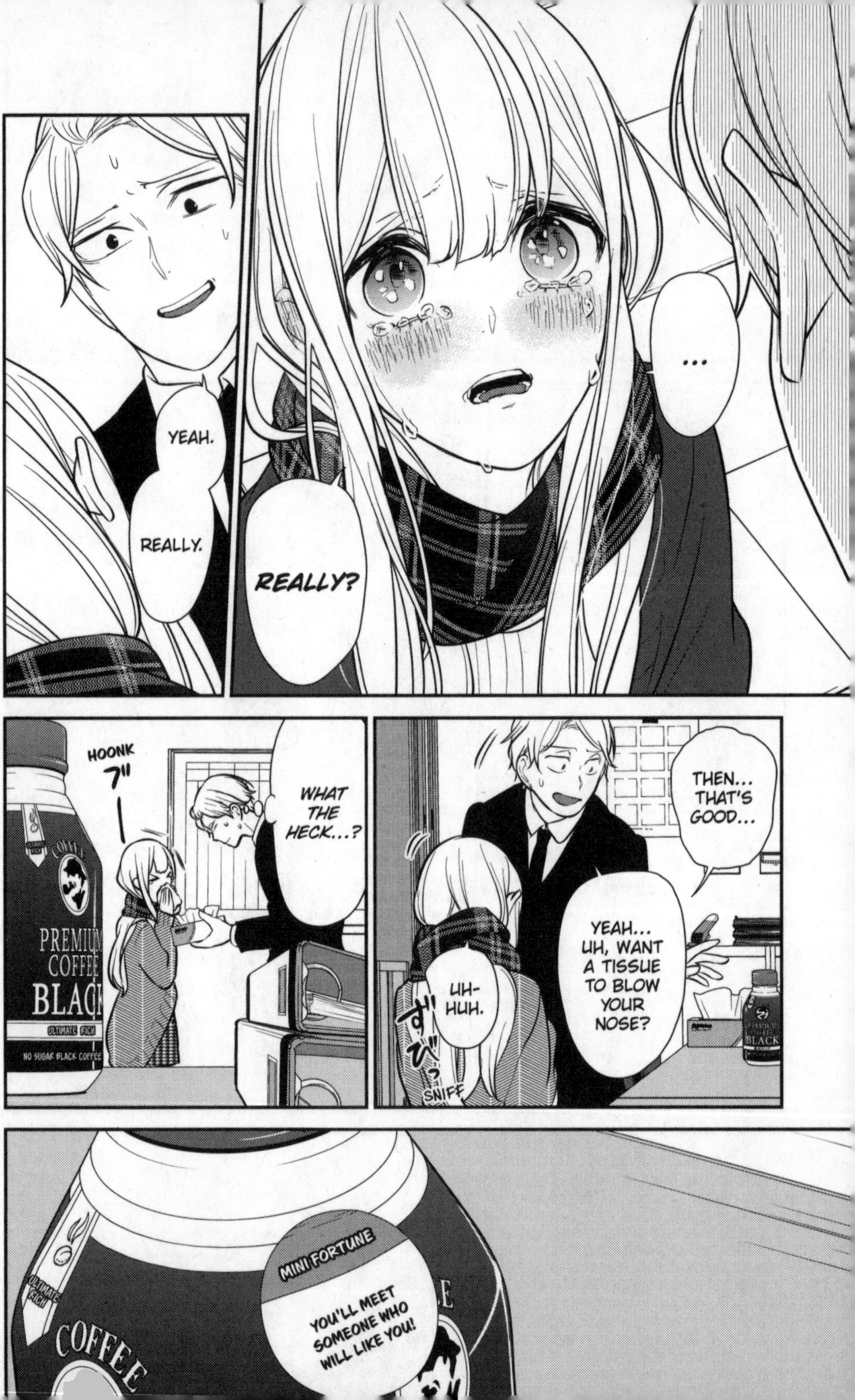
...
REALLY?
YEAH.
REALLY.
THEN... THAT'S GOOD...
YEAH... UH, WANT A TISSUE TO BLOW YOUR NOSE?
UH-HUH.
SNIFF
BLACK
WHAT THE HECK...?
HOONK
COFFEE
PREMIUM COFFEE BLACK
ULTIMATE RICH
NO SUGAR BLACK COFFEE
MINI FORTUNE
YOU'LL MEET SOMEONE WHO WILL LIKE YOU!
ULTIMATE RICH
COFFEE

★ SPECIAL THANKS ★

TAKANAGA-SAMA
YOSHIMURA-SAMA

SHINOHARA-SAMA
ENOMOTO-SAMA
TANAKA-SAMA
ISHIKAWA-SAMA

AMAKAWA MANARU-SAMA
FUKU-SAMA
MIZUKI-SAMA
KOMATSU KOUSUKE-SAMA
TACHIBANA YUTAKA-SAMA
KOBAYASHI KEI-SAMA


COVER & SPECIAL EDITION DESIGN
HIVE-SAMA

EVERYONE IN MY FAMILY

 AND

TO ALL MY READERS

Volume 11
coming soon!

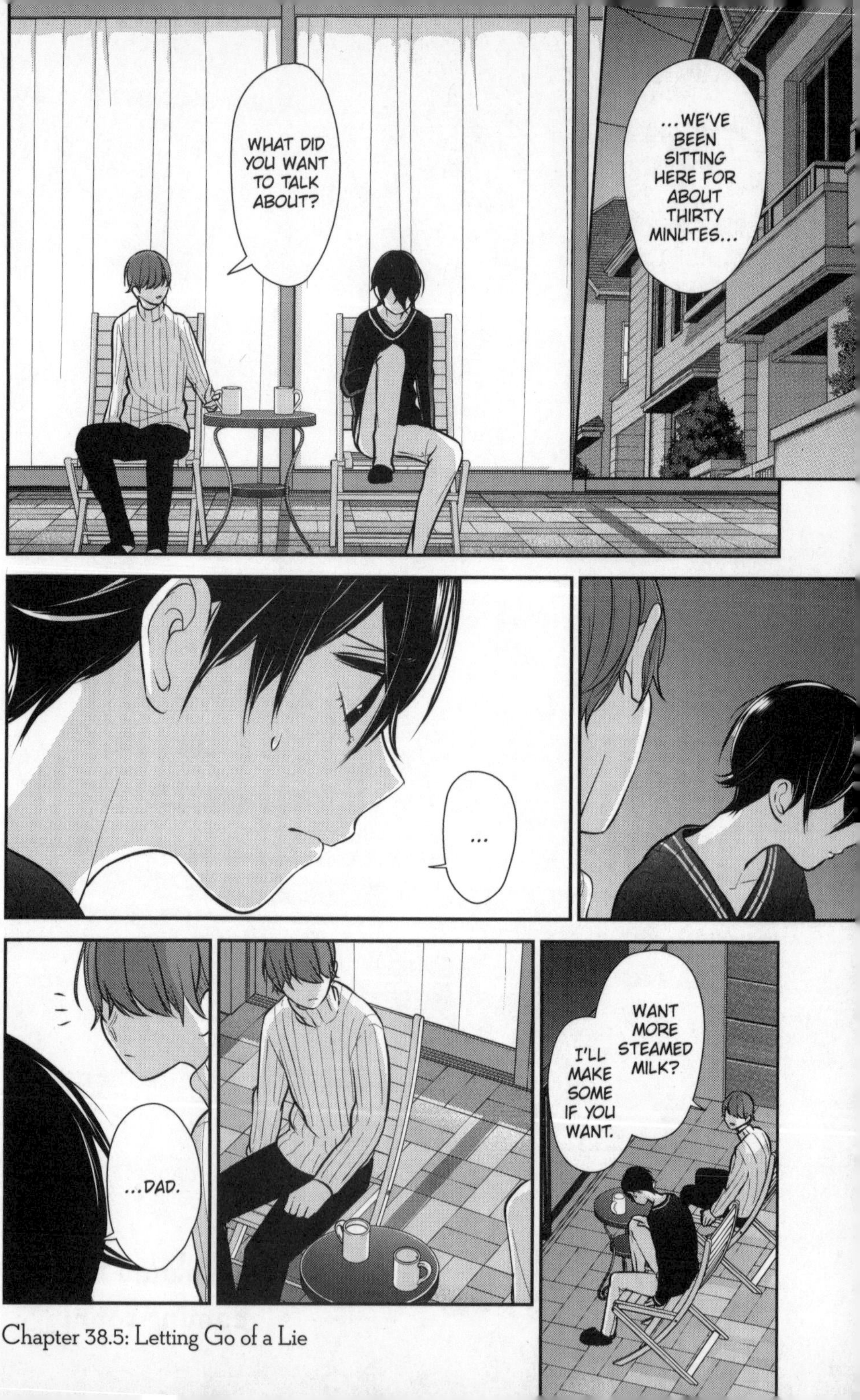
...WE'VE BEEN SITTING HERE FOR ABOUT THIRTY MINUTES...
WHAT DID YOU WANT TO TALK ABOUT?
...
WANT MORE STEAMED MILK?
I'LL MAKE SOME IF YOU WANT.
...DAD.

Chapter 38.5: Letting Go of a Lie

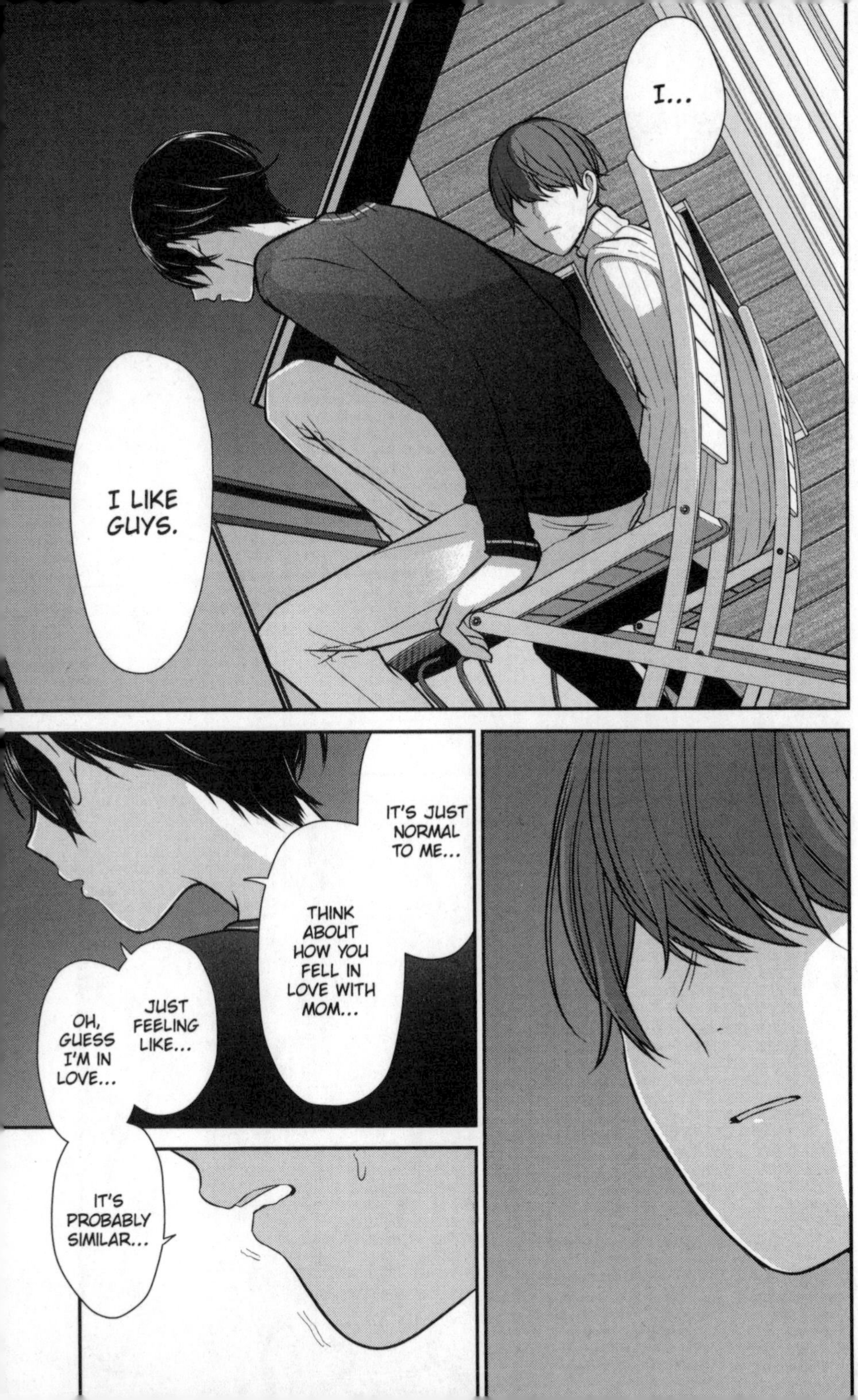
I...
I LIKE GUYS.
IT'S JUST NORMAL TO ME...
THINK ABOUT HOW YOU FELL IN LOVE WITH MOM...
JUST FEELING LIKE...
OH, GUESS I'M IN LOVE...
IT'S PROBABLY SIMILAR...

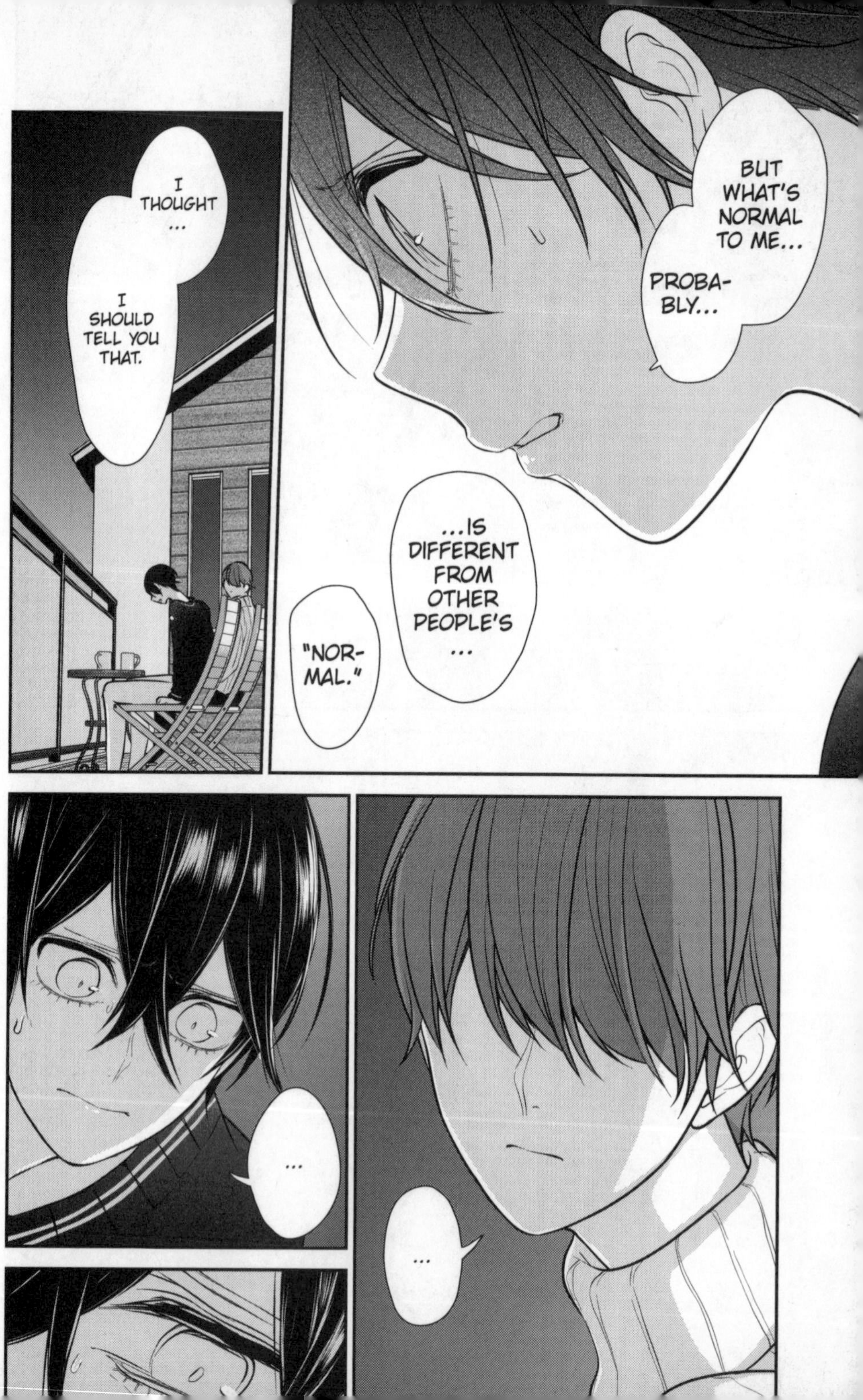
BUT WHAT'S NORMAL TO ME...
PROBA-BLY...
...IS DIFFERENT FROM OTHER PEOPLE'S ...
"NOR-MAL."
I THOUGHT ...
I SHOULD TELL YOU THAT.
...
...

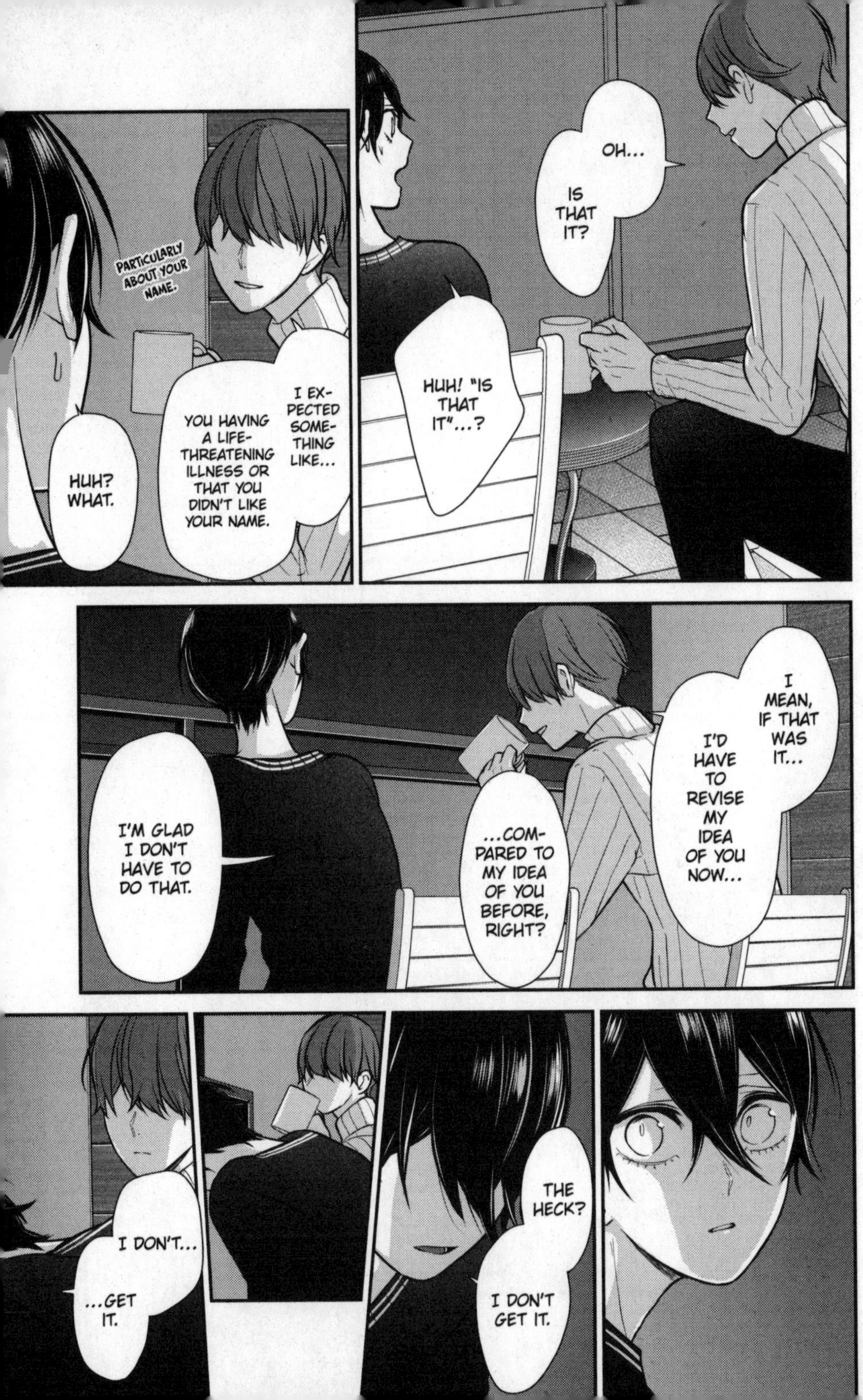
OH...
IS THAT IT?
HUH! "IS THAT IT"...?
I EXPECTED SOMETHING LIKE...
YOU HAVING A LIFE-THREATENING ILLNESS OR THAT YOU DIDN'T LIKE YOUR NAME.
PARTICULARLY ABOUT YOUR NAME.
HUH? WHAT.
I MEAN, IF THAT WAS IT...
I'D HAVE TO REVISE MY IDEA OF YOU NOW...
...COMPARED TO MY IDEA OF YOU BEFORE, RIGHT?
I'M GLAD I DON'T HAVE TO DO THAT.
THE HECK?
I DON'T GET IT.
I DON'T...
...GET IT.

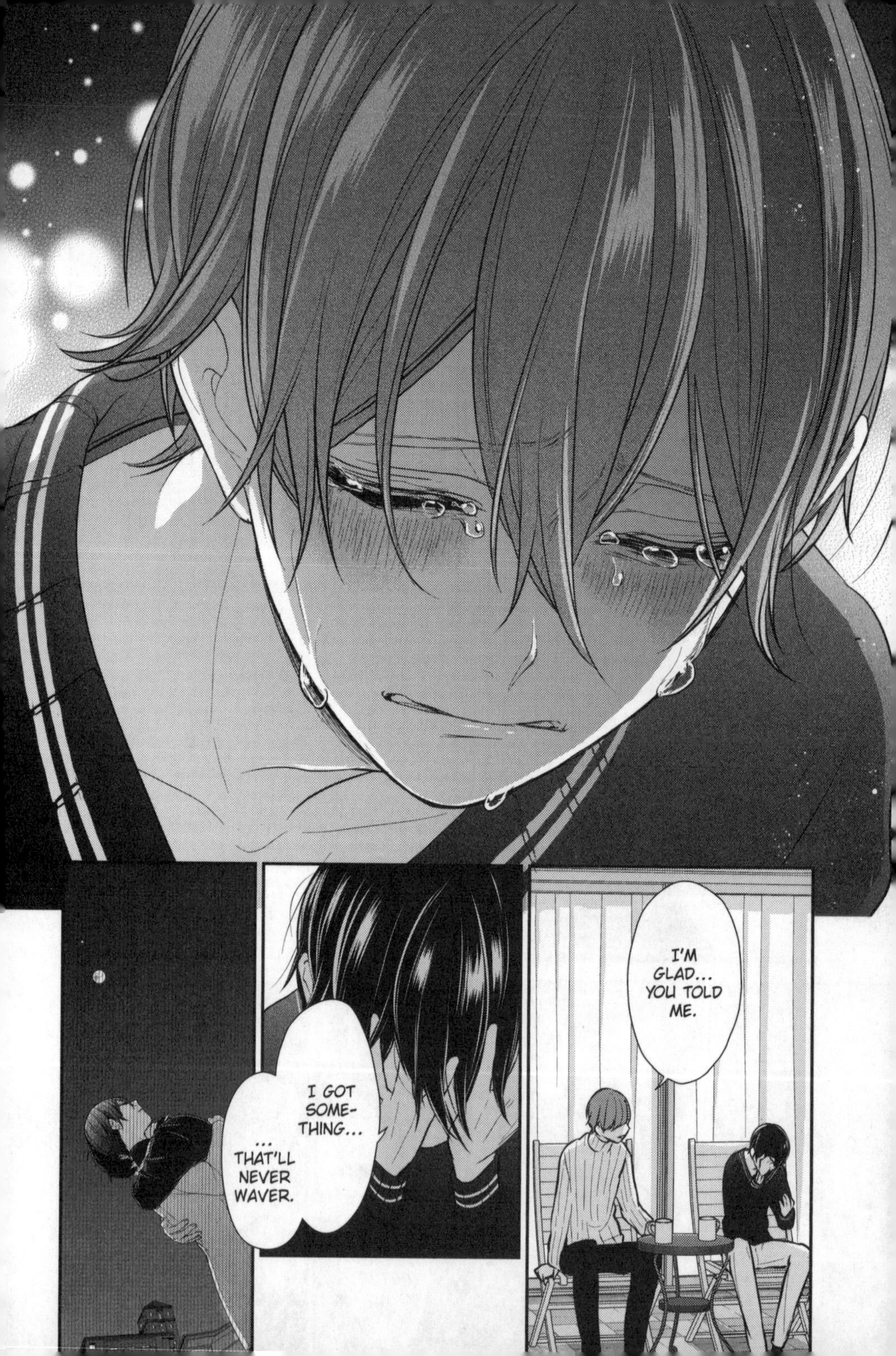
I'M GLAD... YOU TOLD ME.
I GOT SOMETHING... ...THAT'LL NEVER WAVER.

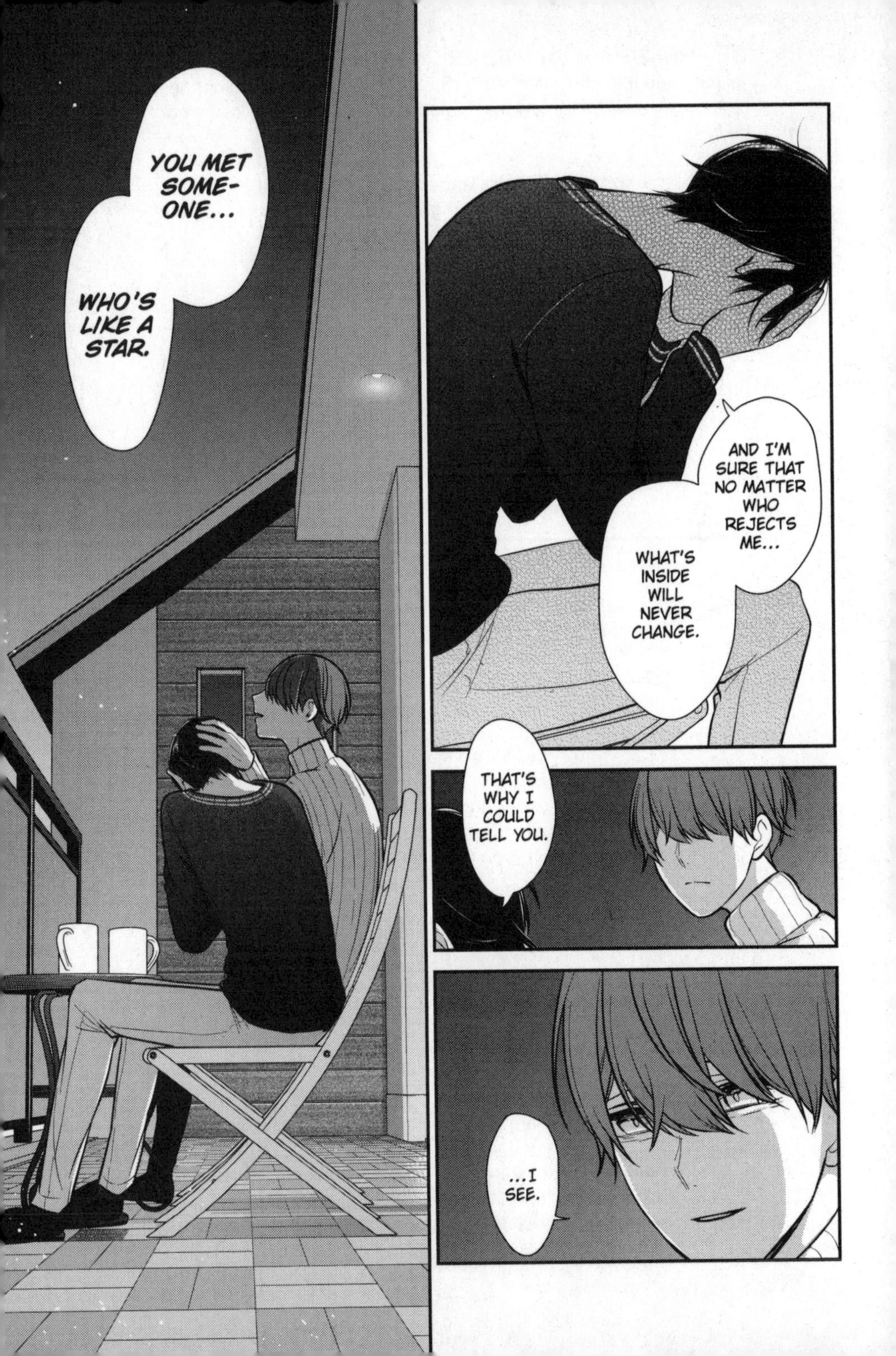
AND I'M SURE THAT NO MATTER WHO REJECTS ME...
WHAT'S INSIDE WILL NEVER CHANGE.
THAT'S WHY I COULD TELL YOU.
...I SEE.
YOU MET SOME-ONE...
WHO'S LIKE A STAR.

A Kodansha Comics Trade Paperback Original
Love and Lies 10 copyright © 2020 Musawo
English translation copyright © 2021 Musawo

All rights reserved.

Published in the United States by Kodansha Comics, an imprint of Kodansha USA Publishing, LLC, New York.

Publication rights for this English edition arranged through Kodansha Ltd., Tokyo.

First published in Japan in 2020 by Kodansha Ltd., Tokyo as *Koi to uso*, volume 10.

ISBN 978-1-64651-057-3

Original cover design by Tadashi Hisamochi (hive & co., Ltd.)

Printed in the United States of America.

www.kodansha.us

9 8 7 6 5 4 3 2 1
Translation: Jennifer Ward
Lettering: Daniel CY
Editing: Tomoko Nagano
Kodansha Comics edition cover design by Phil Balsman

Publisher: Kiichiro Sugawara

Director of publishing services: Ben Applegate
Associate director of operations: Stephen Pakula
Publishing services associate managing editor: Madison Salters
Production managers: Emi Lotto, Angela Zurlo